ACTING GAY

BETWEEN MEN ~ BETWEEN WOMEN
LESBIAN AND GAY STUDIES
Lillian Faderman and Larry Gross, Editors

BETWEEN MEN ~ BETWEEN WOMEN
LESBIAN AND GAY STUDIES
Lillian Faderman and Larry Gross, Editors

Gary David Comstock, *Violence Against Lesbians and Gay Men*

Lillian Faderman, *Odd Girls and Twilight Lovers: A History of Lesbian Life in Twentieth-Century America*

Richard D. Mohr, *Gays/Justice: A Study of Ethics, Society, and Law*

Kath Weston, *Families We Choose: Lesbians, Gays, Kinship*

Judith Roof, *A Lure of Knowledge: Lesbian Sexuality and Theory*

Acting Gay

MALE HOMOSEXUALITY
IN MODERN DRAMA

JOHN M. CLUM

Columbia University Press
New York

Columbia University Press
New York   Oxford

Copyright © 1992 Columbia University Press
All rights reserved

Library of Congress Cataloging-in-Publication Data

Clum, John M.
    Acting Gay : male homosexuality in modern drama / John M. Clum.
        p.   cm.—(Between men—between women)
    Includes bibliographical references and index.
    ISBN 0-231-07510-3
    1. American drama—20th century—History and criticism.
    2. Homosexuality and literature—History—20th century.   3. English
    drama—20th century—History and criticism.   4. Gays' writings,
    American—History and criticism.   5. Gays' writings, English—
    History and criticism.   6. Gay men in literature.   I. Title.   II. Series.
    PS338.H66C58   1992   91–45663
    813'.509353—dc20   CIP

Casebound editions of
Columbia University Press books are
Smyth-sewn and printed on permanent
and durable acid-free paper.

Designed by Teresa Bonner
Printed in the United States of America

c 10 9 8 7 6 5 4 3 2 1

BETWEEN MEN ~ BETWEEN WOMEN
LESBIAN AND GAY STUDIES
Lillian Faderman and Larry Gross, Editors
Eugene F. Rice, *Columbia University Advisor*

Advisory Board

John Boswell
YALE UNIVERSITY

History

Claudia Card
UNIVERSITY OF WISCONSIN

Philosophy

Richard Green
UNIVERSITY OF CALIFORNIA,
LOS ANGELES

Psychology

Gilbert Herdt
UNIVERSITY OF CHICAGO

Anthropology,
Sociology, Political Science

Barbara Johnson
HARVARD UNIVERSITY

Literature

Rhonda R. Rivera
OHIO STATE UNIVERSITY

Law

Between Men ~ Between Women is a forum for current lesbian and gay scholarship in the humanities and social sciences. The series includes both books that rest within specific traditional disciplines and are substantially about gay men, bisexuals, or lesbians and books that are interdisciplinary in ways that reveal new insights into gay, bisexual, and lesbian experience, transform traditional disciplinary methods in consequence of the perspectives that experience provides, or begin to establish lesbian and gay studies as a freestanding inquiry. Established to contribute to an increased understanding of lesbians, bisexuals, and gay men, the series also aims to provide through that understanding a wider comprehension of culture in general.

For Walter S. Melion
Without whom . . .

CONTENTS

Preface   xi

Acknowledgments   xvii

PART 1 • Bodies and Taboos

Chapter One *Seeing Gay*   3

Chapter Two *AIDS Drama: Displacing* Camille   39

PART 2 • Codes and Closets

Chapter Three *Closet Pederasts*   85

Chapter Four *American Dreams*   139

PART 3 • Staging "A Culture That Isn't Just Sexual"

Chapter Five *Dramatizing Gay Male History*   197

Chapter Six *Fashioning a Gay Self*   245

Notes   277

Annotated List of Resources   303

Index   311

PREFACE

In this book, I have sought to interpret the central works of gay male drama written by English and American playwrights. Gay American playwright Lanford Wilson has said "The theater is really the only public forum a gay writer has."[1] For this reason, it has been a particularly important voice in gay culture and has often acted as its mirror. Plays I discuss in these pages reflect transformations in the roles gay men have played in twentieth-century American and English society.

The history of homosexuality in drama records a series of moves back and forth from the unspoken to the spoken, from the unseen to the seen. Homosexual desire is affirmed in Marlowe and acknowledged in Jonson and Shakespeare. It is at least suggested in comedies of the Restoration. For most of the history of theater, the gay playwright's unspoken compact with producers and audiences entailed keeping his homosexuality offstage or presenting homosexuality in a coded manner so that heterosexuals in the audience needn't notice it. The history of the silences and codes used in the presentation of homosexuality in dramas of the thirties, forties, and fifties mirrors the changing position of gay men offstage. Playwrights like Tennessee Williams were able to create rich, powerful drama out of their sense of difference, even when that difference, though a wellspring of their genius, could not be given positive voice.

In the past twenty years, homosexuality in drama has moved from shame-filled hints and indirection to proud assertion. Heterosexism, which used to be upheld as the norm, is now driven offstage in a comforting fantasy not fully enacted outside the theater.[2]

A short list of openly gay playwrights on this side of the Atlantic—Robert Chesley, Christopher Durang, Harvey Fierstein, William Hoffman, Albert Innaurato, Larry Kramer, Craig Lucas, Terrence McNally, Robert Patrick, Doric Wilson, and Lanford Wilson—attests to the vitality and centrality of contemporary gay drama. As I write this, the two most celebrated, longest-running nonmusicals on Broadway are *Prelude to a Kiss,* by gay playwright Craig Lucas, which challenges conventional notions of sexual identity through the presentation of a heterosexual romance, and *Six Degrees of Separation,* by heterosexual playwright John Guare, which satirizes the values of an upper-middle-class family through the depiction of its interaction with a gay character. Both these plays can be considered gay drama.

The term *gay drama* refers to two kinds of plays written for two kinds of audiences. One type is the post-Stonewall play, which is written primarily for gay audiences and which speaks to their shared experience. Such works—I am thinking here of some of the dramas of Robert Patrick and Doric Wilson—are purposely coterie plays, not intended for an "outside" audience. If one wants to study a body of work that reflects the attitudes and language of the out-of-the-closet, politicized, New York gay at a certain period in time, these "inside" plays provide a far more reliable gauge than, say, Jerry Herman and Harvey Fierstein's hit musical *La Cage aux Folles* (1983), which was seen by a great many more people.

However, the playwrights who have achieved the greatest exposure, through both stage production and publication, are those who, for a combination of personal, artistic, and economic reasons, choose to write for the commercial mainstream theater, and who, as a result, must mediate between gay and straight members of their audience. In a similar fashion they must mediate between their own vision and political stance as gay people and the often conservative, heterosexist vision of many in their audience. Still, as the list of authors above attests, in the past decade mainstream drama and gay drama have gradually fused.

The other type of gay drama is the pre-Stonewall play written for the mainstream theater by a homosexual playwright. Such a work may seem to capitulate to the prejudices of its audience but actually reflects the internalized homophobia of the playwright. The reticence and heterosexism seen in such "closet dramas" as those by playwrights like William Inge and Tennessee Williams are not cynical, hypocritical ploys for commercial success but expressions of the playwrights' negative feelings about their own homosexuality.

Closet dramas are bridges to post-Stonewall gay drama from those "outside" melodramas by heterosexual playwrights that exploit taboos about homosexuality while presenting homosexual stereotypes. These plays place homosexuality within the conventions of the dominant genre of mid-twentieth-century English and American drama, the realistic "problem play," in which a social or psychological aberration that threatens a community is introduced only to be, in the end, expunged. In the history of this genre, homosexuality is all too often presented as the "problem" that must be solved or eliminated by the final curtain. In general, the history of representations of homosexuals and homosexual desire is one of integration into, compromises with, and extension of this dramatic form, which has transmitted and affirmed the values of its audiences for more than a century. In part 2, I will show how two such commercial "problem plays," Mordaunt Shairp's *The Green Bay Tree* (1933)[2] and Robert Anderson's *Tea and Sympathy* (1953), distilled the homosexual stereotypes of their respective times and described the limited roles for gay men in their two societies. In the United States, a number of gay playwrights, such as Harvey Fierstein and Albert Innaurato, continue to be drawn to validations of the conventions and assumptions of realism, while British gay dramatists, such as Noel Greig or Paul Godfrey, from whom Shakespeare and Brecht are as viable models as Ibsen, have favored appropriating nonrealistic models for drama. Since the realistic problem play has been, to a great extent, appropriated by television, I include discussions of a few of television's attempts to dramatize the "problem" of homosexuality.

A tradition of cross-fertilization between British and American drama makes their pairing a natural, if not seamless, subject. Most of the plays discussed in this volume have been produced in both Great Britain and the United States. American playwright Martin Sherman lives and writes in London, where his gay plays *Bent* (1979) and *A Madhouse in Goa* (1989) received their premieres. Londoner Noël Coward wrote *Design for Living* (1933) for Broadway. Many of the British plays discussed in this volume have been produced in New York and in regional and university theaters across the country. American plays like Harvey Fierstein's *Torch Song Trilogy* (1980) and Larry Kramer's *The Normal Heart* (1985) have been produced successfully in London. I do not presume an identity of gay cultures in Great Britain and the United States. I explore their difference to the extent that they affect dramatic creation and production.

The book is divided into three sections. The two chapters of part 1, "Bodies and Taboos," center on the presentation of physical aspects of homosexuality and their relationship to the norms of the society that the audience represents. The first chapter focuses on three commonly staged visual images of homosexuality: men kissing, male nudity, and men in drag. The second chapter focuses on a discussion of a group of AIDS dramas that exemplifies the difference between "outside" drama, which presents the gay man and the Person With AIDS as problems that invade "normal" society, and "inside" drama, which focuses on the adjustment of the Person With Aids to his changed sense of himself, his past, and his possibilities. I place these plays in the context of a nineteenth-century play that is the paradigm in popular drama of representations of the relationship between sexual freedom and illness—*La Dame aux Camélias* by Alexandre Dumas.

Part 2, "Codes and Closets," is a survey of dramas written between 1930 and 1968 that in various ways opened up a space for homosexual characters while, paradoxically, maintaining the closet. These plays are either problem plays by heterosexual playwrights or plays by homosexual playwrights that deal with homosexuality in an elliptical or coded manner and that also dismíss the possibility of exclusive homosexuality.

Part 3, "Staging 'A Culture That Isn't Just Sexual,'" focuses on dramas written in the past three decades in which homosexuality is presented directly. This section is also divided into two chapters. The first, chapter 5, treats plays that present incidents or figures central to gay history or gay culture. The final chapter is a discussion of dramas of contemporary gay life.

Gay men are, in the last decade of this century, very much in the spotlight, but we still face more catcalls than applause. Nonetheless, we are onstage for good. For many of us, the issue now is to be seen as legitimate members of a large, varied cast, not leading players in dramas that deny, denigrate, or threaten our very existence.

ACKNOWLEDGMENTS

I am indebted to a number of friends and colleagues for their help and support during the process of researching and writing this book.

First, to my English Department chairman, Stanley Fish, for generously giving me some extra time off from teaching for writing and to English Department administrative assistant Marjorie George and secretaries Miriam Crenshaw and Roz Wolbarsht for their generous, cheerful help.

To David Ball for support, feedback, and computer hacking.

To Duke University colleagues Ronald Butters, Cathy Davidson, Yussef El Guindi, Jane Gaines, Robert Hobbs, Frank Lentricchia, Elgin Mellown, and Dale Randall for their helpful conversations and feedback.

To Richard Mohr for help and encouragement from the beginning, for his blue pencil and doggedness toward the end, and for his many delightful phone calls throughout.

To my editors at Columbia University Press, Ann Miller, Anne

McCoy, and to my meticulous, knowledgeable, and insightful copyeditor, Janet Boulton.

To students whose conversations have been educational, in particular: Mary Ann Armstrong, Christopher Busiel, Shane Butler, Julia Walker, and Abby and Julie Wolf.

To friends and colleagues elsewhere: Alan Bray, Katherine Burkman, Peter Gill, Robert Gordon, Clifford Hindley, Timothy Murphy, Suzanne Poirier, and Phyllis Randall.

To the writers whose work laid the foundation for this book, in particular: Kaier Curtin, William M. Hoffman, Donald Loeffler, and Don Shewey.

To my mother, Edythe B. Clum, my sister, Jean Wotowicz, and her husband, Jan, for their love, help, and support, lo, these many years.

And to my partner, Walter Melion, for his encouragement, his insights, his critical acumen, and his ministrations during this difficult birth.

ACTING GAY

Bodies and Taboos

Bette Bourne, François
Testory, and Beverly Klein
as the three incarnations of
the castrato La Zambinella
in *Sarrasine* by Neil Bartlett.
Produced by GLORIA in
London, 1991. Photo: Sean
Hudson. Reprinted by
permission of GLORIA.

Seeing Gay

"I saw! I know! You disgust me. . . ."
Blanche DuBois, in Tennessee Williams,
A Streetcar Named Desire

The history of the representation of homosexual desire onstage is a series of moves from nothing, to innuendo and gesture, to discussion without any physical signs of attraction or affection, to, finally, showing. The continuing shock value of open demonstrations of homosexual affection or desire shows not only the continuity of heterosexism but also the theatrical principle that bodies contain the greatest potential danger for a contemporary audience, and theater's power stems from its danger.

An emphasis on the centrality of the physical aspect of drama is particularly crucial to a discussion of gay drama, for what might be seen in gay drama is what is usually, for much of the mainstream theatrical audience, unseen. Even speculation about what it would be like to see a homosexual act or, worse, an expression of gay love, is commonly kept locked in a cerebral closet.

What is "seen" in gay drama can be frighteningly erotic or erotically frightening to some members of the audience, and what Martin Esslin rightly calls "the profoundly erotic nature" of performed drama will be central to this discussion.[1] As Herbert Blau asserts, "The erotic capacity of theater is not of secondary importance. It is right there, in the bodies."[2]

Don Shewey has written provocatively about the erotic relationship between audience and actor in live theater: "Apart from the erotic desire aroused by performers we find sexually attractive, our desire is provoked by a curiosity about people very different from ourselves."[3] What happens when a man or woman in the audience sees attractive actors perform a frightening, alien act of physical intimacy for which the audience member may have words, but which he or she has never seen? This question defines not only the erotics of gay drama but also its politics.

The act an audience sees may have been created by one or a number of writers of the dramatic text that is the produced play: actors, director, playwright, designers. Any student of theater knows that the play the audience sees and hears has been "written" by a number of people other than the author, as well as by the social and physical conditions of performance. A gay director might find a homosexual subtext in a heterosexual drama, just as a heterosexual director can, even unwittingly, eliminate the homoeroticism of a gay script. A gay actor might find a gay subtext to a script, while a homophobic actor, or an actor fearful of what playing a gay character could do to his career, might turn a gay character into a stereotype or remove all traces of homosexual desire from his character.

Moreover, the composition of the audience itself writes a great part of the play. It affects both the erotic dynamics of the production—how the audience views representations of gay sexuality and the extent to which the audience feels, resists, or simply does not respond to the erotics of the spectacle—and the politics of the production. Herbert Blau notes: "Gathered in the audience—which elicits thought to the degree that it resists definition—are issues of representation, repression, otherness, the politics of the unconscious, ideology, and power."[4]

The history of the homosexual in drama is the history of the shifts in the dominant society's perception of "repression, otherness, the politics of the unconscious, ideology, and power." These are the very issues central to gay drama. But in an audience of both heterosexuals and homosexuals, these issues will be seen from different points of view, as in fact they will also be seen from different points of view by liberated, politicized, homosexuals and conservative, closeted homosexuals. Much of what follows in this study explores the erotic and political dynamics of the relationship of performed work to its audience—and the way playwrights, directors, and actors manipulate these dynamics.

Shakespeare's Gay Merchant

A case in point is William Shakespeare's *The Merchant of Venice* (1596), as directed by Bill Alexander for the Royal Shakespeare Company in 1987.[5] At the end of scene 1, in which Antonio has promised to find Bassanio money so that he can join the ranks of Portia's suitors, Antonio embraces Bassanio and kisses him passionately. Bassanio pushes Antonio away, the two men look at each other in silence for a moment, then Bassanio runs off, leaving Antonio alone and again melancholy.

This short scene, lasting little more than fifteen seconds, presents what has become a common contemporary interpretation of the Antonio-Bassanio relationship. The older Antonio still loves his young former ephebe, Bassanio, who now, for reasons of sexual inclination, romantic love, financial need, appetite, or a combination of all four, has eyes only for Portia: hence Antonio's melancholy. Antonio, having given Bassanio his body sexually, will now have to "lend my body for his wealth" (V,i,249).[6] Antonio's kiss provides the motivation for his generosity and sacrifice. Portia's knowledge of Antonio's love for Bassanio complicates her later actions, including her welcome of Antonio into Belmont and her acceptance of his bond supporting Bassanio's fidelity:

> ANTONIO: I dare be bound again,
> My soul upon the forfeit, that your lord
> Will never more break faith advisedly.
> PORTIA: Then you shall be his surety. (V,i,254)

This final challenge of Portia's is delivered in this production with a clear understanding of what Antonio has been to Bassanio, but it is now his soul that is his surety, not his body or his wealth, as his relationship with Bassanio will now be purely spiritual. One wonders though whether the callow Bassanio is capable of a spiritual relationship with man or woman.

In speaking of Bill Alexander's production of *The Merchant of*

Venice, I invoke a contemporary "play" that ignores recent historical writings about the use of terms of love between men in Elizabethan society.[7] Alexander's interpretation of relationships between men, building on the word *love,* is decidedly "contemporary," but since he is working with contemporary actors playing before a contemporary audience, one with whom the actor shares a contemporary sense of the meanings of the words he is speaking, this approach is wholly valid. Alexander's production of *The Merchant of Venice* is a "gay play." The title character is homosexual, and his love for Bassanio becomes a dominant, though unspoken and unwritten force in the play.

Presenting a homosexual dimension to the relationship between Antonio and Bassanio also allows the actors to explore the complex relations of homosociality and homosexuality in the male groupings in the play and the ways in which the men's relationships marginalize the women to whom they proclaim love.[8] Sexual or not, love between men is in Shakespeare's Venice and Belmont more powerful than male-female love. (Indeed, Bassanio's love for Portia and Lorenzo's for Jessica seem to have more to do with money than with love. Antonio could afford not to be married.)

In Alexander's production, there is irony, too, in the relationship of Antonio's homosexuality to his virulent anti-Semitism. The final image is of Antonio silently dangling a necklace with a cross on it over Jessica's head. Jessica had dropped the necklace, and Antonio mockingly returns it to her. Antonio demonstrates that for him Jessica cannot "pass" as Christian. Yet at the end, after the members of mainstream society have exited, both Jessica and Antonio are left onstage, isolated from that society to which the Jew and the homosexual can be only partially connected.

A gay critic can argue with this *Merchant of Venice* for its lack of a historical understanding of homosexuality,[9] though the thoughtful interpretations of the script's sexual and anti-Semitic politics that infused Alexander's production are more interesting than the pretty noninterpretations of the 1989 Peter Hall production. Alexander's presentation of the Antonio-Bassanio relationship at least puts the merchant of Venice somewhere near the center of the play named after him.

The challenge of Alexander's production was in what the audience saw, not in what they heard, emphasizing the centrality of seeing to the theatrical experience. As Herbert Blau notes: "The words fly up and the body remains below, in its seeming legibility, and we still tend to preserve, along with the carnal authenticity of the actor, the primacy of the visual. Thus we think of the audience, first, as coming to *see* a play."[10] This primacy of the visual is all too often lost in drama criticism. Antonio's kiss, performed in Bill Alexander's *Merchant of Venice,* may not have been indicated or justified by a traditional reading of Shakespeare's words, but the fact remains that it had more theatrical power as a seen action than it would have if it had been described or celebrated in a hundred lines of verse.

In the remainder of this chapter, I want to examine three ways in which homosexuality can be figured visually in ways variously shocking and affirming to differing interpretive communities in the same audience:[11] kissing, frontal nudity, and drag.

Kissing Scenes

The relationship of body to word, action to dialogue, and actor to audience in gay drama, as well as the threat of gay physicality to some members of the audience, can be seen in two gay sex scenes in plays by Martin Sherman, a respected gay playwright who has succeeded in the commercial theater with a minimum of artistic or political compromise.

Sherman's *Bent,* the 1979 drama of the persecution of gays in Nazi Germany and a theatrical rallying cry for gay men, has become so central to contemporary drama that it even appears in a leading anthology for "Introduction to Drama" courses as the quintessential gay drama (albeit with an apologetic prefatory note).[12]

Bent contains one of the most celebrated sex scenes in contemporary drama. Two men, prisoners at Dachau in 1936, standing at attention under the scrutiny of guards, forbidden to move, much less touch each other, talk each other to orgasm. In a kind of gay version of the love duet from *Tristan und Isolde* without the music, a homosexual act is confined to words:

HORST: I'm kissing you.
MAX: Burning.
HORST: Kissing your eyes.
MAX: Hot.
HORST: Kissing your lips.
MAX: Yes.
HORST: Mouth.
MAX: Yes.
HORST: Inside your mouth.
MAX: Yes.
HORST: Neck.
MAX: Yes.
HORST: Down.
MAX: Yes.
HORST: Down . . .
MAX: Yes . . .

. . . .

HORST: Do you feel me inside you?
MAX: I want you inside me.
HORST: Feel . . .
MAX: I have you inside me.
HORST: Inside.
MAX: Strong.
HORST: Do you feel me thrust . . . ?[13]

After the event one of the men proclaims: "We were real. We were human. We made love. They're not going to kill us" (p. 129). In my experience seeing various productions of this play with various audiences, the response to this scene is usually enthusiastic applause. The audience is won over by the erotically charged dialogue and the virtuosity of acting the scene requires. Though the language is graphically sexual, the audience sees nothing but two fully clothed men standing at attention, looking straight ahead. Gay men (and women) can read the scene as an enactment of the duplicity gays historically have had to stage in their own lives and can enjoy a verbal eroticism seldom presented so candidly in mainstream drama. Heterosexuals can be comforted that homosexual sex has been safely restricted to words, that their restrictions, like the Nazis', have been maintained by the enactment.

In the original London and New York productions, audiences

did not have to deal with knowledge that the actors who spoke these lines were doing any more than "acting" homosexual desire. Richard Gere's Broadway run in *Bent* coincided with the first run of his film *American Gigolo,* in which he played a hustler who "didn't do fags." And ten years ago Ian McKellan, who starred in the original 1979 London production, was not openly homosexual. The audience *saw* no homosexuality in that scene from *Bent.* Casting is one of the most important signs in drama, and it has been a tradition to cast what we might call "openly heterosexual" actors in leading homosexual roles as a way of defusing the threatening aspects of the play for a mainstream audience.[14] In the 1990 London revival starring McKellan and Michael Cashman, both now openly and politically active gay actors, performances of *Bent* were even more affirming experiences for gay men and more richly challenging, perhaps more threatening, for their fellow audience members (and, given the strictures of Section 28,[15] the National Theatre revival of *Bent* was nothing less than an act of defiance).

Sherman's *A Madhouse in Goa* (1989)[16] reverses the tactic of *Bent* by presenting a simulated homosexual act onstage that is belied and complicated by the language used during the act. In *A Madhouse in Goa,* an extremely uptight young Jewish American travels alone and miserable around the world after his graduation from college, trying unsuccessfully to conquer his self-hatred and his grief at losing his first love. David, our central character, is now—1965—at a small inn on Corfu where, in the central scene of the play, he is ravished by a handsome young Greek waiter whose English seems to be limited to pop lyrics:

COSTOS: [*sings*] 'In the jingle-jangle morning, I'll come following you.'
    He speaks in a murmur as he explores DAVID's *body.*
    Do you feel the jingle-jangle? You come following through under the boardwalks? What a day for a daydream. All my thoughts are far away. Do you believe in magic? Homeward bound, I'm homeward bound. . . .
DAVID: Oh . . .
COSTOS: These boots are made for walking . . .
DAVID: Ohh . . .
COSTOS: California dreamin' on a winter's day . . .

DAVID: Ohhh!
   [*David has an orgasm.*][17]

In the 1989 London production, David's throes of orgasm at this point were most convincingly portrayed by Rupert Graves, a young actor who is known for his convincing enactments of homosexual desire. On the night I saw the play, despite the fact that the act of manual sex was hidden under a blanket, the result of this scene was not the jubilant applause that usually greets the words-only sex scene in *Bent,* but the noisy, extremely dramatic exit of a couple from the third row of the stalls. First the husband stormed out in a fit of moral outrage or, most likely, homosexual panic. Then the wife stalked up the aisle while audibly holding forth on the disgusting waste of money she had been forced to witness. Another, unplanned scene had been added to the play by this couple, one that demonstrated the danger of bodies over words as the scene onstage dramatized the growing gulf between word and act even in moments of intimacy (where, some might say, words are always irrelevant). It was seeing what is usually unseen and, for many, taboo that inspired the demonstration of outrage. One of my London students said in class that he shouldn't have had that scene "forced on" him, an interesting and apt turn of phrase that well defines the position of passivity in which an audience places itself, a position that is noticed only when an audience member is threatened with something he or she does not want to face—like embodied homosexuality.

The two scenes from Martin Sherman's plays demonstrate the difference between verbalizing homosexual desire and enacting it physically through what might be called, now with a double entendre, homosexual acts. These acts, whether created by playwright, director, or actors, are calculated to "force themselves" and the homosexual desire they represent on a mainstream audience without losing or totally alienating that audience. In a society that still does not tolerate any overt sign of affection between men, a gay audience will see them as affirming while heterosexual members of the audience will be confronted by that which their laws and mores have kept relatively invisible.

The only sex act in Harvey Fierstein's *Torch Song Trilogy* (1981), the most commercially successful "gay play," is a hilarious mockery of backroom anal sex performed by one fully clothed actor. There is virtually no kissing between lovers. Fierstein knows well that bodies are far more threatening than words.

Sexual desire is not the only dimension of the homosexual experience, but it is the core of that experience. It is sexual desire and acting upon that desire that puts the homosexual into conflict with dominant power structures. It is where we must begin. How does one dramatize homosexual desire? Can one represent desire without words? One can "force on" an audience sexual acts, kissing, embracing, looking. Or one can enact those opposites which have also been central to the experience of many homosexuals: *not* looking, *not* kissing, *not* embracing. Or one can enact the cause of these negations: heterosexism, which can be dramatized by acts of brutality, acts that sometimes result from the negation of one's homosexual desire.

One of the more interesting aspects of homophobia is, as Richard Mohr points out: "People in general find gay love—kisses of parting at the train station and the like—sicker even than gay sex."[18] The sight of two men kissing each other on the lips can evoke enormous fear and hostility in some audience members. Anyone who sat in a movie theater when Peter Finch and Murray Head kissed in *Sunday, Bloody Sunday* (1971), or when Michael Caine and Christopher Reeve kissed in *Deathtrap* (1982), or when Harry Hamlin and Michael Ontkean kissed in *Making Love* (1982), will remember the audible, hostile response such images provoked. Everyone knows that sex between men happens, but the sight of two men kissing is often seen as a transgression of the gender order, taken by many to be "natural."[19] A kiss is a sign of affection, of love, not merely of lust. A kiss, to paraphrase the old song, isn't just a kiss. Hence its theatrical power.

In the 1990 film *Longtime Companion*, written by gay playwright Craig Lucas, a group of gay friends watch together as a television soap opera, appropriately titled "Other People," presents a kiss between two male lovers (the scene has been written by one of the characters). The camera cuts from the televised kiss to the reaction of the gay friends, to the window of an appliance store where a battery of television screens offer the image of two handsome men kissing. The kiss is a triumph for the gay men, though a qualified one, as AIDS has begun to take its toll on their society. The only viewers we see are two women who watch the kiss curiously through the store window, but we hear, in the same shot, the whoop of delight of an unseen group of gay men (is it the writer and his friends or an offscreen group of men who can see the television sets through the store window or a surrogate for the gay men in the audience?). The missing audience is that of straight men. Like much of the film, the scene is about performance and audience, as it shows the power of that kiss on writers, actors, and audiences, except the audience that would treat the kiss with the greatest fear and hostility—heterosexual men.

It is often recorded in psychological studies of homosexuality and homophobia that young men will perform all sorts of sexual experimentation with each other except kissing, for kissing would define their actions as homosexual. The same is true of prisoners, military men, and male prostitutes. The homosexual act that defines the actor as homosexual is the kiss on the lips.[20] C. A. Tripp, in *The Homosexual Matrix,* still one of the classic studies of homosexuality and heterosexism, writes:

> Part of what needs to be accounted for is the fact that murder, graft, and a host of violent crimes, though strongly taboo, fail to stir the intensely personalized emotions that can still be aroused by the homosexual. A main reason seems to be that homosexuality can touch people, can involve them vicariously, in ways that serious offenses do not. Its individual actions include components common in everyone's behavior, here seen in a violational context. Thus, for most people, one of the most disturbing images in homosexuality is that of two men kissing, for it is easily imagined and sharply at odds with what is expected.[21]

The kiss is an act that brings alien homosexual desire into the realm of the known and thus asserts a threatening parity between homosexual and heterosexual desire.

"Embedded" in the meaning of kissing scenes in drama is the question of whom the audience sees kissing. A heterosexist audience not only experiences the inevitable tension between actor (real person) and character (fictional creation) but adds to that experience the iconic reading of the kissing men as homosexuals and nothing but homosexuals. There may be, for some, sentimental stirrings evoked by the kiss. Others in the audience may admire the courage of the actors, who usually take great pains to establish their heterosexual credentials in their Playbill biographies. (Indeed, the number of actors who feel compelled to mention in the program the women to whom they are married or engaged or with whom they are cohabiting—irrelevant information at best—is a sign of the current fear in the theater of being taken as gay or, as a corollary assumption, HIV positive). In *Longtime Companion,* the lead actor on a soap opera, now thrown into an onscreen gay romance by the script, is terrified of what will happen to his career. He has been so successful in keeping his own gayness secret that even the gay writer of the soap opera thinks he's straight.

Some members of an audience watching a male-male kiss will lose track of characters and actors and see in the kiss not a moment in a drama, but a generic homosexual act: "Two men kissing!" A kiss between two men, then, can be used to unleash the force of the audience's gut response to homosexuality. The history of male-male kissing scenes in American drama shows that playwrights are always aware of their power and either exploit or try to defuse their shock value.

At the climactic moment of Arthur Miller's 1955 play, *A View from the Bridge,* Brooklyn longshoreman Eddie Carbone pins his wife's cousin, Rodolpho, to the wall and kisses him on the mouth, an action that on the Broadway stage in 1955 was far more shocking than it would be in a revival. Miller and his colleagues used this shock tactic not only to support the pathology of the central character but also to echo the shock of broken taboos central to Greek tragedy.

Eddie has raised his niece, Catherine, and, as Catherine has grown up, he has become so infatuated with her that he can no longer have sexual relations with his wife. Partly to placate his rightfully suspicious wife, Eddie has brought her two cousins over from Sicily illegally and gotten them jobs on the waterfront. Rodolpho, the younger cousin, a thin, blond, somewhat androgynous young man, becomes increasingly involved with Eddie's beloved Catherine, and this attachment puts Eddie into an Othello-like jealous rage against Rodolpho.

Paradoxically, Eddie's jealousy emerges as the suspicion that Rodolpho is homosexual and merely exploiting Catherine to get his American citizenship. Such a suspicion supports jealousy of Rodolpho while denying that he could be a sexual threat:

> EDDIE: I'm tellin' you sump'm, wait a minute. Please. . . . I'm tryin' to bring out my thoughts here. Couple of nights ago my niece brings out a dress which it's too small for her, because she shot up like a light this last year. He takes the dress, lays it on the table, he cuts it up; one-two-three, he makes a new dress. I mean he looked so sweet there, like an angel—you could kiss him he was so sweet.[22]

To Eddie, Rodolpho's effeminacy "ain't right" because it isn't masculine, yet it is a threat to his possession of Catherine. It also "ain't right" because it places Rodolpho in the feminine position of sexual passivity: "you could kiss him he was so sweet." Though this remark is a common ("Aye, madam, it is common") means of describing an effeminate man, one that denies him even the supposed sexual aggressiveness of the homosexual, it also hints at the possibility that Rodolpho's effeminacy might really be attractive to Eddie.

Rodolpho's transgression of stereotypical masculinity makes him, to Eddie, homosexual, though Eddie has no words for that. He doesn't need those words. The script assumes that effeminacy and homosexuality are so linked in an audience's mind that mention of one implies the other.

Rodolpho is given many of the attributes of the fifties homosexual stereotype—he is thin and blond, has a high voice, enjoys women's company, and needs his burly older brother to fight his battles for him—but of course Rodolpho is not *really* homosexual. Homosexuals are usually invisible—or dead—in fifties drama, even when they are invoked, and Miller seems as frightened of mentioning the word, of invoking more than a hint, as Eddie is.

Eddie's kiss is meant to be a brutal humiliation and exposure of Rodolpho's lack of manhood, which of course is synonymous with homosexuality:

> RODOLPHO: She'll be my wife. That is what I want. My wife!
> EDDIE: But what're you gonna be?
> RODOLPHO: I show you what I be.
> EDDIE: Come on, show me! What're you gonna be? Show me!

RODOLPHO *flies at him in attack.* EDDIE *pins his arms, laughing, and suddenly kisses him.* (p. 63)

All Eddie Carbone's sexual problems are expressed in that kiss: his thwarted desire for his eighteen-year-old niece, his shame at not being able to perform sexually with his wife, his terror of Rodolfo's challenge to his notions of manhood, and his attraction to Rodolpho. It is an act demonstrating the vulnerability of Eddie's sense of his masculinity; it is also a brutal act, but much of Arthur Miller's writing exists to vindicate crass patriarchal brutality.[23]

To prevent Rodolpho from marrying Catherine, Eddie betrays him and his brother Marco to the immigration authorities. Miller, true to form, sees all this nastiness as *Eddie's* "tragedy." At the end of the play, Alfieri, the lawyer who has served as a kind of Greek chorus, praises Eddie's "purity":

> But the truth is holy, and even as I know how wrong he was, and his death useless, I tremble, for I confess that something perversely pure calls to me from his memory—not purely good, but himself purely, for he allowed himself to be wholly known and for that I think I will love him more than all my sensible clients. (p. 86)

The words in which Miller tries to gift-wrap Eddie's brutality can soften the blow only if Eddie's action can be justified. What would justify that action? Rodolpho's homosexuality, of course. The play argues that it is all right for a young man not to be macho; it does not argue for his right to be what he is accused of being. The kiss is a nasty mockery of an unspeakable—and unactable—reality that the play, by implication, decries as much as Eddie does. It is a negation, on Eddie's part and on Miller's, of even the possibility of the reality the kiss mocks. We shall see in chapter 4 how typical Miller's tactics are of the American drama of his time.

Miller is writing his "modern" form of Greek tragedy in *A View from the Bridge,* complete with quasi-chorus. The hint of homosexuality is his counterpart to the horrible violation of taboos in Greek tragedy—like incest (also hinted at) or eating one's children.

Miller's attitude toward homosexuality can be attributed in part to the time and place of his plays and audience; it may also mirror the attitude of a well-meaning liberal of the forties and fifties. In his quasi-autobiographical play, *After the Fall* (1964), the insecure, beautiful singer, Maggie, is "for Negroes and Puerto Ricans and truck drivers,"[24] but violently against "fags." In one of their final feuds, Maggie accuses her husband:

MAGGIE: Fags wear pants like that; I told you. They attract each other with their asses.

QUENTIN: You calling me a fag now?

MAGGIE, *very drunk:* Just I've known fags and some of them didn't even know themselves that they were. . . . And I didn't know if you knew about that.

QUENTIN: That's a hell of a way to reassure yourself, Maggie. (p. 99)

Maggie's accusation is taken as the last word in cruelty, the ultimate castrating comment. Fags aren't men and therefore can't satisfy the sex goddess. Of course, in Maggie's reasoning, any man who does not show sexual interest in her is a "fag." Miller turns Maggie's homophobia against her. Is this possible because the heterosexist taunts are coming from a woman? In the recent, highly successful London production, Maggie was played by a black actress, so the heterosexism took on a richer, more ironic dimension. However it is seen, the "fags" in *After the Fall* are totally in Maggie's imagination. They do not visibly exist onstage any more than they existed in *A View from the Bridge.*

Eddie's kiss indicated, paradoxically, a feared but invisible, unthinkable homosexuality. Commercial gay works make gay characters more visible, but they are often cautious, even contradictory, in their use of the kiss. At the highly melodramatic conclusion of the first act of Mart Crowley's *The Boys in the Band* (1968),[25] the heterosexual Alan, in a fit of outrage, gay bashes the effeminate Emory while screaming a catalogue of homophobic epithets. As the two are separated, Harold, the guest of honor at the ill-fated birthday party, arrives and is kissed passionately by the hustler who has been bought as a birthday present. Crowley is quite aware of the shock value of this moment for many in his audience and exploits that value. The kiss is presented not as something gay men would naturally do but as something outrageous, more outrageous than the violence that preceded it (and for some audience members, Alan's violent attack would be "natural," justified). Because of Alan's presence, the self-hating homosexual characters see the kiss through heterosexist eyes—that is, the eyes of most of the audience. Harold's laughter at his "present" becomes sinister, bizarre, and the freak-show aspect of the play is reinforced.

In the film of Harvey Fierstein's *Torch Song Trilogy* (1988), the only onscreen passionate kiss is between Arnold's present and past lovers, Alan and Ed. In other words, the kiss is not connected to the love the film nominally affirms, but to betrayal. A male-male kiss is still unacceptable.

Lanford Wilson, whose plays are challenges to many American taboos, created a far more affirming kissing scene in his *Fifth of July*.[26] In 1980, Wilson revised his 1978 off-Broadway success for Broadway, with its larger, more diverse, and more conservative audience. The central character in *Fifth of July*, Ken Talley, lost the use of his legs in Vietnam and is terrified of going back to teaching because of how the students will look at him. Ken is also a homosexual, who has, because of his fears about his handicaps, a troubled relationship with his extremely intact lover, Jed. *Fifth of July* is one of the few commercially successful "gay plays" in which homosexuality is not the, or even a, problem for the leading characters or the people around them, and Ken and Jed's relationship is no more fraught than those of the heterosexual characters in the play. If homosexuality isn't a problem, how is it spoken about in drama presented before a Broadway audience for whom homosexuality, if it is anything at all, is a problem? More difficult: how does one *show* homosexuality in a nonproblematic way? Wilson's answer was a kissing scene.

If Lanford Wilson traded in stereotypes, Ken's paraplegia would be a physical manifestation of the moral, emotional, spiritual handicap of homosexuality. But Jed, who spends most of the play shirtless and in cutoffs, is physically as healthy a specimen as one can envision. That potential stereotype, then, is canceled out. Of course, part of showing anything onstage involves casting, and if, as was the case, Ken is played successively by William Hurt, Christopher Reeve, and Richard Thomas, both the handicap and the homosexuality are made palatable, unthreatening, by being in some sense erased. Superman a queer paraplegic?

Wilson, however, did not want Ken and Jed's homosexuality so easily ignored. To make sure the audience must deal with it, he wrote in a passionate kiss between Ken and Jed. In the original production at the Circle Repertory Company in the heart of Greenwich Village, that kiss came as a rather matter-of-fact event fifteen minutes into the play.

Wilson and his director, Marshall Mason, wanted to keep the kiss in the Broadway production, but they knew it was likely to evoke a response that would disrupt the play for a few moments (titters and macho noises). During the preview process, in which a play is revised on the basis of audience reaction, the kissing scene was moved to a number of different places, and audience reaction was gauged. Finally Wilson and Mason decided to put it at the beginning of the play, when an audience is still settling in. The idea was to get the response out of the way at the very outset rather than court the possibility of audience outbursts later on. At the rise of the curtain, Ken is seated at a desk (no sign yet of his artificial legs or crutches). Jed enters, crosses to Ken, and, after two lines, they kiss. Their physical relationship is established unambiguously.

Wilson knew that the sight of two men kissing was as potentially shocking in 1980 as it had been in 1955 when *A View from the Bridge* was first produced. The hostile response of some audience members had to be anticipated and accommodated without seriously compromising Wilson's desire to present, without problematizing, gay lovers. But the kiss is crucial in making gayness onstage more than a safe matter of words. The kiss in *Fifth of July* defines, affirms, and challenges. Its shock value is used to serve a purpose opposite to that of the kiss in *A View from the Bridge*. But an uneasy compromise had to be made with the audience, which became a factor in shaping the dramatic text.

The Gay Body

In John Guare's 1990 success, *Six Degrees of Separation*,[27] the major theatrical shock comes when Ouisa Kittredge, an affluent upper-middle-class New York housewife, opens the guest-bedroom door and discovers that her house guest, who she thinks is Sidney Poitier's son, is in bed with a male hustler. She—and the audience (from a safe distance; the bedroom is veiled by scrims)—see not the usual bodies properly hidden under the covers, but two men engaging rather energetically in an act of oral sex. This would be enough to make clear that Ouisa's house has been invaded by an outrageous, alien sexuality. However, for the next three or four minutes, the naked hustler chases the housewife around the living room and lunges at her husband, Flan.

In one sense the scene is farcical: Ouisa screams "He has a gun! He has a knife!" which is obviously untrue (the hustler is adorned only with socks), but expressing fear in phallic symbolism, however comic, may be the most appropriate response for Ouisa. In another sense, Guare has presented an image that is most unsettling, not just to Ouisa, but to most of his audience, who watches not just a naked man but the naked body of an aggressive gay man. The hustler's last words are a furious "Fuck you" directed to the husband as he grabs the lapels of Flan's bathrobe. In this circumstance "Fuck you" is not just an epithet: it is a sexual threat.

The Kittredge's house guest, a young black man who appeared on their doorstep the previous night claiming to be a friend of their children, is not who he claims to be. His Brooks Brothers shirt is not a genuine sign of class, but a borrowed, perhaps stolen, prop. Paul is a feared unknown—a gay black stranger, an alien who brings into the Kittredge house and sexless marriage a threatening, alien sexuality.[28]

Why did John Guare feel that such a barrage of frontal nudity, in addition to the simulated sex act, was crucial to this moment in his play? What is the threat of that naked body and in what ways does that body read as gay?

Like the male-male kiss, male nudity can cause audience members to lose sight of character and actor and see only an iconic phallic presence. Moreover, nudity creates self-consciousness as audience members focus momentarily on their own responses. That moment briefly changes the dynamics of theater, as the audience fragments into different interpretive communities and the dramatic illusion is lost in favor of a real physical presence.

What the audience sees as the hustler runs around the room is a naked male body, which to some extent takes precedence over the character the actor is playing. At one performance, a friend of mine overheard a woman sitting nearby comment, as the hustler ran around the stage, "I didn't know they flapped like that." Anatomical curiosity took precedence over focus on character or dramatic action in a reaction that is probably not uncommon. Indeed, there is no character except a nameless generic hustler, and the audience doesn't even know the man is a hustler until they are told so later. There is simply a nude male actor up there, but what does he figure? The audience sees what is usually unseen onstage, the penis, in this case attached to a man who refuses to be clothed; he remains nude throughout the scene and uses his nudity as a tool of aggression. Clearly he is unafraid of being seen, and even likes it, as does the mysterious Paul, who tells Ouisa, "It gives me a thrill to be looked at" (p. 38).

The character—and actor—insist upon being viewed, which in itself is a challenge to traditional gender roles. In her book on the male nude, Margaret Walters asserts, "There is still a rigid division between the sex that looks and the sex that is looked at."[29] Of course, men are supposed to be the lookers, not the objects of the gaze. Thus the willfully nude male is placing himself in the passive position of object of the gaze. But our hustler can hardly said to be passive, as he chases the Kittredges around the living room with only his nakedness as a weapon.

The real, physical presence of the nude body and the audience's awareness that the actor knows he is being seen is what makes theatrical nudity so powerful. The audience member is not an unseen (by the object of their gaze) voyeur, but a seen, known, though (usually) anonymous onlooker. And many people do not know how to look at the penis, do not think they should look. Yet the actor willingly and knowingly displays it to us. There is a personal transaction in such a scene onstage unlike that of a nude scene in a film. As Barbara Freedman defines it:

> What do we mean when we say that someone or something is theatrical? What we mean is that such a person is aware that she is seen, reflects that awareness, and so deflects our look. We refer to a fractured reciprocity whereby beholder and beheld reverse positions in a way that renders a steady position of spectatorship impossible.[30]

The notion of the "gay body" as some kind of "third sex," neither male nor female, has long since been discarded. The gay body is, indeed, no different from the straight body (for all one knows, the

naked actor who played the hustler could have been heterosexual).
The homosexual act had to be displayed in some way to indicate
that this is the body of a homosexual. Or is it? Does engaging in a
homosexual act for money make a man a homosexual? Many hustlers would say no. The enactment and the male body raise the
issue of what is a homosexual, or at least they explode the myth of
the distinctly marked homosexual body. Yet that naked body does
come to figure the homosexual body.

Margaret Walters maintains that, for complex reasons, in modern
Western culture "the exposed body is emotionally charged and
potentially subversive."[31] Once the notion of subversiveness is introduced to a discussion of the male body, we are on our way
toward a linking of that body with homosexuality. The unclad body
emphasizes the physical equivalence of gay and straight men; but
the nakedness, the forcing of the gaze and narcissistic enjoyment of
that gaze, the forbidden freedom of the uncovered penis, and the
assumption that viewing the penis is a pleasurable act all represent,
not male sexuality, but gay sexuality. Hence the proliferation of
nude men in mainstream drama about homosexuals and in mainstream gay drama. The danger in the willfully nude male body is
homosexuality.

John Guare is a heterosexual playwright focusing on the point of
view of upper-middle-class, heterosexual New Yorkers. The only
passion expressed is voiced by the young men with whom the
mysterious black, Paul, has slept. Trent Conway, the young man
who taught Paul how to ingratiate himself with Trent's rich New
York friends tells one of his peers: "Paul stayed with me for three
months. We went through the address book letter by letter. Paul
vanished with the L's. He took the address book with him. Well,
he's already been in all your houses. Maybe I will meet him again. I
sure would like to" (p. 79). Rick, the young actor Paul conned, tells
the audience: "We took a carriage ride in the park and he asked me
if he could fuck me and I had never done anything like that and he
did and it was fantastic. It was the greatest night I ever had and
before we got home he kissed me on the mouth and he vanished"
(p. 91).

Sexual passion in Guare's play is homosexual passion, forbidden
but fascinating, rendering even nominally straight men, like Rick,

sexually passive. "I didn't come here to be *this*," Rick says, before committing suicide. *This* is not homosexual, but sexually passive, unmanned. (That Rick feels compelled to kill himself puts *Six Degrees of Separation* back into the dramatic conventions of dramas of the forties and fifties.)

The uncovered penis, the naked male body, figures the power of what Paul represents—sexual chaos, mystery, the unknown, homosexuality. *Six Degrees of Separation* was an enormous success in New York, selling out even after its move from the small Mitzi E. Newhouse Theatre to the cavernous Vivian Beaumont. It is a mainstream play, written by a playwright who proclaims his heterosexuality in both program blurb and dust jacket and written for the white, upper-middle-class audience it depicts (it takes place in an elegant apartment overlooking Central Park, a few blocks from the Lincoln Center theater in which it was performed). In the world of Guare's play, blackness provokes a mixture of liberal guilt and uncertainty, but gayness provokes chaos. The phallus still has the same power it had in Greek and Roman theater, but nowadays that power is tied not to sexual potency and fertility but to homosexual pleasure.

In *Six Degrees of Separation,* Guare is appropriating what has become almost a convention of both mainstream and coterie gay drama, male nudity. The sight of the nude man as a scopular object, the viewing of the male nude as a pleasurable activity, is a common element of gay theater. Gay men do not react with shock at the sight of a naked man any more than heterosexual men react with shock at the sight of a naked woman. One question is the extent to which the nudity in *Six Degrees of Separation,* like the nudity in the sixties musical *Hair* or in Peter Shaffer's highly successful *Equus* (1973), is responsible for the play's considerable commercial success. The titillation of watching the forbidden is one of theater's traditional attractions.

Classical American gay drama—works by Tennessee Williams and William Inge—were "daring" because the man was presented as the object of the gaze. Stanley Kowalski, in undershirt, gaudy bowling shirt, and silk pajama pants, exists to be looked at, and the women in Williams' *A Streetcar Named Desire* (1947) look and respond. Even Blanche's denigration of Stanley is tied to an appreciation of his physical presence: "A man like that is someone to go out with—once—twice—three times when the devil is in you."[32] The women look and the man is looked at; this pattern is central to Williams' work. Maggie the Cat, walking around in her slip in Williams' *Cat on a Hot Tin Roof* (1955), may be erotically charged for some members of the audience, but she isn't really the object of the gaze. Brick is. Maggie looks at him and comments on his beauty: "I wish you would lose your looks. If you did it would make the martyrdom of Saint Maggie a little more bearable. But no such goddamn luck. I actually believe you've gotten better looking since you went on the bottle."[33]

Brick certainly isn't the only male character in Williams to be the object of the gaze: there are, among others, Val Xavier in *Orpheus Descending* (1957) and Chance Wayne in *Sweet Bird of Youth* (1959). William Inge follows the same pattern: it is the hunky man who upsets households and communities in *Picnic* (1953) and *Come Back, Little Sheba* (1949). Straight men could fantasize about the sexual attractiveness and power these male characters had, and women in the audience could identify with the women in the play, but gay men knew what these plays were about. Inge and Williams wrote sexual fantasies that celebrate male beauty and sexual attractiveness by reversing the usual roles of seer and seen, placing the point of view in the eyes of the female characters. The plays may have been—should have been—somewhat unsettling, but in the fifties the men kept their pants on.

When gay drama "came out" off Broadway in the seventies, nudity became almost a convention, as female nudity became a convention for the movies. Liberation meant the freedom to look at naked men onstage and to admit that that was pleasurable. Robert Patrick's work is full of men taking their clothes off, though Patrick often satirizes the narcissism and exploitation involved in New York gay culture. In *T Shirts* (1978), three gay men undress and group together to watch their reflection on the television screen:

> TOM: When there's light just on you, you reflect real bright in the TV screen.
> KINK: We really do look just like three pretty little Maxfield Parrish nudes.

TOM: Even Marvin's pretty.
MARVIN: Isn't it nice? I discovered it the other day.
(*They admire themselves,* TOM *especially, try two or three different poses.*[34]

As the handsome, young Tom continues to pose nude, long after his older companions have put their clothes back on, Patrick satirizes a world in which the handsome stranger becomes not merely the object of displaced sexual fantasy, as in Williams and Inge, but a real sexual possibility, the handsome young gay who will get ahead through his looks and sexual availability. When one of the older, less good-looking characters comments glibly that looks aren't everything, Tom quickly rejoins: "Yes, they are. Don't give me that tired shit. They are so. If you've got looks, you can get anything else. And if you don't, there isn't anything else worth having. I'm sick of that crap. Looks *are* everything" (p. 38). Yet the world Tom's looks allow him to enter will also exploit him: "When a society's only values are good looks and money, sooner or later people are going to wind up exchanging one for the other," and the result is "a conglomerate as heartless as Con Ed" (p. 35). Marvin, who offers this social wisdom, also admits, "If I had the slightest chance of getting in on any of it, you wouldn't hear a peep from me!" (p. 35).

Like most commercial playwrights, Patrick has it both ways in *T Shirts,* both titillating and criticizing his New York gay audience. He satirizes a society that puts undue value on looks, but he buys into that society by offering looks for money, by offering the sight of the naked Tom to his audience. He defuses Marvin's analysis of his culture by having Marvin admit, "The only reason I'm reactionary is because I get no reactions" (p. 35).

Patrick's *Mercy Drop* (1973, published 1979), not only moved toward a climactic nude scene but featured on the cover of the published version a production shot featuring a nude young man (the actor Kevin Breslin as Johnny).[35] Clearly the sight of the nude male was considered as integral part of reading the published text as it was of seeing the produced play.

In *Mercy Drop,* as in much other gay drama, being the object of the gaze empowers:

JOHNNY: I was thinking I was naked and helpless and small and alone
    behind locked doors in an uncaring city in the arms of a strong

and hungry meat-eating animal—and there was nowhere to go and no one to call and nothing that I could do—but one thing—and I did it!

JOHNNY *spins in* MARVIN's *arms and stands tall and gorgeous.*

JOHNNY: I spun in your arms and stood tall and proud and I said: "I am Venus, Aphrodite, Cytherea, Kypris, the foam-born, goddess of love and beauty, and I have been trapped these fifteen years in this boy's body—and you and your touch have freed me—for this you shall forevermore be my poet and my puppet, my favorite, fop and fool."

JOHNNY *stands radiant. Suddenly he flings* MARVIN *to the ground.*

JOHNNY: And you knelt! You knelt!

MARVIN: And I was conquered.[36]

Johnny's empowerment comes from his celebration of his own nakedness, which fully reveals his androgyny. The slender, "girl-ishly beautiful" (p. 5) adolescent with long hair and soft face also has a large penis. He comes to see himself not as the passive boy, not even as the classical passive boy, the subservient Ganymede, but as the powerful Venus, whom men worshiped and served. Johnny moves from masculine passivity to feminine power as Marvin kneels before him in worship and submission and also in preparation for oral sex. Johnny's naked body is the most vivid image of what he represents in the play. At the same time the presentation of that image onstage and the use of that image to market the published text represents another aspect of gay culture in the seventies, the marketing of the heretofore forbidden image of the male nude as object of desire.[37]

Such combined exploitation and exploration of the metaphoric possibilities of the male nude became a convention of gay theater in the era between Stonewall and the age of AIDS (as we shall see later, AIDS playwrights like Robert Chesley use the nude body in very different ways). By 1980, gay drama had moved into mainstream venues, where nudity provided shock value for part of the audience as it provided the expected titillation for the gay clientele.

In the first scene of Martin Sherman's *Bent* (1979), Max, suffering from a hangover, is surprised and mystified when a blond, naked man emerges from his bedroom. Wolf is Max's trick from the night before, his naked body the sign of Max's sexual promiscuity. But

Wolf is also the first victim of the Nazis: by the end of the scene he has been shot and his throat has been cut. As his nudity represents the most visibly overt sexuality in the play, so his murder is the first bloody action. Wolf embodies both the threatened gay sexuality and the brutal physical violence of the Nazis.

Why does Wolf have to appear naked? Why not in underpants or a jock strap? The answer is that they would cover the focal penis, which figures homosexual desire and the promiscuous gay underworld in which Max lives at the beginning of the play. For some in the audience it represents the sexual freedom a criminally repressive society will destroy; for others it represents an alien, threatening sexuality.

At the beginning of the second act of Terrence McNally's oft-rewritten *The Lisbon Traviata* (1985), Stephen, the unhappy opera queen, comes into his apartment early in the morning and confronts the naked body of his partner's new lover. Stephen's passion is almost entirely displaced onto opera, particularly the cult of Maria Callas. "Opera is about us, our life and death passions—we all love, we're all going to die. Maria understood that,"[38] Stephen tells the naked Paul. The irony of the scene is in the talk of and music of opera juxtaposed with the physical reality of the naked Paul. Mc-Nally's opera queens do not live in the world of physical reality but of camp fantasy. The displacement of their emotions onto opera and dead divas cuts them off from real life-and-death passions. The naked male body is in many ways the opposite of the opulent, sentimental fantasy of Maria Callas: performed opera is about transcendence of the flesh. What Stephen and his fellow opera queen, Mendy, have in common with Callas is that, like her, they live in unhappy isolation. Pleasure in male sexuality, represented by Paul's nakedness, is replaced by the sentimentalizing of opera's version of (male-created) feminine passion.

The gay Spanish filmmaker Pedro Almodovar's use of actor Antonio Banderas is a case study in how nudity can figure gayness. In two of Almodóvar's films, *La Ley del Deseo* (*Law of Desire*) (1987) and *Átame* (*Tie Me Up, Tie Me Down*) (1990), the handsome young Banderas plays a psychopath, brutally and sometimes murderously trying to possess fully the object of his infatuation (the two characters are different in class and sexual orientation but identical in motivation and even in their penchant for home repair). In *Law of Desire,* Banderas, who plays a gay man obsessed with a gay film director, appears partially clad or naked in many of his scenes, the object of the gaze. His desire to possess the filmmaker is presented as murderous pathology but also feminine, a gay male version of Glenn Close's character, Alex, in the film *Fatal Attraction* (1987).

In *Tie Me Up, Tie Me Down,* he is, except for one shot of him from overhead as part of a fragment image of a sex scene, fully clothed, while the leading lady is often nude or seminude. Though his character is equally possessive and pathological, he is presented neutrally. Almodóvar seems to think making the nude Banderas the passive object of the gaze changes his sexuality, makes him more passive, feminine, like the nude willing victim in *Tie Me Up.* It is also clear that *the film* is a (failed) attempt at reaching a mass audience larger than that for the overtly gay *Law of Desire* and that male nudity would be scary for members of the former audience and a turn-on for the latter.

Like men kissing, male nudity still has shock value for many in a "mainstream" audience, while it offers long forbidden pleasure to gay men.

Drag

When the audience entered Stratford-upon-Avon's Swan Theatre for the 1989 production by Danny Boyle for the Royal Shakespeare Company of Ben Jonson's seldom performed *Epicoene, or the Silent Woman,*[39] they saw clothes strewn about the stage. When Clerimont and his page entered half clad, the audience realized that the clothes strewn about the stage were not so much the signs of a sloppy master and servant as of sexual urgency. The page was indeed Clerimont's "ingle." But the youth, reversing Elizabethan convention, was embodied by a young woman, not a boy. As the Elizabethan theater defused the danger of embodying a heterosexual relationship by casting boys as women,[40] this production began by defusing the contemporary horror of pederasty by casting an androgynous young woman as the boy. The audience could see the idea of the sexual relationship of Clerimont and his "ingle" without dealing with a literal embodiment of a potentially shocking relationship.

A viewer might think that Boyle was buying iri to the old, inaccurate cliche of male-male sexual relationships as a parody of male-female relationship. However, it became clear when Epicoene, the title character, appeared, that Boyle was playing a much more elaborate game with his audience's assumptions about sex and homosexuality. The androgynous young man who played Epicoene (not a regular member of the RSC but cast for this role only) was quite intentionally the most beautiful "woman" on the stage, though no effort was made to disguise his obviously masculine voice, thus underscoring once again the gap between body and word. The program listed the actor, John Hannah, as "Hannah John," but the voice let the audience in on the joke before the end of act 3.

What was being presented here? First, the misogyny in Jonson's script was underscored by this beautiful transvestite surrounded by grotesque women. One might ask whether the production was commenting on the misogyny in Jonson's script or reinforcing it, but one could not avoid noticing the way in which the production confounded its presentation of the unfortunate, ancient mixture of gender and homosexuality by ending with Dauphine Eugenie, the architect of Epicoene's disguise, rolling arour ! on the floor with the now unwigged and unfrocked Epicoene, clearly masculine and clearly Dauphine Eugenie's "ingle." With the kiss of Dauphine Eugenie and his half-clad male lover, the joke on old Morose was turned into a joke on the audience—and also a challenge to it. Homosexual desire and transvestism have been untied, and one has, in the embrace of the two young men, the only nongrotesque presentation of sexuality in the play.

Clearly the creators of this production of *Epicoene* were mindful of the mainstream audience, gradually exposing to them the text they saw in Jonson's script, a text that saw the world of the play as a network of misogyny and homosexual desire. The production mocked the misogyny in Jonson's play while celebrating the homosexual desire with which the misogyny maintains an unstable relationship. To a mainstream audience member, this might have seemed a subversive production. It not only subverted, as farce traditionally does, patriarchal authority and sexuality but subverted as well the heterosexual norm that farce traditionally upholds.

This production of *Epicoene,* then, had two characters in drag: a woman dressed as a boy and a man dressed as a woman, which is a modification and expansion of the central joke in Jonson's dark comedy. It is difficult to imagine the erotics of *Epicoene* in Jonson's theater, in which boys played all the parts: "Its mannish women no less than its 'ingles' and its 'manikins' were boys, of course, whose undeveloped or precocious sexuality would have lent an edge to its audience's attention—satiric, paedophilic, what you will—inseparable from Jonson's textual emphasis on Jonson's cross-gendered comic types."[41] At the least, the erotics of performance were different from, or complicated, the erotics of the script. Having a woman play the "ingle" as a "trouser role" in 1989 ties the scene to another tradition in theater (in the late seventeenth and eighteenth centuries, trouser roles allowed women to display more of their bodies than traditional women's roles, thus truly reversing the erotics of the scripted situation), while it defuses the danger of the pederastic relationship, which is taboo on stage and off. Epicoene himself is another matter. In this 1989 production, the man in drag playing *Epicoene* brought into the production the politics of drag and its relationship to homosexuality.

The fact is that, unlike kissing scenes and the uncovered penis, drag may figure homosexuality but is not, for a heterosexist audience, transgressive. It merely underscores the connection between homosexuality and effeminacy. The Harvey Fierstein-Jerry Herman musical, *La Cage aux Folles* (1983), was a hit despite its lead characters' being a homosexual couple, because one of the gay men spent most of the show in a dress and was almost completely woman-identified. The musical was about a middle-aged married couple whose son is about to get married to the wrong girl. Gay men could take the drag queen's song, "I Am What I Am," as a song of gay pride, but the heterosexual audience saw a reinforcement of the usual stereotypes of gay couples ("Who's the man and who's the woman?").

Fierstein's *Torch Song Trilogy* (1981) reinforces the same stereotypes. The leading character is a drag queen who aspires to being the ideal Jewish mother. Arnold's values are those of the typical

Wednesday-matinee audience. With his overweight body and gravelly voice, Arnold is an unusual drag queen, a textbook example of what Richard Dyer calls *inbetweenism*[42], which he sees as a dwindling species: "Once the E.R.A. and gay civil rights bills have been passed, me and mine will find ourselves swept under the carpets like the blacks done to Amos, Andy, and Aunt Jemima."[43]

The powerful final scene in *Epicoene* offered the unmasking of the young page in drag and the embrace that followed. The drag was merely part of a nasty trick, not an expression of the gender identification of the character. The putting on of drag by the central character in *La Cage aux Folles,* "with a rare combination of girlish excitement and manly restraint" (how in between can you get?), is moving from the humdrum male life to a glamorous fantasy world as it is a move from aging to eternal youth: "So when my spirits start to sag/ I hustle out my highest drag/ And put a little more mascara on."[44]

Drag defuses the threat of homosexuality. Albin's "big switch" to the glamorous Zaza is fulfillment of the wish "to be someone who's anyone other than me." As the audience watches Albin don his drag, they see a middle-aged man become a expensively, garishly dressed caricature of a woman—a living example of inbetweenism. Moreover, drag is merely "dressing up." In Albin's song, we see him "put on" a costume in no physical way connected to his "real self." It is a theatrical act placed within the context of theater.[45]

Moreover, drag places Albin's homosexuality and his thirty-year relationship with his partner in a familiar pattern. The dress of one character—and the playing out of that character's wifely and maternal feelings—equates the "marriage" with heterosexual marriages. In his liner notes for the original cast album, Harvey Fierstein writes: "Here, amidst the age-old triangle of mother, father, and child, we found our justification, our universality, our reason to create." In making Albin a devoted mother, Fierstein denies his maleness and, in a central way, his homosexuality. Drag makes homosexuality safe.

Still, drag can be more than a reinforcement of a stereotype of the effeminate homosexual; it can be a defiance of rigid definitions of sexual identity. Here is where "La Cagelles," the chorus of the musical *La Cage aux Folles,* complicated the audience's response.

The singing, dancing drag artists were so convincing in their gaudy, often revealing costumes, one could not spot the one or two women in the chorus until the curtain call. To confuse gender more, offstage women's voices were mixed into the sound of the chorus the audience saw. Drag here was not caricature—as it was for Albin—but convincing imitation.

While the use of drag in La Cage aux Folles shows the slipperiness of gender definitions, it never unties the link of homosexuality to effeminacy. Albin's lover was not a drag artist but was always played by an actor whose heterosexuality was never in doubt. The presence of Gene Barry, television's Bat Masterson, as a homosexual kept things safe for the suburban audiences. Homosexuals wear dresses—or act like they should wear dresses. Categories are kept intact.

In the 1988 Broadway hit, M. Butterfly, drag, ironically, denied the homosexuality of a seventeen-year affair between two men. The audience is to believe that a French diplomat, Rene Gallimard, conducted his affair with a Chinese transvestite totally believing that women's clothes covered a woman's body. At one point Gallimard allows that his belief might have willfully erased the shadow of a doubt: "Did I not undress her because I knew, somewhere deep down, what I would find? Perhaps. Happiness is so rare that our mind can turn somersaults to protect it."[46] Here and elsewhere, David Henry Hwang, the playwright, turns not-very-convincing rhetorical somersaults to keep his homosexual affair heterosexual, to keep the focus on the way Western men see Asians and the way men project their own fantasies onto women. Hwang has his characters spell everything out for the audience; this is not the most interesting way to write a play, but it keeps the audience from drawing its own conclusions. When a judge asks the transvestite how he could fool his lover for so long, the man answers: "One, because when he finally met his fantasy woman, he wanted more than anything to believe that she was, in fact, a woman. And second, I am an Oriental. And being an Oriental, I could never be completely a man" (p. 83).

Hwang displaces the usual heterosexist baggage of effeminacy onto Asians and exploits Western disdain for Asians. When Song undresses in front of Gallimard and offers himself—as a man—to his lover of seventeen years, Gallimard answers: "I'm a man who loved a woman created by a man. Everything else—simply falls short" (p. 90). The plodding literalness of Hwang's play also keeps it heterosexual. If the play acknowledged the subtext that Gallimard loved a man in woman's clothing, it would have had more complexity. Taking Gallimard's assertions at face value, as the play expects its audiences to do, is like accepting the denials of "outed" gay performers.

Hwang's play is most interesting for what it shows about the taste of Broadway audiences. Homosexuality is hinted at but safely displaced; so a play managed to be about the long-term romance of two men while denying that it is about that at all. The white man is safely heterosexual, duped by a wily drag queen who he thought all along was a woman. There are strong similarities between M. Butterfly and Six Degrees of Separation (1990), the next serious American drama to be a commercial success. Both are about nonwhite homosexual con men who dupe upper-middle-class whites. In both, the nonwhite gay man is there to provide a catalyst for a commentary on the heterosexual, white experience. The homosexual is basically a crafty actor who gains acceptance, even love, by conning heterosexuals. The homosexual is not who or what he seems. Drag in M. Butterfly is a means of commenting on Gallimard's patriarchal view of women and Asians. Yet the homosexual is still a man in a dress.

In performance, Song changes from drag into western men's clothing onstage, an act that usually elicits applause from the audience. What are they applauding? A man's ability to wear men's clothing? The convincing nature of the female masquerade Song enacted during the first two acts? Or the fact that this man has finally moved into gender-appropriate clothing?

It is only in his afterword to the published text that Hwang acknowledges that his play could have a different meaning for homosexuals. But that meaning, as he sees it, has to do only with the way "Rice Queens" (Caucasian gay men who are attracted to Asian men) treat their Asian lovers, who inevitably, for reasons of racial self-hatred, see themselves as "the women" in the relationship.

The work of serious gay theater artists over the past forty years has defied the sort of formulations drag has represented in the commercial theater. In recent years some of their work has developed a wide, mainstream audience. Charles Busch's Vampire Lesbi-

ans of Sodom ran for years off Broadway, and Charles Ludlam's *The Mystery of Irma Vep* has become a staple of professional theaters across the country and was recently produced in London. Ludlam's play is an example of how drag can be used to confound the very formulations of which it inevitably becomes part.

In *The Mystery of Irma Vep,* each of the two actors plays male and female characters in a quasi-Victorian "penny dreadful" that travesties the sex roles central to Gothic romance. What becomes clear in performance is that both the male and female characters are "drag" enactments, cartoons of the ways in which the characters play out their sex roles. The title character, Irma Vep, is another character in disguise, but when "Irma" is unmasked, the other character is not sure which of the characters played by the actor playing "Irma" has been revealed:

> LADY ENID (*Reaches up and rips off* IRMA's *face, which is a rubber mask, revealing the other player*): Edgar?
> JANE: No, Jane!
> LADY ENID: Jane! You?[47]

This metatheatrical moment owes its success, as do a number of inside jokes in the play, to the multiple, role-within-role-playing that is a great deal of the fun of *The Mystery of Irma Vep,* but it also underscores the fluidity of gender the role-playing asserts. Irma could be Edgar or Jane who, after all, are embodied by one actor. Edgar and Jane, like Irma, are disguises. In Stan Wojewodski's 1991 production at Center Stage in Baltimore, "Irma" was played by the actor who plays Edgar and Jane, but not with the rubber mask the script calls for. Instead, the actor is in drag, including a pillbox hat and veil, but without a wig (the actor's own short hair was clearly visible).[48] Enid's misperception that Irma was Edgar was the audience's as well. Gender role playing became all the more complicated.

In serious works, like writer Neil Bartlett's and composer Nicholas Bloomfield's musical theater piece *Sarrasine* (1990), it can be part of a deconstruction of gender and of the relationship between erotic desire and art.

In choosing Honore de Balzac's 1830 story *Sarrasine* for his theater piece, Bartlett is also paying homage to the work of literary theory that inspires such a pluralistic reading, Ronald Barthes' elaborate analysis, *S/Z*.[49]

In Bartlett's free adaptation of Balzac's story, it is the present and the elegant Mme. de Rochefide has come to Venice to hire the famed singer Zambinella to sing for her. De Rochefide had heard Zambinella sing once, when she was nineteen years old and has been ever since obsessed with the purity of that voice and fascinated with the castrato's sexual ambiguity: "She was dressed as a woman, but everyone said, 'You know he's not a man.' . . . And I remember thinking that is too beautiful to be a man."[50] Mme. de Rochefide's use of *that* to free La Zambinella from conventional gender definitions connects to her fascination with what she sees as the purity and perfection of the eunuch artist.

La Zambinella appears first as a two-hundred-and-fifty-year-old eunuch: "His face and body are ruined, sexless." His body is covered by a "shapeless gown made from what looks like an old theatre curtain." With his theatrical bearing, full makeup and rings on every finger, he is the incarnation of the aging diva. When La Zambinella finally speaks, however, it is in the crass language of a cynical showgirl: "I don't care if everybody is waiting they can wait all fucking night I'm not doing it right?" This first incarnation of the aging castrato was played by the famous drag queen Bette Bourne, founder of the performing group "Bloolips." Soon, two more versions of La Zambinella join Ms. Bourne: Zambinella as the young diva, as he appeared to the young French nobleman Sarrasine in Balzac's story (played by a man, Francois Testory). This second incarnation is the most ambiguous. Testory changes from gown to showgirl costume, to spangled g-string, to an eighteenth-century Italian aristocratic boy's outfit. Testory represents Zambinella as protean object of desire. Finally, we see Zambinella as a worldly wise chanteuse (played by singer Beverly Klein). Bourne usually speaks and sings in English; Testory, in Italian; Klein, in French. These three embodiments of Zambinella appear together for most of the musical play. Together they represent the complex, illusive castrato.

The Zambinellas present Mme. de Rochefide with the score of an opera based on the story of Sarrasine and demand that she participate with them in its enactment. As three performers play Zambinella, Mme. de Rochefide plays herself and the young nobleman Sarrasine, who falls in love with Zambinella and abducts her but discovers that she is a man and is killed by henchmen of Zambinella's protector, the Cardinal.

The various stories collected in *Sarrasine* center on the primary transaction of theater, performance for money. Zambinella was castrated for money, performs for money, and receives money from his lovers. He remembers his lovers by counting the rings they gave him as payment for his sexual favors. Mme. de Rochefide pays for this final performance of Zambinella. Yet within these transactions, beauty is created and love is inspired. The story of Sarrasine is also one of erotic desire and gender. Sarrasine became enamored of what he thought was a beautiful woman. In the Balzac story, he screams at the person he now sees as a sham woman: "Monster! You who can give life to nothing. For me, you have wiped women from the earth."[51] Bartlett's Sarrasine is twice removed from the audience. He is enacted by Mme. de Rochefide's reading of his lines, and he is seen through Sarrasine's descriptions and reactions. Sarrasine is the audience member who falls in love with a performance—a perfect musical performance and a performance of feminity. Zambinella is masculine and feminine, though neither male nor female. He/she is protean, enlarged and freed by his/her gender ambiguity. Bartlett says that "the castrato is sex itself, the ultimate sexual myth. Straight men, gay men, women—everyone fell in love with the castrato."[52]

In Balzac's story, Zambinella admits to being heartless, unable to love. In Bartlett's work, Zambinella may not be able to experience love, but he/she, the artist, can dream it: "I dream of it every night and when I dream I can see love . . . I want it. I ache for it. For loves different to any you have every known; loves stronger than any you could every imagine." Sarrasine's love is destroyed when he discovers that Zambinella does not fit his gender definitions; she is a monster or an "illusion." She is denied reality. But Bartlett's musical play celebrates illusions, dreams, art as the sites of love. Like many works of gay theater, it echoes Blanche DuBois's proclamation, "I don't want realism. I want magic!"

> If your dreams aren't dreams of Love,
> How will you live
> When you're awake?

In waking life, though, power comes from being unknowable, unattainable. At the end, Mme. de Rochefide says: "No one will have known me. I am proud of that." The "perfect," unknowable Zambinella has, for her, provided moments of beauty and inspired dreams of love.

In Bartlett's piece of theater magic, the young, nineteenth-century sculptor is given the body and voice of a middle-aged woman. The castrato is given male and female bodies, masculine and feminine characteristics. Zambinella's female drag created the illusion of a woman, but hides that fact that he is a man. His male costume creates the illusion of a man, but hides his lack of male genitalia. Drag, then, is not feminine apparel hiding a male body. It is another question mark in a work that offers no stable answers. *Sarrasine,* like Zambinella, is fascinating, yet ultimately impossible to establish clearly. It shows the way drag, traditionally used to parody women and reinforce gay sterotypes, can be used to unmoor seemingly fixed gender categories.

"I saw! I know!"

The epigraph for this chapter is Blanche DuBois' response to seeing her husband, Allan Grey, in bed with another man: "I saw! I know! You disgust me. . . ."[53] "Seeing" a homosexual act for Blanche is "disgusting." For Ouisa, in *Six Degrees of Separation* (1990), seeing is terrifying, a prelude to what she thinks will be a violent attack and robbery. But between *A Streetcar Named Desire* (1947) and *Six Degrees,* "seeing" has moved from an act recounted in exposition to an act seen by the audience. The kiss in *A View from the Bridge* was shocking in 1955, but it was not an enactment of homosexual desire, which still could not be shown onstage. However cautiously or elliptically presented, as in *Fifth of July* (1978), the enactment of homosexuality is more than words. Like homosexuality itself— indeed, like sexuality—it is a matter of bodies and seeing, and it is here that a discussion of gay drama must begin. However, before the kissing scenes, the nudity, and the drag, there was a history of coded representation of homosexuality that reinforced a sense of identity and community for the homosexuals in the audience while maintaining the heterosexists' sanctions, taboos, and superstitions about homosexuality and homosexuals.

"Robert Chesley in New York, 1983." Photo: Mark I. Chester. Reprinted by permission of Mark I. Chester.

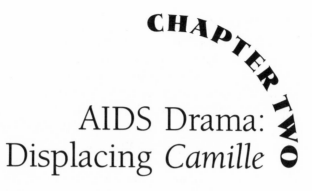

AIDS Drama: Displacing *Camille*

"I have lived for love and now I am dying of it."
Marguerite Gautier, in Alexandre Dumas, fils,
La Dame aux Camélias

"Something bad is happening.
Something very bad is happening.
Something stinks—
Something immoral—
Something so bad that words
Have lost their meaning."
Dr. Charlotte, in William Finn, *Falsettoland*

AIDS drama would seem to be more likely material for the final chapter of a narrative of gay drama to the present. I want, however, to resist the reinforcement of AIDS eschatology; the gay community is very much alive. More to the point, it is in AIDS drama and AIDS discourse that we see most clearly the continuation of nineteenth-century constructions and metaphors of disease and what Paula Treichler calls "the myth of the homosexual body." Gay AIDS dramas dismantle the misapprehensions about AIDS while affirming the Person With AIDS. They also, in the process, deconstruct oppressive constructions of homosexuality that have been perpetuated by popular dramatic representations.

Acting AIDS

During a rehearsal of a play of mine, an actor playing a character who is HIV-positive asked me whether it would be all right if he had the makeup people paint some Kaposi's sarcoma lesions on his hands so that the audience could see his "condition." Without the signs of an AIDS-related disease, how could he show anything? AIDS itself is invisible, known only by its effects—physical, psychological, and social. HIV-positive status, too often equated in our society with full-blown AIDS, is yet more invisible, a dormant virus that will rouse at a signal from an unseen alarm clock.

My young actor faced the problem of acting AIDS. Enactments of AIDS and people with AIDS reflect the ways in which AIDS is, to use Paula A. Treichler's term, "an epidemic of signification." But the signification of AIDS is fraught with complexities. Ironically, we cannot depict AIDS: we can depict only the symptoms of those diseases the immunovirus allows to infect and ravage a person. We can show more easily the social and political status of the Person With AIDS. AIDS itself is invisible, unactable.

Is the very fact of the body of a Person With AIDS the most powerful theatrical sign of the condition? In London in 1990, a theater company heralded its presentation of *Hamlet* starring a Person With AIDS in the title role. What did *Hamlet,* more about social and political corruption and disease than about physical disease, have to do with AIDS? How was acting *Hamlet* a political statement for a Person With AIDS? Was it not the same statement of courage and artistic devotion in the face of almost insurmountable difficulties that it was when Ian Charleson, dying of HIV-related infections, perilously played Hamlet at the National Theater the year before? The difference is that Charleson's condition was not known outside the theatrical community until his death. For most of his audience, the fact of AIDS was not one of the signs of Charleson's performance. The second *Hamlet* was more about performing with AIDS than it was about Hamlet.

Acting the part of a Person With AIDS focuses the audience's attention on the body and the person's drastically altered relationship to his body. It also focuses attention on the person's altered relationship to society. AIDS discourse not only reflects a horror of

he upper-middle class inhabited by most characters in gay
. Tom is a baker, his shirt still covered with flour as he sits in
ce station and tells of the events that led to his arrest.
m has lived for three years with Johnny, and he remembers
y Johnny's physicality, his energy, his twitching, his hyperac-
It is clear throughout the monologue that Tom inhabits a
flective, physical world: "I'm your kinna guy, fellas, I won't
about it. We do what we do, we do what's gotta be done."[6]
e audience, like the unseen police, are led to believe that
s confession will be about murdering the already dying Johnny,
d with pain, but Tom's confession is far less conventional.
Johnny died in Tom's arms, Tom "cut a place on his cheek
e he used to dig and on his chest where he used to gouge out
e red marks and in his hair. And when the blood came I licked
him" (p. 75). Tom, who has tested negative, hopes the inges-
of his lover's blood will kill him, but the act is also the ultimate
sical communion—literally sharing the loved one's blood and
infection. Wilson uses "came," the past tense of "come," to
gest the sexual dimension of Tom's act and the way in which
S forces sex into the past and into associations with infection.
ike Chesley's plays, *A Poster of the Cosmos* is presented totally
ugh words—exposition—but at its center is a vivid, harrowing
sical image, a reverse vampirism in which receiving blood of a
ed one is deadly.
The title of Wilson's play not only refers to the defunct soccer
m Johnny loved but testifies to the elusiveness of even the most
ncrete language. The title contains physical reality one step re-
ved—a picture of a soccer team—as Tom's narration, his words,
th express and belie the physical power of his act, which is for
uch of the play misunderstood by the audience. The word *Cosmos*
both specific-physical and universal-metaphysical, the dual worlds
the love Tom feels for Johnny.
The denouement of much AIDS drama is often a symbolic enact-
ent of the disappearance of the body, as if acting the effects of the
ondition would somehow be unbearable or sacrilegious. Yet enact-
g disappearance places the Person With AIDS, rather than his
dversaries, in the position of being the "problem" of traditional
alistic drama—the problem that has to be removed by the final

physicality but also reinforces the political dimension of the physical. It takes us back to the body of the person infected with the virus and to the problematic body of the homosexual as well. "Whatever else it may be," Paula Treichler writes, "AIDS is a story, or multiple stories, read to a surprising extent from a text that does not exist: the body of the male homosexual."[1] For Simon Watney, AIDS is "embodied as an exemplary and admonitory drama, relayed between the image of the miraculous authority of clinical medicine and the faces and bodies of individuals who clearly disclose the stigmata of their guilt. The principal target of this sadistically punitive gaze is the body of the homosexual."[2] And the signs—the debilitation, the lesions—become in this drama evidence of the moral and physical "disease" of homosexuality. Who is the audience for what Simon Watney calls "the spectacle of AIDS"? Those already inclined to marginalize—or worse—the homosexual, whose sexual activities have been brought out of the closet for this spectacle of retribution. Who is the author? The same audience whose ignorance, prejudice, and power are reinforced by this drama.

The body of the AIDS patient, then, becomes a principal player in a moral allegory as primal as *Everyman*. AIDS is not disease, but retribution. The lesions caused by Kaposi's sarcoma are signs of corruption. Therefore the Person With AIDS should be isolated but not offered any of the benefits of society: compassion, government support for medical treatment. But he also should be used as the sign for the inevitable result of "giving in" to homosexual desire.

What separates drama from literature is the need for the body, though, as I pointed out in the first chapter, the body depicting the gay man needn't be a "homosexual body." Thus the very impossibility of fixing the homosexual body is dramatized by having a heterosexual play a homosexual. Enacting the diseased body is equally difficult, thus the physical problem of AIDS drama, which has its antecedents in earlier dramatizations of disease.

In Robert Chesley's play *Hold,* Dog imagines his dead lover and reminisces with him while slowly taking off all his clothes and revealing that he is "exotically spotted with a considerable number of Karposi's Sarcoma lesions."[3] It is likely that Chesley, the most intensely physical of gay playwrights, wanted the part played by an actor with KS rather than one with lesions painted by a makeup person, which forces the audience to come to terms with the physical reality and disfigurement of the AIDS-related disease, the sign of AIDS itself. What is left for the central character in *Hold* is the naked body, signed with lesions, the physical embodiment of the remembered passion of a lover whose mind was ravaged by an opportunistic infection. Dog is painfully aware that his partner is now a figment of his imagination, seen but not physically felt: "I wish you were really here, Lad. Your *body,* living. And your mind. . . . I wish I weren't just imagining the warmth of your belly against my back, your arms around me, your cock bobbing against my butt" (p. 156). What is most missed is touch, which cannot be fully remembered or fantasized. Yet to the audience, the naked body of the lover is as real as Dog's body. The theatrical experience is different from that of the central, imagining character; it is actually more physical.

The vividness and physical intensity of Chesley's play center on the vision of two naked men, which becomes not an overture to desire but the unveiling of the site of memory, grief, and affirmation. In the published text of his AIDS plays, Chesley does not let his readers escape the physical reality of AIDS; the photograph of Chesley on the last page (159) of the published text shows him shirtless, exposing the numerous lesions that mark his body, even circling the tattoo on his arm that is a playful, more willful ornament. This photograph is in contrast with the picture on the back cover of Chesley, dressed in leather jacket and Levis, cigarette in hand, posed against the corner of a brick wall as if he were on sexual display (see p. 39). To his right, around the corner, is a bare, lightly painted, well-lit expanse of wall. To his immediate left, in the shadows, is a wall decorated with appropriate graffiti. A dark, shadowy figure painted on the wall seems about to strike Chesley. To its left are the words "The Undead." The two photos, both built on what should be provocative, celebratory displays of the body, offer another drama of AIDS that figure Chesley's lament for the sexually liberated past.

Chesley's AIDS plays focus on physicality and fantasy, on memories of a Whitmanesque fantasy world of men communing in a "holy madness" of sex, which is an act of "breaking down walls": "Our spirits were enthralled with the dream of breaking down *all*

walls between *all* men. So many men, so
Fuck a guy, find his beauty and touch it, sh
Chesley's plays reflect their author's cha
AIDS crisis. *Night Sweat* (1984), which was t
play, is an angry fantasy of a world in whic
who have lost all hope go to the Coup de (
while enacting their favorite sexual fantasy
other infected men, but in the Coup de Grâ
equation sex = death dominates absolutely.
the fatal "ultimate experience" are hope, love
to live. Richard, the despairing principal ch
the "ultimate experience" by being forced to
a vital element of life:

RICHARD: But I'm going to die!
TOM: Yes, yes. But meanwhile you're going to
   moment you die! (TOM *embraces* RICHARD.)
   love in every possible, safe and sensible wa
   most delicate cruising to the heaviest S & M

The title, *Night Sweat,* bridges past sex and
Chesley's play affirms sexual liberty and celeb
AIDS. It celebrates the possibility of a present
so through vivid enactment of sexual acts that
tions of both Eros and Thanatos but later are
The play ends with a celebratory dance that
and gender definitions as it defies death.

Few playwrights in the history of drama h
depicted the world as sensually as has Robert Cl
saddest, his plays have an erotic charge that is
discursive AIDS plays—one might say in mo
wants to restore sensuality; first in defiance of A
of experiencing AIDS. His plays are about phys
from life celebration to masturbatory fantasy to n
Lanford Wilson's *A Poster of the Cosmos* (1988)
with Chesley's work in its intense sense of the pl
as well as in its psychological and spiritual dimen
plays, *A Poster of the Cosmos* is written in the p
and experience of the speaker of this extended n

curtain. Ironically, even in gay drama the Person With AIDS is often "expunged," a victim of the inexpressibility of AIDS, the fear of disfigurement and death, and the exigencies of post-Ibsen drama.

At the end of William Hoffman's play *As Is* (1985), the white hospital curtain is pulled around the bed that now contains Rich, the Person With AIDS, and his partner, Saul. This act hides not only the sexual act that is the resolution of the play but also the body of the Person With AIDS. The rest of Rich's story is narrative, told by the hospice worker. The Person With AIDS disappears from the stage at the end of Andy Kirby's *Compromised Immunity* (1985), leaving his male nurse to narrate the lessons learned while holding a scarf—a remnant of the now-invisible object. Jean Claude van Itallie's *Ancient Boys* (1989) has its central character enact a ritual suicide that is also a disappearance: "*He slips into the see-through pyramid, and, from the inside, pulls the last piece into place. He puts a crystal on his forehead. We see him on his back, his arms folded across his chest. The lights fade on him.*"[7]

In the play *Andre's Mother* (1988), by Terrence McNally, the final ceremony for Andre's friends and family is releasing his soul, now represented by white balloons: "When you let go, it means you're letting his soul ascend to Heaven. That you're willing to let go."[8]

Ironically, disappearance is often what the character with AIDS wants, an escape from being seen with the visible signs of the disease, a horror especially for men for whom appearance has been crucial. Rich, in Hoffman's *As Is*, tells Saul: "What's so hot about living when you're covered with lesions and you're coming down with a new infection every day? . . . If it gets too bad, I want to be able to quietly disappear."[9] The beautiful Peter, in Richard Greenberg's *Eastern Standard* (1988), tells his sister that he has decided "to diminish without witnesses."[10] Disappearance is the only way to have a glamorous farewell, or at least a farewell that preserves the memory of one's glamour. There are no beautiful death scenes (*pace* Larry Kramer), as in *La Dame aux Camélias*, only an absence, a closing of the curtain, a fade out of the lights—or an ascending white balloon.

Equations

In writing about AIDS drama, one is writing about drama's relation to disease, particularly communicable, sexually transmitted disease. And realistic drama's relation to disease is a reflection of a society's relation to disease, expressed in language that is not only a tool for healing the body but also a means of policing the body. In his superb study, *Disease and Representation: Images of Illness from Madness to AIDS,* Sander L. Gilman maintains: "The social reality of disease is constructed on the basis of specific ideological needs and structured along the categories of representation accepted within that ideology."[11] Therefore, "the infected individual is never value neutral" (p. 7). Medical historian Charles Rosenberg has written, "The desire to explain sickness and death in terms of volition, of acts done or left undone—is ancient and powerful."[12]

Since realistic drama is usually postulated on some scheme of moral, social or psychological cause and effect, diseases in drama tend to have moral, social, or psychological causes, thus mirroring society's tendency to link disease and morality. It is not surprising, then, that causality becomes central to AIDS drama, as it is central to much of AIDS discourse, in which the cause of AIDS becomes not the retrovirus but the mode of transmission: nonprocreative, transgressive sex. Homosexuality and AIDS have been not merely joined into a causal relationship in the minds of many people but actually equated, as Allan M. Brandt points out:

> Now AIDS threatened heterosexuals with homosexual contamination. In this context, homosexuality—not a virus, causes AIDS. Therefore homosexuality itself is feared as if it were a communicable, lethal disease. After a generation of work to strike homosexuality from the psychiatric, diagnostic manuals, it had suddenly reappeared as an infectious, terminal disease.[13]

This is not surprising, since homosexuality has been linked to metaphors of disease for more than a century and, because of that link, has been feared as something "catching."

The connection between homosexuality and disease, tied to the move of homosexual acts into the realm of medical discourse in the late nineteenth century,[14] is a corollary to a more general linking of sexual promiscuity with disease that was evident in nineteenth-century literature about syphilis. Brandt has written exhaustively and powerfully about the ways in which "venereal disease became a metaphor for late Victorian anxieties about sexuality, contagion, and social organization"[15] These Victorian anxieties are precursors of AIDS hysteria in the late twentieth century; the infection has been the focal point of right-wing sexual hysteria, justification for a return to the "old ways" and "traditional family values," which are seen as charms to ward off evil homosexual spirits and as the only true vaccination against AIDS/homosexuality.[16] This shibboleth moves AIDS into the discourse of family as well as of morality and medicine, and since American drama is essentially domestic, AIDS drama places its characters into the discourse of family values.

Thus AIDS entwines us in a series of equations:

AIDS = homosexuality
AIDS = disease
Homosexuality = disease
Homosexuality = AIDS
Nonmarital, uncontrolled sex = disease
Transgression of family values = disease

The Person With AIDS also becomes linked in a causal relationship to his sexual past, particularly to the "liberated" gay past. The unabashed enjoyment of erotic pleasure that was the focus of gay life for many in the sixties and seventies has been presented by our enemies as a Sodom (literally as well as figuratively) for which gay men are being punished, a notion underscored by the human penchant for simplicity in causal explanations. Even for those, like Susan Sontag, who do not believe such canards, the past becomes fearful territory:

> The fear of AIDS imposes on an act whose ideal is an experience of pure presentness (and a creation of the future) a relation to the past to be ignored at one's peril. Sex no longer withdraws its partners, if only for a moment, from the social. It cannot be considered just a coupling: it is a chain, a chain of transmission, from the past.[17]

But for many gay men, the past was a time of unabashed enjoyment of erotic pleasure. To denigrate that past is to denigrate a way of life, an ethos. For the generation that lived through the erotic age, finding a meaningful present in an age in which sex has become not only deeroticized but terrifying involves retrieving and affirming the past and purging it of the stigma of guilt, sin, and corruption with which AIDS and heterosexism have stained it.[18]

For a society that sees AIDS as a moral disease, the cure is a return to what Julia Kristeva calls "the Law of the Father," a discourse and a set of values that reinstate patriarchy. Society must be purged of its problem, which is sexual transgression, and the "proper" patriarchal, heterosexist order must be restored. AIDS plays, like many gay plays, ask whether, within the framework of realistic drama, it is possible for a new order to be established that replaces the Law of the Father with an order that allows the gay man place and power. Can the Law of the Father be seen as the "problem" and thus expunged? Can realistic drama, with its dependence on causality, allow space for a celebration of the past?

"Marguerite Is Ill"

In mainstream popular drama, particularly television drama, the gay Person With AIDS is heir to the fate of the nineteenth-century "fallen woman," doomed to the punishment of fatal disease. I offer an extended reading of Alexandre Dumas, fils' dramatization of his novel La Dame aux Camélias (1852) because this ever-popular play demonstrates how realistic drama has, from its beginnings in the mid-nineteenth century, placed sexually active characters within the realm of disease as well as that of the normative discourse of sexual morality. La Dame aux Camélias reveals how a popular drama can seem to be opening a space for a character who lives outside of conventional sexual morality while proving that such a space is impossible.

La Dame aux Camélias has also achieved status as a camp classic, a position confirmed by Giuseppe Verdi's opera La Traviata (1853), by the Garbo film version, Camille (1936), and by Charles Ludlam's celebrated travesty version onstage. The 1990 revival of this central work by Ludlam, who died recently of AIDS-related infections, must have inspired at least some members of the audience to see the play as an AIDS narrative: it has always been easy to read *La Dame aux Camélias* as a gay narrative.

Dumas' heroine, the doomed courtesan Marguerite Gautier, is the ancestor of the gay character with AIDS in mainstream drama. Her ancestor among "fallen woman" is the sinister creature called Marwood in eighteenth-century bourgeois drama, whose goal was the corruption and destruction of male and female innocence.[19] Marwood was a female Satan, despairing and destroying. Marguerite, suffering the ravages of her sexuality and the disease that figures her behavior, becomes a relatively passive figure, more to be pitied than condemned.

Marguerite, in living for "love," lives for pleasure, behavior that is presented as symptomatic of a social and moral disease that leads to actual, physical disease. The beautiful, available body of the courtesan is a site of attraction and pleasure but also a site of corruption and disease. The woman is passive, but so is the man, lured by the beauty and sexual freedom of the woman. The only active roles are those of denial and renunciation.

To see women and sex this way is to see them through the eyes of patriarchal morality. Marguerite must please austere father figures, including a very fatherly God. Ultimately, it is her acceptance of their authority and judgment that allows her to be seen as a sympathetic victim rather than as a social outcast who deserves her suffering. It is her understanding of her responsibility for her disease that makes the death scene "the ultimate tearjerker," to use Charles Ludlam's term.

Marguerite may have originally found the life of a courtesan an escape from her impoverished existence as a poor embroideress, but now it is an addiction, an illness: "If I were to begin to take care of myself, my dear man, I should die. Don't you see that it is only the feverish life I live that keeps me alive?"[20] Marguerite's life is "feverish," diseased, but to lose the disease is to lose her life. The disease is linked to a life outside the economy and ethos of the middle class—a life of pleasure, of spending money without earning it, of sex without love, a life of the senses—but Marguerite articulates her society's estimation of the physical and spiritual price she pays for moving outside the dominant economy: "because in the midst of this restless existence of ours, our senses live, but our hearts are stifled" (p. 133).

In the novel on which the play is based, Dumas replaces biological with moral causality, presenting the disease as a metaphor for Marguerite's "nature" but also as the cause of her compulsions: "Her illness, subdued but far from conquered, continued to stir in her those feverish desires which are almost invariably a result of consumptive disorders."[21]

Dumas obsesses on the ravaged body of Marguerite. Her coughing blood and wasting away are not enough: he is compelled to exhume her rotting corpse a year later: "A foul odor emerged, despite the aromatic herbs with which it had been strewn. . . . The eyes were simply two holes, the lips had gone, and the white teeth were clenched. The long, dry, black hair was stuck over the temples and partly veiled the green hollows of the cheeks."[22] These details of decomposition are not unique to Marguerite, of course, but the effect of such a description of the dead courtesan's face is to link her real and metaphoric "illness" with ugliness and disfiguration. Dumas thus figures Marguerite's illness not as consumption but as syphilis, a disfiguring, deadly venereal disease. In his book, *Disease and Representation: Images of Illness from Madness to AIDS,* Sander L. Gilman displays the title-page illustration of a mid-nineteenth-century French edition of a poem, "Syphilis." A young man is kneeling, holding the left hand of a well-dressed courtesan. A bouquet of flowers lies at her feet. In her right hand, the courtesan holds a mask up to her face. The mask is of a beautiful woman; the face is a rotting death's head. Gilman uses the illustration to show how, by the nineteenth century, vice and disease are equated and become linked to the courtesan: "The female is seen as the source of pollution, but also as the outsider, the prostitute, the socially deviant individual."[23] The picture could be an illustration of the meeting of Marguerite and Armand.

In both novel and drama, Marguerite's disease is not the only double bind that traps her: she is also caught in an impossible nexus of forbidden promiscuity and forbidden monogamous love. She renounces her beloved Armand and returns to her former life in a noble sacrifice to his father, so that he can ensure the successful marriage of his chaste daughter, Armand's sister. Her sacrificial move back to promiscuity is a move back to the city and to her disease. The Marguerites of the world cannot be allowed to infect family life. Marguerite's disease becomes dangerous—to herself and others—when she falls in love and becomes a threat to middle-class life. She stepped out of place and out of line. In speaking of Violetta Valery, Verdi's operatic version of Marguerite Gautier, Catherine Clément writes:

> She is sucked into unmarked swamps, interstices that are neither bourgeois, nor workingclass, nor noble. Places of circulation where women get stuck in the mud; ones they will never get out of. The family's son can take a spin there, he will get out just fine, having seen life; but the woman never gets out. . . . Because she wanted to leave, Violetta must pay the required price, her life itself.[24]

No one has to tell Marguerite this. She knows it. Old Duval need only give the right cues for Marguerite herself to articulate society's "wisdom": "And so, whatever she may do, the woman, once she has fallen can never rise again. God may forgive her, perhaps, the world never. What man would wish to make her his wife, what child to call her mother. It is all true, what you have told me" (pp. 140–141).

Marguerite's redemption can come only through sacrifice. She is allowed neither promiscuity nor monogamy, and since chastity is not her choice, her fate is death. And she takes on the judgment of such agents of society as wealthy old men with chaste daughters. But the agents of power in her world are seen not only as right and just but also as merciful. Old Duval forgives Marguerite—from a distance. The courtesan keeps to her place outside the structure of the middle-class family, in her own subculture, where she is both contained and expendable. Nature and God will mete out the inevitable punishment.

The play, like the novel, was thought to be a "true picture" of life in the Parisian fast lane, the demimonde. Everyone knew the identity of the prototypes of the characters. The authority of history, of real names and events, validates the moral scheme of the fiction. However, the events of realistic drama obey not nature and God but the old Duvals who are their representatives. The mores of society allow Marguerite no escape from either the disease of hedonism or the attendant disease of consumption. The only noble act allowed her is renunciation, but still she must die, a fact she accepts nobly: "I have lived for love and now I am dying of it" (p. 163). She has lived for sex, which previously she carefully separated from love, but she dies from love for Armand. Or she dies because of her return to sexual activity, the "feverish" life. But consumption is not a venereal disease, though here it is a potent code for one, a respectable, contagious disease figuring the results of pollution of body and spirit. And she knows her death is "God's will": "Believe me, God sees more clearly than we do" (p. 163). What is it God sees? Marguerite's harsh self-judgments prefigure the expressions of internalized heterosexism voiced by gay characters in pre-Stonewall plays like Mart Crowley's *The Boys in the Band* (1968).

The myth enacted here lives on through AIDS discourse.[25] The pleasure ghetto of gay life infects the middle class through AIDS, perhaps even infecting innocent heterosexuals and children if it is not contained. AIDS, homosexuality, and nonprocreative sexuality are equated as diseases and spreaders of disease.[26] Austere father figures like Jerry Falwell can "hate the sin but love the sinner"—if from a distance. The libertine must keep her or his place, must not infect. And the source of sexual infection, pollution, is feminine, or worse, homosexual. Sander L. Gilman points out how AIDS discourse modifies the traditional gendering of venereal disease: "The male is not only the sufferer, but also the source of his own pollution. Here we have the conflation of the male and female images traditionally associated with sexually transmitted diseases such as syphilis."[27]

The "truth" of *La Dame aux Camélias* resembles what Simon Watney describes as the commonly accepted "truth" of AIDS, which "resolutely insists that the point of emergence of the virus should be identified as its *cause*. Epidemiology is thus replaced by a moral etiology of disease that can only conceive homosexual desire through a medicalized metaphor of contagion."[28]

Marguerite Gautier's rotting face is the figure for her sexual behavior, itself diseased, "feverish," and potentially infectious. Her disease is both the cause of her behavior and its effect. But, from our point of view, Marguerite's illness can also be seen as her internalization of the judgments of her society. The truly subversive figure would have at least a sense of irony about her expressions of the justness of her own doom. Charles Ludlam, who loved Garbo's *Camille* and had one of his greatest successes as Marguerite, could justify the tears shed over the lady by his belief that, "At the heart of the dramatic event lies the spirit of masochism."[29] Masochism, however, is also a pathological state all too often identified with gay men.

Onstage Marguerite's disease is signified by a cough, an occasional fainting spell, and words, as if any more overtly physical tokens of her illness would be unbearable, improper. The disease loses its vivid embodiment and its figurative relationship with syphilis but not its equation with her "feverish" sexual behavior.

The View from Outside

There are two ways in which AIDS dramas may try to revise or explode the connected sets of equal signs that constitute a certain kind of AIDS discourse. A well-meaning mainstream work, written for a predominantly heterosexual audience, may present a compendium of the facts while insisting on the preeminent qualities of love and compassion that can burst the bonds of prejudice. Gay AIDS drama defies the moral causalities and upholds the value of the liberated life before AIDS.

In mainstream popular drama, however well-meaning, AIDS and people with AIDS are ground into the mill of the problem play, and the Person With AIDS, not the virus or the social problems the person faces, is the problem. The Person With AIDS, in other words, must carry, as he too often does, the baggage of nineteenth-century causalities. I devote this section to television dramas because it is on television that we see most clearly that mainstream mixture of well-intentioned liberalism, shaped by the industry's sense of public values, and popular thinking about homosexuals and homosexuality. Television is, for our time, the major purveyor of middlebrow, "outside" drama.

The 1980s ended on prime-time television with a New Year's Eve re-run of a made-for-television biography of Liberace, who died of AIDS in 1987. Somehow this combination of ostentatious wealth, showbiz glitz, and AIDS more aptly encapsulated the decade than the network executives, to whom I don't attribute much sense of irony, could have envisioned. In a sweet but bizarre scene, after we have suffered with Liberace through his unhappy liaison with a cynical cokehead, Scott Thorsen, who "outed" Liberace by suing him for palimony, we find the pianist at his pool with another beautiful young man, this time an intense brunet (brunets tend to be intense and steadfast in TV's version of gay life). Staring at the Speedo-clad youth posing beside his pool, Liberace claims to find his "personality" attractive, and with a clasping of hands, they vow "friendship." The young man accompanies Liberace through his illness and vows to keep his secret from the world. We are to assume that this friendship between Liberace and the youth is just that, that Liberace has not infected his young friend. In good television morality, the wages of sex is disease, and love between men must remain, in the age of AIDS as before, asexual (even when the young man looks magnificent lounging by one's pool in a Speedo and is on salary).

In one of the teleplay's final moments, Victor Garber's eerie facsimile of Liberace is gaunt, wasted, slumped in the back seat of a limousine; his devoted chauffeur companion eyes him protectively through the rear-view mirror. *Liberace: Behind the Music* did not judge its subject: after all, Liberace was a product of television. Instead it made him the object of pity, the pathetic lonely man who looked for love in the wrong places. In the final scenes, he is allowed chaste love, but only when his death is imminent. This is, in other words, *La Dame aux Camélias* revisited; as camp, in its own way, as Ludlam's *Camille,* but endearingly ignorant of its own silliness.

An Early Frost, written by Ron Cowen, is the best-known AIDS drama, having appeared on network television in 1985 and been distributed on videotape. It is, as one would expect of prime-time commercial television, an "outside view," however well-meaning as an effort to present gay men with AIDS in a compassionate way. As such, it demonstrates both the virtues and the limitations of television's appropriation of nineteenth-century problem drama. However well-written and well-intentioned, *An Early Frost* yet manages to keep in place all the discursive connections that entrap AIDS and people with AIDS. The teleplay is a celebration of traditional sex roles and of middle-American marriage, which is briefly threatened but eventually reaffirmed. The way in which the teleplay seems to question but ultimately upholds established values is an object lesson on the relationship of television "realism" to any social problem that stretches "traditional family values."

Under the title of *An Early Frost,* we see the "normal" routine of the Pierson family, who live in that generic television house we have seen continuously since "Father Knows Best" in the fifties, though one is never clear exactly where the Piersons live. We know only that it is a plane ride away from Chicago, thus a safe distance from "urban problems" like homosexuality. It could be a suburb, a town, or a small city. Of course, geography is irrelevant. The Piersons live in Televisionland.

Within this world, gender and family roles are clearly delineated. Nick, the macho father, runs a lumberyard with his son-in-law, who has taken the role of the oldest son in the family business and home. In his spare time, Nick fiddles with the car. In the living room, his wife, Kathy, gives piano lessons—though she seems to know only one piece of music—thus having a career that allows her to express her "feminine sensitivity" without leaving the home. Social life and rituals center in the living room, with bridge games and anniversary parties bringing together this family, which includes a daughter and a son-in-law and the wife's mother, who gives the wife a matrilineal support group to compensate for her pathologically stolid husband. Traditional values are upheld but are not based on any visible ethnicity, religion, or social group. Gender roles are acted out: husband gets up before dawn to work out; wife cans vegetables, demonstrating her link to a traditional past, despite her cigarette smoking, her music, and her slacks.

Yet casting complicates the typical picture somewhat: Gena Rowlands and Ben Gazzara, with their barrage of Actors Studio mannerisms and urban accents, hardly seem comfortable as the people-next-door. Moreover, Rowlands played a lesbian in an earlier TV film, *A Question of Love* (1978). Middle America needn't make a complete identification with these folks; the casting says "serious drama," not television "real life." And Kathy's "artiness" (she is a graduate of a music conservatory who married and settled down instead of pursuing a career) makes her a bit suspect on Main Street: "Don't worry, folks, the Piersons aren't People Like Us."

The doorbell rings at the Pierson's twenty-fifth-anniversary party, heralding the arrival of the problem-play's mysterious visitor, the disrupter of the family pattern, the prodigal son, Michael (not the butch diminutive "Mike," like his father's "Nick," but "Michael"). On this family visit, Michael announces that he has just been made junior partner in his law firm: the Ivy League education the family gave their son has begun to pay off. When his mother asks whether Michael has met any nice girls, his answer is coyly evasive: "Well, I haven't been a monk."

In the next sequence we see "the problem" that will upset the Pierson household: Michael's Chicago home life and his diagnosis of AIDS, which will be presented not as Michael's problem but as his parents'. Michael wakes up in a beautiful lakefront high-rise condo straight out of *Metropolitan Home*. It is contemporary and cold, not the least "homey." This is the generic yuppie apartment of television and film—beautiful, sterile, and vulnerable to threat from outside. Michael is awakened by his handsome lover, Peter, who holds out Michael's cup of morning coffee and playfully rouses Michael for his day at work. Can it be a coincidence that Peter's plain-colored open-necked sport shirt and slacks resemble the out- fits Michael's mother wears?

Michael and Peter are television's version of an acceptable gay couple.[30] Michael is the "straight" homosexual: handsome, charm- ing, sensitive, and totally devoid of effeminacy. He is also painfully aware that his homosexuality does not fit into his own personal vision of the American dream. His gay life is a secret at work and with his family. Peter is the male counterpart of the girl a mother dreams of for her son. He is handsome and nurturing, he does the wifely jobs of shopping and cooking, and he succeeds, most of the time, in laughing off Michael's closeted behavior. While Michael is a lawyer, Peter, openly gay, runs a chic boutique that sells merry- go-round horses, jukeboxes, and other camp items, presumably to other very rich urban gays. He sells a form of nostalgia, but in a contemporary, sterile store disconnected from the roots of the nos- talgia. Michael and Peter have it all—looks, money, success, mar- riage, vacations in Hawaii—but the setting shows that something is missing. According to the narrative, what is most missing is real membership in Michael's family circle, something Peter wants and Michael dreads. When Peter asks Michael whether he has told his family about their relationship, Michael counters: "I don't talk about sex with my family and they don't talk about sex with me." Michael understands well how the typical middle-American family will read his relationship with Peter.

In the urban fast lane, the wages of sex is death. Michael was sexually active before he met Peter, and Peter has had a few flings when Michael was overbusy at the law firm. Michael now has *pneumocystis carinii,* a rare pneumonia that has become a calling card of full-blown AIDS. The diagnosis of AIDS is disclosed at the hospital by a kindly doctor who presents the objective, but compassionate, medical view and accepts the relationship of Michael and Peter, who is sitting at Michael's side as a good spouse should be. Later, in spite of an ignorant hospital worker who leaves Michael's food outside his door, and ambulance drivers who refuse to take him to the hospital, it is made clear that the medical establishment is, as usual on television, knowledgeable, kind, tolerant, and supportive. Hospital rooms are big enough for a basketball game. This is an OK place to leave your son, an important factor as the teleplay progresses.

When Michael returns home, a guilt-ridden Peter confesses to his flings. This is the only time the invisible "gay scene" of bars and nonmonogamous sex is invoked, and Michael responds with all the wrath of the wronged wife. Peter has betrayed their relationship. He has also given Michael an easy reason for his illness: "You're sorry. And I have AIDS."

After breaking up with Peter, Michael returns to his family, and the real play, set in the locus of the traditional family, begins. The problem has now come home and must be faced. Michael tells his parents that he has AIDS and that he is gay, as if the two facts were necessarily equated. Significantly, he tells them at night, outside the house. The reactions to the information underscore the differences and problems in what we might see as an already dysfunctional family. Dad rears back to punch his son; Mom steps in to protect.

It is clear from their reactions that the fact of Michael's homosexuality is far more upsetting than his terminal illness and that the narrative must provide some explanation for this nonviral "problem." Michael is blessed with a set of parents straight out of Freud: doting mother and distant father. Thus Michael can be blamed for his immorality and his parents can be blamed for not raising him properly. In addition, Michael's pregnant sister starts acting out her own little psychodrama against her mother and refuses to see Michael (he might infect her unborn baby). Michael's mother and her mother seem to be only healthy, caring people. For the first three-quarters of the teleplay, Mother knows best and must work out a solution to the problem of holding her family together. Her real mission is to get all members of the family to do the right thing. When asked by Michael whether she approves of his gayness, she responds: "No. The thing is, you're my son. I wouldn't let anything in the world separate us." Family is all.

In an abortive attempt at reconciliation, Michael goes to visit his father in the lumberyard and tells him that he is "ashamed" (of his sexuality? of AIDS?). But shame is not enough for Nick, who feels that his son is now a stranger. All Nick has to offer is disapproval and dismissal. But when Michael convulses from an attack of toxoplasmosis, Nick can carry his son down the stairs and into the hospital, though he won't visit him there.

While recovering in the hospital from his second opportunistic infection, Michael has come to terms with both his illness and his sexuality through his friendship with a real queen, and a nonupper-middle-class one at that, a former chef named Victor. At first, Michael is revolted by Victor, who not only displays the very visible signs of Kaposi's sarcoma and chemotherapy but also exhibits the flagrant signs of stereotypical Hollywood homosexuality: effeminacy, an irreverent, self-protective wit, campiness, and a fondness for Susan Hayward movies. Michael's first response to Victor mirrors Nick's sullen, macho response to Michael's homosexuality. Coming to terms with Victor is coming to terms with his own difference.

When Peter makes a surprise appearance at the Pierson household and is invited by Michael's mother to stay a few days, Nick glowers. Peter may be Michael's loving partner, but he also represents an alien world. When Michael's mother notes that Michael's first apartment was more like a closet than a home (truer than she knows) Michael and Peter are reduced to a fit of giggling that brings them closer together but further alienates Nick, who never laughs.

The women love Peter (of course!), but disapproving Dad must have a middle-of-the-night confrontation with this interloper—the Father and the Other. We're back in the haunts of Camille. Ultimately, Peter, like Marguerite, bows to the power of the Law of the Father. He shows Nick a picture of him and Michael on a fishing trip (see, Dad, we're just normal guys), then tells Nick that Michael will need his father's strength and stolidity if he is to fight his illness. Peter can take over the mother's nurturing role, but he cannot do the macho bit. The scene between the father and Peter, as played by Ben Gazzara and D. W. Moffett, is a duet between burly bass and countertenor on the verge of tears. Peter may be sweet, but he's not the man Michael's father is. The narrative is moving toward its inevitable reinforcement of the Law of the Father.

Michael realizes that his place is with Peter, who loves him and will take care of him, but by the time Michael talks of returning to Peter in Chicago, he is already harboring thoughts of suicide, the aftermath of the death of his friend Victor. Victor is alone and lonely, as movie and television queens always are and are supposed to be, and Victor, tidily, dies off camera. There is no more space for him in the world of television than a brief moment of pity. Michael, realizing not only his own future but also his difference, goes into a fit of suicidal despair.

Michael is saved from suicide by his father, and the climax of the play is his fight with his father: "I'm not the man you wanted me to be. Well, I don't give a damn what you think anymore, because I'm a better man than you'll ever be, you son of a bitch." This classically Oedipal moment leads to his father's loving embrace and the admission that he doesn't want his son to die. Michael has received enough lessons in manhood from his father to put up the good fight. Ultimately the family rifts are healed not by the mother's intervention but by the father's action and his hypermasculinity. Mother is literally pushed aside in the scene of father-son reconciliation. It was his son's feminine shame and cowardice that most bothered Nick, it turns out, not merely his homosexuality, which might be forgiven if not accepted, would Michael only act like a man. In this drama of sexual stereotypes, Michael-the-homosexual is allowed the best of father and mother. He needs his father's strength but needs also the "feminine" sensitivity to admit to Peter that he loves him. The marriage of Michael and Peter may be a better one than that of Nick and Kathy, but television can only suggest this when AIDS dooms such a union.

At the end of *An Early Frost,* the family is healed. Michael can play duets with his mother (the same piece, now four hands), sister can embrace Michael, and Mom and Dad can stand arm in arm as Michael's taxi leaves to take him back to Chicago and Peter and AIDS-related infections. The drama is resolved for the Pierson family by Michael's leaving the scene. The interruption of their family pattern has been disposed of, lovingly and affirmingly, but disposed of nonetheless, in the manner of realistic drama. Michael is driven around the corner on a rainy night as an ominous rumble is heard on the sound track. He has gone back to the world he belongs in, and the family is no longer disrupted. Mom and Dad stand side by side on their front lawn. Michael has disappeared from the scene, and their "family values" have been upheld: they will lose their son, but everything they stand for will have been vindicated.

What is affirmed ultimately in *An Early Frost* are the values and authority of television itself: tolerance, love, marriage, and family. While those values at first seem feminine, they must be tied to masculine toughness and action: father still knows best. Homosexuals are to be accepted, but they don't live on the tree-lined streets of Televisionland: they live in cities, with all the other serious social problems that deserve tolerance and distance. Michael, his homosexuality, his AIDS, have all been seen from the point of view of Televisionland. Michael's own point of view is less and less the focus as the teleplay progresses: he and AIDS get pushed literally out of the picture. What the family has to go through is far more important because more typical. Television knew how to handle the problem so that everyone Felt Good at the end and so that the authorized point of view—that of the TV Couple arm in arm on their front lawn, secure in their rightness—triumphed.

In *Our Sons* (aired in May 1991),[31] the mothers of a gay couple are single, working women; Audrey (Julie Andrews), a successful executive living in a beautiful beachfront house in San Diego, California, and LuAnne (Ann Margret), a waitress in a Fayetteville,

Arkansas, bar who lives in a mobile home with an American flag hanging in front. The focus of the telefilm is on the relationships that these women from different sides of the tracks forge with the only men in their lives, their gay sons.

LuAnne threw Donald (played by Željko Ivanck), her seventeen-year-old son, out of their home when she discovered he was gay. He is now twenty-eight, has somehow become a successful architect, and is dying of AIDS-related diseases. His devoted lover is James (Hugh Grant), Audrey's son, a composer and cocktail pianist-singer. Unlike LuAnne, Audrey has always claimed to accept her son's homosexuality, though, as he tells her, "We would need spiked boots, Mother, you and I, to step over what has been swept under the rug since I was eighteen years old. Mountains." Audrey has never faced her disappointment that James is gay, never accepted Donald as James' partner, never faced her anxiety about the possibility that James may be infected. James, as uptight a WASP as his mother, will not be tested for HIV antibodies.

Through Audrey's mediation, a favor to her son, there is a reconciliation between LuAnne and Donald: LuAnne admits that she was wrong and Donald forgives her. Before Donald dies, and through LuAnne's candor, Audrey comes to realize that she needs to accept James fully. Homosexuality and AIDS have again been equated, though the script makes clear it is wrong to accept middle-American hatred of homosexuals and the attitude that gays bring AIDS on themselves. It is equally wrong to settle for liberal tolerance, for loving someone "in spite of" his sexual orientation. The script's heart is in the right place, but the ending is a peculiarly Oedipal one. LuAnne takes her son's coffin back to Arkansas, thus signaling her acceptance of his life and her willingness to be honest with her friends about her "queer" son. Audrey and James are now a couple.

James had complained at the beginning of the film that Audrey accepted James' sexuality when he was unattached but never accepted his relationship with Donald. Before Donald dies, LuAnne shows him a picture he drew as a child of a castle. LuAnne remembers that they pledged to live in that castle, which would be "full of magic." Both mothers wanted exclusive relationships with their sons, a demand the film in no way judges. At the end, Audrey gets her wish. If James is HIV-positive, and the script hints that he is, Audrey can care for him:

JAMES: I might need you.
AUDREY: Oh, God, I hope so.

There is no hint that James might find another partner. While the dialogue has moved Audrey to an acceptance of James' life and his right to a loving relationship with another man, the action moves him out of other men's beds and back into mother's arms. The one song we hear James sing is "Someone to Watch Over Me." At the end, as he and his mother stand together, the tune plays again on the soundtrack. The "Someone" is clearly Mother. Michael, in *An Early Frost,* at least got to go home to his lover.

There is camp fun in seeing Julie Andrews arrive at an Arkansas trailer park in a limousine and in seeing Andrews and Ann Margret square off. Hugh Grant was imported from England to play James, probably as a sop to gay audiences (Grant was one of the stars of the 1987 film version of E. M. Forster's novel *Maurice*), but while his character, as befits Julie Andrews' son, is very stiff-upper-lip British, he was directed to play James in an American accent, which emphasizes the incredibility of his character. The commercials for various vaginal ointments made clear that the advertisers saw *Our Sons* as a "women's film," ignoring the buying power of the gay viewer, a group advertising agencies never think of targeting. The film sees AIDS and homosexuality from a mother's point of view, not from a gay man's. From the *New York Times'* usual patriarchal position, television critic John J. O'Connor wrote:

> "Our Sons," then, might be expected to leave the gay community reasonably pleased. Perhaps even a little gratitude would be in store. Don't count on it. Many homosexuals today are not about to be satisfied with occasional crumbs from the groaning board of popular culture. They are fed up with seeing their very existences viewed primarily as "controversial." Even the occasionally more sensitive films use distancing ploys, exploring not the lives of homosexuals but the anguished fretting of their parents or friends.[32]

O'Connor grudgingly acknowledged a valid anger. In the most popular of popular cultures, AIDS and the homosexual have become inextricably entwined, as they have in the most hateful heterosexist expressions during the past decade. The daring move would be for television to dramatize the lives of male homosexuals who are not HIV-positive, who cannot be thrust into a pre-Stonewall world and discourse by AIDS. But the captains of the television and advertising industries do not see the gay viewing audience as reliable potential consumers of their products. Lesbians and gay men remain outside the mainstream.

Rapprochement

In the mid-eighties AIDS was the focus of most gay drama, as the diverse population known as the "gay community" began to be unified in its attention to an epidemic that ravaged lovers, friends, neighbors, and acquaintances. Gay drama about AIDS to some extent dispenses with the Law of the Father, or at least with the father, and with the dismissive resolutions of conventional problem plays. The voice of the straight world is now the sibling or caregiver. In both William Hoffman's *As Is* (1985) and Larry Kramer's *The Normal Heart* (1985), a gay character must come to terms with his older brother as father surrogate, as the voice of society. For Ned in *The Normal Heart,* his brother represents the exclusivity and judgments of the straight male: "You can only find room to call yourself normal,"[33] but Ned's brother apologizes, accepting the errors of vision he and the straight world he represents share. In *As Is*, Rich's straight brother cries for forgiveness from Rich. The old judgments of parents are gone, and siblings must accept the new law of love and compassion.

Andy Kirby's *Compromised Immunity,* a 1985 production of London's estimable Gay Sweatshop,[34] effects a rapprochement between the dominant "straight" world and that of a gay Person With AIDS. In the fashion of popular British drama à la Peter Shaffer, the play alternates scenes with narration, here split between the two protagonists as they forge a friendship. Peter Dennett, a young heterosexual nurse, is assigned to his East London teaching hospital's first AIDS patient, a feisty thirty-six-year-old civil servant, Gerry Grimond. Gerry at first treats Peter with a combination of wariness and hostility:

GERRY: You know nothing about AIDS!

PETER: Stick around and teach me then. And if you want my sympathy, you'll have to start treating me like another human being. Imagine I'm gay if it makes it any easier.[35]

But Peter has his own prejudices. In explaining why Gerry was nasty to the female nurses, he demonstrates his acceptance of stereotypes:

PETER: Homosexuals don't get on with women, sexual rivals you see. You're both after men.

GERRY: So you don't get on with lesbians then?

PETER: I don't even know any.

GERRY: You work with at least two. . . . It might help if you stopped pontificating about what gays are and are not and do and do not prefer. (p. 56)

The play explores the AIDS = homosexuality equation from within. Peter's problem is not dealing with the hospital's first AIDS patient: it is dealing with a homosexual. Gerry's problem with AIDS is not merely medical: it has weakened his resistance to shame, which is "how you feel about how other people feel about what you are" (p. 60). "It took years to build up a resistance to the way people treated me as gay and now that's as compromised as my physical immunity" (p. 61).

Despite the fears of his girlfriend, who doesn't like Peter dealing with an AIDS patient, and against his own professional ambitions, Peter continues to treat Gerry, whose depression leads him to attempt suicide. Peter realizes that treating Gerry has a spiritual as well as a medical dimension. He tries unsuccessfully to spur the conscience of Gerry's estranged lover. At a gay disco, he meets a young man and convinces him to become Gerry's friend. That young man, Ian, reconnects Gerry to his gay friends and, thus, to life. "Do you know why I'm still here? Because they are coming, because some of the doors I shut have started opening again. I'm gay and I'm dying. I know I said being gay doesn't matter any more. But it does. Ian helped me realize that" (p. 77). Peter cannot cure Gerry, but he has helped Gerry reclaim his identity and his life. Gerry has taught Peter "about being more than an ill person" (p. 79). A rapprochement has been effected between the straight world, its medical discourse and authority, and the world of the gay man with AIDS.

Unlike the angrier American plays, Kirby's *Compromised Immunity* is optimistic—even sentimental—about productive professional and personal relationships between people with AIDS and the heterosexuals who take care of them. The play is more focused on forging links between the gay and straight communities than on providing a critique of the medical and political Establishment's responsibility for the AIDS crisis. Is it that in an Englishman's eyes Peter and Gerry are linked by class loyalties that transcend other rifts? Would the play be different if Gerry were upper-middle class and the hospital was in Queen's Square or Harley Street?

Broadway's people with AIDS are upper-middle class, which is a logical result of the demographics of the "legitimate" theater. They, too, are integrated into the dominant society with surprising, if not particularly convincing, ease.

Richard Greenberg's *Eastern Standard* (1988) is a masterfully written contemporary comedy, celebrated by mainstream heterosexual drama critics as an accurate picture of contemporary life for New York City yuppies. The title reinforces the sense of typicality and authority Greenberg's play invests in its characters. In the world of *Eastern Standard,* gay men and straight men and women are united by education and class in ways that make their differences in sexual orientation relatively unimportant. Straight Stephen confides his relational failures to his gay friend, Drew, for whom Stephen sometimes finds male blind dates. Phoebe's handsome brother, Peter, is also gay. Most of the play explores the new romances of Stephen and Phoebe, and Peter and Drew on the sands of the Hamptons.

Peter has AIDS, which he announces to his sister with a death sentence, "I'm going to die soon."[36] For beautiful, vain Peter, who can make such an announcement over lunch at a chic restaurant, dealing with AIDS, like everything else, is dealing with an image problem: "Nobody ever looked at me without thinking I'd live forever" (p. 21), and Peter would rather disappear from the scene, put himself "in the hands of strangers who'll never have seen me as anything but a bag of bones and lesions" (p. 63). He doesn't want his conservative mother (there is no father to worry about) to know that he has AIDS (and is gay) because: "My mother has a certain way of seeing me. . . . I rely on it" (p. 50).

Peter has, we are told, "slept with the entire free world." The link between this hyperbolic promiscuity and his AIDS is never directly made, but he describes his past life to straight Stephen in a way that makes it sound both attractive and superficial:

> You'd see someone, you'd find him early; and you didn't think—is he going to like me, is he smart, will we have anything to talk about? No, you thought: there's my evening. And the glitter in his eyes, taking you in as if you were a newly discovered continent. And it might last an hour, or sometimes a day, or some amazing times a month, but it never got stale, because the minute you felt yourself start to become boring, you'd just click away—scarcely even saying goodbye. And never— never—any regret, because there was always someone else who'd fall in love with you a few minutes away. (p. 69)

Peter's description of his past, the longest set speech in the play, is an example of a convention of AIDS dramas, the "aria of reminis-cence," in which the Character With AIDS celebrates his past pro-miscuity or laments the impersonality of the urban gay lifestyle. Jean Claude van Itallie's *Ancient Boys* (1989) offers a vivid example of a more mournful reminiscence, as two friends lament the separa-tion of love and desire in their society:

> REUBEN: If I ever slept with anybody I'm close to, it'll be you. I love you. But I don't sleep with my friends. I just sleep with—not even men—with parts of men: thighs in denim, an ass in chaps, a big chest . . .
> LUKE: Ditto. Ditto. I've tried to get away from all that by vowing I'm not sleeping with anybody I don't have a feeling for. So I end up not sleeping with anybody.[37]

Peter's description of his past in Greenberg's *Eastern Standard* is less poignant, less judgmental. Yet in a play about finding and celebrating the possibility of loving relationships, the aria sings of an empty, vain world, earning straight Stephen's response: "I'm sorry—but it sounds awful." The apology allows Stephen a liberal stance, but the judgment is only conditionally rebutted: "Once in a while it was."

Peter spends much of the play eluding Drew's romantic overtures, as he wants to elude the shame of the spectacle of his AIDS, his disfigurement. But miraculously, between scenes, Drew commits to caring for Peter, and Peter, who has never had a serious relationship in his life, accepts Drew's love. In a self-reflexive moment, Drew and Peter present the "moral" of *Eastern Standard,* the grace of dealing with "unmet expectations":

PETER: I was looking for an escape. And you'd sort of hoped for a lover without complications.

DREW: These utopian scenarios tend to fall apart in the second act. The strong among us adjust. (p. 104)

And Drew swears his version of "till death do us part":

PETER: When are you going to leave me?

DREW: When you aren't there anymore. (p. 105)

At the finale of the play, the two couples drink a champagne toast "to couples," as they prepare to go back to the city and the compromised life.

It may seem odd to compare this sweet yuppie romance with the classic "tearjerker," *Camille,* but Peter, the beautiful libertine, is miraculously converted to romantic love and a gay "marriage" that is qualified by his fatal illness. His past is presented both as a vision of erotic freedom and of heartlessness. Peter and Drew are redeemed, too, by living outside of the gay world, which is only presented as promiscuous sex unsupported by any social or cultural life or sense of identity. Membership in the upper-middle class dissolves all other differences, and the norms and values of that class are never challenged even by those who transgress them. Popular drama has not come far since *La Dame aux Camélias* opened in 1852.

Redeeming the Past

Gay AIDS dramas, though different in style and focus, tend to share two crucial elements: a reaffirmation of the pasts of the characters, and the affirmation of a radically changed present that not only vindicates but celebrates gayness. In many ways, William M. Hoffman's *As Is* (1985) is the paradigmatic AIDS drama in its reflection of a changed world. *As Is* is not only about dealing with an ominous, conditional present but about forging new links to the past, as Saul and Rich live through personal revolutions:

RICH: Remember Sunday afternoons blitzed on beer?
SAUL: And suddenly it's Sunday night and you're getting fucked in the second-floor window of the Hotel Christopher and you're being cheered on by a mob of hundreds of men.[38]

The litany of "Remember" is replaced by "I used to" as Saul and Rich continue their celebration of their sexual past:

SAUL: God, I used to love promiscuous sex.
RICH: Not "promiscuous," Saul, nondirective, noncommitted, nonauthoritarian—
SAUL: Free, wild, rampant—
RICH: Hot, sweaty, steamy, smelly—
SAUL: Juicy, funky, hunky—
RICH: Sex.
SAUL: Sex. God, I miss it. (p. 521)

Saul and Rich merge as their memories of the past merge, and during the course of As Is, past and present intertwine as Saul and Rich go backwards and forwards through their relationship. The play opens with the division of the spoils after their separation and ends with the couple climbing into bed together to reconsummate their reforged relationship. This movement from divorce to consummation, both forward and reverse, underscores what AIDS has done to time and memory.

Rich and Saul are a marriage of WASP and Jew, poet with a hunger for freedom and loyal homebody. They are, as the division of spoils demonstrates, affluent, another dream gay couple whose world was one of tasteful but grand consumption. Even their professions, photographer and poet-caterer, represent the affluent urban world of expensive furniture, art, and parties. This was the traditional "gay world" about to be changed by AIDS, governed by hedonism, consumption, and above all by taste. Thus the postseparation negotiations over who gets the cobalt glass, the Barcelona chair, and the Cadmus drawings, remnants of a marriage lost when Rich left steadfast, domestic, kvetching Saul for a feckless, beautiful young man, a muse for his poetry. When Rich visits Saul to divide their possessions, he has AIDS and has been rejected by his new lover, the clients on whom his catering business depends, friends, and family:

SAUL: You'll stay here with me.
RICH: Till death do us part.
SAUL: I love you. (p. 514)

Rich may mock "Till death do us part," but this crucial but oft-forgotten marriage vow is exactly what he and Saul forge during the course of the play, even overcoming their fear of sex to find some way of sharing physical intimacy. Saul will take Rich "as is": "I'll be here for you no matter what happens" (p. 548). Without denigrating the past, Saul and Rich affirm the devotion and commitment of a loving, caring relationship. Like Drew and Peter in *Eastern Standard,* Saul and Rich forge their new life together in a qualified world, a far cry from the carefree past that they can neither relive nor forget.

As Rich and Saul move from divorce to remarriage, they move forward from memories of their voluptuous past to memories of that moment when the nightmare touched their lives:

SAUL: I was at the St. Marks baths soaking in a hot tub when I first heard about AIDS. It was how many years ago? My friend Brian—remember him—was soaking, too, and he told me about a mutual friend who had died the week before. It was "bizarre," he said. (p. 522)

Saul's reminiscence is followed by another litany, this time of "The first time . . ." stories of AIDS touching people's lives. The nameless characters who recount their tales place Rich and Saul in a larger perspective: a Person With AIDS and his lover. Later, when Rich recounts the story of his life as a gay man, from closeted adolescence to coming out to his relationship with Saul and the "shallow, callow and selfish" Chet, we see his life as the typical experience of a New York gay man celebrating his physicality. One night as he runs through lower Manhattan, training for the New York marathon, his joy becomes religious: "I'm running and telling God I didn't know he was that good or that big, thank you Jesus, thanks, thanks. . . . The next morning I woke up with the flu and stayed in bed for a couple of days and felt much better. But

my throat stayed a little sore and my glands were a little swollen"
(p. 523).

If the present is not sickness, as it is for Rich, it is the fear that
consumes Saul, particularly when he goes to the old night spots:
"They remind me of accounts of Europe during the Black Plague:
coupling in the dark, dancing till you drop. The New Wave is the
corpse look" (p. 509).

At the end of the play, after Saul denies Rich the pills that would
allow him to commit suicide (controlling the way one dies seems to
some the only control left), Rich accepts his present, dependent
relationship with Saul and envisions not only the ultimate future
after death but an immediate future as a poet. With that, he and
Saul negotiate the consummation of their remarriage in the limited
privacy of Rich's hospital room.

As Is is not only a play about coming to terms with disease and
with one's love for a partner but also a play about coming to terms
with one's past without guilt or regret. Sexual promiscuity is not
lamented as a probable cause of Rich's contracting AIDS but is
celebrated, its loss lamented. AIDS is lamented, but Rich learns to
celebrate the life he has left. Sex is not merely equated with death
but is reintegrated into Rich and Saul's relationship. The play is also
about proving depth of commitment and concern, thus confound-
ing notions of superficiality and fecklessness.

As Saul brings Rich the pills that could kill him, he has an
epiphany-like vision in a puddle outside a Greenwich Village sex
shop: "In this dirty little puddle was a reflection of the red neon
sign. It was beautiful. And the whole street was shining with
the most incredible colors. They kept changing as the different signs
blinked on and off. . . . I don't know how long I stood there. A
phrase came to me head: 'The Lord taketh and the Lord giveth' "
(p. 548).

Saul can see beauty and a reason to live in a puddle, and Rich
can revive his need to write. Art will no longer come from the form
of a beautiful youth but out of a compromised world. And love will
not be the search for a muse but the realization that people must
love each other "as is."

The final move toward reconsummation of their relationship in
Rich's hospital bed is the triumph of desire, now qualified and

modified, in the new world. Rich's body is now far from the perfect object of desire: "I have Kaposi's sarcoma, a hitherto rare form of skin cancer. It's spreading. I have just begun chemotherapy. It nauseates me. I expect my hair will fall out. I also have a fungal infection of the throat called candidiasis, or thrush. My life expectancy is . . ." (p. 542). Sex will now be something different from the wild celebration of the past. Now careful, frightening, but affirming their commitment.

While Hoffman uses the affirmation of the past as one element in refashioning life in the age of AIDS, Robert Chesley is more insistent on the justification and celebration of past eroticism. Yet Chesley's best-known play, *Jerker, or The Helping Hand: A Pornographic Elegy with Redeeming Social Value and a Hymn to the Queer Men of San Francisco in Twenty Telephone Calls, Many of Them Dirty* (1986), finds little space for the present. Nor does it find space for a larger social context for its characters, who live in problematically hermetic worlds.

Jerker uses the AIDS-age phenomenon of telephone sex to underscore the alienation from their past and from each other that gay men now experience. J. R., a handicapped Vietnam veteran, calls Bert, a businessman whom he has seen in bars, and they share masturbatory fantasies. While the physical isolation and separateness of the characters and the solitary practice of masturbation are poignant reminders of the reduction of eroticism in the age of AIDS, the scenes celebrate the power of sexual fantasy to join these men, whose experience is described by Edmund White in his essay, "Esthetics and Loss":

> Onanism—singular or in groups—has replaced intercourse. This solitude is precisely a recollection of adolescence. Unloved, the body releases its old sad song, but it also builds fantasies, rerunning idealized movies of past realities, fashioning new images out of thin air.[39]

J. R. and Bert's fantasies are of adolescence, of sexual play between brothers in a rural setting, an idealized past of physical pleasure without regret, fear, or disease. But even this shared fantasy cannot fend off the plague. First Bert cries over the death of a friend, and his anger and grief lead to the first nonsexual conversation, as Bert vents his anger over denigrations of the past:

But, you know, everyone's putting it down nowadays. 'The party's over! The party's over!' Well, fuck it all *no! That wasn't just a party!* It was more: a *lot* more, at least to some of us, and it was *connected* to other parts of our lives, *deep* parts, *deep* connections. I'm not going to deny that drugs were part of it, and I *know* for some guys it was—or turned out to be—hell. But that's not the whole story. For me, for a *lot* of guys, it was . . . *living;* and it was *loving.*[40]

J. R.'s past also includes Vietnam, the cause of the crutches that lean against his wall. Vietnam, which maimed him physically, taught him "what immoral means": compared with Vietnam, sexual activity is "all that is *good*—really, truly *basically* good. Something in me *knows* that, knows that it's just the exact opposite of the evil I've seen" (p. 475).

In *Jerker* the only bearable erotic fantasy is of sex before AIDS. As J. R. and Bert fantasize a pure, outdoor adolescence, a rural idyll, another friend's masturbatory fantasies have to be in the pre-AIDS past: "He can't even fantasize what he wants to do with another man unless it's before . . . all this" (p. 476). Bert asks the central question for men terrified of AIDS and robbed of their past, "What does that leave us, huh?," and J. R.'s response affirms the saving emotions that remain: "Loving can't be killed: it's stronger" (p. 476). Yet Chesley wants to affirm that the sexual encounters of the past were also love—that love isn't only disembodied feeling. Bert recounts in considerable detail a sexual encounter he had in 1979, before the plague. The value of Bert's memory is not only the present sexual pleasure it gives him and J. R. but the affirmation it offers: "Getting me to remember—that it was love. And . . . a virus can't change that" (p. 483).

A virus can change the present and the future, however. Bert gets sick, and in the final scenes of the play, J. R. can reach only Bert's answering machine, which plays a Judy Garland song that now takes on ironic significance:

> So as long as you've begun it,
> And you know you shouldn't have done it . . .
> Oh, do it again— (p. 490)

The voice of Judy Garland, whose death was a catalyst for the Stonewall riot, sings a song about forbidden sex. The lyric that once meant sex that was naughty—wrong—now hints at sex that is literally deadly. Always a song of defiance, it now affirms sex even in the face of death.

Both the power and the poignancy of *Jerker* are contained in the fact that J. R. never gets to give Bert the loving comfort he offers. Finally, when Bert is only a voice on his answering machine, J. R. gives his phone number. J. R. likes "anonymous encounters." He is writing "a history, a history of love among strangers" (p. 479), and anonymous encounters are what he wants to affirm. "And *nobody* can say it's without meaning: just that both parties have voluntarily chosen to limit the *medium* for meaning—limit it to what's good, limit it to sex" (p. 479).

At the end, speaking to Bert's answering machine, J. R. proclaims his love for Bert, but Bert and J. R. never have the embrace or the assurances of Hoffman's lovers. The world they celebrate also isolates because it offers no liberating vision of the present or the future. The sexual freedom decried as a cause of the spread of the AIDS virus is celebrated as it must be to offer the gay man anything but guilt, regret, and a rejection of his own experience. But there are limitations to the fantasies Bert and J. R. offer each other.

The attitude of the characters in *Jerker* mirrors that of Ghee in Harvey Fierstein's *Safe Sex* (1987): the enemy is "now": "We can never touch as before. We can never be as before. 'Now' will always define us. Different times. Too late."[41] *Safe Sex,* the centerpiece play of the trilogy of the same name, has two lovers precariously balanced on a giant seesaw. Mead wants to hold Ghee, who is obsessed with his Safe Sex list of do's and don'ts. Of course, any move of one partner toward the other upsets the precarious balance of the seesaw and sends both crashing to the ground. Human connection, at least for gay men, cannot stay aloft in the age of AIDS. In a lengthy monologue, Ghee compares "then" when "We had great sex, but argued politics," with "now," when "we enjoy politics but argue sex" (p. 56).

In the first play of the *Safe Sex* trilogy, Manny and Jake, Manny is haunted by the fact that he is a carrier, that sex with him is deadly. He can only lament the past: "A moment of silence for what we used to do and how it felt" (p. 12). Manny's lament becomes a litany as he sits static throughout the play in a lotus position, echoing and expanding his own mantra: "A moment of silence for what can't be done. Another for what can't be undone. A moment of silence for letting go of dreams. And one for stifled lives. For loss. For want. And a toast to those who can change. Who have changed. Who want to change and not forget" (p. 21).

Manny cannot forget nor can he change. His obsession with loss and with his own status as "carrier" has rendered him immobile, unfeeling. But sex to him was nothing but physical satisfaction: "Separation was my only rule" (p. 17). AIDS has enforced the separation without the physical gratification. When Jake offers him affection, solace, and comfort, Manny rejects him—and his own humanity:

> JAKE: People shouldn't be alone.
> MANNY: I'm not people anymore. (p. 23)

Ghee, in *Safe Sex,* is spared the same isolation by Mead's insistence that they embrace. By moving together toward the center of the seesaw, they maintain balance, stay aloft. One—two—can embrace, love safely, even "now." Fierstein's toast is for people who can "change and not forget."

"Till death do us part"

To "change and not forget"—the phrase is the epitome of what is essential to survival and growth in AIDS drama. Change is moving toward an affirmation of love, a physical and spiritual embrace that overcomes the internalized homophobia and fears of commitment that were the crippling detritus of the past. AIDS drama may not be erotic, but it is unabashedly romantic, even at its most violent.

It is a tragic irony that AIDS can validate gay relationships by showing the sacrifice and devotion of the caring partner toward his lover. In *An Early Frost,* Michael can go "home" to his lover, Peter, because their love has been tested by Michael's illness. In *As Is,* Rich realizes that Saul's domesticity and kvetching are what he needs now, not Chet's beauty and fecklessness.

The question in AIDS drama is, "Will you still love me when I'm deathly ill and covered with lesions?"

RICH: But what happens when it gets worse? It's gonna get worse.
SAUL: I'll be here for you no matter what happens.
RICH: Will you?
SAUL: I promise. (*As Is*, p. 548)

PETER: When are you going to leave me?
DREW (*turns to him; simply*): When you aren't there anymore. (*Eastern Standard*, p. 105).

The sign of moral failure is to give up on a relationship, as Gerry's lover, Hugh, does in Kirby's *Compromised Immunity,* or as Chet does to Rich in *As Is.*

A discussion of Larry Kramer's *The Normal Heart,* which ends with a deathbed marriage, brings us back full circle to problems of AIDS discourse discussed earlier in the chapter.

The Normal Heart, a thinly veiled drama à clef, chronicles Kramer's own battles with the closety Gay Men's Health Crisis, which reflected the New York gay community's resistance to giving up on promiscuity as the primary tenet of gay liberation despite the ravages of the AIDS epidemic, and his battles with the indifference of Mayor Koch's administration. Throughout the play Kramer's message of sexual abstinence is shouted, as it was emblazoned throughout Kramer's editorials and letters during the eighties. Ned Weeks, Kramer's character in the play, is a contemporary, gay Cassandra, whose dire but accurate prophesies are scorned by his fellow gays: "After years of liberation, you have helped make sex dirty again for us—terrible and forbidden."[42]

The Normal Heart ends not with Ned's dismissal from the Gay Men's Health Crisis, which he founded, but with his marriage to the dying Felix. Interwoven with scenes depicting the political battle over AIDS are scenes chronicling Ned and Felix's romance.

Ned meets Felix when he goes to the *New York Times* to challenge gay reporters to cover the AIDS story, which is being buried on the back pages if treated at all. Felix is a fashion writer who tries to keep closeted on the heterosexist *Times* but who writes about "gay designers and gay discos and gay chefs and gay rock stars and gay photographers and gay models and gay celebrities and gay everything. I just don't call them gay" (p. 41). While Felix is not eager to "come out" at the *Times,* he is eager to establish a relationship with Ned.

Kramer uses the Ned-Felix relationship to show what was wrong with gay relationships in the age of liberation and how old, self-destructive behavior patterns doom current partners. On their "first date," Felix reminds Ned that they had sex in the baths years before and that Ned rejected any further contact, "I really am not in the market for a lover," a line he repeats on this date with Felix. Felix, the "strong" partner in this conventional dramatic gay relationship, responds with the lesson Ned must learn if he is to bring his political platform into his own life: "Men do not just naturally not love—they learn not to" (p. 53). They learn from the heterosexist world in which they are raised, but the message is reinforced by the promiscuous urban gay world in which sex is "okay as long as we treat each other like whores" (p. 53).

Ned is instantaneously cured of the neuroses that had him running "after people who didn't want me and away from people who do" (p. 49), and he and Felix move in together. But there can be no happily-ever-after in Kramer's jeremiad. Ned and Felix must pay for their promiscuous past even though Felix, like Marguerite Gautier, judges his past actions in a way consonant with society's judgment: "I sometimes make mistakes and look for love in the wrong places" (p. 53). Looking for love in the baths is extremely naive, but one shouldn't die for such romantic idealism. Yet die Felix must, for Kramer is intent to show that true love is as doomed by the AIDS virus as are the constantly shifting liaisons of the leaders of the Gay Men's Health Crisis.

Kramer gives Felix a death scene that Dumas or Giuseppe Verdi would have admired. After Felix dispenses some final bits of wisdom and advice, he and Ned are married by a doctor in the presence of Ned's now-apologetic brother. There can be no love relationship, only a deathbed marriage. Gay men are once again doomed to be alone. "È strano!"

Kramer has trapped himself in his own rhetoric. There is no space for resolution of the crisis that obsesses him, no space for the love that could be a counter to the promiscuity he excoriates as not only exploitative and destructive—as he presented it in his novel *Faggots* (1978)—but now also deadly. We can feel pathos for the death of the sweet, handsome, noble Felix (played, by the way, by D. W. Moffett, who a few months later would play Peter in *An Early Frost*), but who or what is at fault? Kramer, too, confuses the mode of transmission with the virus itself. In doing so, he buys into all the destructive confusion of AIDS discourse. Anger isn't enough.

Kramer's political confusion is expressed not only in the text of the play but also in the texts that form the play's setting. However naturalistic the script seems, Kramer has set his play within walls on which are painted statistics that are also accusations: of indifference or worse on the part of Mayor Koch and the city government, of the federal government, and of the *New York Times*. Moderate gay groups, like the Gay Men's Health Crisis, are damned by inference in the longest passage, filling an entire wall, which describes the futile AIDS strategy of polite cooperation and "backstairs diplomacy" with Washington officials. This strategy is likened to the one the American Jewish Committee followed during the Holocaust, when more radical action against a seemingly indifferent American government might have saved more European Jews. Raising the specter of the Holocaust clarifies Kramer's politics. Is AIDS being used, through design or negligence, as a "final solution" for homosexuals in America? If so, then radical action is the only possible response and protection, and that action can be effective only if gay men are willing to "come out." But surely this argument could be presented without turning the attack so completely against the gay community. An effective call to arms does not divide, it unites, something Kramer himself realized in 1987: "In reading over my collected diatribes of the past years, I realized I am still unable to resolve this fundamental problem—how to inspire you without punishing you."[43] As we shall see, Kramer found a more effective, more focused vehicle for his anger than the theatrical diatribe.

Into the Streets

Principal dramatic form of the decade (owing to AIDS):
the memorial service.
"Theater: The Best of the '80's," *Village Voice*,
January 2, 1990

In an article in the October 1989 issue of *American Theatre,* Alisa Solomon writes:

> Recently, AIDS has fallen off as a central subject for new drama. It's no wonder. When, for instance, spectacle and public ritual are so movingly combined in the image and action of the Names Project Quilt, conventional theatre seems redundant—at best a pale imitation of the formal, mass expressions that help give shape to real grief and anger. Time and again the spirited protesters of ACT UP have demonstrated that the theatre of AIDS is in the streets.[44]

That Solomon's article on ACT UP (the AIDS Coalition to Unleash Power) was printed in the best chronicle of the current state of American drama gives credence to her argument. From the vantage point of the early nineties, AIDS drama looks like it has run its course. Its apex was reached in 1985, that strange banner year for gay men.

1985 was the year the AIDS crisis allowed a space for gay men on television. On "Dynasty," Steven Carrington fell in love with Luke, who thanked the Carrington family for letting him sit at their table, a symbolic moment that suggested that gay men, hats in hand, might find a place in America's living rooms and cultural consciousness. It was the year Laura Z. Hobson's novel *Consenting Adult* (1975) was moved from the world of New York Jewish intelligentsia to Televisionland and Marlo Thomas. It was the year of the most daring of television dramas, *Welcome Home, Bobby,* in which a teenage boy, who had been having an affair with an older man, made clear to his family that his sexual partners were going be his choice. In these television programs, as in *An Early Frost,* the young gay man battled his strong father while a noble mother mediated. The son won, but his days in Televisionland were numbered.

Television had another vision that year, one that drastically revised the public image of AIDS and of gay men for middle America. "Dynasty" viewers were not only watching handsome blond Steven go through fits of ambivalence over his sensitive brunet lover, Luke, but they also saw the ravaged remains of Rock Hudson as he carried on, in and around the stable, with Steven's stepmother. It took an actor to focus America's attention on AIDS. Even the actor in the

White House, who refused to mention AIDS for the first five years of the epidemic, had to acknowledge his friend's death.

Hudson's death also gave his *Giant* costar, Elizabeth Taylor, a new role as spokesperson for the American Foundation for AIDS Research, which was established with a grant from the ailing Hudson. In a brilliant piece of gallows humor, the late Stephen Chapot described sitting in the balcony with three other Persons With AIDS, watching the spectacle of an AIDS fundraiser featuring Elizabeth Taylor. Chapot's essay is a stunning piece, exposing the absurdity of a spectacular Hollywood benefit performance, another kind of AIDS theater:

> The show is everything you would expect from this town in a crisis. No one mentions the word AIDS until twenty-five minutes into the show, and when it comes, it's mentioned by the director of the AIDS Project. Someone snickers. "She dresses like my old aunt." They present an award to a man in a wheelchair who has brought his own oxygen. This is an audience that gives a man a standing ovation for dying in public. . . .
>
> When Taylor does make her appearance, she promises "to spend the rest of my life fighting AIDS." I chuckle, "So will I, honey, so will I."[45]

1985 was also the year in which Robert Chesley's *Jerker* takes place, and in which William Hoffman's *As Is* and Larry Kramer's *The Normal Heart,* the most commercially successful AIDS plays, received major New York productions. *As Is* moved from the Circle Repertory Theatre in Greenwich Village to Broadway and then on to a lugubrious television production (1986). *The Normal Heart* earned the record of being the longest-running production at Joseph Papp's New York Shakespeare Festival, and rumors spread that Barbra Streisand would produce a film version.

Two years later, AIDS as theater had transformed itself radically. In San Francisco, activist Cleve Jones, while recuperating from stab wounds inflicted by fag bashers who had seen him "come out" on TV's "60 Minutes," devised the idea of the AIDS quilt. His panel, the first panel of the quilt, would be a memorial to his friend, actor Marvin Feldman. In October of 1987, almost two thousand panels of the AIDS quilt were displayed on the Mall in Washington, D.C. In a moving ceremony, the names of the people celebrated by quilt panels were read out. Among the readers was playwright Harvey Fierstein and producer Joseph Papp. The ceremony, the reading of names, and the unveiling of the giant pattern of tributes was one form of AIDS theater. The sense of communion that comes from being in an audience, of sharing an event—that sense that theater shares with religion—is a crucial part of the experience of the quilt. It is not like looking at a painting, or a quilt on display in a crafts gallery or museum. The communal viewing of the quilt, the sharing of the emotions it evokes, is central to the experience.[46]

A more lively form of AIDS theater was the brainchild of Larry Kramer, whose rage led him from editorial vituperation, to the Gay Men's Health Crisis, to *The Normal Heart,* to a chaotic farce about the First Family of the eighties, *Just Say No* (1988), an attempt to parody what was already absurd, to founding ACT UP, which has proved that the protests and street theater of the sixties can be useful in the conservative eighties and nineties.

Just Say No was a testament to the limitations of theater as an effective expression of Kramer's anger. A bizarre farce, with characters who clearly represent the Reagans and Mayor Koch, the play was more an exercise in what we now call "outing" (exposing closeted homosexuals who are supporting oppression of other gays) than focused drama. Kramer's introduction to the published version of *Just Say No* is far clearer than the play itself, showing that during the AIDS crisis, Kramer grew as an essayist, while his ability to form a coherent drama dwindled. It is not surprising that the next Larry Kramer production to appear at the New York Shakespeare Festival (in the summer of 1990) was *Unnatural Acts,* a theater piece based on excerpts from the essays collected in his *Reports From the Holocaust,* with, as a curtain raiser, a fifteen-minute dance-theater piece performed to selections from the speeches of Jesse Helms.[47]

By the time *Unnatural Acts* was produced (1990), Kramer would be better known as AIDS polemicist and activist than as playwright. ACT UP grew out of a speech Kramer gave on March 10, 1987. Two weeks later, ACT UP had its first demonstration on Wall Street, replete, significantly, with props built in the shops of the New York Public Theater. Kramer describes the public demonstrations of ACT UP as theater: "Each action is like an enormous show. We're divided

into committees, doing banners, logistics, media, just like a producer would hire people for scenery, costumes, publicity."[48]

The purpose of the production is to garner the largest audience
possible through doing something so theatrical that the media cannot resist covering it. In his history of the tragic farce of the
American medical and pharmaceutical Establishment's handling of
AIDS, Bruce Nussbaum credits ACT UP with providing the impetus
for forcing the National Institutes of Health and corporations like
Burroughs-Wellcome to act with a modicum of competence and
responsibility.[49] Now there are ACT UP chapters all over the country, even in the front yard of Burroughs-Wellcome and Jesse Helms,
Raleigh-Durham, North Carolina.[50]

ACT UP demonstrations dramatize the AIDS crisis through vivid
theatrical metaphors played out where decisions are made—on
Wall Street, in the headquarters of drug companies, and at medical
conventions. In doing so, they prove the power of theater but also
come up against its limitations, as drama tends to play to the
already-converted and seems to have little effect on those who need
conversion. For over twenty years, theater people have lamented
the inability of political theater to do more than validate those in
the audience who share the playwright's opinions. ACT UP has
redefined political theater for the age of mass media. It has shown
that theaters are not places to effect social change: theater is a more
effective tool for shocking people into awareness of key issues when
it is taken out of its conventional home. In *AIDS Demo Graphics,*
Douglas Crimp writes:

> For AIDS activist artists, rethinking the identity and role of the artist
> also entails new considerations of audience. Postmodernist art advanced
> a political critique of arts institutions—and art itself as an institution—
> for the ways they constructed social relations through specific modes of
> address, representations of history, and obfuscations of power.[51]

Crimp is speaking of the visual arts, and his volume is a vivid
record of how they have been galvanized into use by and for ACT
UP and other AIDS activists. His statement, representative of many
by contemporary critics, raises questions about the institution of
theater in a time in which old prejudices and associations need to
be exploded.

AIDS theater, then, is played out most effectively in the real world, sometimes with stars like Rock Hudson or Liberace, sometimes with chronically enraged playwrights like Larry Kramer, but most vividly by a cast of thousands, proving, as Hudson inadvertently did, that there are millions of gay men who are not known by the usual, stereotypical signs. They may be forced into being known, or—better—may choose to be known. Like a Cecil B. DeMille spectacular, the power of AIDS as theater is the power of numbers: the cast of thousands in the streets at a gay-pride rally or an ACT UP demonstration is the most powerful sign that the gay community is big and ultimately unbeatable.

Street theater has been a central part of gay life, from the informal and formal costumed processions of Halloween, that celebration of disguise that has become the gay holiday, to the display of sexual and social identity of the gay-pride march. Now gay street theater has been galvanized by AIDS, given a purpose. The flamboyant, celebratory masking has been transformed into potent performances of unmasking aimed at those who are doing nothing, or less than nothing, about AIDS.

AIDS drama onstage, so important in the mid-eighties, may have served its purpose. But AIDS theater, with the world as its stage, is still being powerfully played. It is a potent antidote to "the spectacle of AIDS."

PART 2

Codes and Closets

Alfred Lunt, Lynne
Fontanne, and Noël
Coward in Noël Coward's
Design for Living (1933).
Photo from the Billy Rose
Collection, New York
Public Library at Lincoln
Center.

Closet Pederasts

"When the audience watches it here, I want them to
say to themselves, 'It's homosexual. Nothing is said
about it but it's there. It must be there. That's the
only explanation for these characters and their story.'
So that's what I want. I want to create something
without stating it."
Jed Harris, on his production of *The Green Bay Tree*

"He was an expert on the adolescent male body. He'd
completed an exhaustive study of his subject before I
met him. During the course of one magical night he
talked to me of his principles—offered me a job if I
would accept them. Like a fool I turned him down."
Sloane, in Joe Orton, *Entertaining Mr. Sloane*

This chapter focuses on the presentation of homosexuality in British
dramas from the 1930s until 1968, when the section of the Licensing Act of 1737 that mandated the censorship imposed by the Lord
Chamberlain's office was revoked. In these plays, one sees how the
depiction onstage of gay characters was the result of cautiously
showing what could not be shown, and saying what could not be
said. By both suggesting and denying the existence of homosexuals,
the plays of this period dramatize and maintain the closet. Such
"closet dramas" could be written by heterosexuals exploiting the
potentially sensational subject matter or, in the case of Harold
Pinter, toying with the very restrictions involved in presenting homosexuality at all. Or they could be written by gay playwrights like

Noël Coward, dependent on the popularity and rewards of commercial success, or Joe Orton, desiring success like Coward's but wanting as well to place homoerotic desire at the center of his plays. All the plays discussed in this chapter were also produced in New York (Coward's *Design for Living* was first produced, in 1933, on Broadway) and were, thus, influential in establishing American stereotypes.

Actors and the Closet

In December 1990, British actor and gay-rights activist Ian McKellan became Sir Ian McKellan. While McKellan is hardly the first homosexual to earn a "Sir" before his name, he is the first to proclaim his gayness openly beforehand and to campaign against government attempts to reinstate the closet onstage and offstage. When filmmaker Derek Jarman excoriated McKellan for accepting the knighthood and thereby supporting the heterosexist policies of the government, which McKellan had rightfully attacked, eighteen other British theater people—producer Cameron MacIntosh; playwrights Martin Sherman, Nicholas Wright, and David Lan; and fifteen directors and well-known actors—"came out" and supported McKellan's knighthood as a crucial moment in English gay history. "Never again," their overly optimistic statement read, "will public figures be able to claim that they have to keep secret their homosexuality in fear of damaging their careers."[1] The previous summer, actor Alec McCowen (one of the signers of the letter supporting McKellan) announced that his appearance in a dramatization of Christopher Isherwood's *A Single Man* was his coming out, since the play, about a middle-aged gay man's dealing with the loss of his lover, mirrored McCowen's own recent loss of a lover to AIDS.

While skeptics may note that the statement supporting McKellan was signed only by well-established "personages"—no young actors felt it was safe to sign the statement—optimists can read a number of meanings into these British theatrical comings-out. They are at once a defiance of growing strictures against the public admission of homosexuality in England and an acknowledgment that few Britons care whether theater people are gay. Many simply assume that they are—an equation of homosexuality and artists "in a country in which homosexuality is tolerated as an eccentricity but not accepted as a way of life"[2] that may explain how the British government can both honor a gay activist and enact laws to silence gay activism.

What these British theater people have done in publicly proclaiming their homosexuality is what many American theater people most fear. Here, "outing," announcing that a public figure is homosexual, is a weapon used by activists to attack closeted public figures who, by their silence, support the oppression of their fellow gays.[3] Why is it that American actors have to be dragged out of the closet, while British artists see the importance to the gay community of their visibility as gay people? Why is it that, when outed, gay American actors vehemently deny their sexuality and even, in some recent cases, get married to a woman in an attempt to invalidate the allegation? Why is there less of a price to pay for coming out in Britain than in America? In our society, despite the success of Harvey Fierstein and a few other playwrights, many thespians feel that any tie between the theater and homosexuality must be publicly severed, despite the fact that many of our leading playwrights, composers, lyricists, directors, and designers are and have been homosexual.

While American actors have mastered "playing the closet," many English actors understand the political and theatrical power of coming out. Coming out is a kind of performance, a public proclamation of one's gayness akin to the public demonstration of salvation in an evangelical revival. It is a public joining of private and public life, a public refusal to perform the intricate but limiting roles heterosexist society wants gay men to perform: maintaining silence and denying what others do not want to know or playing the role people want and expect, preparing "a face to meet the faces that you meet," as Eliot's Prufrock so aptly puts it. The performance may be of "playing straight" or playing a stereotype of homosexuality that heterosexist society can grasp. Coming out is a performance that resists a number of other performances.

Much of the public is protected by the performances associated with the closet from knowing what they do not want to know and, therefore, not having to deal with what they do not want to deal with. Eve Kosofsky Sedgwick notes "the degree to which the power of our enemies over us is implicated, not in their command of knowledge, but precisely in their ignorance."[4]

The closet itself is less a place than a performance—or series of performances, maintained by the heterosexist wish for, and sometimes enforcement of, homosexual silence and invisibility. Like any good performer, the closeted individual seeks approval by giving his audience what they want, but in the process he performs his shame at being homosexual.

In this chapter and the next, I will focus on the paradoxes endemic to the dramatic closet. The stage closet resembles one of those garish magician's cabinets that gaudily dressed assistants wheel around the stage: "Now you see him; now you don't." For theatricality—metatheatricality—is essential to the language of the dramatic closet. The phantom homosexual is the character who imaginatively transforms his environment, who turns reality into stage set as a background for his performance. As the homosexual resists conventional categories of sexual identity, the stage homosexual—and the closeted play—are known (only sometimes) by their resistance to the strictures of realistic theater. Dramatizing the closet is also dramatizing the theater of the closet.

One of the most common clichés encountered in discussions of any creation of homosexuals is the "gay sensibility," a universalizing term suggesting that flamboyant, ironic theatricalization, like limp wrists, is a genetic quirk all homosexuals have to one extent or another. This misconception not only denies that homosexuals, like heterosexuals, have more differences than similarities but also minoritizes art as "sissy" because it is more "natural" to homosexuals. I suggest that what has been called the "gay sensibility" is actually a "closet sensibility," an awareness of performance because of the need to perform, and a mockery of the roles one is expected to perform. Closet sensibility seems universal, "natural" to the "unnatural" homosexual, because it is a set of responses to being stereotyped.

Closet drama is tied to two complementary aspects of the closet: the denial of the existence of homosexuality within the audience's social sphere, which is being depicted "realistically" onstage, and the maintenance of stereotypes that assure audiences that the homosexual can easily be recognized and, should he intrude on normal society, marginalized.

The Closet and the Police

The only truly successful representation of the closet is invisibility and silence—no homosexuality at all; however, like all the other titillating taboo subjects exposed onstage in the twenties and thirties,[5] the horror of homosexuality proved to be an irresistible lure. Realistic drama could afford audiences a glimpse of the forbidden, then banish it from the stage. Historically, homosexuality had moved from the silent and invisible to the unspeakable and unshowable.[6] The theater's challenge was to suggest and indicate without actually acknowledging the existence of the forbidden subject. This is the first visible dramatic closet: the invocation of homosexuality without naming it—or the problematizing of homosexuality without acknowledging its existence. It could be read by those who wanted to see it, particularly homosexuals.

In the United States in the 1930s, depictions of homosexuality were limited, if not eliminated, by legal sanctions against representing homosexuality onstage. These sanctions had been unnecessary until the appearance of such representations. Inspired by a public outrage that had been fueled by the reaction of a moralistic press to Mae West's play *The Drag* (1927) (which never got closer to Broadway than Bayonne, New Jersey) and a sensationalistic melodrama about lesbians, *The Captive* (1927), a translation of a French play by Edouard Bourdet, legislators added the Wales Padlock Act to the New York State Penal Code. The act outlawed plays "depicting or dealing with, the subject of sex degeneracy, or sex perversion." The threatened penalty, if a theater housed a play that "would tend to the corruption of youth or others," was the padlocking of that theater for a year and, potentially, the revoking of its operating license. All persons involved in any way with these productions, or with any "obscene, indecent, immoral, or impure production," were guilty of a misdemeanor.[7] Though it was nominally directed against any stage obscenity, the Wales Padlock Act was supported by the "threat to society" posed by *The Captive,* a play that was hardly an advertisement for the joys of lesbian behavior. The melodrama was

considered dangerous merely because it acknowledged the existence of such behavior.

What seemed most dangerous to the City Fathers was not what
happened onstage but the fact that gay characters onstage attracted
numbers of gay people to the audience, thus creating a visible
presence and, therefore, a threat to the enforcement of invisibility.
It is clear from newspaper accounts that the out-of-town productions of *The Drag* and *The Captive* attracted a large proportion of
gay men and women, and the exposure of the public to displays of
"vice and the vicious" on both sides of the footlights probably
contributed to the outcry. Heterosexist Jeremiahs seemed to believe
that the frightening fiction of homosexuals onstage spawned the
horrible reality of numbers of homosexuals in the audience. In
declaring *The Captive* obscene, Justice Jeremiah Mahoney cited police reports that at one performance 60 percent of the audience was
female, "and groups of unescorted girls in twos and threes sat
together." One of the dangers of *The Captive,* it seemed, was the
creation of an environment in which women socialized without
male companionship or supervision. Mahoney wondered whether
obscenity laws should not protect "the young and immature, the
ignorant and sensually inclined," for "many people must be protected from their very selves."[8] Neither *The Captive* nor *The Drag*
gave those "sensually inclined" men and women very much on
which to base a positive self-image, but it was an image, and so,
though the plays reinforced attitudes about the horror of unnatural
sexuality, they did provide gay people with at least a grudging
acknowledgment of their existence. Even presenting homosexuals
in a negative light opened the closet door a crack.

In Great Britain the Lord Chamberlain's office had, since 1737,
exercised censorship over all theatrical scripts. This censorship was
originally intended to stifle antigovernment satire but later became
more concerned with matters of "decency." Until the Licensing Act
was finally revoked in 1968, the Lord Chamberlain was expected to
keep homosexual characters and relationships off the British stage.
You could evade the Lord Chamberlain's watchful eye only by
producing a play in a private club (the Royal Court Theatre had to
be turned into a club in order to present John Osborne's *A Patriot
for Me.*)[9]

On the American or British stage, then, homosexual characters and relationships could be inferred from the behavior of the actors, though it could not be discussed openly. Such inference could best be shown by a combination of selections from the catalog of gay male stereotypes:

Effeminacy (mincing, limp wrists, lisping, flamboyant dress)
Sensitivity (moodiness, a devotion to his mother, a tendency to show emotion in an unmanly way)
Artistic talent or sensibility
Misogyny
Pederasty (as we shall see, this became the stereotypical formula for homosexual relationships, with its connotations of arrested development and pernicious influence)
Foppishness
Isolation (the homosexual's fate, if he or she remained alive at the final curtain)

Stereotypes are both necessary and highly problematic. They are necessary because homosexuality does not, like racial or ethnic identity, have any visual signs. Therefore, to represent homosexuality, a catalog of signs was needed, particularly when a character's homosexuality could not be enunciated. As Richard Dyer points out:

A repertoire of signs, making visible the invisible, is the basis of any representation of gay people involving visual recognition, the requirement of recognizability in turn entailing that of typicality. Though not indispensable, typification is a near necessity for the representation of gayness, the product of social, political, practical, and textual determinations.[10]

The purpose of these stereotypes, which assume the validity of certain "universal" signs, is to make homosexuality visible and recognizable. But there is no "truth" to the stereotypes themselves nor to the assumption underlying them: gay people are as different from each other as heterosexuals are.

Further, these problematic stereotypes exist not only to indicate gayness but also to privilege the heterosexual who believes he can identify and marginalize the homosexual. In addition, they help gay people, who can "pass" in a heterosexist society by not enacting the stereotypes. The homosexual character is often trapped in a ritual of purgation—of identifying and eliminating. Visual stereotypes allow the playwright and performers to enact this ritual without ever naming what is considered unspeakable.

As we shall see throughout this chapter and the next, homosexuals were both invoked and marginalized by the very structure of realistic drama. Feminist drama critics maintain that realistic drama necessarily upholds a certain order, one that is as dangerous for gay men as it is for women: "Narrative closure reinstates the preexisting order after instigating its temporary crisis."[11] Jill Dolan reminds us that "if there is an enigma in realism, its structural shape is bent toward unraveling and expunging it."[12] In a structure in which the homosexual is inevitably what Alan Sinfield calls "the outlaw-intruder who threatens the security of the characters and, by inference, the audience,"[13] the purging of the homosexual gives the play closure. Gay playwrights could infuse this formula with irony but could not totally reject it without rejecting the form altogether.

Now You See Him?

Mordaunt Shairp's *The Green Bay Tree,* performed in London and, very successfully, on Broadway with Laurence Olivier in 1933, is a play about a homosexual character and possible homosexual relationship that never mentions or even directly alludes to homosexuality. Shairp managed to succeed where most of his predecessors had failed: he slipped a play about a homosexual relationship past the scrutiny of the Lord Chamberlain and into production and, a few months later onto Broadway without invoking the Padlock Act. Focusing on an elderly homosexual's "tutelage" of an impressionable young man, the play is perforce written in innuendo and depends on stereotypes and judgmental language to make clear the homosexuality that is not written into the script. In discussing *The Green Bay Tree,* Shairp was careful to make his heterosexuality known—in press interviews, he told how he first shared the idea for his play with his wife.[14] This drama about homosexuality was to be seen by the authorities to be clean of any tinge of homosexuality.

The Green Bay Tree, which was to define the formula for the British stage homosexual, established in its Broadway production a recognizable stereotype that dominated American stage and screen for twenty years. It also incorporated homosexuality into the realistic "problem play." In the melodramatic world of *The Green Bay Tree,* the threat of homosexuality lies in the possibility of corruption through pederasty. The worst result of that corruption is, apparently, effeteness verging on effeminacy, a quality that in Noël Coward's *Design for Living* is both chic and sexually ambivalent. In Shairp's play, that sinister effeteness—and hints of pederasty—are the only overt signs of homosexuality in a play that manages to keep its principal subject closeted.

Mr. Dulcimer (no first name, though he is known as "Dulcie," a name precious enough to give him away) is a very wealthy bachelor who lives in elegantly appointed quarters in London. For fifteen years he has been guardian and adoptive father to David Owen, a poor Welsh boy Dulcimer heard sing at an Eisteddfod. Dulcimer fell in love with the purity of the lad's voice and bought the boy from his drunken father for £500. The angelic quality of David's voice, of which the audience hears a recording, signifies the innocence Dulcimer has corrupted, for, since he "bought" the lad, he has shaped him in his own image, teaching him to love his effete life in London and at his country home, Silver Gates (a name suggesting both opulence and imprisonment). Obviously Dulcimer was a good teacher, for David, renamed Julian Dulcimer, is now a handsome twenty-six-year-old ornament, a testament to his training: "My aim was to make him like, and to be unable to do without, what was best for me."[15] For some reason (and this is the most incredible aspect of the play) Julian falls in love with a young veterinarian, Leonora, who took care of his beloved dog, David (clearly his dog has his old name to show that David/Julian is little more than a house pet to Dulcimer). The action of the play centers on the conflict between the effete Mr. Dulcimer and the no-nonsense Leonora over possession of Julian. The role of The Woman here is crucial, as it always is in realistic problem plays focusing on homosexuality. Here the woman is the strong, positive adversary of the evil, homosexual influence. In order to save Julian from Dulcimer, Leonora also must save him from the effete, affluent world into which Julian has been placed and make him a productive member of the middle class.

The "problem" in this melodrama is the sexual corruption of a working-class boy by an older upper-middle-class man. Alan Sin-field notes that it was common for upper-middle-class homosexuals in this period to seek lower-class sexual partners.[16] The romance of cross-class relationships had been central to the literature of gay romance since Edward Carpenter had appropriated Walt Whitman's poetry as a model for loving men around the turn of the century. *The Green Bay Tree* vitiates the myth of the vitalizing sexual force of the working-class man; it also declines to celebrate relationships that cross class lines, relationships that had been an integral com-ponent of early gay literature (E. M. Forster's *Maurice* [1913, pub. 1971] is the classic example), and it does so by linking them to pederasty. Shairp connects the age and class differences in his central relationship of Dulcimer and Julian to the corruption of working-class youth, a reworking of the theme of danger lurking for working-class girls, a staple of nineteenth-century melodrama.

The establishment of cross-class pederasty as the model for evil homosexual relations is a crucial aspect of the formula Shairp evolved. Another is the codified presentation of unstated homosexuality. Shairp is meticulous about stage directions, presenting judgments on his characters that the actors are clearly meant to communicate to the audience. Nowhere is this judgmental language clearer than at the entrance of Mr. Dulcimer at the opening of the play:

> He is a man of about forty-five, immaculately turned out, and wearing at present a double-breasted dinner jacket. He speaks exquisitely, in a clear voice, and with now and then a slight drawl. He has a habit of looking at you from under his eyes, and though a complete dilettante, he has an alert, vibrating personality. A man who could fascinate, repel and alarm. Instantly we know that he is the one thing missing in the room, and he seems to know it, too, for he stands a moment inside the doors, almost as if he were 'taking a call' for having created it. (p. 55)

It does not take a very subtle reading to see the mixed metaphors embedded in Dulcimer's description. His entrance clearly presents him as an actor, a performer in an environment he has made his stage set. An earlier stage description describes Dulcimer's living room as "*artificial*," but it "*reflects his personality, his sensitiveness, and his delicate appreciation of beauty*" (p. 55). The setting contains not only Dulcimer's tasteful living room but also his hothouse garden;

Shairp has mastered the Ibsenesque use of setting as commentary on character. Dulcimer has created a stage on which to perform and, as he is willing to admit, an artificial world in which he can nurture the perfect hothouse flower in Julian.

Dulcimer is the interior decorator as stage designer, but a decorator whose taste is too fine to be shared with the world. The performer and the "complete dilettante," the fop as homosexual, are the stereotypes Shairp uses throughout the play to indicate Dulcimer's homosexuality. An aesthetic sense is connected to *delicateness* and *sensitivity,* words that suggest both effeminacy and its corollary, weakness. Dulcimer is first seen arranging flowers with his butler, Trump, who has obviously been trained to "play" the butler to the hilt. Trump is a fellow performer on Dulcimer's stage, playing a version of Lane, Algernon's butler in Oscar Wilde's *The Importance of Being Earnest* (1895), and that play, with its associations with the "degeneracy" of its creator, ominously echoes throughout Dulcimer's hothouse. Peter Burton points out that Shairp "is setting up Dulcimer as the epitome of effeminacy" and that the opening scene of flower arranging "quickly telegraphs the information to the audience that 'Dulcie' is not a 'real man,' that he must therefore be decadent and, thus is not to be trusted."[17] Indeed, the "effeminate" activity of arranging flowers is the most sinister sign of Dulcimer's effect on Julian. At the end of the London production of the play, Dulcimer's death mask smiles over the set while Julian arranges flowers, a sure sign of his destruction at Dulcimer's hands.[18]

Still, Dulcimer's "performances" raise him out of melodrama and make him a vibrant character. In one extraordinary scene, he stages an elaborate masquerade by inviting Julian and Leonora to dinner and then setting the living room up as a restaurant, complete with menus and with Trump as a haughty *maitre d'.* Julian loves the game, even one-ups Dulcimer by sending Trump for a blank check for the bill, but Leonora sees it as another manifestation of Dulcimer's sinister, unnatural behavior.

Dulcimer's penchant for performance is intended to reflect the aesthete's love of artifice and hatred of the natural—an echo of Oscar Wilde. Like the voice in Eliot's *Wasteland,* Dulcimer hates spring, "that cruel, terrifying time," with its "shattering . . . reassertion of the principle of life" (p. 57). This opposition to nature—

and, by implication, to heterosexuality—turns the fop into a de-mon. The first stage direction presents him as reptilian: "*a man who could fascinate, repel and alarm*" (p. 55). Later, Leonora says, "You fascinate me like a snake fascinates" (p. 82). Earlier, she described Dulcimer as being "rotten to the core" (p. 76). David's father de-scribes Dulcimer as "wicked. He's evil. You don't realize how evil he is" (p. 95). What do we see Dulcimer do that is so evil? He has molded David-become-Julian in his own image and thinks of Julian as his possession, a not-uncommon trait for a father figure in Edwardian drama. The "crime" is not merely the molding but the uncloseted candor with which Dulcimer describes his influence on Julian. Here the mask is off: "I have created comfort and beauty and constant change of scene out of money and a cage for Julian's soul in which he sings to me as sweetly as in that stuffy Welsh school-room all those years ago" (p. 93). The "sensitive hothouse flower" (p. 81) is also a bird in a gilded cage. Only a truly diabolical figure would revel in caging souls, though Dulcimer has also provided the money that will guarantee that Julian's cage will be gilded and that he will live in the style to which he has become accustomed for the rest of his life. But there is no place in that scheme for a woman—even one called Leo—and Dulcimer ultimately wins the battle for possession of Julian on economic grounds. He fights for Julian, "because he is to me youth and charm and companionship. I admit the claims of these indefinable things. I must have them" (p. 93).

Dulcimer sees Julian as another possession for his perfect stage set, but there is more in Dulcimer's too-rational explanation of Julian's place in his life: "But I must have a focussing point for all my activities and interests and self-expression. That focussing point is Julian. If you take him away, I'm lost. I admit that. Like you, I have feelings, but with Julian in my life, I'm never troubled by them. He keeps them constant and satisfied" (p. 94).

This is an oblique way of saying that Dulcimer loves Julian and cannot live without him. The coolness of expression is an aspect of Dulcimer's soulless character but also a function of the Lord Cham-berlain's censorship. The meaning of the play and the "horror" of Dulcimer's character are meaningful only if we "translate" this line to its most emotionally and physically powerful meaning. What makes Dulcimer so "evil," so dangerous, is that which is never spoken, except in one hint from Leonora: "This man has got hold of Julian body and soul" (p. 94). It is that hold on Julian's body that is so repellent, yet that hold is never seen or discussed beyond that line. Why else would he fight ruthlessly to possess handsome Julian, as we are led to believe he has possessed him since David/Julian was eleven? The luxury is merely the outward trapping of the "diabolical sexual thrall" in which Julian is being held. Contemporary critics saw clearly what was hinted at in *The Green Bay Tree,* and Dulcimer's death by means of his own "exquisitely jeweled revolver" (he is killed by Julian's real father, a drunk-turned-evangelist who is enlisted by Leonora to "save" Julian) is poetic justice.

Julian is not saved, however. Having been "perverted by Dulcimer, Julian at the end *becomes* Dulcimer, arranging flowers sent up from Silver Gates and bantering with Trump:

> TRUMP (*looking up at the mask*): Mr. Dulcimer always said, sir, that a man could never settle down until he'd got women out of his life.
> JULIAN: I expect he was right. He nearly always was. (p. 97)

Except for the butler, who stays on when he discovers that women will not invade the household, Julian is alone at the end of the play, but since he has taken on Dulcimer's identity, one senses that he will soon be taking a trip to Wales to find his own sweet-voiced eleven-year-old. This ending provides an interesting twist on the purging of the outsider essential to the structure of the realistic problem play. Dulcimer, the corrupter, is killed in his own home. Leonora is removed from the scene: she is the outsider in Dulcimer and Julian's world because of her "normal" middle-class values and heterosexual desires. Julian, at the final curtain, is safely ensconced in his hermetic world, removed from "normal" society, sealed in the gilded cage where he belongs. A gay audience could see the denouement not as a sinister picture of corruption but as the survival of the homosexual. Only a portion of the audience will read flower-arranging as a sign of degeneracy.

Yet, while *The Green Bay Tree* presents Dulcimer's elegant surroundings as a gilded cage, the only alternative environment the audience sees is the squalid, Spartan flat of Julian's born-again father and the only alternative career, veterinary medicine, a ludicrous choice for someone of Julian's upbringing and temperament. As in much popular melodrama, an outlandish set of circumstances and alternatives is presented with utmost earnestness; laughter is precluded.

The issue presented with such earnestness is Julian's corruption at the hands of a diabolical homosexual, yet all one can do with homosexuality in *The Green Bay Tree* is "sense" or "presume," since nothing is overt beyond what the director and actors perform. Reports of the original London production suggest that there was much overt effeminacy in the playing of Dulcimer and Julian, but this could be passed off as high camp, which had been an aspect of British drawing-room comedy for centuries and was not always overtly tied to homosexuality. However, when in 1933 Jed Harris produced the play for a Broadway audience, which has always equated camp with effeminacy, he cut out even the hints of homosexuality yet still wanted the audience to "know" that his characters were homosexual. He told his cast at rehearsal:

> As you know, in London the entire production was dominated by homosexuality. There was even swishing onstage. I'll have none of that. We've [Harris and his house playwright, Edward Chodorov] been removing all of those references. When the audience watches it here, I want them to say to themselves, 'It's homosexual. Nothing is said about it but it's there. It must be there. That's the only explanation for these characters and their story.' So that's what I want. I want to create something without stating it.[19]

The few overt references to Julian's "fate," like Leonora's line: "I hope I shant meet you one day in Piccadilly with a painted face, just because you must have linen sheets" (p. 92), were cut from the Broadway production. The audience was left to infer from long glances and meaningful silences: "They'll know. It's better if they figure it out than if we tell them."[20] Harris even cut the final tableau of Julian arranging flowers as being too "swish": "I'll bet half the audience left the theater convinced that they actually saw Larry [Olivier] arranging the flowers."[21] The onus of reading homosexuality was on the audience, not the producer, whose show could be padlocked. Yet the assumed audience ability to read homosexuality into the gestures and innuendoes, to decode the cryptic production, shows that Harris knew his audience had some awareness of homosexuality and some understanding of its stereotypes.

The Green Bay Tree managed a moderately healthy run without provoking the legal problems of earlier plays about homosexual relationships, though it hinted at a relationship that was not only homosexual but pederastic as well. While a number of contemporary reviewers denied that there was anything sexual in the relationship of Dulcimer and his ward, critic Robert Garland saw what Jed Harris wanted him to see:

> Reading the reviews printed while I was out of town, I gather that *The Green Bay Tree* has nothing to do with the way of a man with a man. Well, if it has nothing to do with that, it has nothing to do with anything.
>
> If it has nothing to do with that (and "that" is an incident not unknown to the public in general and to patrons of revues in particular), Mr. Shairp's play is the most meaningless play ever written by anybody.[22]

Indeed, if the play is not about "that," it is about destruction by meticulous good taste. But meticulous good taste is code for effeminacy, which equals "homosexual." If Julian has taken Dulcimer's place at the end, then the audience is to infer that Julian has become Dulcimer in all ways. But inference is all the play allows. The meaning of *The Green Bay Tree* is contained in its stereotypical imagery, which audience members could choose to read as they wished. Homosexuality is in the eyes of the beholder and can be "presented" indirectly and nonverbally.

For American audiences, *The Green Bay Tree* established the stereotypical picture of the homosexual as wealthy, effete—and British. He would be played in Hollywood by Charles Laughton or George Sanders. Slightly Americanized in Alfred Hitchcock's films, he would be one of the effete psychopathic killers of *Rope* (1948) and *Strangers on a Train* (1951).

Lifestyles of the Rich and Famous

Noël Coward's *Design for Living,* also produced on Broadway in 1933, is another exercise in the masterful manipulation of "reader response." One sees—and hears—what one wants to see and hear. Overtly, the play centers on Gilda, who during the course of the play has relationships with three men: a painter, Otto; a successful playwright, Leo; and an older, staid art dealer, Ernest. Gilda plays musical beds, moving from Otto to Leo to Otto again, then marrying Ernest, and finally giving up her marriage to Ernest to run off with both Otto and Leo. One can see the play as merely a sophisticated sex comedy about free love in the Bohemian set, in which Gilda is the most unconventional character.

However, the "naughtiness" of Gilda's promiscuity is eclipsed by the hints that Otto and Leo were also romantically involved before Gilda came into their lives:

ERNEST: Otto and Leo knew each other first.
GILDA: Yes, yes, yes, yes—I know all about that! I came along and spoilt everything.[23]

Now this exchange could be read, as the play has often been read, even by contemporary critics, as an expression of Gilda's awareness that she is the disruptive force in an intense homosocial relationship. The issue, according to this reading, is how to resolve Otto and Leo's friendship with the facts that they both love Gilda and that she loves both of them. However, two more pieces of evidence discourage that reading. The first is Leo's explanation, in the first scene, of the tangled web of affection the play depicts: "The actual facts are so simple. I love you. You love me. You love Otto. I love Otto. Otto loves you. Otto loves me. There now! Start to unravel from there" (p. 21). The other is the famous photograph of Otto, Leo, and Gilda (Noël Coward, Alfred Lunt, and Lynn Fontanne) linked together on the sofa at the end of the play, in a menage that illustrates exactly what Ernest has called a "disgusting three-sided erotic hotch-potch!" (p. 138). The three bodies are all intertwined, and Leo, not Gilda, is in the middle, draped half across Otto's body, half across Gilda's. The truth of the relationships of the central characters is in this design of bodies (see p. 84).

Design for Living was a sophisticated comedy by England and America's most popular playwright, and it starred him and the glittering couple Alfred Lunt and Lynn Fontanne. Did the genre of sophisticated comedy with such stars defuse the danger of the relationship the play depicted? The play itself is a defense of the lifestyles of the rich and famous, asserting, as much celebrity gossip had done for years, that stars live by another code. As Otto tells Gilda:

> We are different. Our lives are diametrically opposed to ordinary social conventions; and it's no use grabbing at those conventions to hold us up when we find we're in deep water. We've jilted them and eliminated them, and we've got to find our own solutions for our own peculiar moral problems. (p. 72)

The weakness of the play is its incessant, didactic harping on the validity, if not superiority, of the trio's own moral code. Ultimately, the butt of the play's jokes is any representative of a morality that denigrates the trio's mutual devotion.

Coward has kept Otto and Leo's sexual relationship hidden in the exposition, and they use terms of endearment that could be read as terms of friendship. The only hint we get of the physical aspect of their relationship is the recounting of a violent argument, in which Leo pushed Otto into a bathtub and doused him with cold water. Their one scene together seems to be a drunken lament over the loss of Gilda, but buried in that scene is another clue:

> LEO (*haltingly*) The—feeling I had for you—something very deep, I imagined it was, but it couldn't have been, could it—now that it has died so easily.
>
> OTTO: I said all that to you in Paris. Do you remember? I thought it was true then, just as you think it's true now. (p. 89)

Yet within a few lines, Coward covers his tracks by having Leo qualify their relationship: "Do you honestly believe I could ever look at you again, as a real friend?" (p. 89). A gay auditor would understand that "friend" has always been a slippery euphemism in gay parlance and continue to read the scene as a presentation of a homosexual relationship; straight audience members could hear that line as a disclaimer of hints of homosexuality. Here decoding is necessary to read Otto and Leo as either friends or lovers. Coward lays enough hints to allow either reading, though the play makes less sense if Otto and Leo are "just" friends.

The most definitive sign of homosexual behavior in *Design for*

Living is Otto and Leo's camp behavior, an echo of the sort of performance that was presented as sinister in *The Green Bay Tree*. In act 3, after Gilda has married Ernest and found a place for herself in New York society (represented by a trio of dreary, witless people), Otto and Leo arrive, dressed to the nines, and proceed to perform a bitchy camp spectacle that, as they planned, drives the guests from Gilda's living room:

> LEO: I always thought Madame Butterfly was over-hasty.
> OTTO: She should have gone out into the world and achieved an austere independence. Just like you, Gilda.
> GILDA: Don't talk nonsense. They both talk the most absurd nonsense; they always have, ever since I've known them. You mustn't pay any attention to them.
> OTTO: Don't undermine our social poise, Gilda, you—who have so much.
> GILDA (*sharply*): Your social poise is nonexistent.
> LEO: We have a veneer, though; it's taken us years to acquire; don't scratch it with your sharp witty nails—*darling!*
> *Everybody jumps at the word "darling."*

Gilda's guests, the New York elite, are discomfited by the way Otto and Leo banter, refer to themselves constantly as a couple, assert that they both lived with Gilda, and, most shocking, use that sophisticated endearment *darling*. In this scene, Otto and Leo are the gay couple horrifying a straight party, but their goal of winning Gilda defuses the danger of forbidden overt homosexuality. The invited guests aren't developed enough to be the targets of satire. They are stand-ins for the audience, composed of similar, wealthy New Yorkers. Their discomfort is the same most members of the audience would feel at such a display of camp behavior. The audience is put in the position of laughing at its own responses.

In his discussion of the play, which is infused with his usual ambivalence toward the homosexuality he exploits and sensationalizes, John Lahr writes: "Coward's comic revenge at the finale [in which Gilda's outraged husband, Ernest, falls on his face as he storms out] is the victory of the disguised gay world over the straight one."[24] However, Coward's focus in *Design for Living* is not on homosexuality: Gilda is not a man in disguise. It is precisely on the freedom not to be defined by codes of sexual behavior—not to have to be heterosexual or homosexual. In that the play is most revolutionary. It is the triangle—and the focus on Gilda's anguish and confusion—that hides Otto and Leo's relationship for some, defuses its danger for others. Coward, like Harold Pinter and Joe Orton, removed the danger of homosexual relationships by making his characters bisexual. In doing so, he dramatized the instability of sexual desire. Homosexual desire is there for those who care to see it, neither asserted nor problematized. However, neither is it eroticized nor connected to the possibility of an exclusive homosexual relationship. Like Orton, Coward does not in his plays deny homosexual desire or love, but he does deny exclusive homosexuality as a social identity.

Coward wrote of the audience reaction to *Design for Living*: "People were certainly interested and entertained and occasionally even moved by it, but it seemed, to many of them, 'unpleasant.' "[25] Even glittering star turns and Coward's mots could not hide the hint of homosexuality and the fact that any disapproval of his triangle was either mocked or chastised.

Design for Living had a moderate success in New York, and the Lord Chamberlain eventually allowed it to be produced in London in 1939. A sanitized film version was released in 1933.[26] Still, it was not one of Coward's most successful plays, despite the starry cast, and was not revived until the sexually liberated seventies. In the 1930s, hints of homosexuality among the smart set might be titillating on the larger canvas of a Hemingway or Fitzgerald novel, in which such behavior is a relatively minor detail, but center stage it was too close for comfort for all but the Ottos and Leos in the audience. Coward was never so daring again.

For both Noël Coward and Mordaunt Shairp, homosexuality, whether the stuff of high comedy or moralizing melodrama, was linked to a world of wealth, elegance, and sophistication. The homosexuals were the descendants of the fops of Restoration comedy and, more to the point, of the bachelors in Wilde's *The Importance of Being Earnest*, fashionable in their limited worlds, lacking in erotic charge but containing coded hints of sexual transgression. Coward and Shairp also mastered the art of suggesting without speaking the unspeakable, which for the characters in *The Green Bay Tree* included pederasty and transgression of class. The comic mode of *Design for Living* allowed Coward more latitude than the simplistic melodrama of *The Green Bay Tree*. Coward also was writing his play for both a heterosexual and a homosexual audience, while *The Green Bay Tree,* though it attracted homosexuals delighted to see any version of themselves on the stage, offered them nothing but a negative stereotype.

Transition: The Homosexual and the Woman

The new generation of British playwrights who appeared in the 1950s were more overt in their presentation of homosexual characters, but this meant, unfortunately, only more fully developed, more articulate versions of the stereotype defined in *The Green Bay Tree*. The homosexual male, seen or unseen, was the effete, feminized male. In dramas of the 1950s, he became identified with female characters and "feminine characteristics."

Among the unseen characters against whom Jimmy Porter rails in John Osborne's watershed play, *Look Back in Anger* (1956), is the homosexual, Webster, who is identified as a friend of Jimmy's wife, Alison. Webster completes a trio of aristocratic men associated with Alison: her father, lost in memories of his powerful position in India during the waning days of Empire; her brother, Nigel, stupid but confident of the power that is his birthright; and her friend Webster, the homosexual. Aristocratic men do not have the "burning virility" associated with Jimmy's rage. The damaging qualities of the aristocracy—moral rectitude, ruthless policing of class boundaries, and, paradoxically, cowardice—are identified with on- and off-stage women. Webster, the homosexual, may be afflicted with a "disease" endemic to his class—a dramatic cliché, as we have seen—but his homosexuality also makes him an outsider and something of a rebel against the morality of his class.

Webster is the only member of Alison's class Jimmy credits with "guts" and "sensitivity."[27] Yet Jimmy has mixed feelings about the group he calls the "Greek chorus boys" (p. 35) and the "Michelangelo brigade" (p. 36)—terms veiled enough to placate the Lord Chamberlain. While he admires their "revolutionary fire" (p. 35), he doesn't like the way they keep reminding people of their difference:

He (Webster) doesn't like me—they hardly ever do. I dare say he suspects me because I refuse to treat him either as a clown or a tragic hero. He's like a man with a strawberry mark—he keeps thrusting it in your face because he can't believe it doesn't interest or horrify you particularly. As if I give a damn which way he likes his meat served up. I've got my own strawberry mark—only it's in a different place. (p. 36)

The man of "burning virility" is not threatened by homosexuals. He accepts them so long as they don't mention their sexuality, a typical "liberal" point of view. Jimmy is a man of categories as he lives in his attic room with his "mate," Cliff, in the other chair, and his wife or mistress at the ironing board. His heterosexuality makes him terrified of and hostile to the women to whom he is attracted, but Jimmy's sexual pathology is not, as it would traditionally be in the United States, linked with heterosexism.

Osborne's presentation of Webster marks a transitional stage in the dramatization of homosexuality and homosexuals in the English theater. Webster has the old connection with aristocracy but is presented positively. He is the pal of the woman, not the man. Moreover, like Tennessee Williams' homosexuals, he exists only in the closet of exposition. In England, the theatrical closet was still policed.

In Peter Shaffer's *Five Finger Exercise* (1958), we move from the presentation of homosexuality as a moral problem, exemplified in the diabolical and judgmental language of *The Green Bay Tree,* to homosexuality as a psychological problem, the result of a dysfunctional family and the cause of destructive, neurotic behavior.

Five Finger Exercise[28] is the first of a number of Shaffer's plays in which homosexual desire, though unstated, plays a crucial role. Shaffer, who is habitually drawn to simplified Freudian interpretations of human behavior, presents a family that is a textbook Freudian model for the development of a homosexual: a gruff, self-made father in conflict with an overaffectionate mother filled with cultural pretensions that she projects onto her children, particularly her eighteen-year-old son, Clive. When both Clive and his mother become attracted to a young German man who has been hired to tutor the fourteen-year-old daughter, a clash develops that finally destroys the tutor and leads the son to realize fully his membership in a destructive family. Shaffer makes clear that Walter, the tutor, is heterosexual; homosexual desire is never requited in Shaffer's work, thus never more than a source of anguish. Moreover, Clive's crush on Walter leads him to destroy Walter's position in the household and threaten his parent's already fragile marriage. Homosexual desire puts Clive in the position usually given to young girls in problem plays like Lillian Hellman's *The Children's Hour* (1934) and Arthur Miller's *The Crucible* (1953), that of being the purveyor of destructive information. Walter, the heterosexual, is trying to act honorably on a deeply felt desire to be part of a family. Clive, the self-hating neurotic (read homosexual) can only destroy. He and his sexuality are the products of the dysfunctional family, which is presented as basically the fault of the mother, who cuts Walter off when she realizes that he sees her not as a potential sexual partner but as "a second mother." In a quasi-Freudian causality, the woman is to blame for making her son less than a man. Father, however boorish, does know best.

Clive's homosexual desire is expressed in alternating bursts of hostility and cloying dependency. Given that there is no possibility of his desire being requited and, seemingly, no other possible object for it, Clive is the stereotypical miserable, frustrated, malicious homosexual, spiteful of Walter's "normality." His hyperemotionalism is related to his mother's affectations and theatrical behavior. Not surprisingly, the emotional climax of the play is the confrontation of mother and son, who are infatuated with the same young man.

If Clive in *Five Finger Exercise* is the miserable, neurotic, destructive, effeminate, latent homosexual, Geoff in Shelagh Delaney's *A Taste of Honey* (presented in 1958) is the kindly nellie who is the heroine's best friend, another common stereotype. After Jo, the heroine, has been left by her promiscuous mother and made pregnant by a sailor, Geoff moves in to be Jo's companion. He is derided by Jo's mother and her mother's boyfriend. He is a "pansy," a "lily," and a "fruitcake." Yet Jo takes Geoff in. He is, after all, safe: "I always want to have you with me because I know you'll never ask anything from me."[29] Geoff is supposedly homosexual, but he doesn't have any relationships with men, reinforcing the shibboleth that the only acceptable homosexual is celibate. Only his friendship with a woman keeps him alive: "Before I met you I didn't care one way or the other—I didn't care whether I lived or died" (p. 80). Homosexuals may not be sexually attracted to women, but they cannot live without them. Though Geoff has Jo's best interests at heart, he is thrown out when Jo's wayward mother returns. Jo does not get the opportunity to fight for Geoff's presence. Like the traditional outsider, the "problem" in realistic drama, Geoff is expelled from the stage before the final curtain. The close friendship of a woman and a gay man is rejected as a possibility. Yet, at the final curtain, Jo is singing a song Geoff taught her, the artistic legacy of the homosexual.

Neither of these 1958 plays conceives of the possibility of an affirming homosexual friendship, much less a homo*sexual* relationship. One way or the other, the homosexual is isolated by either his "sensitivity" or his effeminacy.

Pinter: Pederasty Revisited

Harold Pinter's *The Collection* (1961) presents interesting variations on established gay stereotypes. A great deal of the obliqueness of *The Collection* stems from the games it plays with television and stage censorship (the drama first appeared on TV) while it extends the stereotypical representation of homosexuals seen in *The Green Bay Tree*. Pinter's play actually gains its force, as Pinter's work often does, from the indirection the subject matter required. *The Collection* is also of particular importance because here, more than in any other Pinter work, homosexuality is tied to the male homosociality and misogyny that are central to Pinter's heterosexuals.

The Collection is set in the fashionable London neighborhoods of Chelsea and Belgravia, where well-behaved, affluent homosexuals were acceptable, even trendy neighbors, and in the women's fashion industry, in which homosexuals occupied key positions. The drama opens in an elegant Belgravia house occupied by Harry, a middle-aged man who owns a fashionable women's clothing business, and Bill, a dress designer. Bill is both much younger than Harry (Bill is in his twenties) and from quite another social world. "I found him in a slum, you know, by accident. Just happened to be in a slum one day and there he was. I realized he had talent straight away. I gave him a roof, gave him a job, and he came up trumps."[30] Harry's remark contains an innuendo Joe Orton would have admired: the "talent" Harry noticed on first sight probably had little to do with dress design. Harry's history of his slum meeting with Bill (which seems to have taken place some years before, when Bill was a teenager) echoes the pederasty and transgression of class boundaries that formed the dynamic of the relationship between Dulcimer and Julian in *The Green Bay Tree*.

Bill, the slum boy turned dress designer, is the only character in the play definitely out of Pinter's usual social milieu—the working class and the socially displaced—though in being "reformed" he has lost any obvious signs of class. Bill's language, in particular, has lost its identifying characteristics. It is studied and, as a result, lacking in affect: "Every woman is bound to have an outburst of . . . wild sensuality at one time or another. That's the way I look at it, anyway. It's part of their nature. Even though it may be the kind of sensuality of which you yourself have never been the fortunate recipient. What?" (p. 151). Simon Trussler sees the artificiality of Bill's dialogue as a deficiency on Pinter's part: "Mostly, the characters talk not like members of the upper-middle class pretending to be classless, but like upper-middle-class characters imitating people in plays."[31] But Bill is a lower-class character trying to sound posh. Taking the boy out of the slums has made him grammatical and languid, but Bill's new style of language only masks his hostility. The problem for the audience is not that Bill's language isn't convincing—it isn't supposed to be; he's a creature of Harry—but that one cannot imagine Bill going to work. Harry notes that Bill is "supposed to be able to use [his] hands" (p. 124), a stereotypical reference to his origins, but all we ever see is an ornament, one capable, on occasion, of being a flirt.

While the dynamics of Harry and Bill's relationship are left to innuendo, any intimacy they may have shared is clearly on the wane. What is left is the empty familiarity of an old married couple sharpened and threatened by Harry's jealousy and possessiveness. Harry goes off to parties every evening, leaving Bill home alone, because—according to Harry—Bill's "got a slum mind" (p. 155) and isn't fit to socialize with Harry's friends. Since Bill's manners would delight Lady Bracknell, Harry is more likely worried about

Bill's slum sexual appetite. There remains a definite authoritarian structure, reinforced by class and age differences. Bill makes breakfast and is expected to fix the broken stair rail. He is also expected to honor Harry's possession of the house and himself. Yet *The Collection* would be more interesting if there were some sign, or at least memory, of an erotic charge in their relationship. It may be that the constraints of censorship supported Pinter in staging a safe, nonerotic homosexual relationship, which was all he could conceive of. The audience is left, as they are in *The Green Bay Tree,* with hints of a sexual relationship: the profession, the neighborhood, the affluence, the circumstances of their meeting, the age and class differences, the domesticity, the jealousy. One reads homosexuality by a process of elimination: why else would these men be living together?

The relationship is more strained by the Pinterian intrusion of James, who seems intent on upsetting Harry and Bill's domestic life as well as his own. James' initial four a.m. phone call, answered by Harry, gives the only clear hint in the play of a sexual relationship between Harry and Bill:

JAMES: Is that you, Bill?
HARRY: No, he's in bed. Who's this?
JAMES: In bed?
. . . .
HARRY: Do you know it's four o'clock in the morning?
JAMES: Well, give him a nudge. Tell him I want a word with him.
    (p. 121)

The call also, like James' subsequent arrival on Harry's doorstep, insinuates a relationship between James and Bill that arouses Harry's possessiveness and jealousy and is the motive force for Harry's antagonism toward Bill, which is expressed in alternate fits of irritability and camp playfulness. It is Harry who raises the possibility that Bill may have been unfaithful on a recent trip:

HARRY: Did you meet anyone last week?
. . . .
BILL: I didn't speak to a soul.
HARRY: Must have been miserable for you.
BILL: I was only there one night, wasn't I? (p. 125)

But James plays on Harry's jealousy, as he plays sexually charged games with Bill. In the second television production (1976), directed by Michael Apted, Bill (played by Malcolm MacDowell) picked up what he thought were James' (Alan Bates) sexual clues and flirted very obviously with him, assuming the visits from James would end in bed, or at least with both of them on the living-room floor. James sadistically toys with Bill's assumption, as he toys with Harry's jealousy and his wife's guilt.

Harry's response to James' encroachment on his territory is to get more authoritarian—"Don't touch that paper" (p. 138)—and to go camp, playing theatrical variations on James' appearance at Harry's doorstep. His fantastic descriptions of James are so bizarre as to be frightening, but there is anger under the play:

HARRY: He didn't dance here last night, did he, or do any gymnastics?
BILL: No one danced here last night.
HARRY: Aah. Well, that's why you didn't notice his wooden leg. I couldn't help seeing it myself when he came to the front door because he stood on the top step stark naked. Didn't seem very cold, though. He had a waterbottle under his arm instead of a hat.
BILL: Those church bells have certainly left their mark on you.
HARRY: They haven't helped, but the fact of the matter is, old chap, that I don't like strangers coming into my house without an invitation. Who is this man and what does he want? (p. 140)

Bill's response, characteristically, is passive-aggressive evasion, and any information he imparts to Harry (and he must impart some) takes place when Harry follows Bill upstairs.

James is obsessed with every detail of the recent Leeds hotel-room fling that Bill and Stella are supposed to have had, an event that may have happened or that Stella may have made up as an act of passive aggression against an overly suspicious husband. We never discover exactly what happened at the Leeds hotel nor, more important, why Stella confessed to it or fabricated it. What is clear is that the relationship of James and Stella is a heterosexual mirror of the one between Harry and Bill: an aggressive, possessive man and a partner whose silence and evasions are tools of manipulation and possibly revenge. However, the only character credited with "wild sensuality," uncontrollable sexual force, is Stella, the woman, who remains the most enigmatic character.

When James comes to play the wronged husband with Bill, the scene turns into a combination of flirtation and violence. Pinter practices his own form of passive aggression by ending scenes like this one before we can see a character's response. The first scene between Bill and James ends with Bill still lying on the floor, James still standing over him, and Bill supporting James' suspicions:

JAMES: You were sitting on the bed next to her.
Silence.
BILL: Not sitting. Lying. (p. 137)

A blackout ends the scene with the focus on Bill's response, which is both hostile and provocative. Does James want vengeance for Stella's infidelity, or does he want to enjoy Bill himself? However, the central unanswered question is: What happens next? How do James and Bill get out of this potentially sexual pose?

James' acquaintance with Bill gives him a weapon to use against Stella:

He reminds me of a bloke I went to school with. Hawkins. . . . Hawkins was an opera fan, too. So's whats-his-name. I'm a bit of an opera fan myself. Always kept it a dead secret. I might go along with your bloke to the opera one night. He says he can always get free seats. He knows quite a few of that crowd. . . . I mean, you couldn't say he wasn't a man of taste. He's brimming over with it. . . . After two years of marriage it looks as though, by accident, you've opened up a whole new world for me. (p. 144)

James, obsessed by his wife's relationship with Bill, avenges his wife by claiming a relationship with Bill, thus appropriating his wife's lover for himself. The allusions to an old school chum, to Bill being an opera queen (a claim for which there is no evidence), to James' having kept his love of opera (a euphemism for homosexuality) a "dead secret," and to Bill's excess of taste—"He's brimming over with it" (p. 144)—are hints of homosexuality, the sort of pre-Wolfenden code by which gay men operated, as well as an elaboration of the stereotype of the affluent, elegant gay man already operative in the delineation of Harry.

In the next scene James is having another tete-à-tete with Bill, which Harry later claims to have orchestrated so that he can talk with Stella. Yet the opening of this scene is more flirtatious than the

previous encounter. The undertones of sex lead to Pinterian menace, as Bill picks up the cheese knife and describes it in phallic
terms: "Hold the blade. It won't cut you. Not if you handle it
properly. Not if you grasp it firmly up to the hilt" (p. 150). While
Bill uses the knife as the catalyst for a sexual invitation, James sees
the cheese and fruit knives as weapons in a bizarre version of the
duel that, in a bygone day, would have reestablished his honor.
Still, references to the knives remain phallic:

> BILL: What do you do, swallow them?
> JAMES: Do you?
> *Pause. They stare at each other. (Suddenly)* Go on! Swallow it!
> JAMES *throws knife at* BILL's *face.* BILL *throws up his hand to protect his
> face and catches knife, by blade. It cuts his hand.* (p. 152)

James' later comment that the knife might have cut Bill's mouth
underscores Bill's most potent weapons, words, as he manipulates
the narrative of the hotel encounter in Leeds, first denying, then
assenting because, "It amused me to do so" (p. 154), and finally
claiming that the real truth was that he and Stella spent two hours
in the bar talking about what they would do if they went to bed
together. "Two hours . . . we never touched . . . we just talked about
it" (p. 157).

Bill's story of an encounter far more erotic than a mere hotel-
room copulation is his final revenge for James' manipulation and
violence and for Harry's vicious vituperation, in which he describes
Bill as a slum slug: "He confirms stupid little stories just to amuse
himself, while everyone else has to run around in circles to get to
the root of the matter and smooth the whole thing out. All he can
do is sit and suck his bloody hand and decompose like the filthy,
putrid slum slug he is" (p. 155). Bill's final narrative—that he and
Stella only talked about what they would do—silences Harry, who
has been furiously searching for a denial of the Leeds encounter,
and it gives James a story he wants to believe, though Stella holds
onto what little power she is allowed by refusing to confirm or deny
Bill's story to James.

Bill's encounter with Stella transgresses sexual categories. It is a
betrayal of his relationship with Harry and the homosexuality on
which that relationship is based. Bill's alleged bisexuality makes him

dangerous to all the characters, because it makes him an unstable force. His final story of only talking about sex with Stella may fulfill his own fantasy of having sex with a woman without being in the position of phallic penetrator, a passive-aggressive fantasy that, ironically, empowers him. At the end Bill sits silently sucking the blood from the wound on his hand, an image that is vampiric and narcissistic.

While Bill's passivity becomes connected with his sexual ambiguity, he is in the masculine position of controlling language, of controlling the narrative. Stella, the woman, can only react or deny— yet more passive tactics. Her narrative of her encounter with Bill in Leeds initiates the action but is never heard by the audience and is denied or reshaped by the male characters. Before Bill's final version of the Leeds narrative, James is willing to make peace with Harry and Bill by placing all the blame on Stella: "The fault is really all hers, and mine, for believing her" (p. 156). Bill could have assented to Harry's story, that Stella "made the whole damn thing up," but his final story was his weapon against Harry's possessiveness and cruelty. Harry may be able to keep Bill out of women's beds, but he can't stop him from thinking or talking about such sexual encounters. The homosexual male is still allowed space in the dominant discourse, but the discourse is of heterosexual activity.

Bill, like Harry, knows how to spin a narrative, but while Harry's narratives are fantastic displacements of anger, Bill's are weapons. His power is in his sexual attractiveness to men and to women— "[she] must have found me terribly attractive quite suddenly" (p. 136). Yet Pinter has not presented Bill as an erotic object the way a gay playwright would. The play lacks the erotic charge that would make it powerful and credible.

The Collection is a transitional work that plays with old homosexual stereotypes but also introduces themes and situations that gay playwrights were to eroticize and enliven. Homosexuality is still closeted, still a matter of hints, and must be portrayed through the acting rather than the written script, but it isn't sensationalized. Harry's cautious presentation to Stella of his relationship with Bill is both a dead giveaway and an accurate representation of closeted discourse: "We've been close friends for years" (p. 147). Yet in reality we see not the relaxed familiarity of friendship but the hostility of a sexual relationship on the wane. The interesting, positive move in *The Collection* is to the paralleling and equation of hetero- and homosexual marriages.

The "slum slug," as Harry describes Bill, will become central to Joe Orton's work, but he will be far less passive than Bill Lloyd. Bill has, under Harry's tutelage, become a house pet, as Julian has for Dulcimer. He is like the cat Stella holds and Harry so admires. Orton's slum boys are not so easily domesticated.

Joe Orton, Farce, and the Closet

Joe Orton, clearly influenced in his earlier work by Pinter, infused drama with the homoerotic charge missing from works like *The Collection*. He also kept the sense of ludicrousness found in moments like Harry's description of his meeting with James but moved it out of melodrama and incorporated it into the conventions of farce, which, like the realistic problem play, has a complex relationship with homosexuality.

John Mortimer maintains, "Social conventions are essential to farce,"[32] because farce is about transgression, which requires limits. This is why doors are essential to the setting of farce. In the world of farce, closets, or at least closed doors, abound, and doors never stay fully closed—closets cannot be maintained. The open doors free the libido: sexual ambiguity and confusion of sexual identity seep through the perilously maintained gender order as the behavior of farce characters violates the social order.

In raising questions about the gender order assumed and policed by the closet, farce also raises questions about the stability of hetero- and homosexuality, terms that imply their opposites but that also imply a stability of desire counter to the language and vision of farce. In Shakespeare, bisexuality, hinted at, seems to be happily, if cautiously, absorbed by society, but the characters who feel exclusively homosexual desire (the Antonios of *Twelfth Night* and, perhaps, *The Merchant of Venice*) suffer the typical stage homosexual's fate of isolation when the traditional finale of coupling is enacted. Yet Shakespeare's comedies can hover at the brink of polymorphous perversity. In John Caird's brilliant 1989 production for the Royal Shakespeare Company of *A Midsummer Night's Dream*, Demetrius awakes after the love potion has been placed in his eyes and is about to turn his lovesick gaze onto Lysander when Puck turns his head, in the nick of time, toward Helena. In a cartoonlike, high-speed chain of events, Demetrius starts to turn his head back in Lysander's direction, and Puck has to intervene again. Homosexual desire is barely averted. The moment got one of the production's biggest laughs, but it also reminded one of the possibility of homo-sexual desire lurking very near the surface in many of Shakespeare's comedies. In farce, sexual desire is unstable, settling only with difficulty into the social order some call "natural." Conventional categories are arbitrary expressions of a rage for order.

C. W. E. Bigsby writes: "Farce has always been concerned with the elimination of character, with the creation of an almost hysteri-cal intensity in which character is flung off by the sheer centrifugal force of language and action."[33] In farce, either an individuating characteristic enlarges to engulf the entire character or individuating characteristics disappear altogether. In either case character be-comes type. Since typification is the historical condition of the stage homosexual—a reduction to his homosexuality or to mannerisms an audience associates with homosexuality—the gay character can easily become a farce "type." The converse is that, in removing stereotypical mannerisms, the playwright removes any recognizable (to straight audiences), individuating, "comic" characteristics.

To understand the British farce version of the gay type, we need look no further than the English television comedy, "Are You Being Served?," which is a hit on American public-television stations. (It is so successful in the land of Jesse Helms that the North Carolina public-television network ran three episodes back to back in prime time during its 1991 pledge marathon.) This program, which was produced from 1972 to 1984, takes place in an old-fashioned department store in which the sales and managerial staff are a catalog of farce types. One of the salesmen, Mr. Humphries (played to the hilt by John Inman), is a compendium of the mannerisms of the stereotypical farce queen: limp wrist, flounce, high voice (except when he lowers his voice two octaves to answer the phone with the greeting "Men's wear"), flamboyant clothes, constructed face, ho-mosexual innuendo, a tendency to cry, constant phone calls from his mother with whom he lives, of course, and a passion for measuring men's inseams. Since "Are You Being Served?" takes place entirely in the workplace, Mr. Humphries' sexual life is only, though constantly, suggested (talk of being secreted onto a navy warship for the weekend, for instance). When the opportunity for erotic encounter actually appears, in the person of an admiring customer, Mr. Humphries rolls his eyes heavenward and flutters his hands in a combination of panic and disdain. He isn't even "man enough" to respond to homosexual advances. Like the other characters on the program, he is not eroticized at all, therefore no sexual threat. Mr. Humphries is one of many bizarre types in "Are You Being Served?," yet the program caricatures women and the gay man more than it does its collection of dirty old men. Women are bimbos or grotesques, drawn in as broad strokes as is Mr. Humphries.

Farce is more blatant in its presentation of stereotypes than melodrama. Even American television comedy's rare presentation of homosexuals repeats the same stereotypes. Donald in the cable television series "Brothers" or the gay couple who serve as the parents for Tracey Ullman's teen-age character, Francine, on "The Tracey Ullman Show," are prime evidence. The alternative is the "straight" gay who is neither funny nor interesting but there simply to prove that gay men can be as stolid and dull as heterosexuals, like Michael, the gay baseball player on "Brothers."

Peter Shaffer's farce, *Black Comedy* (1965),[34] his next London and New York production after *Five Finger Exercise,* was an extremely popular presentation of the farce gay type. The play focuses on the catastrophic problem a young artist, Brindsley Miller, experiences while preparing to entertain a famous art patron. To impress the millionaire, the young man "borrows" a roomful of antique furniture and ornaments from his neighbor, a prissy, gay antique dealer, Harold. Harold's arrival, in the midst of the power blackout that gives the play its name, and his discovery of the whereabouts of his possessions, is one of the central threads of the farce. Harold, of course, has an unrequited crush on Brindsley and is not very subtly jealous of the young man's girlfriends, though essentially he is a male old maid. Homosexuality in farce involves effeminacy, misogyny, but also chastity, the opposite of male libidinousness. Harold is an upscale Mr. Humphries, another version of the farce queen, this time created by Britain's most successful writer of closet dramas.

Joe Orton, who had his eye on commercial success, aspired to the box-office grosses of *Black Comedy* but also wanted to avoid its stereotypes:

> I hope that now that homosexuality is allowed[35] people aren't going to continue doing the conventional portraits there have been in the past. I think that the portrait of the queer in Peter Shaffer's *Black Comedy* is very funny, but it's an awfully conventional portrait. It's compartmentalization again. Audiences love it, of course, because they're safe. But one shouldn't pander to audiences.[36]

The safety offered by the farce queen is that of instant, reassuring recognizability. This is what gay people are like. They exist only in beauty parlors, antique stores, and, on occasion, in the men's clothing section of department stores. But, since they have such identifiable characteristics, one is in no danger. Moreover, they aren't in the least erotically provocative. Avoiding the farce queen would be one more tactic in moving the farce—and British drama—toward more danger and greater realism. Orton wrote that he wanted his American production of *Loot* (1965) to be "an amalgam of *Black Comedy* and [Pinter's] *The Homecoming*."[37] Orton wanted farce, but without stereotype or camp. He also wanted the commercial success of Shaffer's comedy combined with the critical praise lavished on Pinter.

The setting and language of Joe Orton's farces (with the exception of *What the Butler Saw* [1969]) is that of the British underclass, of people either on the dole or supported by criminal activity. The language aspires to a respectability that the characters are incapable of attaining. The acting style is to be realistic, not the mannered presentation of farce. Orton told one director of *Loot*, "We must make this absolutely truthful as it would happen in life."[38] Yet the "absolute truth" of Orton's plays is their sexual underpinnings. His farces don't merely play with gender and sexual confusion: that confusion is their only reality and a challenge to any possibility of order. C. W. E. Bigsby writes:

> In Orton's work sexuality is aggression; it is subversion. It is a challenge to all authority, including, through its emphasis on incest, the authority of the parent, and, beyond that, perhaps of God, who is mocked not

only in *Loot* and *Funeral Games,* but through a truculent rejection of all values except a total freedom of imagination and action.[39]

"Sex is the only way to infuriate them. Much more fucking and they'll be screaming hysterics in next to no time."[40] As this much-quoted diary entry illustrates, Joe Orton saw the graphic depiction of sexual disorder as the primary means to épater la bourgeoisie. The audience and critics of the premiere of *What the Butler Saw* did become "screaming hysterics." Stanley Baxter, who played the libidinous Dr. Prentice, recalled: "They [Orton's vociferous detractors in the gallery] really wanted to jump on the stage and kill us all."[41] While it is not clear how much of the fury could be credited to a misguided production or to the highly publicized circumstances of the playwright's death, Orton got his wish. He would have loved the headline of one review: "DEAD PLAYWRIGHT BOOED BY GALLERY."[42] The reviews echoed the moral outrage American critics were expending on Edward Albee: "Orton's terrible obsession with perversion, which is regarded as having brought his life to an end and choked his very high talent, poisons the atmosphere of the play. And what should have been a piece of gaily irresponsible nonsense becomes impregnated with evil."[43] Harold Hobson's language here verges on the purple as he blames Orton's sexuality (a "terrible obsession with perversion") for his death (blaming the victim once again) and for "poisoning" the play.

Hobson's attack shows how Orton's life, death, and work had become, like Oscar Wilde's, inextricably entwined, another moral parable of the wages of (homosexual) sin. Like Oscar Wilde, Orton became a major "uncloseted" playwright whose life, as a result, was for many more important than his work. John Lahr's exploitation of Orton has only exacerbated this problem. His biography of Orton, *Prick Up Your Ears,* begins with the sensational details of Orton's death, as if that death is the crucial fact in understanding Orton's work (actually it is important only to a biographer of Orton's lover and killer, Kenneth Halliwell). The movie made from Lahr's *Prick Up Your Ears,* a film in which Lahr himself (at his own suggestion, according to Alan Bennett, the screenwriter) became a major character, focuses on Orton the homosexual and sheds virtually no light on Orton the playwright.[44] Bennett was aware of this problem, noting in his introduction how difficult it is to depict on film the act of writing.[45] Yet even the relationship of Orton and Halliwell, on which the film focuses, is presented as a grotesque version of the British stage stereotype of homosexual relationships. Older Nellie Halliwell initiates a working-class boy into homosexual sex and makes the boy his intellectual protégé. Butch Orton transcends his learning both sexually and artistically, becomes a success, and constantly cuckolds Halliwell, who stays home and cooks and cleans. Moreover, the casting of Alfred Molina as Halliwell turns him into a grotesque, which photographs of Halliwell don't support. Molina looks like Orson Welles as the bald, aging, Citizen Kane lumbering through Xanadu in a snit over Susan's defection. The film claims to present the story of Orton and Halliwell as one of the archetypal troubled first marriage of a successful man who no longer needs the spouse who helped him through the early stages of his career: "The idiosyncrasies of the relationship apart, one sees many marriages like this."[46] But one doesn't *see* many relationships as physically grotesque as the marriage of Orton and Halliwell is presented as being, and there is a great difference between the divorce court and murder-cum-suicide.

Who is the audience for *Prick Up Your Ears?* Gay liberationists might see the film as a corrective tale about the dangers of aping heterosexual marriages. They certainly would be disappointed if they expected gay eroticism. Heterosexists, if they went to the film at all, would see evidence for their own prejudices and stereotypes. The casting of Gary Oldman might attract others to a homosexual version of *Sid and Nancy* (the 1986 film version of Sid Vicious' life and death, in which Oldman starred), another sensationalist version of life in the sixties fast lane. The only people who would be disappointed are admirers of Joe Orton's plays. *Prick Up Your Ears* remains on the shelves of video stores when most "gay-oriented" videos disappear, if they have appeared at all, because it is a naughty, titillating picture of gay life for heterosexuals. The Lahr version of Joe Orton popularized in the Frears-Bennett film needs at least an alternative. Orton would have preferred Frears' previous film, *My Beautiful Laundrette* (1985), in which the erotic attraction of working-class youths is candidly and sexily portrayed.

Yet the identification of life with work was not the only thing that turned critics like Harold Hobson against *What the Butler Saw*. Worst of all, for Hobson, Orton's farce dares to be more than "gaily irresponsible" nonsense and thus "becomes impregnated with evil." The "evil" is the sexual violence and polymorphous perversity that the manic action of farce always at least intimates. Like other gay playwrights, Orton was attacked for being superficial, and thus undermining the seriousness of art, and for having too much of the wrong content, and thus not being superficial enough.

Not only did Orton want his audience—and, by extension, his critics—to become "screaming hysterics" but he declared that the outrageous sexual activity depicted in his plays was "the only way to smash the wretched civilization"[47] corrupted by an insane sexual morality and the worship of propriety. When a friend confessed his guilt about his homosexuality, Orton responded: " 'Fucking Judeo-Christian civilization!' I said, in a furious voice, startling a passing pedestrian."[48] Underlying the farce in Orton's work is the anger of a Ben Jonson, turned not against human appetite but against the morality that curbs it: "Reject all the values of society," Orton told his friend, "and enjoy sex."[49] Here in a nutshell is the conflict in Orton's plays. Jonathan Dollimore notes Orton believed, as many in the sixties did, "that sexual transgression and deviance could radically challenge an existing, repressive social order."[50] Society's farcical attempts to curb human appetite were the primary targets of his satire. It is society that is unnatural, not society's notion of unnatural behavior.

The world of Orton's plays is one of unstable sexuality but also one in which the clash of appetite with futile but brutal attempts at social order lead to real violence. People bleed and die in Orton's farces. The police are not the Keystone Cops or the benignly stupid constables of traditional farce. They beat their "suspects" into submission:

TRUSCOTT *kicks* HAL *violently.* HAL *cries out in terror and pain.*
TRUSCOTT: Don't lie to me!
HAL: I'm not lying! It's in church!
TRUSCOTT (*shouting, knocking* HAL *to the floor*): Under any other political system I'd have you on the floor in tears!
HAL (*crying*): You've got me on the floor in tears. (*Loot*, p. 235)

Yet Truscott is easily bought off and more than willing to send an innocent man to jail. Representatives of authority are as arbitrary and self-serving as the people they police.

Violence is not restricted to officers of the law. Sexual violence is common behavior, the guilty secret that people closet. The closet was not, for Orton, the site of homosexuality but, in the tradition of farce, of any disorderly sexual behavior. In *What the Butler Saw,* the closet becomes the setting for primal familial scenes that would make Sophocles blush, for the family in Orton's plays is the chief example of an arbitrary social order masking a network of desire and violence at odds with the ideals of the society that maintains it. Peter Shaffer's *Five Finger Exercise,* in the simplistic tradition of Freudian melodrama, posits a dysfunctional, destructive family as the cause of homosexual desire. Orton sees the family as a much more complex, volatile combination of repression and desire. The nuclear family that is rejoined at the end of *What the Butler Saw* was literally created in a closet. Its dynamics are an acting-out of the impulses fantasized in Edward Albee's *Who's Afraid of Virginia Woolf?* (1962): a promiscuous wife and intellectual husband spawn children with whom they become sexually embroiled.

In the linen closet at the Station Hotel, one of those monstrous old hostelries attached to a train station, a chambermaid was seduced, which led to the birth of twins. Eighteen years later the same woman finds herself in the same closet with (unbeknownst to her) the son she bore as a result of the previous incident. The encounter is photographed by a hidden camera installed by the young man, who is now attempting to blackmail his "victim," who tells the boy: "When I gave myself to you, the contract didn't include cinematic rights."[51] When she narrates the closeted assignation to her husband, her role changes from willing partner to innocent victim of an unsuccessful attack: "When I repulsed him he attempted to rape me. I fought him off, but not before he'd stolen my handbag and several articles of clothing" (p. 374). The "victim's" alibi is not totally convincing, particularly given her reputation for nymphomania. Later she tells Dr. Rance, the personification of authoritarian, arbitrary social order:

MRS. PRENTICE: The youth wanted to rape me.
RANCE: He didn't succeed?
MRS. PRENTICE: No.
RANCE (*shaking his head*): The service in these hotels is dreadful.
(p. 390)

Mrs. Prentice is much more masterful than Pinter's Bill Lloyd at shifting narratives. Her accounts of the closeted event supplant an "official" version of the story with the "real" narrative of the consensual act, and rape becomes another morally and legally charged term that implodes from misuse during the course of the play. The closet has become not only a place of licentious, incestuous behavior but also the scene of a narrative that hides the sexual appetite and behavior of the woman in question. Even the first closeted event, which led to the birth of her twins, is shrouded in obfuscating language. Two lines after stating that she was raped, Mrs. Prentice says: "I paid for my misdemeanor by conceiving twins" (p. 445), thus acknowledging her complicity in the event. Her husband, who we discover was the alleged rapist, claims that he "debauched" a young lady in the closet, an old-fashioned term that denotes an act short of the violence of rape but that credits him for the young lady's loss of chastity. The event was so exciting that the man wanted to spend his wedding night in the same closet: "If you'd given in to my request, our marriage would never have foundered" (p. 446). The "happy ending" of the play rejoins the parents with their children, who have been more or less willing partners in real and attempted incest, and husband with wife, who from now on will "never make love except in a linen cupboard" (p. 446).

Like the homosexual events in Tennessee Williams' plays, the closeted events in *What the Butler Saw* are not depicted but are enclosed in the play's exposition. The sexual action of the play, like that of much sex farce, is repeated *coitus interruptus*. Nor is the closet a place of homosexual activity, which is only suggested by the compliant young man who, in the style of Orton's young men, will do anything if the price is right. His actions imply a willing homosexual passivity to match his heterosexual aggressiveness: "During my last term at school I was a slave of a corporal in the Welsh Fusiliers" (p. 433). Homosexual activity is shamelessly integrated into the chaotic welter of sexual experience. Even the voice of authority, Dr. Rance, hints that pederasty is not totally unknown to him: "Boys cannot be put in the club [i.e., get pregnant]. That's half their charm" (p. 410). Yet male homosexuality is no more stable than heterosexuality. The outspoken Nick claims: "No position is impossible when you're young and healthy" (p. 370). Like the healthy, bisexual Bobby in Tennessee Williams' *Small Craft Warnings* (1972), Nick has no hang-ups about sex: he is candidly bisexual. Nor does he share his elder's penchant for masking sexual appetite in perversions of morally charged language. In Orton's farces, polymorphous perversity is the way of the world channeled by arbitrary order into fixed categories.

"Unnaturally," Dr. Prentice adheres religiously to his heterosexuality, though his fellow agents of order try to dissuade him:

> RANCE: It might have been wiser if you hadn't rejected the young fellow's blandishments.
> PRENTICE: Unnatural vice can ruin a man.
> RANCE: Ruin follows the accusation not the vice. Had you committed the act you wouldn't now be facing the charge.
> PRENTICE: I couldn't commit the act. I'm a heterosexual.
> RANCE: I wish you wouldn't use these Chaucerian words. It's most confusing. (p. 411)

Prentice's saw about "unnatural vice" is countered by Rance's gruff pragmatism, which separates acts from moral discourse. Ruin is a matter of words, of being accused, and words can be manipulated until they lose their moral force. "Unnatural" suggests that there is intrinsically "natural" behavior. When Nick (dressed as a girl) asks Dr. Rance, "What is unnatural?," the response, given the current confusion of gender identity, is the opposite of what he intends and suggests that clothing is society's tenuous means of stabilizing gender identity and sexual orientation:

> RANCE: Suppose I made an indecent suggestion to you. If you agreed something might occur which, by and large, would be regarded as natural. If, on the other hand, I approached this child—(*he smiles at* GERALDINE [who is dressed as NICK].)—my action could result only in a gross violation of the order of things. (p. 416)

Unconvincing sexual disguise has made it "natural" to proposition the boy. In other words, socially constructed ideas of gender identity define what is "unnatural." No wonder Rance thinks the word "heterosexual" is Chaucerian—archaic and dirty. "Heterosexual" and "homosexual" are arbitrary, like "natural" and "unnatural." When Geraldine, disguised as Nick, declares: "I must be a boy. I like girls," Rance responds, "I can't quite follow the reasoning there" (p. 413). Rance may be authoritarian, but he is properly skeptical about fixed gender definitions and the word "unnatural."

Jonathan Dollimore maintains that the terms "natural" and "unnatural" have, historically, been mechanisms for social control and that Orton clearly perceives the central paradox of the term "unnatural":

> The unnatural then becomes a most insidious and paradoxical manifestation of evil: it is at once alien to, and yet mysteriously inherent within, "the human condition." This contradiction surfaces in two especially revealing (and related) anxieties of the post-war period. The first concerns the family, which was presented on the one hand as incontrovertibly natural and on the other as terribly vulnerable to deviant sexual desire, especially from within. The second concerns the homosexual, who was seen on the one hand as a monstrous invert, utterly alien to normal beings, and on the other as capable of corrupting such beings almost on sight.[52]

In *What the Butler Saw,* the closet is not only a site of transgressive sexual behavior but also a manipulation of the normative language of dominant society to hide the sexual appetites and behavior patterns society calls "unnatural." Order is maintained through either linguistic sleight-of-hand or brute force, but even force is a matter of language: "Who are you to decide what reality is?" (p. 440).

The family, the normative center of dominant moral and sexual discourse, is represented by the sexual network of the Prentices: parents who feel nothing toward their children but lust.

GERALDINE: I lived in a normal family. I had no love for my father.
RANCE (*to* DR. PRENTICE): I'd take a bet that she was the victim of an incestuous attack. She clearly associates violence with the sexual act. . . . Did your father have any religious beliefs?

GERALDINE: I'm sure he did.

RANCE (*to* DR. PRENTICE): Yet she claims to have lived in a normal family. (p. 382).

The irony of Orton's farce is that Rance's seemingly illogical reading of incest into Geraldine's familial situation is true. Yet Rance's Freudian narratives are confused with the best seller he wants to write (he's a kind of fictional Peter Shaffer). For Rance, Freudian analysis and sensational fiction are identical—arbitrary orders that belie chaotic reality.

In *What the Butler Saw,* homosexual behavior is as "natural" as heterosexual behavior, though heterosexual marriage is a grotesque aberration and exclusive homosexual relationships impossible. Alan Sinfield is right in observing the paradox of Orton, who lived a homosexual life and had a kind of homosexual marriage but who did not present the possibility of exclusive homosexuality in his work. In Orton's plays men have sex with each other, but within the framework of masculine camaraderie, a combination Orton alternately mocked and condoned. He feared above all that his characters would be played onstage with elements of effeminacy. In his notes for an American production of *Loot,* Orton wrote:

> I don't want there to be anything queer or camp or odd about the relationship of Hal and Dennis. Americans see homosexuality in terms of fag and drag. This isn't my vision of the universal brotherhood. They must be perfectly ordinary boys who happen to be fucking each other. Nothing could be more natural. I won't have the Great American Queen brought into it.[53]

Nor did he want his female characters played as "one of Tennessee Williams' drag queens."[54] Rance, in *What the Butler Saw,* asserts: "There are two sexes. The unpalatable truth must be faced. Your attempts at a merger can only end in heartbreak"(p. 415). Orton did not like effeminacy or camp caricatures. Men were to be masculine. Orton's untying of homosexuality from the farce queen is as much his own erotic desire for masculine men and dislike of effeminacy as it is a political statement.

In Orton's plays, masculine men are bisexual. In *Loot,* even the law assumes that "perfectly ordinary boys" will have sex with each other: "Two young men who know each other very well, spend their nights in separate beds. Asleep. It sounds very unlikely to me" (p. 233). Though homosexual behavior is assumed to be "natural," Hal and Dennis are sexually omnivorous. As the brutal policeman, Truscott, tells Dennis: "You scatter your seed along the pavements without regard to age or sex" (p. 244). While this bisexuality may seem transgressive, it also denies the possibility of exclusive homosexuality. Orton's boys—Sloane, Hal, Dennis, Nick—are never gay. One wonders whether Orton's insistence on bisexuality wasn't the result of his fear that audiences would tie homosexuality to the effeminacy he despised. Or perhaps, as Alan Sinfield suggests, Orton the dramatist was still, to some extent, in the closet:

> On the other hand, "we're all bisexual really" is the commonest evasion. Hal and Dennis are said to be indifferent to the gender of their partners. . . . That was an unusual and disconcerting thought; it takes the implications of cross-dressing and superficiality quite literally; it could be utopian. But it also keeps a distance from very many actual homosexuals; it was not how Orton lived, or others that he knew.[55]

In the portrayal of Ed, the middle-aged pederast in *Entertaining Mr. Sloane,* Orton wanted to defy the stereotypical assumption that, "the moment you wanted sex with boys, you had to put on earrings and scent."[56] Orton's own self-image—of the leather-clad he-man who liked sex with working-class types in public lavatories—was, like the images of homosexuality he projects in his plays, a counter to the effeminate stereotype, as well as an eroticizing of his own working-class origins. Yet in Ed he also mocks the hypermasculine mythology and athleticism with which Ed not very successfully masks his lust for the teen-age hustler, Sloane:

> ED: Developing your muscles, eh? And character (*Pause.*) . . . Well, well, well. (*Breathless.*) A little bodybuilder, are you? I bet you are . . . (*Slowly.*) . . . do you (*Shy.*) exercise regular?
> SLOANE: As clockwork.
> ED: Good, good. Stripped?
> SLOANE: Fully.
> ED: Complete. (*Striding to the window.*) How invigorating.
> . . . .
> ED: Do you wear leather . . . next to the skin? Leather jeans, say? Without . . . aah . . .
> SLOANE: Pants?

ED (*laughs*): Get away! (*Pause.*) The questions is are you clean living? You may as well know I set great store by morals. Too much of this casual bunking up nowadays. Too many lads being ruined by birds. (p. 87)

Ed's interest in Sloane's "manly" athleticism is, as Sloane well knows, an interest in Sloane's body, as his morality is merely a means of covering his own lack of interest in women and an attempt to encourage that lack of interest in Sloane. By the end of the play, even the word "principles" has become only a euphemism for sex: "He was an expert on the adolescent male body. He's completed an exhaustive study of his subject before I met him. During the course of one magical night he talked to me of his principles—offered me a job if I would accept them" (p. 135).

The linguistic perversions practiced on homosexual desire in Orton's plays are those practiced by most pre-Stonewall drama in masking taboo homosexuality. The difference here is that the language does not succeed in masking the desire. Unlike the farce queen or the closeted pederasts of "serious" drama, Ed in his eroticizing of boys is blatant. And Sloane, who is naked from the waist down when Ed first sees him, is eroticized and fetishized, for Ed's—and the audience's—benefit. In the second act, he is posing on the sofa in the leather pants, the image of Ed's fantasy. Orton's principal contribution to mainstream British drama was the homoerotic charge given homosexual relationships that had been presented, if at all, as sexless. Orton dramatized homosexual desire, not just homosexuality. Like his American counterparts, Williams and Albee, Orton makes the young man the object of the gaze, but he is more blatant; he makes the youth the object of the male character's gaze and thus forces the audience to see him as a gay man might see him. Simon Shepherd notes how in *What the Butler Saw* Nick is framed in the doorway in states of undress and finally appears in a fetishistic costume, underpants and a police helmet, one of many such images of sexy boys.[57] Shepherd also notes that a "straight" production of an Orton play can cancel out its homoeroticism by ignoring the importance of the gaze and the fetishizing of the boys.[58]

Sloane, the object of desire, is young, compliant, bisexual, murderous when threatened. He is a rough-trade fantasy come to life.

At the end of the play, he is in sexual thrall to Ed and his grotesque sister, Kath. The menage that ends *Entertaining Mr. Sloane* is another travesty of a family. Kath treats Sloane as both lover and son and, when she becomes pregnant by Sloane, tells him he's going to have a baby brother. Ed plays big brother and lover. When their father is kicked to death by Sloane, brother and sister see this murder only as an opportunity to possess the boy, "not eternally. . . . Just a few years" (p. 148), until he loses his youth and, therefore, his attractiveness.

Orton could not, or did not want to, untie the relationship between homosexual desire and youth. The object of desire is a teen-age criminal. His partners are either his own age or older men who pay for his compliance. Yet the sex lacks affect, as does much of the sex in Orton's diaries:

> The bed had springs which creaked. First time I've experienced that. He sucked my cock. Afterwards I fucked him. It was difficult to get in. He had a very tight arse. A Catholic upbringing, I expect. He wanted to fuck me when I'd finished. It seemed unfair to refuse after I'd fucked him. So I let him. We lay in bed and talked for a while. . . . As I lay on the bed looking upwards, I noticed what an amazing ceiling it was.[59]

In his diaries Orton becomes the performer in his own series of sexual and domestic scenes. It seems clear that he wanted them to be published and that they, like the highly posed, staged photographs of himself as erotic object, were to be a central aspect of his work. Orton was not a performer in the way Wilde was: he did not make public appearances and lecture tours. Nor did he, like Coward, star in his own plays, even though he had trained as an actor. Yet he was in the process of manufacturing an image that, thanks to the devotion and exploitation of John Lahr, has almost overpowered the plays.

The diaries form the picture of Orton as a proto-gay liberationist, if a rather joyless one. The ironic detachment of Orton's descriptions of his sexual activity may represent a literary pose or Orton's lack of emotional investment in his couplings. Yet sex with a fourteen-year-old Moroccan boy is described in much more erotic detail, not just because of the hashish or the sex itself, but because of

the defiance and rebellion involved in the act of sodomy and pederasty:

> He went off perfectly satisfied, and not for the first time I reflected that
> having had a boy of his age in England I'd spend the rest of my time in
> terror of his parents or the police. At one moment with my cock in his
> arse, the image was, and as I write still is, overpoweringly erotic, and I
> reflected that whatever the Sunday papers have said about *Crimes of
> Passion* was of little or no importance compared to this.[60]

The excitement of pederasty was partly a measure of its illegality,
perhaps one reason for its consistent appearance in Orton's plays.
Domestic bliss, even with people of the same sex, wouldn't make
the audience "screaming hysterics." The family, after all, is in Orton's work a violent, incestuous network. Sodomy and pederasty
were the best revenge.

Orton's first produced play, *The Ruffian on the Stair,* despite its
too-blatant signs of Pinter's influence, provides a prelude to all that
will follow in Orton's work. From its first provocative lines, the play
places a homosexual subculture within a supposedly heterosexual
setting:

> JOYCE: Have you got an appointment today?
> MIKE: Yes. I'm to be at Kings Cross station at eleven. I'm meeting a man
> in the toilet.
> JOYCE: You go to such interesting places. (p. 33)

The public toilets, setting for the dark gropings and bizarre, furtive
dialogue that fascinated Orton, are presented within respectable
dialogue. Throughout the play, it is the ordinary presentation of
transgressive characters and situations that give the play its resonance. Mike, it turns out, is a hit man; Joyce is a former prostitute
whose fidelity obsesses him: "I'd kill any man who messed with
you" (p. 32). Joyce has lived and worked under a series of names:
Madelein, sometimes Maddy, and Sarah. While names provide a
minimal sense of identity to people who are almost ciphers, they
are arbitrary, changeable.

Joyce has read in the paper a record of an "accident involving a
tattooed man. He had a heart, a clenched fist and a rose all on one
arm. And the name 'Ronny' was on his body in two different places"

(p. 32). The signs imprinted on the victim's body—mixed images of sentimentality, eroticism, and violence on the victim's arm and the two appearances of "Ronny" somewhere on the victim's body (Joyce's discretion, or that of the newspaper account, leaves the locations to our imagination)—take primacy over the body itself and its identity. Physical details become the only shreds of identity. When the victim's brother appears on Joyce's doorstep, he asks:

WILSON: You've heard of him?
JOYCE: I've heard of his tattoos. (p. 34)

And he then provides more suggestive physical information:

WILSON: He wore white shorts better than any man I've ever come into contact with. As a matter of fact, strictly off the record, I'm wearing a pair of his white shorts at this moment. They're inconvenient . . . because . . . (he blurts it out)—there's no fly. (p. 34)

Later, Wilson tells Mike: "We had separate beds—he was a stickler for convention, but that's as far as it went. We spent every night in each other's company. It was the reason we never got any work done" (p. 49–50). The separate beds, a sop to "convention," are a flimsy cover for the incestuous relationship between the twenty-three-year-old victim, killed by Mike, and Wilson, his seventeen-year-old brother. Mike's moralistic response to Wilson's admission receives a typically Ortonesque rebuttal:

MIKE: There's no word in the Irish language for what you were doing.
WILSON: In Lapland they have no word for snow. (p. 50)

Wilson's reply implies that the "unspeakable"—homosexuality, in-cest—may be all-pervasive. His feelings for his brother certainly were overwhelming: "I used to base my life round him. You don't often get that, do you?" (p. 50). In an understatement, he admits: "I get a bit lost without him, I don't mind admitting" (p. 59).

The young ruffian sets about terrorizing Joyce and ravaging the hallway outside Mike and Joyce's flat. He also plays on Mike's sexual possessiveness of Joyce, calling Joyce by her "trade" name, Maddie, and describing the time his brother had sex with Maddie. Yet Wilson's tactics are not vengeance, but a goad to Mike to kill him.

The play's first director, Peter Gill, told John Lahr that *Ruffian on the Stair* was "the only play where he [Orton] tried to write about genuine homosexual emotions."[61] Wilson's grief is real, however awkwardly stated, and his only purpose is to get the man who killed his brother to kill him as well: "You've got a gun. Kill me with that" (p. 54). Yet Orton's finale is a bizarre combination of farce and melodrama. Wilson tries to stage a moment of passion with Joyce so that Mike, in a fit of jealousy, will kill him. (Since his brother had sex with Joyce, sex seems to Wilson to provide another means of following in his brother's footsteps.) For her part, Joyce is moved to embrace Wilson not by erotic feelings but by pity for the boy. Mike crashes through the door and shoots, but the first shot destroys Joyce's beloved goldfish bowl. From the point when the second shot kills Wilson, the play moves back into Orton's realm of farcical linguistic displacement. "This is what comes of having no regular job" (p. 61), Joyce proclaims before she breaks down, not because of Wilson's death or the realization that Mike *had* killed Wilson's brother, but because her goldfish are dead. Mike's final speech exercises a rhetorical flourish that, instead of justifying his murder of Wilson, reduces it to banality: "I'll fetch the police. This has been a crime of passion. They'll understand. They have wives and goldfish of their own" (p. 61).

The murderer will be let off for his justifiable crime of passion. But the only real passion, other than possession, was that of young Wilson for his brother. The "murder" was really a carefully planned suicide. To confuse matters more, Joyce is not Mike's wife, though he is as possessive of her as a husband, and the equation of wives and goldfish is the clearest sign of the emotional sterility of Mike and Joyce's world.

In one sense *The Ruffian on the Stair* places the possibility of homosexual love above the arid, potentially violent heterosexual relationship, though Wilson's brother was engaged, and so his and Wilson's relationship was thus already coming to an end. Love, however, is an obsessive displacing of identity onto another person, a loss of self. Wilson's only identity is as brother and lover to the dead Frank. Wilson's alienation is one manifestation of a common plight. Mike says of an appointment: "I'm seeing a man who could put me in touch with something" (p. 43), and his jealous attachment to Joyce is based on a fear of loneliness: "I was so lonely before" (p. 57). Left alone in the flat, Joyce talks to herself about the "humiliating admissions" she has made in her life: "You'd think it would draw me closer to somebody. But it doesn't" (p. 40). The only brief moment of connection in the play—Joyce's tender kiss on the cheek of the boy she pities—leads to the grotesque, deadly denouement.

For all their anomie, Joyce and Mike are whore and killer, a literal version of Orton's typical heterosexual couple. And Wilson, the "boy hairdresser," as he was called in an earlier draft (an adaptation of a novel by Orton and Halliwell), is passive, self-pitying, and ineffectual, a far cry from the rough trade Orton eroticizes in his later plays. He can only adore the masculinity and athleticism of his brother, fetishized by those flyless underpants Wilson wears. Wilson's self-inflicted martyrdom is, in Orton's world, more aberrant than the aggressiveness of Sloane or Nick.

The Ruffian on the Stair falls into the traditional structure of realistic drama. Wilson, the homosexual intruder, is shot at the play's climax. Homosexuality is destroyed, yet what is left is a grotesque parody of "normality."

Orton said that Peter Gill's stage production "came over as a sad little play,"[62] which is hardly what he wanted. His notes to Gill make clear that he wanted a combination of "comedy and menace," but they also leave no doubt that Orton saw his characters as unintentionally funny. Their humor, however, could be achieved only through a totally realistic, deadpan performance: "Unless it's real it won't be funny."[63] Orton was as distanced from his own characters as he was from the sad characters he encountered in the toilets. Wilson's love for his brother was as humorous to Orton as the more overtly bizarre conversations of Mike and Joyce.[64]

Ruffian on the Stair is not a farce as *Loot* and *What the Butler Saw* are, yet it treats its most serious moment as farce, and the emphasis on the grotesque—the violent yet funny physical action, the disconnection between language and action—are the seeds that will flower in Orton's later plays. What one does see in this early work is the way in which homosexuality is embodied not in a conventional, sexless stereotype but in obsessive desire rendered with attention to erotic detail. One also sees the mixing of erotic desire with family:

pederasty and incest combined in the love of the two brothers. The representative of the force that disapproves of homosexual desire and that killed Wilson's brother-lover is a hired killer, a murderer who is also the voice of conventional morality in the play.

Contemporary gay critics tend to attack Orton for his pre-Stonewall limitations of gay political awareness and social critique. Simon Shepherd notes that "not only was Orton the sort of queer most easily accommodated by straight society, but his adventures celebrate the social and sexual power of the penis."[65] One could add that his plays, like his adventures, are exercises in phallic power. Thus Orton's "contempt for the effeminate, and indeed for women"[66] aligns him with the prejudices behind traditional gay stereotypes even as he was exploding those stereotypes. Alan Sinfield notes that Orton's sexual conservatism was linked to a theatrical conservatism: "His attitudes to homosexuality and theatre tended to assume the milieu of Coward or Rattigan,"[67] which limited him to West End aspirations and left him ignorant of the burgeoning of fringe gay drama. Sinfield's criticism is somewhat naive: Orton aspired to the fame and fortune of his closeted predecessors, and that could be achieved only in the mainstream, commercial theater.

Joe Orton, then, is not the great gay comic writer some heterosexual critics would make him but a transitional figure in gay drama. He rejected the queen stereotype of traditional farce but had no positive vision of homosexuals with which to replace it; he dramatized guiltless homosexual desire but never portrayed homosexual love.

Peter Shaffer and the Endurance of Closet Drama

By the time of Orton's death in 1967, censorship had just about ended its long run in Great Britain, and with the advent of gay liberation at the end of the decade, homosexuality could not be treated merely as an open secret. Closet drama was no longer necessary. Yet the genre did not totally fade out of existence. The most popular British "serious drama" of the 1970s (in New York) was Peter Shaffer's *Equus* (1973), a spin on the tradition of British closet drama. In *Equus,* an unhappy middle-aged psychiatrist is assigned a visionary seventeen-year-old boy who has blinded six horses in a stable. Through a series of psychiatric sessions and flashbacks, the analyst discovers that the boy made a religion out of the horses, involving sexual arousal and sadomasochism, and blinded the horses after they witnessed him try (and fail) to have sex with the girl whose father owned the stable.

The girl is very forward in trying to seduce the boy, whose sexual fantasy life has centered on his horse-gods, who are, of course, always masculine (portrayed by tall, athletic men with metallic headpieces in the shapes of horses' heads). The boy's "religion" is romanticized by the doctor as something far more vibrant than his own clinical life and passionless marriage. The doctor sees the boy as a link to the Dionysian ecstasy of ancient Greece, but his job is to cure his patient of this passionate eroticizing of masculinity, which he does, knowing that he has reduced the boy's life to the "Normal":

> I'll give him the good Normal world . . . blinking out nights away in a non-stop drench of cathode-ray over our shrivelling heads! I'll take away his Field of Ha Ha, and give him normal places for his ecstasy. . . . With any luck his private parts will come to feel as plastic to him as the products of the factory to which he will almost certainly be sent. Who knows? He may even come to find sex funny. . . . Trampled and furtive and entirely in control. Hopefully, he'll feel nothing at his fork but Approved Flesh. *I doubt, however, with much passion!*[68]

The psychiatrist's lament over his enforcing of the "Normal" comes after the doctor has covered the boy's naked body. In covering his nakedness, he covers the boy's passionate, aberrant sexuality and his own closeted homosexuality, which has led him to fixate on the boy. The young woman, the cause of the boy's crisis, has been banished from the stage, but "curing" the boy is forcing an adaptation to normal, heterosexual sex. The boy's "religion" is sublimated homosexuality, the result of being raised with a working-class version of the parents in *Five Finger Exercise*—parents who fit the Freudian pattern for homosexual development. The doctor is a repressed homosexual who comes to envy the passion of this seventeen-year-old boy in the way many teachers in the late sixties and early seventies envied and desired their students, whose adolescent freedom they romanticized. It was this fashionable idealization of youth, combined with a denigration of rationality and a celebration of the sixties-style penchant for the spiritual—with the added attraction of an extended nude scene with male and female nudity that led to the success of *Equus*. But under it all is a story of repressed pederasty. *Equus* was a more contemporary reworking of Shaffer's spectacular historical drama, *The Royal Hunt of the Sun* (1964), which had at its center the conflict between a disillusioned middle-aged man and a beautiful semiclad Inca king who thought himself a god;[69] it was a precursor of *Amadeus* (1979), a dramatization of the obsessive love-hate relationship of the established, middle-aged traditionalist, Salieri, and the young, sexually active, eternal adolescent, Mozart. The hope for faith or genius is always a young man who throws a cynical middle-aged man into intellectual and spiritual crisis.

Unlike *Five Finger Exercise* and *Black Comedy*, Shaffer's later plays never present homosexuality directly—or even hint at it; that might have limited their commercial potential. Yet they present a closeted vision of experience and a vision of closeted individuals thrown into crisis by a young man whose very presence challenges their hard-won normality. It could be said that Shaffer keeps rewriting Herman Melville's *Billy Budd*, with the roles of Claggart and Vere combined. The young man becomes a martyr, but he is also the focus of attention. The older man is forced to regard and ultimately to destroy what he doesn't feel he should have. It could also be said that Shaffer keeps manufacturing variations of Shairp's *The Green Bay Tree*, in which the older man doesn't get the boy.

Reflecting on my early experience as a rapt audience member at John Dexter's productions of *The Royal Hunt of the Sun* and *Equus* helped me understand the homoerotics of theater. Dexter's highly theatrical productions foregrounded the homoerotic dimension that was repressed in the script itself. The productions kept one's visual focus on the lithe, often partially clad youth, in *Royal Hunt* on Atahuallpa and even more in *Equus* on the boy, who was clearly presented as the object of the psychiatrist's—and the audience's—gaze. Dexter's productions clarified, for those who wanted to see, what Shaffer's plays were really about. And so a closeted script was uncloseted in production. Both *The Royal Hunt of the Sun* and *Equus* ended with a vision of an older man standing or kneeling by the prone body of a young man, lamenting what he had lost. Shaffer has a gift for romanticizing, disguising, and mass-marketing homosexual repression that makes a reading of his works a fitting conclusion to a chapter on British closet drama.[70]

℞ Aidan Quinn as Stanley
Kowalski with one of
Blanche DuBois' costumes
in the 1987 Circle in the
Square revival of *A Streetcar
Named Desire*. Photo by
Martha Swope. Printed with
permission of Martha
Swope.

CHAPTER FOUR

American Dreams

GRANDMA: And will you look at that face!
YOUNG MAN: Yes, it's quite good, isn't it? Clean-cut, midwest farm boy type, almost insultingly good-looking in a typically American way. Good profile, straight nose, honest eyes, wonderful smile
. . .
GRANDMA: Yup. Boy, you know what you are, don't you? You're the American Dream, that's what you are.   Edward Albee, *The American Dream*

"A man knows a queer when he sees one."
Bill Reynolds, in Robert Anderson, *Tea and Sympathy*

When homosexuality was invoked in pre-Stonewall American drama, it was related to the American concern with "manliness," with a model of masculinity and male bonding that homosexuality endangered. This contrast of homosexuality with masculinity still prevails. It explains the public shock at the illness and death of Rock Hudson in 1985. Before the headlines about Hudson's trip to Paris to be treated for AIDS, most Americans would not believe that tall, lanky Hudson was homosexual (though his sexuality had been known in gay circles for decades). Paula Treichler quotes a *USA Today* article in which a man stated: "I thought AIDS was a gay disease, but if Rock Hudson can get it, anyone can."[1] Hudson was "manly": he couldn't have been gay. The disclosure of Hudson's gayness, a result (as it so often is) of the disclosure of his having AIDS, created a series of narratives, one of which blurred comforting distinctions between masculinity and homosexuality.

Other aspects of the AIDS drama in which Rock Hudson was a central character are pertinent to a discussion of homosexuality in pre-Stonewall American drama. Hudson was adept at "acting straight" on and off the screen. The public fascination with his death arose not merely because he played macho roles or because he was a movie star or because he had AIDS but because he was a closeted movie star.[2] Like many good dramas, Hudson's story was one of discovery, of being "found out." Hudson's "outing" and death proved that the closet is no refuge. Like much gay drama, the moral of Hudson's outing has different meanings for heterosexist and homosexual audiences. To the former, it is a saga of secret guilt and public retribution—the wages of sin are disclosure and death. The closet is no refuge. To many gay men—and women—Hudson's experience demonstrated the futility and, to some extent, the cruelty of the secret life. The closet is no safe haven.

Hudson was an actor, but a central assumption of this book is that closeted individuals are always actors, performing for a reward and approval they don't think they would receive if they were known to be homosexual. Hudson had to choose between being a star and being known as gay, a choice American actors feel they still have to make,[3] as many less public gay men feel they must stay in the closet for fear of rejection of family and friends or heterosexist reprisal. But acting straight also involves internalizing the public's attitudes about homosexuality:

> To accept the closet is to have absorbed society's view of gays, to accept insult so that one avoids harm. Thereby one becomes a simulacrum—a deceptive substitute—of a person: one seems to be a moral agent with ends of one's own and an ability to revise them, but one really is simply a puppet to the values of society.[4]

Like many movie stars, Rock Hudson represented in the late 1950s and early 1960s the masculine American dream. Like most of Hollywood's dreams, Rock Hudson (born Roy Fitzgerald) was as much of a fiction as the characters he played. Roy Fitzgerald's largest acting responsibility was maintaining and protecting the image of Rock Hudson. "Rock," like Tennessee Williams' "Brick," in *Cat on a Hot Tin Roof,* turned out to be an ideal of stolid, unyielding manhood concealing homosexual desire because it is unmanly and, more crucial to stars of the stadium and silver screen, unpopular. While other male stars of the fifties represented a new ideal of male sensitivity, Hudson combined some of their gentleness with old-fashioned stolidity. He couldn't act (real men don't act), but whether holding on to the ranch and Elizabeth Taylor in *Giant* (1956), or assailing Doris Day's virtue in *Pillow Talk* (1959), he was "all man." There is some irony now to viewing *Giant,* in which James Dean, the epitome of the sensitive young man, and Rock Hudson fight over Elizabeth Taylor. Both these embodiments of elements of fifties manhood were homosexual, giving the film a subtext that develops another drama about myths and realities of the American dream of masculinity.

Rock Hudson's drama is a starting point for a discussion of the homosexual texts and subtexts of the plays written in his era, the pre-Stonewall era (Hudson moved in the seventies from the big screen to television). Closets and manhood are the homosexual themes of these plays, yet gay playwrights managed to find space for a critique of the operations of the closet within structures heterosexuals could accept. American gay playwrights deconstructed the image of American masculinity to show its hollowness and cruelty and reconstructed it to include homosexuality. The history of the homosexual in American drama in the fifties and sixties is in large part the story of the reconstruction of the ideal man, the American dream, as object of homosexual desire *and* as homosexual, a task Hollywood had, unknowingly, already undertaken.

The reconstruction includes the homosexual-created character's defiance of the strictures of realistic drama. At the same time, mainstream realistic drama exploited the melodramatic potential of homosexuality while enforcing the norms of heterosexuality and conventional notions of masculinity by raising the possibility of homosexuality but never showing a homosexual character.

Who's the Real Man?

Robert Anderson's *Tea and Sympathy* (1953), an enormously successful Broadway play (the Lord Chamberlain banned a London production) and, later, movie, manages, as many mainstream American plays of the fifties did, to raise the specter of homosexuality without presenting any overtly homosexual characters. Anderson's play, like Arthur Miller's *A View from the Bridge* (1955), both raises and dismisses the possibility of homosexuality. In essence, it pushes its characters back into the closet. Yet the Broadway success of *Tea and Sympathy* suggests that hints of homosexuality inspired a prurient interest in a general audience as long as that audience could feel "safe" from any real threat in an era in which homosexuality was linked with anti-American behavior.

Still, *Tea and Sympathy* challenges the normative equation of sexual orientation and gender (heterosexual = masculine; homosexual = feminine). It does so not to validate homosexuality but to challenge the macho mentality that pervaded America during the 1940s. Ironically, in order to subvert the American he-man mystique, Anderson had to color it with hints of homosexuality. The sensitive male is now the heterosexual, the man's man a latent homosexual, and, as in *The Green Bay Tree,* the woman is the instinctive arbiter of sexual orientation. While this new formulation may extend the definition of masculine behavior, it still maintains homosexuality as the negative of masculine. Homosexuality is still taboo, and *Tea and Sympathy* reinforces this sanction by hinting at the possibility of homosexuality while denying its actuality. This double bind is typical of the treatment of homosexuality in pre-Stonewall American drama. Anderson's play, then, is worth a close examination rather than the usual offhand dismissal it receives for political incorrectness; it is as paradigmatic of the treatment of homosexuality in American drama of the 1950s as *The Green Bay Tree* was of pre-Stonewall English drama.

There are two rooms in the single set for *Tea and Sympathy,* which takes place in a New England boarding school (though it must be a school for slow-witted young men, as their median age seems to be eighteen, an age clearly chosen to make their sexual awareness, and the play's famous final scene, less shocking). The larger space is the living room of the apartment shared by Bill Reynolds, the housemaster, and his wife Laura. This is the space in which Laura, a former actress (therefore worldly, sensitive, and likely to have encountered homosexuals) offers the boys "tea and sympathy." Though Bill is the housemaster, Laura dominates this space in which he and other grown men are disruptive forces. Anderson describes the room as "warm and friendly"[5] and Laura as "compassionate and tender" (p. 4), the dominant, positive, "feminine" qualities the play asserts that men too should possess. The fact that the bedroom is invisible is a sign of the sexlessness of Laura and Bill's marriage.

The bedroom the audience sees is Tom's, which represents through its decor ("an Indian print on the bed, India print curtains for the dormer window" [p. 3]) the taste that makes its inhabitant, Tom Lee, "different." At the opening of the play, Tom is sitting on his bed, playing his guitar and singing "The Joys of Love." Tom is defined by his bedroom, and it is his sexuality that will be the focus of the play, as Laura's visit to his bedroom will affirm Tom's heterosexuality and therefore his "manhood" at the end of the play. While Laura is dressed in soft, warm attire, a cashmere sweater and a wool skirt, even though it is June, Tom is dressed as the typical fifties preppie. Though he obviously does not "fit in," his clothing suggests that he is not totally the "off-horse" he is accused of being.

Typical of a McCarthy-era play, *Tea and Sympathy* is about the danger of name-calling. Like its elder sister, Lillian Hellman's *The Children's Hour* (1934), which had been revived as a covert attack on McCarthyism the previous year, 1952, Anderson's play presents not communism but homosexuality as the "big lie," the nastiest possible attack (a ploy used by Senator Joseph McCarthy's team which was, we now know, a classic case of the pot calling the kettle beige). Tom has been seen "skinny-dipping" with a suspect teacher, and Laura's husband, Bill, is leading the campaign to purge the school of the instructor and to purge his house of the "off-horse," Tom, who is so innocent he doesn't understand what he or Mr. Harris could be guilty of. In Bill's eyes, Tom isn't "all man." He loves music and sings plaintively (shades of Julian Dulcimer); he plays the leading ladies in the school plays. In his first meeting with Laura, he tries on the dress he will wear in a production, appropriately, of Sheridan's *The School for Scandal* (1777), though he clearly takes more interest in Laura's bosom than in transvestism. Tom is called "Grace" by his peers because of his love for Grace Moore in the film *One Night of Love* (1934) (and he isn't gay!). We are told that when Tom's father tried to explain "the facts of life to him," Tom threw up—such revulsion at the thought of sex being presented as healthier than the prurient interest of his peers. When he tries to prove his masculinity by having sex with the town whore, he cannot perform. Yet Tom, the child of a broken marriage, clearly loves the young, beautiful, maternal Laura and plays Marchbanks to her Candida.

When the skinny-dipping scandal breaks, Tom is ostracized by his classmates, and Laura's husband, Bill, becomes obsessed with ridding his school of this pariah. Bill is a real John Wayne type, "large and strong with a tendency to be gruff" (p. 39), but Anderson makes Bill's "manliness" a mask for his latent homosexuality. Bill is a newlywed at forty who apparently showed little interest in women before his sabbatical trip to Europe the year before. Laura's friend Lilly, a sexually outspoken faculty wife, tells Laura of Bill's "safe" past: "Even before he met you, Bill never gave me a second glance. He was all the time organizing teams, planning mountain club outings" (p. 8). Bill's celibacy and professional dedication could be signs that he is the traditional American man's man, but other hints are laid. Bill met Laura abroad on sabbatical, a deceptive time, as Lilly tells Laura: "Teachers on sabbatical leave abroad are like men in uniform during the war. They never look so good again" (p. 9). Yet Bill obviously was a different, frightened person when he met Laura: "I think you're ashamed . . . that you ever let me see you needed help. That night in Italy in some vague way you cried out. . . ." (p. 54). Bill, of course, denies ever feeling anything so weak as fear and now resents Laura's place in his all-male life. Clearly his sexual interest in her has waned now that he is back with his boys: "We don't touch any more. It's a silly way of putting it, but you seem to hold yourself aloof from me. A tension seems to grow between us . . . and then when we do . . . touch . . . it's a violent thing . . . almost a compulsive thing" (p. 112).

Part of being a "man's man" is being able to spot homosexuals, "a man knows a queer when he sees one" (p. 48), but the play supports Laura's claims of even greater powers of perception: "You men think you can decide on who is a man, when only a woman can really know" (p. 173). Like Leonora in *The Green Bay Tree,* Laura has the ability to "spot" homosexuals. In Shairp's play, Leonora's perception was that of any sensible, moral, middle-class person who can recognize evil. Laura's perception is based on a woman's ability to recognize a "real man," a role her husband tries—and fails—to act. In *Tea and Sympathy,* "being a man" is merging masculine and feminine characteristics: "Manliness is also tenderness, gentleness, consideration" (p. 172), qualities Tom possesses and that Bill and Tom's father are trying to scare out of him. Yet even the perceptive Laura equates homosexuality with her sense of what isn't masculine. Homosexuality, however, is no longer "sinister" or "evil," as it is in Shairp's play: it is merely a weakness.

Laura realizes that Bill married her to advance his chances of being headmaster and to mask his own homosexual feelings: "Did it ever occur to you that you persecute in Tom, that boy up there, you persecute in him the thing you fear in yourself? . . . that was the weakness you cried out for me to save you from, wasn't it?" (pp. 175–176). Bill's response is to order Laura out of his apartment and his life, though it is actually Bill, the latent homosexual, who is dismissed from the audience's view. Laura walks up the stairs to Tom's bedroom, where she offers herself to Tom to allow him to prove his heterosexuality and manhood, uttering the curtain line that is almost as universally known to gay men as Blanche DuBois' final words: "Years from now . . . when you talk about this . . . and you will . . . be kind" (p. 182).[6]

Throughout *Tea and Sympathy,* Tom Lee has been marginalized by the "men," and his isolated bedroom becomes an image of that marginalization—almost a closet—until the end of the play, when Laura enters Tom's room and, in essence, brings it and Tom to the center. The master's parlor, the locus for the values of the "man's world" of the school, now stands empty. The play has moved to the little room on the side.

Manliness has been redefined to include those qualities of sensitivity and tenderness that were part and parcel of the 1950s "new masculinity" embodied by "sensitive" film stars like James Dean, Montgomery Clift, and Tab Hunter. But, to validate masculine sensitivity, homosexuality had to be removed by being displaced to the image of the 1940s macho male. Conversely, the sensitive boy's bedroom may be in perfect taste, but his bed contains a woman. Tom says of himself, "I'm no man. Ellie knows it. Everybody knows it. It seems everybody knew it, except me. And now I know it" (p. 179). Laura responds, "You're more of a man now than he ever was or will be" (p. 181). "Only a woman can really know" who is and isn't a man—who is truly heterosexual and who isn't—and Laura, who understands now that homosexuality was "the weakness" Bill "cried out for me to save [him] from" (p. 176), knows that Tom is "all man."

The language of *Tea and Sympathy,* less indirect than the elliptical hints of *The Green Bay Tree* but equally cautious, combines specific accusations of effeminacy and assertions of masculinity with only the vaguest, most indirect suggestions of homosexuality. It's as if, even in plays that titillate with suspicions of homosexuality, the word itself is still as "unspeakable" as it was for Forster's Maurice. Silences—ellipses in the script—are blanks that audience members must fill in for themselves. When her husband tells her of his suspicions about Tom Lee, Laura is uncharacteristically inarticulate: "But, Bill . . . you don't think Tom is . . . (*She stops.* BILL *looks at her a moment. His answer is in his silence.*) Oh, Bill!" (p. 250). Homosexuality can be presented only as a silence. Mr. Dulcimer's sexual initiation of David Owen (if it did happen) is hinted at but presented as horrific, literally unspeakable. The idea that Mr. Harris and Tom Lee might have at least thought about a sexual relationship is, in *Tea and Sympathy,* unthinkable.

Laura's heterosexual initiation of Tom Lee is presented as a noble, even maternal act (her final gesture is putting his hand on her breast). Bill says to her, "You want to mother a boy, not love a man" (p. 173), and, given Laura's earlier marriage to an eighteen-year-old, her present marriage to an "old boy," and her interest in Tom, his comment seems well targeted, but it is Bill's unacknowledged homosexuality that is seen as the problem, not Laura's interest in offering more than "tea and sympathy" to eighteen-year-olds. Initiating a young man into homosexual sex is unspeakable; Mr. Harris is dismissed on the basis of rumors of that heinous crime. Initiating a young man into heterosexuality is noble.[7]

Typical of 1950s dramas, there is no space for homosexual activity in *Tea and Sympathy*. Mr. Harris, the homosexual teacher who swam naked with Tom but never made sexual overtures to him, is fired. (It is interesting to note that Mr. Harris is the only man in the play described as "good-looking," as if that were a label. Or perhaps it's a liberal gesture to suggest that homosexuals may not be men, but they look good!). Bill, the latent homosexual, is too full of denial mechanisms and too in love with the hearty, all-male world he lives in to act on his "weakness." Bill's preference for the company of adolescent boys is a sign of arrested development that is of a piece with his latent homosexuality. Still, in accordance with the rules of realism, Bill is banished from the scene. And Tom, of course, isn't homosexual. *Tea and Sympathy* proves only that a boy can be a sissy without being a queer, a comforting distinction for some mothers in the audience but not particularly helpful for gay men.

Tea and Sympathy was for its time the classic version of mainstream American treatment of homosexuality. Typical of such plays, accusations of homosexuality taint a male society, and the threat of homosexuality is eliminated by the final curtain. Following the formula established in the thirties by *The Children's Hour* and reinforced by responses to the House Un-American Affairs Committee and McCarthy's witch hunts, homosexuality is the one lie so ugly that it can bring down the accuser (remember Joseph Welch's famous rejoinder to one of McCarthy's accusations of homosexuality, "Have you no shame?"). The rise and fall of McCarthyism spawned political melodramas that enforced the closet by suggesting that homosexuality is the worst allegation anyone can make. Thus, alleging homosexuality labels the accuser as cruel, crass, and insensitive. Moreover, the accuser threatens social stability by violating the silence surrounding homosexuality. However, if the accusation is true, the guilty party must be purged from the scene. Parenthetically, we know now that the real drama of the Army–McCarthy hearings was one of the nastier dramas of closeted homosexuality, with one leading character, Roy Cohn, a man who, like Rock Hudson, was subsequently, very reluctantly, "outed" by AIDS and who is a prime example of Richard Mohr's dictum: "Outed people will frequently be spiritual basket cases, whom people would not, or at least should not, want as a model for their soul."[8]

In 1960, two successful Broadway plays centered on the use of homosexuality as the "dirty secret" used to blackmail otherwise honorable politicians. While Gore Vidal's *The Best Man* raises and dismisses the issue without ever having a homosexual appear on-stage, Loring Mandel's dramatization of Allen Drury's novel, *Advise and Consent,* is a vivid example of the fate of the homosexual in a well-meaning, liberal drama of the period.

Brigham Anderson, an upright young Senator from Utah, chair of the committee to ratify the President's choice for Secretary of State, discovers that the candidate has lied about his membership in a Communist Party cell. Anderson, more upset about the dishonesty than the past affiliation, insists on presenting this information to his committee. To stop him, the Secretary-designate, the President, and their supporters are prepared to uncover a secret in Anderson's life, a brief wartime affair with another man, presented as the result of loneliness and sexual frustration, not "real" homosexuality: "It had been almost three years since a personal thing had happened to me."[9] The play is candid about the sexual atmosphere of wartime, when "every vice you can picture is excused, sex and liquor were patriotic" (p. 66). Yet, despite his wife's support and the rightness of his political position, Brig Anderson shoots himself. While this death is presented as a personal tragedy, it also is a dramatic necessity, according to the regulations of popular drama. The dishonest ex-Communist does not get his cabinet seat, but the man who had a brief wartime homosexual fling does the noble thing and kills himself. He accepts the judgment of his corrupt peers—that he is "morally unfit."

Both *The Best Man* and *Advise and Consent* present homosexual activity as an unfortunate side-effect of World War II, a far cry from the affirming stories of homosexuality in World War II recounted by Allan Berube,[10] but in the world of these plays, punishment must be meted out for such unspeakable sins. Mainstream popular drama might by 1960 acknowledge homosexual acts and inclinations, but liberalism had clear limits.

Williams: Masculinity and Homophobia

Three of the four most critically acclaimed and commercially successful playwrights of the postwar period were closeted homosexuals whose plays were supported by the critical establishment so long as they maintained the conventions of closet drama. Of the pantheon of Tennessee Williams, William Inge, Edward Albee, and Arthur Miller, only Miller was heterosexual. Thus the central narrative of homosexuality in American drama of the fifties and early sixties was not in popular melodrama written by heterosexuals but in the plays of highly successful homosexual playwrights who chose to operate in the mainstream theater; they combined their experiences as homosexual men with the conventions of popular drama.

The central figure here, Tennessee Williams, was much more successful at dramatizing the closet than at presenting a coherent, affirming view of gayness. Yet homosexuality in Williams' plays forces the protagonist into a complex relationship with traditional images of masculinity, extending and to some extent subverting those images.

The primary issue for Williams' homosexual characters in his plays of the forties and fifties is the devastating one of exposure, of making the private public.[11] When the idea of homosexuality is raised in the plays, it is usually linked to the brutal exposure of a sensitive man who is often a writer. In A Streetcar Named Desire (1947), Blanche DuBois tells of "coming suddenly into a room that I thought was empty—which wasn't empty but had two people in it . . . the boy I had married and the older man who had been his friend for years."[12] Typically, this extremely discreet description tells us nothing. What room? What were Blanche's husband and his older friend doing? The unspeakable remains unspoken in Streetcar, and the audience is expected to infer a sexual encounter from Blanche's judgmental language: "I saw! I know! You disgust me. . . ." (p. 355). Blanche had seen a private moment and reacted by publicly exposing and humiliating her husband: her outburst was not uttered in the mysterious room but on a crowded dance floor.It was Blanche, not Allan, who publicly exposed the unutterable act. What she saw, knew, and was disgusted by was his homosexuality, and her response is the brutal exposure and repudiation homosexuals have long feared. Blanche's speech-act is the exercise of what Richard Dyer calls "one of the prime mechanisms of gay stereotyping, synechdoche—that is, taking the part for the whole."[13] Blanche cries to Allan, "*You* disgust me," not "your action" or "your sexual betrayal" or "your sexual orientation" but *You.* Allan is reduced to his homosexuality, or, rather, Alan's homosexuality is expanded to be entirely definitive. The all-engulfing homosexual identity engulfs even the artist. "I saw that you are a homosexual—*only* a homosexual. *You* disgust me." Blanche, typical of Williams' characters, cannot exactly name what Allan is. But she can articulate her clear response.

Once made public, the sensitive poet's homosexuality becomes unbearable for him, and he commits suicide, publicly. The audience can accept Allan's self-destruction as poetic justice: there is no place on stage for homosexual behavior, and Allan's story encapsulates the problem-play resolution for fallen women and homosexuals—disappearance and, frequently, death. Creativity and secret homosexuality are intertwined: expose the homosexual and you destroy the artist. And Blanche's own sensitivity is demonstrated by the fact that she is forever haunted by the memory of her act of extreme cruelty, which is, in a kind of poetic justice, repaid many times over by what she suffers through Stanley Kowalski. As she tells Stanley, "I hurt him the way you would like to hurt me." (p. 282). The action of the play transforms this statement: "You will hurt me the way I hurt him."

Through Allan's invisibility and the inexpressibility of what he has performed with his older friend, Allan is a closeted character in one of the richest and most complex closet dramas. *A Streetcar Named Desire,* though without a living homosexual character or overt gay theme, depicts in a codified fashion a paradigmatic homosexual experience.[14] It is the quintessential closeted gay play, and Blanche DuBois is in many ways the quintessential gay character in American closet drama. Williams himself was quoted as saying, "I am Blanche DuBois."[15] Blanche keeps her sanity by making her world theater, "I don't want realism. I want magic!" (p. 385). She knows about paper moons and cardboard skies and paper lanterns, but she also knows that performance is both her allure and her protection. And William's protection of his homosexual subtext is achieved by hiding it within the actions of a heterosexual female character.

Williams' entire play is a series of complex and sometimes paradoxical transformations. A slum in New Orleans takes on the lurid colors of early Technicolor movies (what an irony that the 1951 movie of *Streetcar* was in dingy black and white, but the film is in many ways a gross act of heterosexualization). Blanche tries to transform Stella and Stanley's tiny flat into a theatrical set, while she changes constantly from spinster schoolteacher to coquette to debutante to Marschalin to whore to helpless maiden. She transforms the paper boy into an Arabian prince and Mitch into her Rosenkavalier (is Blanche aware that Strauss and Hofmansthal's Rosenkavalier, Octavian, is a teenage boy, an idealized version of the objects of Blanche's desire?) The Flamingo Hotel becomes the Tarantula Arms, and her promiscuity there becomes her "intimacies with strangers." She knows that her reality and her defense is in her protean gift. When life is theater, role-playing is not lying. Blanche is sane as long as she knows she is acting. When she tells Mitch that she has "old-fashioned ideals," "*She rolls her eyes, knowing he cannot see her face*" (p. 348), a camp gesture that demonstrates her awareness of her acting.[16] Blanche's theatrical descendants are the transvestite heroines of Charles Ludlam and Charles Busch, playing roles in mock B movies but with camp irony.

Stanley, the heterosexual stud who is Blanche's nemesis, makes no such ironic gestures. His brutality is connected to his lack of awareness of his own role-playing. He does not understand the implications of his urge to get those colored lights going, or the potential self-mockery of his silk pajamas. Seeing himself as a single essence, he wants to reduce Blanche to one consistent identity. But even at the end, now perhaps in saving madness, Blanche has transformed commitment to an asylum into a noble gesture, "I have always depended on the kindness of strangers."

Blanche's famous exit line, "Whoever you are—I have always depended on the kindness of strangers" (p. 418), is also a *double entendre* for the promiscuous Blanche, whose wholesale ravishing of the military has had her declared "off limits." Throughout *A Streetcar Named Desire,* a homosexual code is operative. When Blanche tells Stella that she doesn't know how much longer she can "turn the trick" (p. 332), the language may be surprising coming from a Southern aristocrat and high-school English teacher, but it is not accidental. It is the language of prostitution, and Blanche will have to prostitute herself to marry Mitch, an act of reduction out of economic necessity. But it is also the language of homosexuality. When Mitch confronts Blanche with her past and her supposed lies, he says: "I was fool to believe you was straight," a word Blanche repeats, "Who told you I wasn't 'straight' " (p. 385), suggesting a contrapuntal scenario of the unmasking of a homosexual.[17]

Stanley cannot name exactly what he hates about Blanche, what he must repudiate and destroy, but she knows well the hatred of the "gaudy seed bearer," the heterosexual male who can scream at her before raping her, "What queen do you think you are?"(p. 398). To ignore the homosexual subtext of *Streetcar* is to reduce the play, but to see it as the only text is even more reductive. Yet *Streetcar* is a gay play in its theatricalization, not merely dramatization, of experience; its awareness of the power inherent in understanding the slipperiness of language; its playfulness within scenes of impending entrapment and destruction. It is, in short, about the theatricalization of experience as an act of liberation. Such theatricalization does not destroy the closet but makes the closet bearable. The option is exposure and destruction.

A Streetcar Named Desire presents the "real man," the heterosexual stud, as lure and destroyer: it reverses, in other words, traditional gender roles. In the view from the closet, it is the heterosexual man who is watched (the homosexual is not seen at all). The masculine image is that of the object of desire, not the desiring subject, which could, in Inge's and most of Williams' work, be feminine or effeminate. Looking at the heterosexual male does not render him passive; it excites and empowers him. Stanley's physicality is attractive even to Blanche—though she knows its limits and its dangers—but it is also grotesque and funny. His heaving a bloody package of meat at his wife at the opening curtain is a sign that Williams shares Blanche's view of Stanley. His brutality is not simply a matter of class or ethnicity, a mistake made in a number of productions. It is part and parcel of his gender identity as the "gaudy seed bearer." Stanley's working-class origins are necessary to establish an American version of the British myth of the sexual vitality of the working class: Williams saw D. H. Lawrence as one of his literary models.

Stanley's world is *his* stage, no one else's. Only he is allowed to "get the colored lights going." Yet physically attractive, intensely physical men, studs like Stanley, can be as dangerously attractive to gay men as they are to women. Thus proliferate studs in dramas by homosexual playwrights: Inge's Turk in *Come Back Little Sheba* and Hal in *Picnic;* Williams' Val in *Orpheus Descending* and Chance in *Sweet Bird of Youth,* among others; Albee's Nick in *Who's Afraid of Virginia Woolf?* and Young Man in *The American Dream.* These are all men whose power resides in their sexual attractiveness. They are, in the works of gay playwrights, mocked, feared, sometimes martyred, but always lusted after. Since their attractiveness is so central to their identity, their real power exists only when embodied by an actor who can exude that kind of appeal. Directors will tell you that any number of actresses can play Blanche but finding a convincing Stanley is extremely difficult. The audience must find Stanley sexually attractive, or a crucial part of the play is lost. His body is as important as his words and actions.

Stanley is a unitary essence: as the heterosexual male, he needs only to play variations on his role as dominator and penetrator. Blanche's position is more complex. Theatricality is essential. In his essay, "Homosexual Signs (In Memory of Roland Barthes)," Harold Beaver writes:

> "Human beings," [W. H.] Auden has written, "are, necessarily, actors who cannot become something before they have first pretended to be it; and they can be divided, not into the hypocritical and the sincere, but into the sane who know they are acting and the mad who do not." To be natural, as [Oscar] Wilde observed, is such a very difficult pose to keep up. The result is camp: the whole gay masquerade of men and women who self-consciously act; who flaunt incongruous allusions, parodies, transvestite travesties; who are sanely aware of the gap between their feelings and their roles; who continue to proliferate a protean, and never normative, range of fantasies in social dramas of their own choosing.[18]

I could argue with its implicit essentialism, but Beaver's essay does provide a model for explicating *Streetcar.* Blanche chooses sanity, which means, for the homosexual, choosing camp, a theatricality that is a protective covering and a defensive stance toward the hostile, straight world: "Camp is the desire of the subject never to let itself be defined as object by others but to reach for a protective transcendence, which, however, exposes more that it protects."[19] And indeed, in Williams world such theatricality is not protection but exposure. Only Stanley can be theatrical, but, of course, without the irony, the awareness of acting, that makes theater complex and interesting.

A Streetcar Named Desire suggests that those who "aren't straight" must act in order to survive and that they must imaginatively transform a world in which they are rejected into a bearable place. Allan Grey (and how his gray name contrasts with the lurid colors of Stanley's world) and Blanche cannot exist after they have been exposed. Their world is off the heterosexual stage, if they are allowed any world at all.

In one sense, A Streetcar Named Desire is about the place of the homosexual in a world dominated by gaudy seed bearers, but the one visible "gay" character is a heterosexual woman, allowed only the kind of sexual activity homosexuals are allowed in popular drama. Blanche's sad scene with the teenage paperboy figures the pederasty that itself figured the danger and horror of homosexuality in The Green Bay Tree and Tea and Sympathy. And her rampant promiscuity, which caused her to be declared off limits by the army, is "typical" homosexual behavior, though Blanche remembers it without shame, even with some pride.

Like Blanche DuBois, the artist, Sebastian Venable, in Suddenly Last Summer (1958), has an uncontrollable desire for boys and young men. Like Allan Grey, Sebastian is in danger of being publicly exposed by a woman, his cousin and fiancée, and the principal conflict is between her need to tell the truth about Sebastian and his mother's need to keep her beloved son in the closet. But the truth about Sebastian, like the truth about Allan Grey, centers on his death. Sebastian is only memory, manipulated and expressed by the words of the women who knew him.

For the homosexual artist, Suddenly Last Summer weaves an interesting set of variations on the theme of exposure. Sebastian Venable has always been a private artist, wishing to be "unknown outside a small coterie."[20] The privacy of Sebastian's art is a corollary to his sense that his art expresses his religious vision; for the rest of his experience, living was enough: "his life was his occupation" (p. 351). Yet that life was to be even more private than his work: "He dreaded, abhorred!—false values that come from being publicly known, from fame, from personal—exploitation" (p. 353). But Sebastian's private life became a public matter "suddenly" when his cousin, Catherine, saw him killed and eaten by the adolescent boys Sebastian had exploited sexually. To protect Sebastian's privacy, his mother will have Catherine, the witness to his sexual voraciousness and its consequences, lobotomized: "Cut this hideous story out of her brain" (p. 423).

The presentation of Sebastian's private homosexuality and public death is accomplished purely by exposition. Sebastian, the artist-homosexual is invisible, dead, literally cannibalized. The only expressions of his vision are what is left of his poems and the garden his mother maintains as she ruthlessly maintains his asexual image, which makes her the only woman in his life:

> The colors of this jungle-garden are violent, especially since it is steaming with heat after rain. There are massive tree-flowers that suggest organs of a body, torn out, still glistening with undried blood; there are harsh cries and sibilant hissings and thrashing sounds in the garden as if it were inhabited by beasts, serpents and birds, all of savage nature. (p. 349)

This setting not only evokes a Melvillian fallen world (*The Encantadas* [1854], Melville's collection of descriptive accounts of the Galapagos Islands, is mentioned in the play); it represents Sebastian's martyred body and his carnivorous vision of nature. Moreover, the Venable garden, like Dulcimer's hothouse, is part of an interior, in this case of another Victorian mansion. It is both savage and contained, expressive and cut off from public view. Like Dulcimer's hothouse, it is emblematic of its homosexual occupant: "Yes, this was Sebastian's garden" is the first line of the play (p. 14). As the walled garden is both an elaborate closet and the physical remnant of Sebastian, the conflicting stories of his mother and cousin present the public and private selves. The monstrous Mrs. Venable is quite right to see the public exposure of Sebastian's private life as destructive of the image of the artist. The death and the sexual appetite that caused it overshadow Sebastian's poems of summer. *Suddenly*

Last Summer questions whether his mother's fierce protection of Sebastian's closet, or Catherine's truthful narrative, does more violence to Sebastian's memory. The setting suggests that Sebastian's vision should prevail through his work and the memory of his death.

There are no artists in *Cat on a Hot Tin Roof* (1955), though the play is filled with homosexual ghosts. Like *Tea and Sympathy,* the drama focuses on the fraught relationship of homosexuality to conventional ideas of manhood. Its sexually troubled characters are aging athletes, cases of arrested development, as the name "Skipper" suggests. Homosexuality is linked to an inability to grow up into any kind of relationship. However, fortunately, *Cat on a Hot Tin Roof* is far more complex than that, for it contains Williams' most interesting attempt at measuring his characters' troubled relationships against the potential of an abiding love between two men, an attempt that is mitigated by Williams' inability, or disinclination, to forge a positive language for the homosexual love the play tries to affirm.

Cat on A Hot Tin Roof takes place in the bedroom once occupied by Jack Straw and Peter Ochello, a room that expresses both their affluence and their differentness: "*It is Victorian with a touch of the Far East,*" with a "*quality of tender light on weathered wood,*" and dominated by the large double bed the lovers shared for thirty years. For a change, the homosexual's environment is created to present a positive picture: "*It is gently and poetically haunted by a relationship that must have involved a tenderness which was uncommon.*"[21] No hothouse or jungle here! The liberation of the Straw-Ochello relationship is reflected in the walls, "*which dissolve mysteriously into air*" (p. 15). But the positive image the love of Jack Straw and Peter Ochello provides is presented only in the stage directions: otherwise, the silence and invisibility surrounding homosexual desire are maintained. The language we hear is no more positive than the heterosexist discourse that pervades Williams' other work.

The plantation the ailing Big Daddy now controls, which is being fought over by his potential heirs, was inherited from Straw and Ochello. In ways both financial and sexual, the legacy of these two lovers lies at the heart of the play, and the love of Straw and Ochello stands as a counter to the compromised heterosexual relationships we see played out. Straw and Ochello do not carry the freight of negative stereotypes other Williams homosexuals carry: they are not frail, like Blanche DuBois' suicidal husband, nor voracious, like Sebastian Venable; nor are they self-hating, like Skipper, the other homosexual ghost in *Cat on a Hot Tin Roof*. They successfully engaged in the masculine enterprise of operating a large plantation, tying them to a world of masculine discourse and power, not the "feminine" world of artistic sensibility. Yet, beyond the stage directions, there is no positive language for Straw and Ochello, who become in the action of the play the targets for Brick's homophobic diatribes.

Straw and Ochello's heir was Big Daddy Pollitt, the cigar-smoking, virile patriarch who admits to loving only two things, his "twenty-eight thousand acres of the richest land this side of the Valley Nile!" (p. 86) and his handsome, ex-athlete son, Brick, who has turned into a drunken recluse since the death of his best friend, Skipper. Brick externally seems to be one of Williams' studs, but, unlike his father, he cannot play the macho role. The central scene in the play is a violent confrontation between patriarch and troubled son in which Big Daddy tries to get at the truth of Brick's relationship with his friend Skipper.

Williams' stage direction tells the reader that Big Daddy "*leaves a lot unspoken*" (p. 115), as he tells Brick of his young years as a hobo and of being taken in and given a job by Jack Straw and Peter Ochello. The implication of the stage direction, and of other hints Big Daddy gives in the scene, is that homosexual behavior is not alien to Big Daddy, who "knocked around in [his] time" (p. 115). Yet Brick is so terrified of being called "queer," that he cannot listen to what his father is trying to tell him:

BIG DADDY: . . . I bummed, I bummed this country till I was—
BRICK: Whose suggestion, who else's suggestion is it?
BIG DADDY: Slept in hobo jungles and railroad Y's and flophouses in all cities before I—
BRICK: Oh, *you* think so, too, you call me your son and a queer. Oh! Maybe that's why you put Maggie and me in this room that was Jack Straw's and Peter Ochello's, in which that pair of old sisters slept in a double bed where both of 'em died!
BIG DADDY: *Now just don't go throwing rocks at*— (pp. 115–116)

The exchange is a brilliant reversal of expectation: the object of suspicion will not listen to expressions of understanding and tolerance, countering them with heterosexist ranting. Brick is obsessed with his terror of being called a "queer" and conscious of the irony of being expected to perform heterosexually in Straw and Ochello's bed. Big Daddy will allow no attacks on Straw and Ochello, but his defense is interrupted by the appearance of Reverend Tooker, "*the living embodiment of the pious, conventional lie*" (p. 116), which allows Brick's homophobic discourse to dominate the scene. In addition to "queer" and "old sisters," Brick speaks of "sodomy," "dirty things," "dirty old men," "ducking [sic]²² sissies," "unnatural thing," and "*fairies*." Brick's acceptance of the pious, conventional lie is heard in statements that sound like a caricature of the voice of pious respectability: "Big Daddy, you shock me, Big Daddy, you, you—*shock* me! Talkin' so—casually!—about a—thing like that" (p. 119). Yet his stated reason for his shock is not moral, religious, or psychological; it is public opinion: "Don't you know how people *feel* about things like that? How, how *disgusted* they are by things like that?" (p. 119). It is not Brick's heterosexuality, nor moral, legal or religious strictures that make homosexuality such an appalling concept: it is public opinion. Like Inge's characters, Brick lives in mortal fear of exposure.

Brick's homophobia is the core of his sexual and emotional malaise. He is painfully aware that his nonsexual, nominal marriage to Maggie is a far cry from the total relationship the bed signifies, yet Brick occupies a perilous middle state. He does not love his wife, with whom he claims never to have gotten any closer "than two people just get in bed which is not much closer than two cats on a—fence humping" (p. 123), an echo of Big Daddy's loveless sex with Big Mama and an expression of Brick's inability to combine sex with friendship or love; yet he is horrified at the possible perception of a sexual dimension of his friendship with Skipper: "Why can't exceptional friendship, *real, real, deep, deep friendship* between two men be respected as something clean and decent without being thought of as *Fairies?*" (p. 120).

Like the knowing woman in *Tea and Sympathy*, Maggie, Brick's frustrated wife, understands Brick's malaise, that Brick's friendship with Skipper "was one of those beautiful, ideal things they tell you about in Greek legends, it couldn't be anything else, you being you, and that's what made it so awful, because it was love that never could be carried through to anything satisfying or even talked about plainly" (p. 57). Maggie knows that it is Brick's "ass-aching Puritanism" that puts him in such an unhappy position—that he would be better off if he had had the courage to have a complete relationship with Skipper. Maggie told Skipper the truth: "Stop lovin' my husband or tell him he's got to let you admit it to him" (p. 59). Brick blames Maggie for Skipper's death, but Skipper is dead as a result of his own internalized homophobia, and Brick has, as Big Daddy cogently puts it, "dug the grave of [his] friend and kicked him in it!—before you'd face truth with him!" (p. 125).

The bed of Jack Straw and Peter Ochello represents an unstated ideal relationship that seems unattainable for the heterosexual marriages in Williams play. In positing this ideal, the play is subversive for its time, yet the love of Straw and Ochello never seems a possibility for homosexuals either. It is more of a figure of speech than a matter of fact, and a rather paradoxical figure of speech at that, since the only positive words used to describe the relationship are silent hints in the stage directions. The only operative terminology for homosexuals the play allows is Brick's homophobic discourse.

Just at the moment Big Daddy's dialogue with Brick reaches the crucial issue of Brick's relationship with Skipper, Williams offers a lengthy stage direction:

The thing they're discussing, timidly and painfully on the side of Big Daddy, fiercely, violently on Brick's side, is the inadmissible thing that Skipper died to disavow between them. The fact that if it existed it had to be disavowed to "keep face" in the world they lived in, may be at the heart of the "mendacity" that Brick drinks to kill his disgust with. It may be the root of his collapse. Or maybe it is only a single manifestation of it, not even the most important. The bird that I hope to catch in the net of this play is not the solution of one man's psychological problem. I'm trying to catch the true quality of experience in a group of people, that cloudy, flickering, evanescent—fiercely charged!—interplay of five human beings in the thundercloud of a common crisis. Some mystery should be left in the revelation of character in a play, just as a great deal of mystery is always left in the revelation of character in life, even in one's own character to himself. This does not absolve the playwright of his duty to observe and probe as clearly and deeply as he legitimately can: but it should steer him away from "pat" conclusions, facile definitions which make a play just a play, not a snare for the truth of human experience. (pp. 114–115)

Williams begins this statement with a definite interpretation of Brick's panic that places responsibility on the false values of Brick's world, then hedges his bets by qualifying his interpretation, then moves the focus away from Brick to the problems of five people, and finally dismisses definite interpretations altogether in the name of "mystery." The last sentence of William's little treatise thickens the smokescreen: he wants to offer the truth of human experience without facile conclusions or pat definitions. Fair enough, but Williams seems to worry about such things only when homosexuality rears its problematic head.[23] Of course, his printed warning is not shared with his audience, only with his readers, but it allows him to proceed with a scene about homosexuality while denying that is what he is doing. At the end of his statement, he directs that the scene between Big Daddy and Brick be *"palpable in what is left unspoken"* (p. 115). His concern for the unspoken dominates this scene, and what is unspoken here, and in the rest of the play, is the positive force of the love of Jack Straw and Peter Ochello and the unrealized possibility it represents of a positive discourse about homosexual love.

Yet an article Williams wrote in response to critic Walter Kerr's charge that Williams was too evasive, shows that the playwright's understanding of Brick's malaise was much more specific than his vague stage directions indicate:

Was Brick a homosexual? He probably—no, I would even say certainly—went no further in physical expression than clasping Skipper's hand across the space between their twin-beds in hotel rooms and yet—his sexual nature was not innately "normal." . . . But Brick's sexual adjustment was, and always must remain, a heterosexual one.[24]

Love is not an operative term for the men in *Cat on a Hot Tin Roof*. It is a word used only by Maggie and Big Mama; the men are left to wonder: "Wouldn't it be funny if it were true?" (pp. 80, 173). Not being able to accept the love of women, the men cannot accept the unspoken option of sexual love between men. Nor can Williams convincingly offer that option. Heterosexual marriage, however, is either the hostility of Big Daddy toward the overbearing Big Mama or the grotesque charade of "normality" performed by Gooper and Mae.

The paradox in Williams' presentation of his homosexual characters is that the feared homosexuality, for which there is no positive language, also has the potential for creativity, sensitivity, and, as we see in Jack Straw and Peter Ochello, abiding love. Yet the positive potential is, more often than not, invisible and, at best, only hinted at.

How far has Williams traveled from the heterosexist politics of Anderson's *Tea and Sympathy?* The distance is the artistic gap between popular melodrama and deeply felt poetic drama. Sebastian Venable's driven appetite for boys is a far cry from the semicomic Dulcimer's fastidious possession of Julian, as Brick's crippling sexual fears are miles from Tom Lee's easily solved adolescent predicament. Yet Williams seemed as trapped as his predecessors by the enforced reticence of popular drama and the silences and evasions associated with the closet, as unable as those playwrights past to deal candidly and affirmatively with the homosexual characters and relationships he was impelled to present. Was this the deeply felt self-hatred built into his friend William Inge's depictions? Or was Williams more wily than self-hating? *Cat on a Hot Tin Roof* was, and remains, an enormously popular play; Williams demonstrated an uncanny sense of how far into alien territory an audience can be taken. No gay stereotypes have been reinforced, and homosexual love is the measure of the play's relationships, but nothing has been seen or affirmed. Perhaps, like Jed Harris, producer-director of *The Green Bay Tree,* Williams hoped "to create something without stating it." Yet a successful contemporary production does depict the inner turmoil of a self-hating, closeted homosexual. The late Ian Charleson's powerful performance in the National Theatre production was riveting in its intense portrayal of Brick's rage at himself and his terror of being labeled that which he most fears.

While Brick's conflict with Big Daddy provides the apex of *Cat on a Hot Tin Roof,* the central relationship is that of Brick and Maggie, his frustrated wife. Maggie is infatuated with Brick's physical beauty, the focus of much of the first act, which begins with

Brick emerging from the shower. Brick is definitely the object of the gaze, and Maggie's unreciprocated desire for Brick is the central aspect of their relationship. Maggie's objective in the play is to get Brick back into bed with her. The denouement suggests that she will succeed but not that their relationship will ever be one of mutual passion: Brick prefers chaste male companionship. Once again, Williams ends with a compromised version of marriage and procreation, as Brick is forced to turn Maggie's lie about her pregnancy into the truth.

When Williams finally decided—safely after Stonewall—to move his openly gay characters from the exposition to the stage, to give them bodies and voices, he obviously felt uncomfortable and defensive. The printed text of *Small Craft Warnings* (1972) contains an introductory essay entitled "Too Personal?," in which Williams states: "It is the responsibility of the writer to put his experience as a being into work that refines it and elevates it and that makes of it an essence that a wide audience can somehow manage to feel in themselves: 'This is true.' "[25] Not that it is true, but that a wide audience will take it for truth: this focus on reinforcing the stereotypes that constitute the audience's "truth" while writing "personal" drama explains Williams' caginess in both presenting and closeting homosexuality in his early plays and in both presenting and judging negatively his later, visible homosexuals. It is interesting to note that Williams was impelled to write this short treatise on the validity and limits of personal writing as a preface to a script containing an openly homosexual character. He is anticipating charges that such open homosexuality is "too personal."

Quentin, the homosexual character in *Small Craft Warnings*, is immediately seen as out of place in the Pacific Coast bar in which the play is set, not because of his sexuality but because of his effete appearance, which announces him as a stereotypical homosexual out of a 1940s movie: "dressed effetely in a yachting jacket, maroon linen slacks, and silk neck-scarf" (p. 240). Williams has returned us to the stereotype of the homosexual as fop. Quentin's face, "which seems to have been burned thin by a fever that is not of the flesh," makes him a brother to Williams' many aging male beauties, but here the wasting is an outward manifestation of the spiritual desiccation that has resulted from Quentin's sexual promiscuity:

There's a coarseness, a deadening coarseness, in the experience of most homosexuals. The experiences are quick, and hard, and brutal, and the pattern of them is practically unchanging. Their act of love is like the jabbing of a hypodermic needle to which they're addicted but which is more and more empty of real interest and surprise. This lack of varia- tion and surprise in their . . . "love life" . . . [He smiles harshly] . . . spreads into other areas of . . . sensibility. (p. 260)

The result of this emptying is finally the loss of the "capacity for being surprised," which is the loss of imagination and the possibility of creation. Rather than being a component of the artistic sensibility threatened by heterosexuals, homosexuality now destroys the artist. Quentin speaks of himself here in language of textbook heterosexist "objectivity," which is a far cry from the poetic treatment of promis- cuity we find in the language of Blanche DuBois. Desire is no longer the opposite of death, the spur to the imagination.

As Quentin has lost the "surprise" in his sexual life, so has he lost the ability to create. He is now a screenwriter who does rewrites and adaptations, a remove even from the limited originality in- volved in writing a Hollywood screenplay. Emotionless sex and second-rate hackwork connect in his assignment to "make blue movies bluer" (p. 256).

The spiritual waning that cripples the artist reduced to writing soft-core pornography links up here with the inevitable cynicism of the aging homosexual who is so self-hating that he can have sex only with boys who are not homosexual. Quentin is suffering the physical and spiritual ravages of time, the great nemesis in Williams' world. Yet he also suffers for his awareness of the brutality of his sex life. The attraction of youth is the attraction of what has been lost emotionally, and the attraction to young heterosexuals is a yearning for the possibility of an alternative to the "coarseness" of homosexual activity.

Part of that coarseness is the need to keep sex on a financial basis, a matter of distancing and control. The worldly wise Leona, another denizen of the bar, tells Bobby, the boy Quentin has picked up, to take Quentin's payment: "He wants to pay you, it's part of his sad routine. It's like doing penance . . . penitence" (p. 258). Quentin's expression of the place of homosexuality as one cause for his sexual and spiritual malaise is reinforced by echoes from other characters, who present a pathetic image of homosexuality. Leona tells Quentin: "I know the gay scene and I know the language of it and I know how full it is of sickness and sadness; it's so full of sadness and sickness, I could almost be glad that my little brother died before he had time to be infected with all that sadness and sickness in the heart of a gay boy" (p. 254).

Bill, the heterosexual stud who lives by his cocksmanship with women, has to prove himself through fag-bashing: "Y' can't insult 'em, there's no way to bring 'em down except to beat 'em and roll 'em" (p. 241). He at least sees homosexuals as victims of determinism: "They can't help the way they are. Who can?" (p. 242). And Monk, the bartender, does not want gay men in his bar, because eventually they come in droves: "First thing you know you're operating what they call a gay bar and it sounds like a bird cage, they're standing three deep at the bar and lining up at the men's room" (p. 264).

Williams, who once said that he did not want to "deal with the didactic, ever,"[26] has written here a virulently heterosexist play. The only hope for positive homosexual experience is represented by Bobby, the young man who accompanies Quentin into the bar. Like one of Joe Orton's boys, Bobby, Williams' typical fantasy youth, is omnisexual, able temporarily to equate sex with love and enjoy whatever experience comes his way. Bobby has the sense of wonder Quentin has lost, a function of youth, but lacks the sexual specialization he calls Quentin's "hang-up." But Bobby is not homosexual. He is healthily, polymorphously perverse. Like Joe Orton, Williams could romanticize the possibility of such carefree bisexuality but could not present a positive picture of homosexuality.

The wonder-filled youth in *Vieux Carré* (1977) is a young writer, an autobiographical projection of Williams himself, for whom writing and poverty are primary concerns and sex is almost accidental. The drama, like Williams' first success, *The Glass Menagerie* (1944, pub. 1945), is a memory play narrated by the playwright as a young man, here nameless and, alas, faceless. Like much of Williams' later work, *Vieux Carré* is a desperate mining of memory and early fiction ("The Angel In the Alcove" [1943]) for material for a play. The time is the late thirties, when Williams finally had his first homosexual experiences, and the setting is a boarding house in the Vieux Carré in Williams' beloved New Orleans. While the play seems to present Williams' "coming out," that liberation is at best conditional; for *Vieux Carré* is the most vivid evidence for the consistency of Williams' attitude toward homosexuality. In the 1943 story and the 1977 play, homosexual activity is characterized as "perversions of longing" experienced by the young writer and an artist, Nightingale, who is fatally diseased. The narrator, like Tom in *The Glass Menagerie* ruefully remembering events from his young manhood, focuses on speculations regarding his landlady's judgment of his sexual activity with the artist, Nightingale: "I wonder if she'd witnessed the encounter between the painter and me and what her attitude was toward such—perversions? Of longing?"[27] It is interesting that Williams autobiographical artist-narrator seems to internalize the judgmental woman's attitude toward homosexual acts, as it is interesting that he has to imagine a judgmental audience for his sexual initiation.

The "perversions of longing" briefly shared by "the writer" and Nightingale are enacted more spectacularly, though invisibly, by a photographer in the basement with a penchant for "photo sessions" with nude young men. The denizens of the basement are scalded with boiling water poured through a hole in the kitchen floor by the puritanical landlady.

Williams' point of view toward the action of *Vieux Carré* seems as hopelessly muddled as the action itself. At the end, writer and clarinet player head west as the homosexual artist, Nightingale, breathes his last. Has the writer escaped death through his escape with the musician? Williams' last dramatization of the homosexual artist is his most muddled. The move toward affirmation of love between men is tentative.

Donald Spoto quotes Tennessee Williams' most revealing comment about homosexuality in his work:

> You still want to know why I don't write a gay play? I don't find it necessary. I could express what I wanted to express through other means. I would be narrowing my audience a great deal. . . . I wish to have a broad audience because the major thrust of my work is not sexual orientation. I'm not about to limit myself to writing about gay people.[28]

If one's goal is the approbation, and financial reward, of a broad audience, then one must not "force upon" that audience any more than they find acceptable. Like many closeted homosexuals in their "everyday lives," Williams has a fine sense of how much people "want to know." As many people don't want to know that their coworker or neighbor is gay, even when they do know, Williams wrote his major work on the assumption, probably correct, that his audience did not want to know that his plays were, in important ways, built on a closeted sensibility. Awareness of the potential for rejection from one's "audience," led to a series of performances of the closet. Sexual desire for men and rejection of homosexuals are major dimensions of Williams' work, and the "other means" by which Williams expressed homosexuality in his plays are fascinating, if sad. Williams was compelled to write about homosexuality, but equally impelled to rely on the language of indirection and heterosexist discourse. Gaining the acceptance of that broad audience meant denying a crucial aspect of himself.

American Closet Gothic

In 1958, Tennessee Williams contributed a short preface to the published text of William Inge's *The Dark at the Top of the Stairs*. Williams' preface is a strange document, obviously hastily written, but focusing on Inge's predilection for the secrets under middle-American life:

> William Inge, the playwright, like William Inge, the gentleman from Kansas via St. Louis, uses his good manners for their proper dramatic purpose, which is to clothe a reality which is far from surface. This nice, well-bred next-door neighbor, with the accent that belongs to no region except the region of good manners, has begun to uncover a world within a world, and it is not the world that his welcome prepared you to meet, it's a secret world that exists behind the screen of neighborly decorum.[29]

This faint praise by William Inge's mentor, friend, one-time lover, and rival[30] could be a description of the exposure and misery of the closet that is the focus of two of William Inge's one-act plays, in which the use of the closet only supports the impossibility of coming out for his spineless secret homosexuals and the inability to imagine a positive image of homosexuality for their creator.

Like Tennessee Williams, Inge was more successful at writing plays in which sexual desire for a man is focal but displaced onto female characters than he was in writing about homosexual characters themselves, as he did in his later, weaker plays, *Natural Affection* (1963) and *Where's Daddy* (1966).

In *Come Back, Little Sheba* (1949) and *Picnic* (1953), the male is the object of the gaze. Turk, the young athlete in *Come Back, Little Sheba* (1950), poses in his track suit for his girlfriend's drawings, and attention is called to the fact that he's not nude: "The women pose naked, but the men don't. If it's all right for a woman, it oughta be for a man."[31] Marie, the coed who sleeps with Turk, rejects him for a more stable, less sexual man, an inversion of the gender roles in the usual drama of the double standard. In *Picnic* (1953), the working-class stud, Hal, who is the focus of attention, appears "bare chested . . . wearing his T-shirt wrapped about his neck."[32] Hal is the prototype of the "straight" drifter-gigolo Williams developed in *Orpheus Descending* (1957) and *Sweet Bird of Youth* (1959), a heterosexualization of the saintly hustler who looms large in Williams' short stories. In Inge's plays, this semiclad, hypermasculine character is the unsettling force, the outsider who leaves the stage before the play's conclusion.

During the 1950s, the period of his greatest Broadway successes, Inge wrote two one-act plays literally about the "place" of the homosexual; *The Tiny Closet* and *The Boy in the Basement* (both published in 1962). Inge's biographer, Ralph Voss, speculates that the plays, which show a willingness to deal openly and sympathetically with homosexuality not seen in Inge's commercial work, were probably written more as exercises related to Inge's psychoanalysis than as scripts to be produced.[33] The form of the plays, with their heavy, realistic scenic requirements (elaborate for such short plays), also suggests that Inge did not write them for production: they are more short stories written as scripts. Were it not for their subject matter, which would have made production impossible, they could be seen as drafts for television scripts. These two plays seem to be "closet dramas" in more ways than one. Both are dramatizations of shattering invasions of the secret life of lonely homosexual men. They are also symptomatic of Inge's difficulty in tying his homosexuality to received definitions of manhood.

The Tiny Closet takes place in a boarding house in a midwestern city. Its Victorian vintage and decor reflect the values of its inhabitants and its landlady. One of the inhabitants, Mr. Newbold, is, we are told, "always impeccably dressed. . . . He is the sort of man who takes great pride in his grooming."[34] He is also the best behaved of the boarders, a grown-up version of "The Best Little Boy in the World":

> You keep your room spotless, and you're always so correct around the house. My, you're a model guest. You really are. You should open up a class out here at the night school they have for adults and teach 'em how to behave in their rooming houses. The landladies in this town would get together and thank you. (p. 191)

The prissy, well-behaved, aging Mama's boy, Newbold, is obviously, by these signs, homosexual, and his landlady's excessive effusiveness belies suspicion: "If you ask me, it's kinda unnatural for a man to be so tidy" (p. 194). With the introduction of the word *unnatural,* we're in the realm of heterosexist discourse, which will increasingly be turned against Newbold.

At the beginning of the play, Newbold is very upset at the thought that someone might have looked in his closet: "Mrs. Crosby, a closet is a very small space. That's all I ask in this life. That's all I ask, just that tiny closet to call my own, my very own" (p. 190). Newbold's protection of this private space is enough to whet the landlady's appetite and fire up her moral fervor and unconscious gift for paradox: "I'm a real American, and I say, if anyone's got any secrets he wants to keep hid, let him come out in the open and declare himself" (p. 194). To protect America, the landlady and her friend invade Mr. Newbold's closet. Newbold, expecting such an invasion, has snuck back into the house:

> *He has suspected the two women to do exactly what they're doing. He is very nervous. His heart is pounding. He starts up the stairs and then comes down again. He can't seem to get the courage to confront the women. The starch he showed earlier in the play has dissolved. He is perspiring heavily and twisting his hands in fear and excitement. In a few moments we hear the*

women on their way downstairs. MR. NEWBOLD *hurriedly finds a closet to hide in.* (p. 196)

What the ladies find in Mr. Newbold's closet are dozens of beautiful women's hats that Mr. Newbold has painstakingly made for himself. The women bring one of the hats downstairs to admire, but the hats' beauty only underscores hat-making as a subversive activity for a man:

> Why a man who'd make hats and lock them up in a closet, there's no telling what kind of a person he is. He might do any kind of dangerous, crazy thing. . . . I'd rather he was a Communist. At least you know what a Communist is up to. But a man who makes hats? What can you tell about such a creature? (p. 198)

When the women leave, Mr. Newbold emerges from the closet *"shattered"* . . . *"He has become a shy and frightened young girl"* (p. 199). At the end of the play, he puts on a hat and looks at himself in the mirror, but he can no longer find any joy or comfort in posing before the mirror in one of his beautiful hats: *"He drops the hat onto a chair, then himself falls onto the sofa and cries like a helpless child"* (p. 200). Newbold's psychic survival depends on keeping his private self, which is a feminine self, in the closet. Ironically, it is women who cannot find a space for a man who finds joy in creating and wearing feminine accessories. Inge has presented Newbold's secret self and his collapse through visual images, particularly of the closet in which Newbold keeps his secret and the downstairs closet in which he hides after the women have found the hats. Once his closet is invaded, an act that merely forces him into another closet, there is no longer any space for Newbold, and neither his "performance" as a man nor his fantasies of femininity offer any comfort. He is, at the end, literally a "hopeless child," asexual and terrified.

There is no mention of any sexual life for Mr. Newbold. His fantasy defies gender definitions of appropriate behavior but does not transgress the boundaries of desire. Yet his wish to dress as a woman is considered subversive and would have been be read as homosexuality. His danger is in his wish to identify himself privately as a woman. According to the landlady, America itself is threatened by such blurring of sexual boundaries. It is easy to read *The Tiny Closet* biographically, but what is more interesting for our purposes is how codified Inge's presentation of Newbold's plight is. The closeted man is a "girl," not even a full grown woman, suggesting femininity but also presexual innocence. What is feminine is artistic and beautiful but must be kept literally in the closet. *The Tiny Closet* is an expression of the anxieties of a homosexual writer who is afraid that even his artistic expression, his plays, will expose the homosexuality that will destroy his fragile image of masculinity and bring him, not praise, but rejection. There is here a real ambivalence about the very public position of the playwright, whose work must be seen and who has, after all, chosen not to operate in a private sphere. Inge despises the guardians of American morality who "out" Mr. Newbold, but he can see Newbold only as a pitiable victim who capitulates to prevailing values.

Spencer Scranton, the middle-aged undertaker in *The Boy in the Basement,* is not as asexual as Mr. Newbold. Spencer is an undertaker, living and working in another Victorian house "of fussy dignity."[35] Spencer still lives with his invalid father and his powerful, righteous mother. His only personal space is the basement where he embalms the dead bodies: "One dead body after another. That's all my life is" (p. 173). His only moments of freedom are his weekends in Pittsburgh, where he visits gay bars. Unfortunately, on his last trip, Spencer was arrested and had to have his mother wire two hundred dollars, ostensibly to repair the car but really to bribe the arresting officer so that Spencer would not be put in jail and in the local papers. The only bright spot in Spencer's weekday life in his Victorian prison is the regular visit of Joker Evans, the eighteen-year-old grocery-delivery boy who sees Spencer as a "pal," and whom Spencer obviously adores, though he is careful to perform a kind of hearty he-man role for Joker. But Joker, for all his fond joshing and heart-to-heart confidences, sees Spencer as a pal because he sees Spencer as another kid: "I bet in some ways you never grew up, Spence. . . . In some ways, Spence, you're like a kid, too" (p. 173). When Spencer's mother returns home in a fit of fury and self-pity, having discovered where her money went on the previous weekend, Spencer musters the courage to leave home. But Spencer's brief escape from home is nothing more than an adolescent spurt of defiance and freedom. The next morning he returns home "defeated" (p. 179) and embraces his mother: *"Undoubtedly, this is the only person* SPENCER *truly loves"* (p. 180). Right after he returns, the body of Joker Evans, drowned while skinny-dipping with some friends, is delivered for preparation for burial. While his mother asks what he wants for breakfast, Spencer, in his basement, faces Joker's naked body, kisses Joker's hand *"warmly"* and prepares to sever the boy's arteries, *"the hardest thing he has ever had to do in his life."*

In *The Boy in the Basement,* Spencer's homosexuality is demonstrated not by effeminacy but by his arrested development and adoration of a domineering mother, the classic Freudian stereotype. Like Newbold, Spencer is not capable of real strength of will. He will continue to live as his mother's son, even denied the secrecy of his trips to the Pittsburgh bars. His infatuation with Joker Evans is adoration of the embodiment of a masculine normality and an adolescent freedom Spencer can appreciate only vicariously: "You were alive. Jesus! And I wanted you to stay that way" (p. 184). Spencer's homosexuality gives him his only real moment of tenderness, his kissing of Joker's hand, and his only moments of freedom from his mother's domination, but it is not connected to any possibility for happiness or fulfillment. Mother is the primary love object, and Spencer's love for Joker is partly longing for the freedom Joker's youth and heterosexuality afforded him.

In these sad little plays, Inge's homosexuals conduct their lives outside, within, or under "normal" human activities—in closets or basements—and their lives are severely crippled by the sexuality that separates them from the rest of society. At their most articulate, they can only idealize what they cannot have. "Normality" is a performance Mr. Newbold and Spencer must continue if they are to have any happiness at all. Mr. Newbold survives by playing "the good boy," and Spencer can engage convincingly in man-to-man banter, though the real self is in a closet or a Pittsburgh gay bar or a basement embalming room. Manhood is just an act covering the fragile ego of a prissy old maid or a pathetic mama's boy. Underneath the performance, there is no possibility of happiness or of an integrated personality for Inge's homosexuals. Yet Inge's realism allows no space for "normal" heterosexuality either. Mr. Newbold lives in a world of women, and Spencer's vision of normality is killed, the usual fate of the homosexual.

The plays exist as explanations of Inge's own unhappy closeted-ness. They are expressions of despair and misdirected anger. Surprisingly, they posit women as the cause of homosexual self-hatred, which was the result, perhaps of too much Freudian analysis. Yet when Inge tried, later, to write openly gay characters, the results were even more pathetic, as one can see in Inge's version of the pederastic relationship in *Where's Daddy* (1966), a play that brings us almost full circle from *The Green Bay Tree*.

In *Where's Daddy*, Professor "Pinky" Pinkerton, a fat, middle-aged homosexual professor, is—and any irony here is clearly unintentional—the spokesman for "traditional family values." Pinky picked up fifteen-year-old Tom Keen when Tom was an orphaned hustler. The pick-up lasted years, as Pinky became surrogate father as well as lover, paying for Tom's acting lessons and cosmetic improvements. Like Dulcimer in *The Green Bay Tree*, Pinky created something of a monster in Tom, though a heterosexual monster; a self-centered, emotionally limited man who now is going to leave his pregnant wife because a baby might spoil his career chances. Tom's personal limitations are not, like Julian's in *The Green Bay Tree*, the result of being raised by a homosexual: rather they are the effects of his parentless childhood and of the essential vapidity of being an actor.[36] Tom wants to go back to Pinky, which would be a return to immaturity and irresponsibility, but Pinky refuses to take him back, not out of vengeance because of Tom's relationship with a woman, but because Tom should face up to his heterosexual obligations: "You are about to become a father. That means you can no longer be a boy. . . . It's a terrifying step to take, Tom. Some of us never take it, but just grow up into old boys, and go through our lives without dignity or bearing. Take the step, Tom. I beg you. And take your part in this life as a man."[37]

Inge may have finally allowed a homosexual character out of the closet, but only to present the Freudian psychiatrist's view of homosexuality as arrested development. Pinky sees that a homosexual can only grow into an undignified old boy, a living contradiction. The good homosexual believes that "marriage between a man and a woman is a divinely beautiful institution" (p. 62), a sentimentalized, idealized view of heterosexual relationships that denies any possibility of a mature homosexual relationship (the only model for a homosexual relationship is pederasty, with the older man trying to hold onto his lost youth through a boy, preferably a heterosexual boy). Essentially, Pinky's point of view refuses to grant any space to the homosexual. Pinky is a mechanism of abnegation, courting approval of the audience for his awareness of his own inferiority. As a mentor, he must pass onto his ephebe "the truth" about heterosexuality, which inevitably equates with maturity. This is a far cry from the shameless possessiveness of Dulcimer, which looks more and more attractive as one examines the alternatives.

While idealizing heterosexuality, the only language Inge finds for homosexual behavior is that of the outraged mother in *The Boy in the Basement*: "Going to some disgusting saloon, where men meet other men and join together in . . . some form of unnatural vice, in some form . . . of lewd depravity." (p. 177) The moralistic language may seem foolish, even cruel, but it is no more destructive than Pinky's masochistic sentimentalization of heterosexuality. Inge's plays, then, dramatize the closet and are themselves dramatizations of the closet mentality.

The works of William Inge and Tennessee Williams are closet dramas in their evasions, silences, and invisibilites and in heterosexist language with which they surround their homosexual characters. They are also plays about the closet itself and about the terrors of being uncloseted. There isn't much difference between Inge's prissy, effeminate Mr. Scranton, cowering and crying like a child when his closet door is opened, and Williams' macho Brick Pollitt, ranting homophobic epithets to silence the possibility of his father's acceptance of a homosexual bond between Brick and Skipper. Opening the closet door, particularly in the heyday of Williams and Inge, makes one vulnerable to the rejections, insults, and outright violence associated with heterosexism, of which Scranton is a victim and Brick a perpetrator. Not everyone is as tolerant as Big Daddy. Not everyone's closet is the bedroom of a gay couple.

Coming out, in the plays of Williams and Inge, could be linked only to expressions of self-hatred. The playwrights had too successfully internalized the attitudes of their audiences and reviewers. Yet the complex means with which Williams and Inge managed to raise the specter of homosexuality in their earlier, closeted, better work suggests that the restrictions of the dramatic closet were salutary, perhaps necessary, to their writing. It is their rich response to the closet and their mastery of its evasions and projections that made Williams and Inge, in differing degrees, successful writers. For Williams, it was his gift of projecting his personality onto his successful female characters that distinguished his best work: "This mental transvestism is a major key to Williams' art and one of the homosexual artist's principal stratagems for achieving universality."[38] It is also an acceptance of the antipodean relationship of homosexuality and masculinity. "Real men" can be the object of male desire. They can be "trade"—heterosexual men who allow homosexuals to "service" them sexually, usually for a fee. They can also be tortured, repressed homosexuals. But any love between men must be kept offstage. Williams could express his hints of homosexuality more freely than Inge because he was not as trapped in the conventions of realism. His descriptions of settings repeatedly make the point that his plays were not to be visualized realistically. This freed him from the narrative conventions of realistic drama and also gave him the "out" of claiming that his openings of the closet door were part of theatrical, poetic fantasies. In addition to the "mental transvestism" he shared with Williams, Inge had the ability to project a sense of claustrophobia, of compromises characters make for the sake of appearances. When Inge and Williams moved the homosexual subtext from the closet of exposition to the open stage, when they removed the maskings and subterfuges—theatrical tools, after all—which in part made their works interesting, they foundered as playwrights. They couldn't write overtly gay plays that were in any way affirming.

Outing, the Critics, and Edward Albee

The closet was an agreement between playwright and audience and between playwright and critical establishment. Academic critics did not touch upon areas that were to be kept silent or disguised. Even gay critics managed to write about Williams and Inge without violating their artistic disguises: the closets that were created and maintained by academia and the heterosexism that was rife in literary, and particularly dramatic studies, could fill another volume.

For decades, the works of Tennessee Williams, with their not-very-subtle homosexual codes, were celebrated by New York reviewers. In the wane of the brief heyday of American drama, Williams and Inge represented substantial playwrights who could merge art and commerce, a necessity for reviewers, as well as for producers and theater owners. The considerable success of the sanitized film versions of their plays (usually the sanitizing entailed ludicrous attempts to remove all hints of homosexuality from the original Broadway hits) made both playwrights as close to household words as playwrights can become in the United States. The theater needed these playwrights as much as they needed the theater.

By 1963, Williams and Inge had lost some of their control over their material. The closet door was, perhaps unintentionally, opened by the wane in the playwrights' work. The homosexual subtext became less carefully hidden. In Inge's case, his focus on pathological Oedipal relationships and sensitive young men instead of on the macho men and repressed women of his fifties plays raised red flags for critics. Mama's boys meant homosexuals. The cartoonlike middle-aged women and saintly hustlers who began to dominate Williams' plays made homosexual decoding inevitable. And his heroines had aged, making them seem more autobiographical.

One can see from the critical response to the later plays of Williams and Inge, and particularly to the Broadway plays of Edward Albee, that a number of critics saw themselves as guardians of the dramatic closet. By 1963 it was time to warn audiences of the pernicious influences of closeted homosexual drama. In 1963, Howard Taubman, then the *New York Times* reviewer, wrote a "Primer," as a "public service": "Helpful hints on how to scan the intimations and symbols of homosexuality in our theater." Taubman cites Inge's unfortunate melodrama of a son's murderous Oedipal fixation, *Natural Affection* (1963), as a palpable example of a play with "homosexual content," as if any play with a pathologically Oedipal young man who is violent toward women is inevitably homosexual in content, a stereotypical view, to say the least. *Natural Affection* does have one character who feels homosexual desire for another man. But the play is an easy target—a bad play whatever its sexual dynamics. Taubman is more interested in pointing out the hallmarks of insidious, *disguised* homosexual dramas. His telltale signs of homosexuality are worth noting:

> Look out for the male character who is young, handsome, remote and lofty in a neutral way. . . .
> Be on guard for the male character whose proclivities are like a stallion's.
> Beware the husband who hasn't touched his wife for years.
> Beware the woman who hasn't been touched by her husband for years.
> Look out for the baneful female who is a libel on womanhood.
> Look out for the hideous wife who makes a horror of the marriage relationship.
> Be suspicious of the compulsive slut . . . who represents a total disenchantment with the possibility of a fulfilled relationship between man and woman.
> Be alert to scabrous innuendo about the normal male-female sexual relationship.[39]

Taubman concludes by lamenting, "if only we could recover our lost innocence and could believe that people on the stage are what they are supposed to be!" (p. 1). What does it mean to demand that fictional dramatic characters be "what they are supposed to be," unless they are supposed to be heterosexual and to support a myth of universal heterosexual happiness and harmony—the myth of "normality?"

Taubman's warning signs could make his reader suspicious of an enormous amount of "heterosexual" drama, particularly of plays by the *Times'* favorite, Eugene O'Neill, as well as most of Tennessee Williams' work (Taubman's warnings describe *A Streetcar Named Desire* and *Cat on a Hot Tin Roof,* among other plays).[40] However, there was one play on Broadway at the time of Taubman's diatribe that is clearly his target: Edward Albee's *Who's Afraid of Virginia Woolf?* (1962), which had been running since the previous October. The "aloof, lofty" Nick claims that he will "plow a few pertinent faculty wives," though he plans to mount faculty wife Martha not like a stallion but "like a goddamn dog."[41] And Martha could be interpreted as "making a horror of the marriage relationship"; she also claims to be a compulsive slut. Moreover, *Who's Afraid of Virginia Woolf?* could be said to be filled with "scabrous innuendo about the normal male-female sexual relationship," though the scabrous commentary on marriage goes far beyond innuendo.

In the sort of move reserved for homosexuality in the dramas of the closet we have discussed, Taubman defines *Who's Afraid of Virginia Woolf?* as a closet drama, yet, by not mentioning which play he is talking about, keeps the play in the closet. He will mention the unsuccessful *Natural Affection* by name but keeps the hit play shrouded in innuendo. Is he afraid of accusing the large audiences for Albee's play of guilt by association?

In covertly singling out Albee's excoriating attack on the state of American domestic bliss, Taubman attempts to invalidate the play's satire by reducing it to a homosexual code and, at the same time, maintaining the myth of "normal male-female sexual relationships" the play explodes. Perhaps the play hit a nerve in Mr. Taubman that forced him to protect his readers from its pernicious, corrupting influence. Readers needn't worry: Albee's play is *really* about inevitably miserable homosexual relationships, not inevitably happy heterosexual marriages. The belief that homosexuals know nothing about heterosexual marriage, therefore cannot write "truthfully" about it, is one of the most inane weapons in the heterosexist critic's arsenal. Where, after all, do homosexuals come from? They are raised and learn about marriage through spending their childhood and adolescence in heterosexual households. That seventeen or so years of experience should provide some grist for later fiction.

Taubman's covert caveats became interpretive clichés about Albee's play, even inspiring Ingmar Bergman to create a Swedish production in which George and Martha were played by men. Albee was not going to "get away with" the adaptations and transformations allowed Williams and Inge. He had dared to attack too many sacred cows and shibboleths of the American middle class. Yet, despite an overwrought film adaptation and the critical attempt to marginalize the play, *Who's Afraid of Virginia Woolf?* has become a "standard," revived often by professional and amateur theaters across the country.

While Albee's off-Broadway plays, *Zoo Story* (1959), *The Death of Bessie Smith* (1960), and *The American Dream* (1961) had made the playwright critically fashionable, the closeted homosexuality in his Broadway productions inspired the ire of the critics. There was, it seemed, one set of standards for Broadway, another for adventurous off Broadway.

Brickbats were hurled at Albee by respected members of the artistic left. Richard Schechner, soon to be guru of the New York University School of Drama and of sixties avant-garde theater, proclaimed in his journal, *Tulane Drama Review* (later to become *TDR*), the house organ of the theatrical left: "I'm tired of morbidity and sexual perversity which are there only to titillate an impotent and homosexual theater and audience. I'm tired of Albee."[42] The context was a jeremiad against *Who's Afraid of Virginia Woolf?*—to Schechner a dangerous example of dramatic "decadence," "which is likely to have an infective and corrosive influence on our theater."[43] Schechner's choice of metaphors of disease and destructive chemical reaction was typical of the tactics of those who warned against the threat of homosexuality. One can see more vividly in his diatribe than in Taubman's cautious warning the sense of danger and infection the supposed homosexual subtext in Albee's plays inspired. In an extension of the old superstition that pernicious influence can make an unsuspecting soul homosexual—homosexuality as vampirism—it was believed that Albee could taint and corrupt the American theater itself as well as individual audience members.

Albee's next original play, produced in 1965, was *Tiny Alice* (the adaptation of Carson McCuller's *Ballad of the Sad Cafe* intervened). It lit a fire under novelist Philip Roth, the bard of masturbation and Jewish sexual neurosis: "The disaster of the play, however—its tendentiousness, its pretentiousness, its galling sophistication, its gratuitous and easy symbolizing, its ghastly pansy rhetoric and repartee—all of this can be traced to its own unwillingness to put its real subject at the center of the action."[44] *Tiny Alice* is really a "homosexual daydream" (of course Roth is an expert on those) in which a celibate man in skirts is seduced by a strong woman, betrayed by a male lover, and killed by a representative of the law.

Like Schechner, Roth cites Jean Genet as a model for homosexual playwrights. Most of Genet's plays received off-Broadway productions during the fifties and sixties with some degree of success. But, while Genet was openly homosexual in his memoirs and fiction, his plays, except *Deathwatch,* were no more overtly homosexual than Albee's *Tiny Alice,* which bears some marks of Genet's influence.

Genet explored the metaphoric potential of some aspects of the gay experience—drag and camp—but totally outside the conventions of naturalistic theater. The celebration of Genet was partly a result of his status as a chic European playwright outside the loop of commercial theater. It was absurd to think that Genet's linkage of homosexuality with criminality and marginal social status could provide a model of appropriate uncloseted behavior for an American homosexual. Nor could his plays offer a model for a commercial American playwright. The subtext of the invocations of Genet by Albee's detractors is that gay theater belongs off Broadway and that gay men belong outside the mainstream.

Roth calls for an uncloseted homosexual drama: "How long before a play is produced on Broadway in which the homosexual hero is presented as a homosexual, and not disguised as an *angst-ridden* priest, or an angry Negro, or an aging actress; or worst of all, Everyman?"[45] Perhaps the answer is that openly gay drama would be possible when critics stop using words like "pansy." Roth praises Genet but denies Albee the right to the kind of displacements that dominate Genet's drama. He doesn't want magic, he wants realism as pedestrian as his own. It should not be surprising that the chronicler of neurotic heterosexual males should be disturbed by homosexuals invading his turf.

A year after Roth's diatribe, Stanley Kauffman, the new *Times* drama critic, raised the subject of "disguised" homosexual drama again, this time following Roth's example of virulent heterosexism tinging a plea for an openly homosexual theater. On January 23, 1966, eleven days after Albee's adaptation of James Purdy's novel, *Malcolm,* opened to critical brickbats, Stanley Kauffmann's column, "Homosexual Drama and Its Disguises," appeared on the front page of the Sunday *Times'* "Arts and Leisure" section. Kauffman's article was inspired not by Albee's failed work alone but also by the imminent arrival on Broadway of plays by Williams (*Slapstick Tragedies*) and Inge (*Where's Daddy*). None of these plays, as it turned out, would need Kauffmann's help in failing, but it is interesting that this sort of attack would appear in advance of Williams' and Inge's openings.

Kauffmann began by noting that "all of us admirably 'normal' people wish [the subject of homosexuality] would disappear," but since "three of the most successful American playwrights of the past twenty years are (reputed) homosexuals and because their plays often treat of women and marriage,"[46] the subject must be raised. That "reputed" in parentheses looks like a lawyer's addition, but it reflected the *Times'* inability to admit that anyone really was or could be homosexual, a myth the playwrights in question publicly supported.

What bothered Kauffmann was the "*disguised* homosexual influence." He could understand how playwrights, because of the "defiant and/or protective histrionism they must employ in their daily lives" were drawn (passive construction, of course) to the theater. Here superstition and universalizing have already pigeonholed the homosexual and, at the same time, created a paranoid fantasy. Either there are very few homosexuals, since he could allude to only three playwrights, or there are millions being "drawn to" the theater, armed and ready to undermine "normal" life. While Kauffmann could blame society for forcing homosexuals to dissemble, to write plays "streaked with vindictiveness toward the society that constricts and, theatrically, discriminates against them," and while he could forgive "their distortion of marriage and femininity," since "the marital quarrels are usually homosexual quarrels with one of the pair in costume and . . . the incontrovertibly female figures are drawn less in truth than in envy or fear," he drew the line at camp, though he kept the term in the closet along with the playwrights' names. The real crime of homosexual playwrights is that they "exalt style, manner, surface. They decry artistic concern with the traditional matters of theme and subject because they are prevented from using fully the themes of their own experience." While this wildly inaccurate generalization dismisses or reduces the "matters of theme or subject" in Williams', Inge's, and Albee's major work because they were homosexual and leaves them only surface, Kauffmann, with no sense of the irony involved, then joined the chorus of praise for Jean Genet as "one of the few contemporary dramatists whose works are candidates for greatness," because Genet "is a homosexual who has never had to disguise his nature."

I describe Kauffmann's column in detail because it is a prime example of the heterosexist attacks that plagued homosexual playwrights in the decade before Stonewall, an echo as well of some of the posthumous attacks Joe Orton's work received. Moreover, Kauffmann was considered by some an "intellectual" critic of the *New York Review of Books* variety, one who represented a more thoughtful, reflective brand of analysis than newspapers usually offered. But liberal, "intellectual" critics were the most avid exponents of heterosexism. It was, after all, in the *New York Review of Books* that Roth's attack appeared. Kauffmann's column is a classic example of the mixed signals that entrapped American playwrights: a few liberal posturings about society's responsibility for the closet, as if Kauffmann himself weren't maintaining the closet, followed by gross oversimplifications that dismiss the work of the dramatists in question, followed by praise of Genet.

Two weeks later, in response to a spate of angry letters that pointed out the gross oversimplifications in his column, Kauffmann wrote a sequel that softened the heterosexism and raised the volume on the liberal white noise: "I mean simply (to repeat) that homosexual dramatists need the same liberty that heterosexuals now have."[47] Kauffmann's response when homosexual dramatists took the liberty he offered them can be seen in his review, in the *Saturday Review,* of Martin Sherman's *Bent* (1979), in which he consistently, almost defiantly, referred to the characters as "queers."[48] For Kauffmann, Harvey Fierstein's *Torch Song Trilogy* (1981), which places gay experiences squarely within the patterns of heterosexual marriage and child-rearing "is not the first valuable, nonvindictive work, but it takes first place in the field so far" after years of "artistic trash and social vengeance."[49]

Clearly these critics were most offended in the sixties by Edward Albee's work and took it upon themselves to unmask Albee's "vindictiveness," dismiss his considerable strengths as a playwright, and reduce his plays to homosexual codes. Yet postliberation gay critics, with their own, very different agenda have been eager to ride the same hobby horse. In his pioneering study of homosexuality in American literature, Georges-Michel Sarotte goes further than Albee's detractors:

> *Who's Afraid of Virginia Woolf?* . . . is a homosexual play from every point of view, in all its situations and in all its symbols. It is a heterosexual play only in outward appearance, since in 1962 it had to reach the mass public, and also because Albee *does not want* to write a homosex-

ual work. However, as is the case with *all* homosexual writers, his obsessions emerge, despite all he can do, to color.and contravene his best intentions.[50]

Sarotte makes Albee a homosexual in spite of himself. His supposedly affirming thesis is that homosexual writers cannot closet themselves: the "truth" of their vision and experience will out. This universalizing removes from the writer any will and any control over his work. It is a kind of extreme Freudianism in which the subconscious of the author will dominate all his writing. It also reduces Albee's play (and many other works Sarotte discusses) to only one subject and reduces Albee to his homosexuality. If *Who's Afraid of Virginia Woolf?* is only a lengthy feud of two homosexual couples, a better written Mart Crowley's *Boys in the Band* (1968), it is nothing more than the testament to homosexual self-hatred its detractors see. But Sarotte had already one-upped heterosexist critics by titling his chapter on William Inge "Homosexual Spite."

Canadian playwright and drag artist Sky Gilbert echoes Howard Taubman's critique from a militant gay point of view. Like Taubman, he catalogs identifying characteristics of closet drama, "all of which are present in *Who's Afraid of Virginia Woolf?*," which Gilbert calls "Albee's great closet gay play": [51]

1. A quiet, intellectual, slightly effeminate, autobiographical male hero with little or no personality and a mysterious past. . . . The leading character in these cases is, in actuality, a gay man, but because the writer has refused to reveal this, the character remains mysterious, not very fleshed out, but with certain, obvious, stereotypical gay characteristics. 2. Misogyny. The female characters are in effect men in drag, but because the writer is not honest about this, the presentation of women is sexist and misogynistic. 3. Unrealistic and not very closely observed heterosexual relationships that resemble gay ones. Sure, heterosexuals act like this, but this is not a closely observed heterosexual relationship; it is a closely observed gay relationship masquerading as a straight one. So the observations are less piquant, less truthful, more off-putting and confusing.[52]

According to Gilbert, the closeted Albee does justice neither to the heterosexual relationships he claims to be depicting nor to the homosexual relationships he cannot help but depict. What he is hiding is an antigay play, not just a portrait of a gay relationship: "Not only is the play about gay men, it is a critique of their lifestyles and presents many of Albee's antigay feelings, but buried deep inside the closet."[53]

Albee has been attacked from all sides: by Kauffmann for being closeted and, therefore, distorting the truth of heterosexual relationships and by Gilbert for being closeted and, therefore, distorting the truth about heterosexual relationships, women, and homosexual relationships. Yet Albee's plays seem less about sexuality, either homo- or hetero-, than do the more naturalistic plays of Williams and Inge, in which sexual desire is the overt focus. As Foster Hirsch observes: "Typically, sexual drives in Albee become transfigured into mock-religious acts of sacrifice, penitence, immolation; sex is incorporated into a lofty, symbolic framework. . . . Albee's characters customarily use sex either as a deadly weapon in ferocious marital battles, or else abstain from it altogether."[54] Sex in Albee involves recollection of adolescent freedom; for his adults, it is a diminished thing or a weapon. It is linked not to fertility but to sterility: George and Martha's childlessness, Honey's abortions, Tobias' "spilling his seed" in A Delicate Balance (1966). It is not the motivating desire, the agent of chaos, the underlying "truth" that it is in Williams and Inge. To some extent, Albee's plays are interesting because they question the very assumptions of naturalism— rationality, the belief in a "truth" one can grasp, the primacy of sexuality. Critics tied this skepticism, this nihilism, to Albee's sexuality in ways that denied him anything but his homosexuality and looked for homosexual codes where they were perhaps present but not central. They refused to acknowledge the potential validity of Albee's insistence that loneliness and emptiness are universal conditions. That's all right for heterosexual Eugene O'Neill to say, but from a homosexual it is an impertinence.

However, Albee's peek-a-boo alternation of overt references to homosexuality and subsequent denial of homosexuality only tantalized his heterosexist detractors (in the fifties and early sixties gay audiences for the most part were happy with any hint they could get). It didn't take a philosopher to discover that Albee was not so much a philosophical nihilist as no philosopher at all: this is no crime. Playwrights are seldom philosophers and philosophers are even more rarely playwrights. Albee's detractors had a point. Ultimately, what Albee shared with Williams and Inge was that the very elements that make his better plays so theatrically vibrant are those that make them the closeted gay dramas both gay and straight critics agree they are.[55] These are not the only aspects of the plays but account for their power more than the rehashes of truisms about the alienation of modern man.

In *Zoo Story* (1959), which some critics have read as a bizarre homosexual encounter, the "intruder," Jerry, admits that at age fifteen, during an eleven-day affair:

> I was a h-o-m-o-s-e-x-u-a-l. I mean I was queer . . . queer, queer, queer . . . with bells ringing, banners snapping in the wind. . . . I think I was very much in love . . . maybe just with sex. But that was jazz of a very special hotel, wasn't it? And now; do I love the little ladies; really, I love them. For about an hour.[56]

Jerry's adolescent romance was the closest thing to love he has ever felt, but he still claims heterosexuality, though he is incapable of more than a one-night stand with the "little ladies." Heterosexuality seems an accommodation in a world that demands the compromise of unhappy heterosexuality, though it is a world in which "GOD IS A COLORED QUEEN WHO WEARS A KIMONO AND PLUCKS HIS EYEBROWS" (p. 18). Jerry wants Peter to acknowledge and understand his world of marginal people, yet he denies the homosexuality that marginalizes him. The mock sexual and religious crucifixion that ends the play, with its sexual pun, "I came unto you (*He laughs, so faintly*) and you have comforted me" (p. 26), is nominally an example of the combination of love and cruelty that Jerry claims is "the teaching emotion" (p. 19). If *Zoo Story* has a homosexual subtext, it is one of thwarted love through the self-hatred of denied, closeted homosexuality, but the negativism is directed at the homosexual. Homosexual love is an adolescent idyll; adult reality is heterosexual promiscuity combined with misogyny and fear of commitment, or unhappy, castrating marriage and routine. "What is gained," Jerry says in his story of the dog, "is loss," but is that loss as inevitable as Albee thinks? Only if heterosexuality is inevitable.

In William Inge's plays, the beautiful young man was the image and agent of liberation. In Williams' plays, the beautiful young man was the martyr to sexual desire. Both playwrights idealized and sentimentalized male beauty. The dream of their hunks is Hollywood, that apex of narcissism and factory for American dreams, but they are too nice and too innocent to succeed in such a predatory environment. The unfeeling, narcissistic hunk who is the American dream in Albee's 1961 play of the same name is a Freudian nightmare, a result of the classic pattern of domineering, castrating mother and ineffectual father. He is a loveless sexual receptacle, the receiver of the gaze and nothing more. He is the opposite of his twin brother, who was dismembered for not focusing all his attention on his monstrous parents. Albee's title, *The American Dream,* presents this spiritually sterile hunk as an image of cultural aspiration, but the story of the unfortunate twins is really a parable of the Freudian formula for the making of the homosexual.

Who's Afraid of Virginia Woolf? (1962) is a more realistically rendered elaboration of the one-act plays. George and Martha, named to suggest that they are American icons, are fuller versions of the domineering Mommy and castrated Daddy of *The American Dream,* and their treatment of their imaginary son is relegated inevitably to exposition. He is like the castrated, mutilated son of Mommy and Daddy, the twin brother of the American dream, who emerges, fully clothed in the later play as Nick, the cool, smug biologist on the make. In *Who's Afraid,* the ineffectual husband finally triumphs over his monstrous wife by robbing her of her fantasy of motherhood—of womanhood. Nick is ultimately put in the position of Peter in *Zoo Story,* of learning the truths of marginal lives, of the underside of the "normality" he seems to represent; he is forced to see that the truth is that love and violence are intertwined for self-hating people. Martha is a descendant of Ibsen's *Hedda Gabler* (1890), a Daddy's girl trapped in a marriage to a mediocre scholar, and her battles with George echo Strindberg. Albee acknowledges his debt to the Scandinavian naturalists but cannot commit himself fully to their belief in logic and causality. At the heart of the exposition—the imaginary child who is the guilty family secret—is nothing more than a fantasy. Naturalism is both used and undermined—a reflection of the gay writer's usual ambivalence toward the dominant mode of modern theatrical structure, which functions both to explain and to dispense with the outsider, the problem.

In *Who's Afraid,* the outsider who must be humiliated and purged is the handsome, brilliant, but vacuous Nick. What threat does Nick really pose? He is relatively humorless, he is uncomfortable being thrust into the fighting and game-playing of George and Martha, he doesn't love his wife (for whom the playwright reserves the brunt of his contempt), he is ambitious and vain, and he doesn't play the games very well. In other words, he has the makings of a theatrically dull character but doesn't deserve to be punished. Like Williams' Stanley Kowalski, Nick is a version of "masculine," heterosexual, "normality," but Albee disarms Nick. The potent danger is not from conventional virility, but from George's theatrical authority, spearing Martha not with his penis but with snapdragons.

Unlike Williams and Inge, Albee is not good at writing women. Honey is a hateful caricature, a horrid case of arrested development. Martha, like Albee's other theatrically lively women, is, as Sky Gilbert suggests, a drag queen: loud, self-mocking, highly performative (the next Martha, Claire in *A Delicate Balance,* even trots out an accordian at a climactic moment). Martha is a cartoon of a woman, if a woman at all. William's transvestite displacement was successful because he wrote women's voices more convincingly than he wrote men's. Albee did not have the ear, or the sympathies, for such ventriloquism.

What is offered Martha instead of the phallus she desires, at times claims, for herself, or which she at least wants from a man, is a pop gun—a trick, a theatrical device, but it gets her sexually excited:

> (GEORGE *takes from behind his back a short-barreled shotgun, and calmly aims it at the back of* MARTHA's *head. . . .* MARTHA *turns her head to face* GEORGE. GEORGE *pulls the trigger.*)
> GEORGE: POW!!!
> (*Pop! From the barrel of the gun blossoms a large red and yellow Chinese parasol.* HONEY *screams again. . . .*) You're dead! Pow! You're dead!
> . . . .
> (HONEY *is beside herself.* MARTHA *laughs too . . . almost breaks down, her great laugh booming.* GEORGE *joins in the general laughter and confusion. It dies, eventually.*)

. . . .

MARTHA (*joyously*): Where'd you get that, you bastard?

. . . .

GEORGE (*leaning over* MARTHA): You liked that, did you?

MARTHA: Yeah . . . that was pretty good. (*Softer*) C'mon . . . give me a kiss.

GEORGE (*Indicating* NICK *and* HONEY): Later, sweetie.

(*But* MARTHA *will not be dissuaded. They kiss,* GEORGE *standing, leaning over* MARTHA'*s chair. She takes his hand, places it on her stage-side breast. He breaks away.*) (pp. 94–95)

George's theatrical performance of a potency he does not in actuality possess excites Martha to initiate sexual activity, which George rebuffs: "What are we going to have . . . blue games for the guests?" (p. 95). As George has performed a cartoon of the phallus, Martha performs an exaggerated sexual overture in which she is the aggressor, her husband the passive receiver of the "pass" that he must rebuff. While much has been made of the many instances of conventional sex-role reversal in the play, the central dimension of the moment is the presence of the audience. The gun play and the sexual overture are performed, as George's rebuff is performed, for the audience onstage, Nick and Honey. The death of George and Martha's imaginary son is the denouement of a series of scenes they have acted out for each other for years. Near the beginning of the play, before Nick and Honey enter, George warns Martha not to "start on the bit . . . the bit about the kid" (p. 77). The theatrical definition of "bit" is an entertainment routine, an "act," which is exactly what their son is. The insupportable rule is that their act is not to be played in front of an audience, which makes it no act at all. Bits need an audience, and their chosen audience, the young couple, is a parody of heterosexual "normality," and as such a parody of many in the real audience in the Billy Rose Theater. The bit about the son is also a parody of heterosexual "normality," of the family George and Martha cannot have and that they would destroy, as they destroy him in their bits.

The "What a dump" exchanges at the beginning of the play are also performance, by inference acknowledging an audience—why else would George and Martha do "bits" so blatantly? The theatrical "Screw you" at the opening of the door to reveal Nick and Honey switches the focus from real to surrogate audience, as the young people are both audience and target of George's satire. The only private "overheard moments" are at the play's coda, when the audience is to believe George and Martha are alone because they have, for the first time, stopped performing.

The emphasis in *Who's Afraid of Virginia Woolf?* is on performance as superior to real experience. After Nick's exposure and humiliation in "Get the Guests," Nick threatens to join the performance: "I'll play in your language . . . I'll be what you say I am" (p. 136). Nick's very statement, confusing "play" and "be," shows his inferiority to George and Martha. Nick doesn't know how to perform and ultimately becomes the butt of jokes in George and Martha's "bits." Even in the midst of their war, George and Martha join in a musical mockery of Nick:

> NICK: I'm nobody's houseboy.
> GEORGE *and* MARTHA: . . . Now! (*Sing*) I'm nobody's houseboy now. . . .
>   (*Both laugh.*)
> NICK: Vicious. (p. 156)

Onstage, theatricality triumphs, and George and Martha's home is a theater in which the rules of theater prevail. Experience and fantasy, truth and illusion, are turned into art, and the hilarious, fun surface only partially masks Albee's hatred of the Nicks of the world, disgust at the Honeys, and ambivalence toward the Marthas. The play is, in its best moments, as its straight and gay detractors claim, an exercise in camp. Whatever social or philosophical message Albee claimed for the satire in the play, it is greatly an exercise in gay metatheatricality and an exorcism of the claims of heterosexuality. When the bitchiness and game-playing ends, the play's *raison d'être* is eliminated and one is left with an empty, joyless conclusion.

This is not to say that *Who's Afraid of Virginia Woolf?* isn't a brilliant play, but its brilliance is on the surface. Dig too deep and, like Julian in Albee's *Tiny Alice,* you'll find yourself wedded to nothing at all, though Albee insisted on making claims for that nothing as though it were a form of depth. As he couldn't claim his homosexuality, he couldn't claim that surface in his plays is almost everything. The joy is in the bitchy language, in camp feminine diminutives like "snoozette" (what straight man would conceive of such a playful diminutive?), and in the travesty of femininity and sexual appetite Martha enacts.

Albee, like Williams and Inge, couldn't write homosexual scenes. He couldn't believe in their acceptability (Albee saw himself, as Williams and Inge did, as a "Broadway writer"). In a way, it's a good thing for gay men that he didn't; for a gay *Who's Afraid of Virginia Woolf?* would also be antigay, as would a gay *Streetcar Named Desire* or a gay *Picnic*. Albee's gift, to a lesser extent than Williams', was the ability to stage a version of heterosexuality from the "other side" that was theatrically vibrant, more so than many pictures of heterosexual life created from within. Perhaps the complex relationship Albee, Williams, and Inge had toward heterosexuality, as well as toward their own "marginal" sexual status, gave them the tools to theatricalize the other for whom they were The Other. No heterosexual playwright has done it so well since. Still, I must agree with Alan Sinfield that "decoding the work of closeted homosexual artists ought to produce a recognition of oppression rather than a cause for celebration."[57] In the works of Albee, Williams, and Inge, successful drama is produced from, and itself dramatizes, the considerable self-loathing reinforced by the closet.

Frank Rich and the New Closet Drama

In the eighties, Terrence McNally became the house playwright of the Manhattan Theatre Club, which moved from modest surroundings to a theater in the New York City Center and a four-million-plus annual budget. While his openly gay *The Lisbon Traviata* (1985/ 1989, discussed in Chapter 6) was successful enough to merit a move to one of the larger off-Broadway houses, McNally's big hits have been *Frankie and Johnny in the Clair de Lune* (1987), which had a long off-Broadway run and a West End run in London and has been turned into a film with Al Pacino and Michelle Pfeiffer, and *Lips Together, Teeth Apart* (1991), which earned a rave review from Frank Rich and sellout business.

Frankie and Johnny in the Claire de Lune, like Lanford Wilson's highly successful *Talley's Folly* (1980), is a romantic play about a couple of socially inept people in which a man must break down a woman's resistance to a relationship. In Wilson's play, the issue is the viability of a nonprocreative marriage (the woman cannot have children; the man doesn't want to bring children into a world he sees as evil). The Talley trilogy, which culminates in *Fifth of July* (1978), with its central gay couple, ultimately affirms nonprocreative gay and straight relationships, a challenge to the "traditional family." The middle American nineteenth-century farmhouse is inherited by a gay couple. The biological future is the formal garden one of the lovers is developing.

In McNally's *Frankie and Johnny,* the names suggest a gender ambiguity—the names could be masculine or feminine, the couple could be gay or straight. In the preface to the published version, McNally claims that it is his most autobiographical play, a response to the loss of dear gay friends to AIDS.[58] Yet one sees and hears a man and a woman. As a matter of fact, one sees and hears one of the best romantic dramas in years. But there is very little gay in *Frankie and Johnny in the Clair de Lune.* There is one cautious reference to caution in the age of AIDS, yet a few minutes later Johnny (the man) is sucking blood from Frankie's cut finger, a blatant act of unsafe intimacy. Frank Rich called this play "the most serious play yet about intimacy in the Age of AIDS."[59]

McNally's most recent play, *Lips Together, Teeth Apart,* presents two heterosexual couples in a Fire Island house inherited by one of the wives from her brother, who recently died of AIDS-related infections. In *Lips Together, Teeth Apart,* Nathan Lane and Anthony Heald, who played the gay central characters in *The Lisbon Traviata,* are the troubled heterosexual husbands. Gay men are background noise—on Fire Island! They make love in the bushes while the onstage heterosexuals rail—and avoid the pool because they might catch AIDS from it!

Frank Rich, in a rave review, proclaimed, "The play's great generosity can be found in its insistence on letting the audience see each camp through the eyes of the other without distorting either point of view, and, as it happens, without bringing a gay character onstage."[60] *See* is the operative verb in Rich's sentence, yet precisely what the audience does not do is "see" gay men. If anything, McNally is overly generous toward the heterosexuals in his affluent Manhattan Theatre Club audience—and toward Mr. Rich—they are spared the awkwardness of "seeing" gay characters. McNally, who more blatantly than his colleagues, put gay men on the Broadway stage in *Bad Habits* and *The Ritz* now receives praise for pushing homosexuality at least into the wings. Otis Stuart rightly laments that "*Frankie and Johnny in the Clair de Lune* and *Lips Together, Teeth Apart,* which contain not a single gay character, can be seen as the return to the era of the invisible homosexual."[61]

In a recent interview, McNally noted: "Unless you write a play for a specific audience now, you don't know who's sitting out there, whereas in the '60s I knew who came to my plays. We were all against what we saw as the establishment. Now we've become the establishment."[62] McNally does write for a specific audience—the well-heeled, New York "liberal" audiences who support the Manhattan Theatre Club. He has made clear that for him, the New York theater is "the only place to be if you want to work with the best directors, actors, and designers in the American theater."[63] But one also works with the New York audience and must please Frank Rich, the latest *Times* drama critic who, like his predecessors, has a clear sense of the place of gay men on the New York stage. McNally is praised for his "straight" plays and given more qualified eccomiums for his gay plays.

In 1990, playwright Craig Lucas wrote an article for *American Theatre,* "A Gay Life in the Theatre,"[64] and the film about the effect of AIDS on a group of affluent gay men, *Longtime Companion.* He also managed to create a critical and commercial success with *Prelude to a Kiss,* which premiered at the Circle Repertory Company, the old stomping ground of Lanford Wilson, and moved for a long run into the same Broadway theater that housed *Torch Song Trilogy.* Film stars Alec Baldwin, Timothy Hutton, and Steve Guttenberg were willing to play Peter, the heterosexual leading character in Lucas's play while, ironically, lesser-known stage actors played the gay men in Lucas' film. The larger irony is that Lucas could write a successful film about gay men, but his big dramatic success was a heterosexual love story, if one with a twist only a gay playwright could execute sensitively. The "prelude" to a kiss is a whirlwind courtship of Peter and Rita, two yuppies in love. On their wedding day, Rita is kissed by an old man and she and the old man exchange bodies. Peter finds himself with the body of his wife, but with a stranger occupying that body. As his mother-in-law points out, this is not an uncommon experience for a newlywed. He is reunited with the person he loves, now in the body of a cancer-ridden old man. *Prelude to a Kiss* is a sweet, deftly written play with some gentle reflections on mortality and the difference between youthful spirit and aging, decaying flesh. However, in the manner of contemporary commercial theater, it is totally unthreatening, totally accommodating to its audience in ways Lucas did not think would be necessary in a screenplay.

In one moment just before the wedding, Peter's best friend and best man kisses him on the cheek and mouths "I love you" to the groom.[65] The friend claims never to have sex. Is this the typical gay man in the age of AIDS, safely virginal out of fear of disease and playing the closeted, stalwart sidekick to his beloved straight friend? Peter spends his honeymoon having sex with an old man in the body of his wife. What if it had been a gay young man in his wife's body? That might have been too threatening. Frank Rich's proclamation, "I loved this play!" is emblazoned on the front of the dust jacket.[66]

The off-Broadway success of the 1990–1991 season was David Stevens' *The Sum of Us,* an Australian play about the relationship of a butch gay working-class man and his father. Though it is hinted at the end that the son may have found a lover, throughout his only close relationship is with his adoring father, whose voice is privileged through his lengthy monologues. *The Sum of Us* focuses on a father's tolerance of his son's not very active homosexuality and the son's primary relationship with his father. While the only loving, sexual relationship celebrated in the play is that of the father's mother with her lesbian lover, the audience never sees a loving, sexual gay (or straight) relationship.

This is the commercial theater in the nineties—an "outside" comedy-drama of a "good" gay son is a hit and openly gay playwrights now proudly write the sort of play closeted gay playwrights previously wrote. The offstage openness of the playwrights combined with their sensitivity to their audiences wins the praise of Frank Rich and success in commercial theater in which the most powerful, successful producer is an openly gay manufacturer of heterosexist lowbrow musical fantasies.

The return of the closet in the early nineties may be the clearest indication of what Williams' *A Streetcar Named Desire* metaphorically asserts and his more realistic plays bear out—that in traditional, realistic drama, there is no meaningful place for gay experiences or explorations and expressions of what has been inadequately called the "gay sensibility."[67] In the discussions of the contemporary gay drama in part III, we will see that it is in pushing beyond the limits of realism and the expectations and sensibilities of the audience for mainstream theater that gay drama most vividly stages gayness.

PART 3

Staging "A Culture That Isn't Just Sexual"

Simon Russell Beale (Edward) and Grant Thatcher (Gaveston) in Marlowe's *Edward II*. Photo: Michael Le Poer Trench. Reprinted by permission of the photographer.

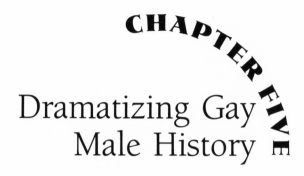

CHAPTER FIVE

Dramatizing Gay Male History

> "The only way we'll have real pride is when we demand recognition of a culture that isn't just sexual. It's all there—all through history we've been there; but we have to claim it, and identify who was in it, and articulate what's in our minds and hearts and all our creative contributions to this earth."
>
> Ned Weeks, in Larry Kramer, *The Normal Heart*

On the 1991 season finale of CBS' *Northern Exposure,* two good-looking, well-dressed men arrive at an Alaska wilderness town. One is bearded and in his early forties, the other fair, a bit younger; their looks, clothing, and comfort with each other make them instantly recognizable to gay men as a gay couple. They want to buy an old house, restore it, and turn it into a bed-and-breakfast. Maurice, the burly ex-astronaut who owns the building and most of the town, smelling money, invites the two men to dinner to help solidify the deal. The couple sees Maurice's well- equipped kitchen, antiques, and large collection of original- cast albums and assumes he, too, is gay. Having found, they presume, a kindred spirit, they feel totally at home, so much so that they hold hands at Maurice's dinner table. The next day, Maurice, thrown by the misperceptions of the previous evening into a major image crisis, gives away his Cuisinart and Broadway albums (if he had any knowledge of gay literature, he would also change his name). When he asks the hip DJ at the local radio station what he would assume about men who loved cooking and show tunes, the immediate answer is, "I'd think they were homosexual."

To protect the town from an invasion of "Nancy boys," Maurice tells the couple he won't sell them the house. Their assumption is that Maurice is a closeted gay who is out to get a higher price. They offer him the house's outrageous list price, throwing Maurice into a conflict between heterosexist principles and greed. Greed wins.

In the final scene, Maurice is buying the two men a drink in the community's bar (Maurice's fears have been assuaged by the knowledgeable DJ's telling him that there were bloodthirsty, militaristic homosexuals in the Ottoman Empire and that excessive fear of homosexuality is frequently a sign of homosexuality). When a couple begins slow-dancing to the jukebox, other couples join in, including the gay couple, who slow-dance with their arms around each other. The camera pans from them, past other dancing couples, including two Native American women, and then moves behind Maurice and the DJ, who stand watching, the DJ with his arm around Maurice's shoulders in a friendly gesture that could have been—but wasn't—misread as a sign of homosexuality. In this situation, Maurice is the outsider, the viewer of an integrated society, but he is accepting the affectionate touch of a male friend.

The gay couple has been integrated into this town of eccentrics without any compromise. They had to buy their way in at an inflated price, but they didn't back down when faced with Maurice's homophobia. More important, they weren't scared to dance; nor did their dancing cause any consternation. This episode of *Northern Exposure* presented a sweet, idealized picture of assimilation. The show did not completely ignore stereotypes—it wouldn't exist without them—but it did mock dependence on stereotypes, and the joke was in the reading and misreading of signs. It offered the healthiest dramatic image of gay men television has yet presented: two men who wouldn't think of being marginalized establishing their place on a dance floor and slowly dancing, arms around each other, like everyone else. Homosexuality was never problematized, nor were homosexuals; it was Maurice who had the problem.

Post-Stonewall gay drama is basically about finding a place on the dance floor, a place in society where a gay man can safely not act straight. It is about the experience of being gay as seen from inside. The situations are often the same as those shown in "outside" drama about gays, but the point of view is now that· of a gay character. If gay men choose to assimilate, as television and much drama assumes they will, the central question remains: What does it mean to be gay? This is a question that has until recently been answered for lesbians and gay men by the dominant culture. What is gay identity apart from sexual-object choice? Canadian dramatist Robert Wallace has written that "the essential strangeness of being gay in a heterosexual society is the common denominator that united the millions of lesbians and gay men openly involved in the construction of "sexual community."[1] Don Shewey adds that this "essential strangeness of being gay is being something other than what one was brought up to be."[2] "It is," Philip Brett notes, "the special characteristic of the homosexual stigma (unlike that of being black or Jewish) that it is almost always reinforced at home and thus the more readily 'internalised.' "[3] This strangeness is reinforced by homophobia, or heterosexism, the resultant rejection, and the potential for violent attack from hostile outsiders.

In part the two gay men on *Northern Exposure* were accepted because they were a couple joining other couples. One of the major questions in the years since Stonewall has been that of relational values: what are the most appropriate gay relationships and what does love mean in a gay context? These issues of alienation, internalized heterosexism, and the possibility of loving relationships are so interrelated that they inevitably become intertwined in gay drama.

A gay couple can fit more comfortably into the world of *Northern Exposure* than into that of the typical "serious" television drama because *Northern Exposure* is not dependent on the conventions of realistic drama, as were telefilms like *An Early Frost* and *Our Sons*. The show is an interesting generic mix—comedy, farce, parody, melodrama, fantasy—that defies linear narrative. The moon over Cicely, Alaska, is full, and characters aren't expected to behave in accordance with realism's laws of rational causality. Homosexuality needn't be problematized, nor do issues have to be resolved in a conventional, realistic manner. In other words, to paraphrase Blanche DuBois, magic takes precedence over realism. This is the thrust of contemporary gay drama; and what unites many gay plays is the dialogue with, defiance of, or elimination of the conventions of realistic drama that would otherwise entrap gay characters. More-over, the plays are unabashedly metatheatrical, revelling in their own theatricality, underlining the essential fact that acting has been, to some extent, an essential part of the gay man's life.

I divide post-Stonewall gay drama into two categories. This chapter will be devoted to the development of an affirming gay history, the next to depictions of contemporary gay life that focus on what it means to act gay.

The Historical Impulse

Eve Kosofsky Sedgwick has defined a potential alternative canon of lesbian and gay male literature as "a literature of oppression and resistance and survival and heroic making."[4] Oppression and resistance and survival and heroic making are the stuff of gay history, and much of gay drama is an expression of what might be called the "historical impulse" in gay literature—the impulse to depict and define the collective past of gay men to affirm a sense of identity and solidarity and to educate the dominant culture about the brutal effects of its heterosexism.

The historical impulse is expressed in Christopher Marlowe's *Edward II* (1594), which not only focuses on the homosexual desire of its central character but also celebrates and affirms Edward's love for Piers Gaveston by linking it with a catalog of celebrated male lovers of classical history and myth:

> The mightiest kings have had their minions,
> Great Alexander loved Hephaestion,
> The conquering Hercules for Hylas wept,
> And for Patrochlus stern Achilles drooped:
> And not kings only, but the wisest men:
> The Roman Tully loved Octavius,
> Grave Socrates, wild Alcibiades.[5]

Such list-making was the central historical act in the early days of gay liberation, when identity and pride came from a symbolic joining with celebrated homosexuals of the past and present. Larry Kramer has Ned Weeks, in *The Normal Heart* (1985), incant such a list of past homosexuals:

I belong to a culture that includes Proust, Henry James, Tchaikovsky, Cole Porter, Plato, Socrates, Aristotle, Alexander the Great, Michelangelo, Leonardo da Vinci, Christopher Marlowe, Walt Whitman, Herman Melville, Tennessee Williams, Byron, E. M. Forster, Lorca, Auden, Francis Bacon, James Baldwin, Harry Stack Sullivan, John Maynard Keynes, Dag Hammarskjold.[6]

Kramer's list manifests the problems inherent in such compilations. What meaning is there in invoking such names? And, once we have the names in place, what do we do with them? After all, many of the people on Kramer's list, including Christopher Marlowe, could not conceive of homosexuality as we understand it,[7] and others who could were not known for proudly asserting their gayness. Yet this cataloging both represents an urge to make historical connections and, to use Kramer's Ned Weeks' words, calls for "the recognition of a culture that isn't just sexual."[8] Kramer's Ned Weeks recited his list as a rebuttal to the charge that his pleas for gay men in the AIDS epidemic to stop their promiscuous behavior were destroying the foundation of the gay community, which was sexual liberation. His list is an assertion that there is more to the gay experience than sex, which forms but one element in a long history of artists, leaders, and heroes. The assertion can be made more effectively as a counter to heterosexist reductions of gay people to their "abnormal," "deviant" behavior.

The *historical impulse* in gay theater—the urge to dramatize the history of "oppression and resistance and heroic making"—is linked in complex and interesting ways with three other central impulses in gay drama:

The *anarchic impulse* to celebrate, sometimes even in its nonlinear structure, creative anarchy as a positive counter to oppressive order.

The *romantic impulse* to posit loving relationships as the norm for gay men—to posit the right to love, not merely the right to sex, as the stake in the battle against oppression.

The *canonical impulse* to celebrate gay creativity by dramatizing the experience of gay artists, thus reinforcing awareness of the kind of pantheon of creative figures that Kramer's Ned Weeks hailed. Those names establish that much of Western culture is gay culture, and they claim a space in this culture for an openly gay identity.

I shall devote this chapter to a consideration of four types of history play. First I shall evoke a canonical model, Marlowe's *Edward II*, which can be seen to point the way toward contemporary gay history plays by evoking a homosexual martyr and defining a conflict between the "official" world and what one might call "the right to love." The second section focuses on three plays that dramatize the complex relationship of homosexuality to privileged all-male societies. In these mainstream plays, the homosexual, seen from outside, cannot be fully integrated into the society in which he places himself. His marginalization is symptomatic of a complex social malaise. I will then discuss three contemporary history plays that focus on three pivotal events in modern gay history: The Oscar Wilde trials, the Nazi persecution of homosexuals, and the Stonewall riot (the Boston Tea Party of gay history). All three of these "inside" plays—Noel Greig and Drew Griffiths' *As Time Goes By* (1977), Martin Sherman's *Bent* (1979), and Doric Wilson's *Street Theater* (1982)—mix a politicized view of history with a project for love between men. Finally, I shall look at some dramatic representations of gay artists that serve as examples of how the canonical impulse merges with the romantic and anarchic impulses.

The Canonical Model

Two post-Stonewall productions of Christopher Marlowe's *Edward II* (1594) have become particularly famous. In 1969, Ian McKellan played Edward in repertory with a play that shows its influence, William Shakespeare's *Richard II* (1595). The production inspired outrage, particularly for the kissing scene between Edward and Gaveston. Tabloid newspapers referred to the moment as the "shock kiss"; and a photograph of the kiss was included in a book called *The Erotic Arts*. McKellan's *Edward II* was videotaped and shown in America as well as in Great Britain. In 1990 Gerard Murphy directed a production for the Royal Shakespeare Company at Stratford-upon-Avon that moved to the RSC's London home in 1991. These productions are not only revivals of a masterpiece but recognitions by gay artists of the centrality of Marlowe and *Edward II* in the gay canon. This centrality has been reinforced by the 1991 film version by the gay British director Derek Jarman.

Marlowe himself has become a gay hero, romanticized by some artists:

> When Edward gets fatally screwed for letting the world go screw itself, you sense Marlowe's unflinching confrontation of his own emotional self-indulgence. Edward chooses to reject his responsibility as a King to his Country, as Marlowe rejected his responsibility as a writer to his talent; and you can't blame either.[9]

He has been seen by gay scholars and critics as a poststructuralist gay hero: "Like the heroes he created, Marlowe lived and died in the impossible project—as author, government spy, and homosexual—of the marginalized, negativized existence permitted him."[10]

Edward II fulfills one of the prime functions of a gay history play; it establishes a pantheon of historical and literary figures who form "a culture that isn't just sexual." The text is based on chronicles of English history, and the text also creates its own chronicles of gay history. *Edward II* places a character motivated primarily by homosexual desire in a world in which this motivation alienates him both politically and domestically.

The "official" view might be that Edward's blatantly sexual love for Gaveston and Spenser can be seen only as fatal political error. In this interpretation, the sex of Edward's love objects is not the issue but rather their class and the power Edward grants them. Edward abuses kingly privilege to defy aristocratic privilege. "Traitor" and "treason" are important words in *Edward II* and the "lovesick" king invites civil war and ignores strife in France. To Edward, everyone who stands in the way of his will is a traitor to his kingship, but ultimately Edward himself, along with Gaveston and Young Spenser, is punished as a traitor to the realm.

If, however, we see *Edward II* as a play about gay history instead of English history, varied alternative readings emerge. Director Gerard Murphy sees homophobia as a crucial element. Murphy thinks that when Edward takes Spenser as his lover

> he has learned a lot about the complexity of the reasons why people hated Gaveston and actually endangers Spenser's life by saying, "You are now my official boyfriend." The turning point is when a messenger comes from the barons and says, "Right, we've got rid of Gaveston and if you want this to end happily you'd better get rid of Spenser." The

underbelly of anti-gay feeling now becomes ulcerous. And Edward's murder, with the poker thrust into his anus, is not accidental.[11]

More historically oriented critics, like Alan Bray and Jonathan Goldberg, see *Edward II* as a case history of the complex Elizabethan attitude toward sodomy, a term that still has resonance and legal power for many gay people. Not only are a number of state sodomy laws still on the books, but in 1982, in the *Bowers v. Hardwick* ruling, the United States Supreme Court declared that Georgia's sodomy laws take precedence over an individual's right to privacy.[12]

No gay critic can ignore the play's lavishly expressed homoeroticism, a subject that heterosexist critics either ignore or decry. Purvis E. Boyette writes that *Edward II* is "about the erotic consciousness and its play through all the tensions of the drama. . . . The homoeroticism of the play expresses a plausible consciousness no dramatist had explored before Marlowe, and for him traditional judgment becomes irrelevant, a fiction he chooses to ignore."[13]

The play begins with a speech by Gaveston, who represents the magnet to which Edward is drawn. In Marlowe's play, Gaveston may be a commoner, a Frenchman, a sycophant, and a ruthless opportunist, but he is also the representative of a free play of imagination and erotic charge presented in language far more attractive than that of the edicts of his dour adversaries, the barons. Gaveston's opening speeches evoke the worlds of beauty, art, and music, but particularly the world of theater:

> Music and poetry is his delight,
> Therefore I'll have Italian masques by night,
> Sweet speeches, comedies, and pleasing shows. (I,i,53–55).

But the theater is one of sexual ambiguity and homoerotic desire:

> And in the day when he shall walk abroad,
> Like sylvan nymphs my pages shall be clad
> My men like satyrs grazing on the lawns
> Shall with their goat feet dance an antic hay;
> Sometime a lovely boy in Dian's shape,
> With hair that gilds the water as it glides,
> Crownets of pearl about his naked arms,
> And in his sportful hands an olive tree
> To hide those parts which men delight to see. (I,i,56–64)

The "my" paints Gaveston as creator, producer, and director of an erotic spectacle in which, as in the Elizabethan theater, boys play women, but in which those boys are also erotic objects in themselves. Stephen Orgel summarizes the Elizabethan attacks on boy actors playing women: "Male spectators, it is argued, will be seduced by the impersonation, and, losing their reason, will become effeminate, which in this case means they will lust not after the woman in the drama, which would be bad enough, but after the boy beneath the woman's costume, thereby playing the woman's role themselves."[14] This, in essence, is what Gaveston intends his spectacle to do to Edward, to allow him to "draw the pliant" (that is, effeminate) king. Alan Bray rightly asks whose parts are those "men delight to see," Dian's or those of the boy actor playing her?[15]

Gaveston's speech establishes a central aspect of his relationship with, and attraction for, Edward. Gaveston is the spirit of theater which is attractive and dangerous. Bruce R. Smith warns: "The lovers' fascination with dressing up, with role-playing, with acting things out threatens to drain the world of substance and set up instead the infinite regressions of Ovid's *Metamorphoses*."[16]

Gaveston's motives are more Machiavellian than they are loving, but of all the characters, only Edward isn't a scheming pragmatist. Still, Gaveston's ornate language and richly erotic vision link him and Edward not only to art and pleasure but to a rich mythological past. This opulent vision could not be further from the matter-of-fact threats of Young Mortimer, the baron who is most militant in his demand that Edward renounce his beloved:

> Come uncle, let us leave the brain-sick king,
> And henceforth parley with our naked swords. (I,i,124–125)

Mortimer's language represents the norm of violently imposed order and brutality, which sees Gaveston in the typically gay role of agent of anarchy: "If you love us, my lord, hate Gaveston" (I,i,79). Simon Shepherd sees Mortimer's hatred of Edward's love for his minions as predicated on the Elizabethan concept of manliness that Edward transgresses not by loving a man but by his uneconomical emotional expenditure: "The ideology of manliness, or masculinity, inscribes the individual within interpersonal competition and denigrates emotion without action."[17] As Edward is in thrall to Gaveston's eloquence, he will become captive to Mortimer's manly action. Both are dangerous; Gaveston's opulent, eloquent shows of love have a sinister dimension that supports the barons' mistrust:

> It shall suffice me to enjoy your love,
> Which whiles I have I think myself as great
> As Caesar riding in the Roman street
> With captive kings at his triumphal car. (I,i,170–173)

Gaveston sees himself as Caesar; Edward is a "captive king." Edward sees Gaveston's performance as one of love—"he loves me more than all the world"—the play presents it much more skeptically.

It is not Gaveston but Young Spenser, his successor in Edward's affections, who is allowed to grow from pragmatist, interested only in his own advancement, to loyal lover. In Gerard Murphy's production, Gaveston was never more than a preening love object: there was no sign that he reciprocated Edward's love. Young Spenser is more complex. He is first seen in bed with his lover Baldock, a sign that homoerotic desire is more than show for this pretty young man, but his conversation is of favor and patronage:

> But he that hath the favour of a king
> May with one word advance us while we live. (II, i,8–9)

Spenser has read his Machiavelli, and he wants advancement for himself and his scholarly lover, but his youthful exuberance is no match for the mature resolve of the barons, who see Edward transferring his affections to a mere boy. Spenser, however, moves from teen-age Machiavellian pragmatist to the voicer of a glorious lament for his martyr king:

> Oh is he gone? is noble Edward gone?
> Parted from hence, never to see us more?
> Rent, sphere of heaven, and fire, forsake thy orb,
> Earth melt to air, gone is my sovereign,
> Gone, gone alas, never to make return. (IV, vi,99–103)

In a world of deceit, Spenser's eloquent lament is a brief moment of honest love. It contrasts with the false tears of Lightborn, the hired assassin, who seduces Edward for the last time. In Murphy's production, Lightborn's execution of Edward was indeed a seduction, the most graphic sexual moment in the play. Lightborn boasts as he prepares to meet the king:

> ne'er was there any
> So finely handled as this king shall be. (V,v,37–38)

Like Gaveston, Lightborn will "draw the pliant king which way I please," a deadly seduction that is a brutal perversion of the act it punishes.[18] Claude Summers observes:

> The "anal crucifixion" combines elements of sexual desire and violent "policy" into a horrible triumph of the will. In so doing, it forcefully juxtaposes the world of erotic freedom and sexual fulfillment represented by Edward's love for Gaveston and the symbolic world of power politics symbolized by the union of Mortimer and Isabella, whose love "hatcheth death and hate."[19]

To embrace his "minions" publicly is to inspire classical heterosexist imagery. In defending the king's youthful love for his minion, Old Mortimer presents homosexual desire not only as a quality that connects Edward to great figures from the past but also, paradoxically, as something he will outgrow: "For riper years will wean him from such toys" (I,iv,400). Young Mortimer evokes the virulent imagery of disease: Gaveston will be killed, "purging" the realm "of such a plague" (I,iv,270).

In the first English drama about a character who is what modern parlance would term a homosexual, that character is imprisoned in sewage, forced to shave in fouled water, and fatally sodomized with a hot poker. In the grand, grisly catalog of deaths in Elizabethan and Jacobean drama, Edward's execution is one of the most gruesome and humiliating, and Marlowe lingers on those final humiliations, not as justice for the petulant humiliations Edward caused others nor as punishment for insults of his beloved but to present his audience with a pathetic, if not tragic martyrdom:

> This dungeon where they keep me is the sink
> Wherein the filth of all the castle falls.
>
>   . . .
>
> And there in mire and puddle have I stood
> This ten days space, and lest that I should sleep,
> One plays continually on a drum;

> They give me bread and water being a king;
> So that for want of sleep and sustenance,
> My mind's distempered and my body's numbed,
> And whether I have limbs or no I know not. (V,v,55–56, 58–64)[20]

Edward's final scream of pain at the combination of rape and death blow is loud enough to "raise the town" (V,v,113).

Like later gay heroes, Edward is shown as a martyr to his own desire, which is presented as being more positive than any other human feeling in the play, except, perhaps, Young Spenser's imprudent devotion. Marlowe's graphic dramatization of Edward's suffering and death begins a pantheon of martyrs to homosexual love as it evokes a glorious history of heroic lovers. Edward is also an agent of disorder in a world where order is brutal, repressive, and unloving. When order is the enemy, anarchy is a just cause.

Admittedly, this is neither an old- nor a new-historical reading of *Edward II* but one that places the play in a canon of gay history plays that set erotic desire and imagination against official repression. What is at stake is not only homoerotic desire but the possibility of the theater of male love envisioned and voiced by Gaveston as a splendid alternative to the dour world of order and power. Edward, like many characters in gay history plays, is both martyr and traitor, but he is incapable of the imaginative liberation Gaveston represents or of the love and loyalty of Young Spenser.

Traitors

Edward II dramatizes the adversarial position of a man who chooses to live through his homosexual desire, which places him in opposition to the representatives of a repressive male authority. Edward's execution is the painful, humiliating punishment of a sodomite, an agent of disorder. Edward is the first gay martyr in drama, branded traitor and destroyed by the dominant society.

Hugh Whitemore's *Breaking the Code* (1986) dramatizes the life of Alan Turing, a British mathematician and pioneering genius in computers. Turing became a hero in World War II by breaking German military codes, in particular one code—created by a machine called Enigma—that the Nazi command used to communicate with its U-boats. Turing's service to his country did not prevent his being imprisoned, shot up with female hormones, and treated as a traitor when his homosexuality was discovered. In the play, when it becomes clear to the uncompromisingly honest Turing that he is an object of constant suspicion and scrutiny, he remarks to his superior:

> Day after day I came up with new ideas, new solutions—the Germans always seemed to be one step ahead of us. But I persevered, and—after years of exhaustive effort—the U-boat Enigma was finally broken. It took much more that mathematics and electronic ingenuity to do that. It needed determination, tenacity—moral fibre, if you like. That's what made it so deeply satisfying. You trusted me then. Why not now?[21]

Turing's sexual orientation made him a security risk, a potential traitor, able to enjoy intimacy and companionship only with young, working-class toughs. His mistreatment at the hands of the government he so ably served (and his subsequent suicide) make Turing another gay martyr, one who is included in Larry Kramer's gay pantheon.[22] Treason, like disease, both physical and mental, has been a controlling metaphor for gay men, but it can also contain the germ of an empowering metaphor. Freedom, and a sense of private revenge, can come from consciously playing out the role one is assigned, but such duplicity traps one in a constant performance. Treason is another closet in which the gay man has the illusion of control.

Both John Osborne's *A Patriot for Me* (1965), and Julian Mitchell's *Another Country* (1981), depict historical figures who chose to become traitors to the privileged societies that nurtured and empowered them but that, ultimately, marginalized them. The two plays focus on masculine societies—the military and the English boarding school—that both enforce and celebrate discipline; however, in these societies tension exists between the forces of order and those of anarchy. The ultimate threat to the discipline that tenuously holds the society together is the openly homosexual character, who is, or is perceived as being, the traitor whose behavior will undermine that society. As the person who threatens to bring into the open his society's hidden secret, he must be contained or destroyed. Yet the central characters of these plays have been raised and trained to want, above all else, positions of power in their societies. If treason is the only way to have power, then these men will embrace the role of traitor. Both *A Patriot for Me* and *Another Country* are as much critiques of the values of aristocratic male societies as they are depictions of the role of homosexuality in those societies. Ironically, as in *Edward II*, the homosexual traitor has more integrity than the supposedly principled men around him.

Osborne and Mitchell draw obvious parallels between their dramatic situations and the British spy and sex scandals of the fifties and sixties. Homosexuality and treason are seen in Osborne's play from the vantage point of 1960s Britain (two of Britain's most infamous spies, Guy Burgess and Anthony Blount, were homosexuals), and the parallels between Mitchell's Guy Bennett and British spy Guy Burgess are obvious.[23] For both writers, from different vantage points, the issue is the link between homosexual and traitor in a society that protects as well as punishes homosexuality.

A Patriot for Me and *Another Country* are separated by the degree of their authors' identification with the homosexual subject matter. Osborne's play was so daring in 1965 that, to avoid the wholesale cuts demanded by the Lord Chamberlain's office, the Royal Court had to be turned into a private club for the run of the play.[24] Yet, however important it was in opening up space for homosexual subject matter in the censored British theater, *A Patriot for Me* presents its homosexual hero from the point of view of a well-meaning but not totally convinced liberal. Its treatment of homosexuality is typical of that of mainstream drama. Mitchell's play, though a commercial success in the West End, is more like gay drama in that it presents its society through the eyes of its homosexual hero.

A Patriot for Me chronicles twenty-three years in the life of Alfred Redl, ostensibly one of the most promising, fast-rising *Wunderkinder* in the pre–World War I Austro-Hungarian army. Redl, though not an aristocrat, the usual prerequisite for speedy ascent in military circles, moves quickly to the top of Army Intelligence. Ironically, Redl's private life as a spy makes him prey to manipulation by Russian spies. Redl never resists being a traitor: as the title suggests, his real loyalty is not to his country, but to his own impulses.[25]

Osborne's play begins and ends with the linking of violent death, heterosexism, and anti-Semitism. In the first scene, Redl, a young lieutenant in the Galician infantry, is in a predawn conversation

with an extremely handsome fellow officer, August Siczynski. Redl
has agreed to be the young man's second in a duel with the
aristocratic von Kupfer, who has offered Siczynski the double insult
of calling him "Fraulein Rothschild," thus labeling him both Jew
and homosexual. It is for the latter insult that Siczynski has challenged von Kupfer.

The setting for this predawn dialogue between Redl and Siczynski is an army gymnasium, the cathedral for the masculine society
in which these officers live. Climbing bars, a thick rope, and a
vaulting horse define the scene. Yet within this space, Redl and his
comrade display, however cautiously, their attraction to one another. These are men with something to hide, yet they are open,
almost intimate, with each other, defining, again paradoxically, both
their need for such intimacy and their awareness of its impossibility:

> SICZYNSKI: What, what does one, do you suppose, well, look for in
> anyone, anyone else, I mean?
> REDL: For?
> SICZYNSKI: Elsewhere.
> REDL: I haven't tried. Or thought about it. At least . . .
> SICZYNSKI: I mean: That isn't clearly, really, clearly, already in oneself?
> REDL: Nothing, I expect.[26]

After this halting verbal exchange, the scene ends with two crucial,
contrasting physical images: the brutal duel between von Kupfer
and Siczynski and the final tableau of Redl cradling the dead Siczynski's body in his arms. By winning the duel, von Kupfer has done
his aristocratic duty of purging his world of Jew and homosexual.
Redl, unacknowledged Jew and homosexual, in cradling Siczynski
is embracing not only a body, one for which he had an unacknowledged attraction, but also a victim of the forces that will always
keep him an outsider. Moreover, his embrace demonstrates the
uncontrollable force of impulse that will always be at war with his
fierce sense of discipline. Redl will always embody both order and
anarchy.

In a real sense, Redl never leaves the gymnasium in which the
play opens. His world is defined by physicality, discipline, and
violence. It is a place with virtually no space for women, yet it
denies honest expressions of love between men. Redl is an almost

schizoid figure in this gymnasiumland. He is constantly described as the most disciplined of men, working all hours and achieving through ability and effort the rank and power that are usually the privilege of the aristocratic birth he was denied. His discipline is also a weapon in his battle against his own sexual impulses: "Tried everything, apparently. Resolution, vows, religion, medical advice, self-exhaustion. Used to flog a dozen horses into the ground a day. And then gardening, if you please, fencing, and all those studies they do, you do, of course—" (p. 82–83). Redl's success, then, is the result not only of ambition and excellence but also of repression of a strong sexual force; but it is homosexuality itself, in both its repression and its expression, that is most linked with violence as Redl moves, in the ten scenes of the first act, from repressed to practicing homosexual. That violence is chronicled in the two scenes that end the act. In the first, Redl attacks a young homosexual at a cafe who says to him, "I know what *you're* looking for," another version of the accusation Siczynski took as a challenge to his honor. Redl grabs the young man by the throat *"with ferocious power."* Yet in the next scene, Redl, after his first sexual experience, cries, "Why did I wait—so long?" But shortly thereafter, Redl is brutally beaten by four friends of his young sexual partner, who steals Redl's money and jewelry and who leaves with the advice, "Don't be too upset, love. You'll get used to it" (p. 67–69). Allowing the erotic dimension of one's feelings for men to emerge is moving from a world of brutal repression and power to one of brutal victimization.

Acting on erotic attraction also makes a person vulnerable to those who know information is power. As Redl spies, he is spied upon by the Russians and is blackmailed into being a double agent, a role he accepts because to do otherwise and be exposed as a homosexual would be to lose the only world in which he feels comfortable, not simply because of its known systems of reward and privilege but also because of the security of its all-male society. When he is ultimately, inevitably, exposed, he commits suicide, not as an acceptance of the strictures against his sexual behavior but for the same reasons he became a double agent: he could not live outside a military society.

Unlike Osborne's earlier central characters, Redl is an almost totally physical person, whose sexual appetite and violent nature lie close to the surface. Physicality is everything to Redl, and his love for young men is in part a connection to his lost physical youth. This also means that Redl's treason is unreflective. It is not a reasoned response to his place in society.

The principal question is what Redl's sexuality has to do with his being a spy, a master of "the treachery that leads to wars. The game" (p. 96). Osborne's answer is that the greatest outsider is the greatest traitor. It is not just that Redl is homosexual—so are many of his comrades. Nor that he hides his Jewish blood—so do many others. But, in addition, Redl has had to master a class system that did not privilege him and will not protect the outsider who made it by will and talent, not by birth. Yet the goal of Redl's life is the creation of a space for the expression of his homosexual desire, which he achieves but with greater and greater indiscretion. Redl has no loyalty to country or class, but he is loyal to his own impulses and to his world—the military, in which those impulses are both repressed and condoned in ways familiar to him.

Redl the outsider is constantly at war. His conflicts with the aristocracy are seen in the vicissitudes of Redl's friendship with von Kupfer, who killed Siczynski but who becomes Redl's aide and protector, lives in Redl's quarters, and wants to be Redl's friend and lover. Redl frames him as a spy (he knows too much). Redl's sexual battles are revealed in the partners he chooses, who are either whores or opportunists. Ultimately it is an old friend who exposes his spying and gives him the pistol.

The old baron, who hosts a spectacular drag ball, a travesty of Viennese aristocratic life, says: "This is the celebration of the individual against the rest, the us's and the them's, the free and the constricted." (p. 77). Osborne takes great pains to make this drag ball, which opens the second act, as realistic as possible (by means of a two-page footnote), and he understands that the contrast between this festivity and the stodgy, aristocratic ball of act 1 defines the attractiveness of the ironic and richly theatrical gay subculture. In the same way, the contrast between Gaveston's language and Mortimer's defines the seductive attractiveness of homoeroticism in *Edward II*. It is only within this splendid, make-believe world that, we are told, Redl can "be himself for once" (p. 83), but Redl finds no more than temporary and partial freedom at this gathering. He remains in uniform, becomes his old, repressed self when confronted by von Kupfer, and leaves after violently attacking an effeminate young man with whom he had joked earlier. The ball makes clear, as Arnold P. Hinchcliffe puts it, that "neither style—Hofburg nor drag—suits him."[27]

A Patriot for Me shows Redl's suicide, like the earlier duel, as a secretly sanctioned means for society to dispense with its uncontrollable elements. In taking his own life, Redl allows his world to rewrite his history in order to control its image. His homosexuality is erased while his Jewish blood, heretofore secret, is published. The homosexuality that seems an inevitable corollary of the hypermasculinity of Redl's world remains the privileged secret of that world.

Yet, with characteristic confusion, Osborne does not see Redl's death as a martyrdom for his sexuality but as the inevitable self-destruction of another Osborne outsider. In A Patriot for Me, as in his previous plays, Look Back In Anger (1956, pub. 1957) and Inadmissable Evidence (1964), Osborne gives mixed signals in his depiction of the homosexual. Homosexuality is Redl's badge of status as outsider-victim, yet it is also a measure of the decadence of his society. Nor can the playwright resist throwing an anachronistic attack on gay liberation into the play: "God, I'm weary of your self-righteousness and all your superior railing and your glib cant about friendship and the army and the way you roll out your little parade: Michelangelo and Socrates, and Alexander and Leonardo. God, you're like a guild of housewives pointing out Catherine the Great" (p. 101–102). Since no one in the play has uttered the "cant" the Countess attacks, the speech seems wildly out of place, unless Osborne is offering a rejoinder to anyone who thinks he is promoting a positive view of homosexuality.

No such mixed signals exist in Julian Mitchell's Another Country (1981), which is also about how the brutality and hypocrisy of a closed, privileged, masculine society, when turned against a homosexual member of that society, creates a traitor. The society in question is the English public school, the training ground for the power elite. Militarism, fake piety, and anti-intellectualism are the hallmarks of this corrupt training ground. The time is the mid-1930s: the Depression is on and Europe is moving toward a world war, but Gascoigne School operates as it always has, oblivious to the movements of history.

We discover volumes about the mores of the young men at Gascoigne School through the suicide of one of them, Martineau, who hangs himself from the chapel bell tower. Martineau was caught with his pants down, literally, in the school darkroom. Reactions to his death are the litmus paper by which we judge the values of the students at Gascoigne's. For most of the select group of young men who run the house, the Prefects, Martineau would have been alive if a teacher hadn't interfered in something that wasn't his business: "If you ask me, it all comes of having masters who aren't old boys. . . . An old boy would have had more sense than to go prowling around Phot. Soc. Dark Room in the evenings."[28] The students have their own code of morality and discipline, and in their eyes, the real crime is "letting themselves be caught" (p. 24). The punishment is flogging with a cane, which is both the infliction of physical pain and a public humiliation. It is punishment and containment of the school's guilty secret, which is rampant homosexual activity.

Another Country is about the subtle and the violent marginalization of outsiders—the believer, the Communist, and the homosexual—who threaten the system of appearances the school upholds. The students are united in scheming to keep the absolutist, Fowler, from attaining authority because he believes in the principles underlying the school's code of discipline. He believes in right and wrong, rather than in the appearance of right and wrong. His view of Martineau's transgression has the simplicity of the extreme conservative, "Immorality is immorality" (p. 24), but his belief in his code blinds him to the fact that his peers use the code to hide their own sexual activity. If there is an investigation into sexual activity at Gascoigne's, it will affect the students' future in the world of power to which they aspire.

Tommy Judd, the Communist, believes that the system represented at Gascoigne's must be overthrown by world revolution. Like Fowler, he has strong principles, but Tommy sees no way for the present system to be honorable. Both Fowler and Tommy Judd can be, and are, defused without violence because their idealism validates the system in which they are placed. As long as they don't have enough power to upset the old order, there is a place for the absolutist and the intellectual revolutionary. But Guy Bennett, the homosexual, is dangerous and must be dealt with violently.

Guy is the only character who understands what Martineau's death means: "Martineau wasn't a hypocrite. That's why he did it [committed suicide]. This ghastly school persuaded him its footling, meaningless rules actually stood for something real. Moral principles! Rules of life!" (p. 34). Guy understands that the system is a game, yet he aspires to be one of the winners. He wants his place high in the Foreign Service. Yet he is aware that, unlike so many men for whom homosexual activity is merely the only sexual release in an all-male society, he, like Martineau, is compelled to *love* another man. This, for him, explains the discovery of Martineau with Robbins in the darkroom:

> For Robbins it was just a game. Assignation—excitement—hands fumbling with buttons in the dark—all perfectly normal! School practice! But then poor Martineau—he went and told him [he loved him]. And Robbins was revolted—disgusted. He shoved him away. *That's* not what he'd come for! And Martineau knocked something over and Knickers came in to see what was happening and—(p. 96)

It was not just another instance of sex, but Robbins' violent response to Martineau's confession of love, ironically, that got them caught. Gay history dramas typically posit love, not sex, as the forbidden, dangerous impulse.[29] Martineau, through suicide, saved himself from a life of humiliation and verbal violence: "Think of that for a lifetime. Think of the names. Pansy. Nancy. Fairy. Fruit. Brown nose" (p. 96). The violence of heterosexist language is, for Guy, more bitter, more enduring, than the violence of caning.

Guy Bennett is in love, as Martineau was, with a boy from another house, and it is the mixture of real love with homosexual activity that brands him as an outcast. More practically, engaging in sexual activity with a boy from another house is seen as the worst of crimes because it increases the possibility of scandal, and containment of scandal is the primary objective of this society.[30] Guy is able to stave off a caning by playing on his peers' worst fear: "I just thought you'd like to know—if one stroke of Fowler's cane lands on my arse, I shall go straight to Farcical [the Master] and tell him the names of everyone I've done it with over the last three years" (p. 86). When Fowler discovers a love letter, Guy must be punished to maintain appearances; he receives the requisite brutal caning and loses his chance for a position of authority in the house. He is punished and contained. Guy's response is to vow to become a traitor. When his friend Tommy Judd tells him, "Either you accept the system, or you try to change it," Guy responds: "Why not both? Pretend to do one while you really do the other. Fool the swine! Play along with them! Let them think what they like—let them despise you! But all the time—" (p. 99). The homosexual will become a double agent, accommodating to society while subverting it. For Guy, treason is revenge against a society that despises him, a form of passive aggression. Martineau committed suicide not because he was discovered but because he knew he was really homosexual and would, as Bennett puts it, "face a lifetime of *that*," "that" being hatred and punishment. Guy Bennett admits to his idealistic, Communist friend that he prefers love to justice. *Another Country* laments the necessity to make a choice between the two.

War

David Rabe's *Streamers* (1976), is the American counterpart to Osborne's and Mitchell's plays about the homosexual in an all-male society. Like *A Patriot for Me,* it is not written from the point of view of the homosexual character but uses the homosexual as a type, an outsider who is allowed provisional space in his environment. *Streamers* powerfully dramatizes the problems of acting gay in a heterosexist community. It is 1967, early in the Vietnam War, a year of racial unrest in Newark and other American ghettos. The Stonewall riots are still two years away. Set in an army barracks that is a way station between American society and the chaos of Vietnam, *Streamers* connects homosexuality to a network of related issues—racism, male bonding, role-playing in a male-dominated society, and the forces causing the Vietnam War. Homosexuality is not a secret to be maintained and contained as it is in the Austro-Hungarian army or the British public school. Attempts to deny the homosexual a place in this fortress of American middle-class values ultimately fail.

The barracks Rabe shows us is a peculiar one containing only four young men whose position in the army (and in American society) has allowed them special status. One is a college-educated "All American Boy" from Wisconsin, another an assimilated black, a third a wealthy urban homosexual who, of course, can't be fully labeled until he stops "playing straight" (the fourth disappears from the scene early in the play). The false appearance of uniformity in the army allows these men to live together as if their differences don't exist. Billy, a college graduate from Wisconsin, falsely claims to be a school drop-out and affects a kind of "street talk" to erase his differences with Roger, who has learned to play the kind of assimilated black who does not endanger whites. Richie, the homosexual, has declared his place among heterosexuals by taping a female pin-up to the inside of his locker door. "Acting" is the operative term for the behavior of all these young men, and acting means finding a common language that denies any differences.

All the young men in the barracks are suffering from some form of pre-Vietnam anxiety that will foreground their real identity and propel the action toward violence. As the play begins, one of them, Martin, has slashed his wrists, an act that will lead to his discharge from the army. The remaining men manifest their anxiety in less overtly self-destructive ways. Roger has been to the camp psychiatrist because of tension headaches, Billy feels "sick-like,"[31] and Richie has moved from hiding his homosexuality under a common language and a *Playboy* pin-up to aggressively performing his difference: "ever since we been in this room, he's been different somehow" (p. 16).

Though Billy's first action in the play, symbolically, is to bring Richie a piece of American pie, Richie's performance of his homosexuality moves him outside the male bond that has been formed between Billy and Roger, a bond Richie sees as phony. When Billy slips and uses a four-syllable word, Richie shows that he is "on to" Billy's affectations: " 'Obliterate,' did you say? Oh, Billy, you better say "shit," "ain't" and "motherfucker" real quick now or we'll all know just how far beyond the fourth grade you went" (p. 14). The gay man, used to playing a role himself, is particularly sensitive to others' role-playing.

What Billy and Roger share, beyond fear of their impending duty in Vietnam and a series of common rituals to overcome that fear (push-ups, cleaning the barracks), is heterosexism. Richie's behavior inspires in Billy and Roger a number of manifestations of their prejudice and hostility. Roger vehemently denies Richie's homosexuality in the face of Richie's protestations:

ROGER: You ain't sayin' you really done that stuff, though, Rich.
RICHIE: What?
ROGER: That fag stuff.
RICHIE: (*He continues looking at Roger and then he looks away.*) Yes.
ROGER: Do you even know what you're sayin', Richie? Do you even know what it means to be a fag?
RICHIE: Roger, of course I know what it is. I just told you I've done it. I thought you Black people were supposed to understand all about suffering and human strangeness. I thought you had depth and vision from all your suffering. Has someone been misleading me? I just told you I did it. I know all about it. Everything. All the various positions.
ROGER: Yeh, so maybe you think you've tried it, but that don't make you it. (p. 28–29)

Roger's denial finally dismisses any protestation from Richie: "Ohhh, ohhh, you ain't no screamin' goddamn faggot, Richie, no matter what you say" (p. 29), before proceeding to vivid descriptions of fag-bashing in his neighborhood.

Richie's adolescent boastfulness about his homosexuality ("I know all about it. Everything. All the various positions") is a means of asserting himself in an alienating environment. Billy finds it necessary to respond with moral outrage. His attitude toward homosexuality is manifested in a long story he tells Roger, within Richie's earshot, about how he and his friends used to take advantage of homosexual men:

So we'd let these cats pick us up, most of 'em old guys, and they were hurtin' and happy as hell to have us, and we'd get a lot of free booze, maybe a meal, and we'd turn 'em on. Then pretty soon they'd ask us did we want to go over to their place. Sure, we'd say, and order one more drink, and then when we'd hit the street, we'd tell 'em to kiss off. We'd call 'em fag and queer and jazz like that and tell 'em to kiss off. (p. 48)

One of Billy's gang began going home with the men who picked him up and eventually admitted that he was a homosexual. For Billy, his friend Frankie's homosexuality was an addiction Frankie could have avoided by not succumbing in the first place: "He had got his ass hooked. He had never thought he would and then one day he woke up and he was on it. He just hadn't been told, that's the way I figure it" (p. 49). Billy's story, the moral of which is "Just say no," is meant to be a cautionary one for Richie, as if he is making sure that Richie, unlike poor Frankie, is told what he needs to be told to avoid being a "fag." As Billy misunderstands homosexuality and Richie, Richie, who has a crush on Billy, misreads Billy's story: "Well, was it . . . about you? (*Pause*) I mean, was it ABOUT you? Were you Frankie?" (p. 71). Billy rightly responds: "You didn't hear me at all!" (p. 71).

Out of a desperate need to assert his confused sense of himself, and out of a genuine attraction for Billy, Richie unconsciously performs what amounts to a parody of Roger and Billy's stereotypical "faggot." The underwear-clad Richie jumps on to Billy's bunk and lies next to him:

RICHIE: And what time will you pick me up?
BILLY: (*He pushes at* RICHIE, *knocking him off the bed and onto the floor.*) Well, you just fall down and wait, all right?
RICHIE: Can I help it if I love you? (p. 14–15)

Richie is not only *being* gay, he is *acting* gay with a vengeance, and in doing so acting what disturbs Billy most about "queers"—their unwillingness to believe he isn't one of them: "So you tell 'em you're straight and they just nod and smile. You ain't real to 'em. They can't see nothin' but themselves and these goddamn games they're always playin' " (p. 17). Billy assumes a reality, which is, of course, straight, and sees gay behavior as narcissistic game-playing, and the presumption that he might be gay as "lookin' out and seein' yourself" (p. 27). Billy's responses to Richie mount from nasty attacks, "you go up and down like a Yo-Yo and you go blowin' all the trees like the wind" (p. 25), to threats of rejection that he presents as "straight talk," "If you don't cut the cute shit with me, I'm gonna turn you off. Completely" (p. 27). Like Brick in *Cat on a Hot Tin*

Roof, Billy has the power to "hang up" on Richie—to deny him any recognition at all.

But Richie's character is built from traditional stereotypes. Even his powdering ritual after showering smacks of effeminacy, as does his half-mocking claim that he's "so pretty." Richie is also the most affluent of the men, as if homosexuality were, as it seemed to be in *The Green Bay Tree*, linked to the corruption of wealth: "But I've just done what I wanted all of my life" (p. 28). Julian Dulcimer joins the army! It is not clear why Richie, who reads film critic Pauline Kael in his free time, has enlisted in the army (all three occupants of the barracks have enlisted), though Roger may be right in assuming that Richie joined the army to "get away from" his homosexual past: "And now you're gettin' a chance to run with the boys a little, you'll get yourself straightened around" (p. 35)—if the boys will teach Richie how to act straight and if Richie can keep up the act!

Into this tense situation comes Carlyle, a frightened ghetto black. As Richie's effeminacy, sexual aggressiveness, and air of superiority are homosexual stereotypes that force a response from straight men, so Carlyle's volatility and hostile language evoke the stereotypical black man white men fear most. Carlyle comes into the barracks to meet another black man, but whites like Richie and Billy are alien and frightening to him. Carlyle catches Roger staring at Billy's pin-up (Roger is trying to figure out whether Richie is what he claims to be), and Roger, to counter Carlyle's accusations of his being attracted to white women, proclaims, "This here the locker of a faggot" (p. 18), leading Carlyle to misread the dynamic among Richie, Billy, and Roger as a kind of sexual ménage he might be able to join: "You and Roger are hittin' on Richie, right? . . . I'd like to get some of him myself if he a good punk" (p. 68). Billy's response, interestingly enough, is not to protest his own "straight-ness," but to defend Richie's: "He's not queer, if that's what you're sayin.' A little effeminate, but that's all, no more, if that's what you're sayin" (p. 68). Billy's denial is a means of protecting the central myth of an all-male society: it contains no homosexuals.

Later in the evening, after a lot of drinking, Richie and Carlyle ask Roger and Billy to leave the barracks so that they can have sex.

Richie wants to make Billy jealous; Carlyle just "wants his nut" and wants to feel part of this group. Roger reads Richie's motivation in purely racial terms: "Richie one a those people want to get fucked by niggers, man. It what he know was gonna happen all his life— can be his dream come true. . . . Want to make it real in the world how a nigger is an animal" (p. 84), but he won't endanger himself by taking a stand on what is happening in his barracks. He tells Billy: "Get up in the rack, turn your back and look at the wall" (p. 82). Billy, however, is impelled to impose his white, heterosexist values and sense of territory: "It ain't gonna be done in my house. I don't have much in this goddamn army, but *here* is mine" (p. 84). Richie misreads Billy's stand as an expression of his latent homosexuality ("Jealous, Billy?"), but Carlyle, in fury and frustration, cuts Billy's hand, and Billy, in retaliation, turns on Carlyle with a straight razor—demonstrating that he too can be irrational, violent. Instead of attacking with the razor, Billy flings it aside and attacks with words that assert his superiority: "I put you down, I put you down—you gay little piece of shit cake—SHIT CAKE, AND YOU— you are your own goddamn fault, SAMBO! SAMBO!" (p. 88). Carlyle responds by stabbing Billy fatally, thus silencing the voice of white, heterosexist middle America.

After Billy's body has been carried out, Carlyle arrested for Billy's death, and a drunken sergeant killed while trying to attack Carlyle, Roger, the assimilated black, and Richie deny any responsibility for what happened. The violence has not taught the survivors anything: Roger still denies that Richie told him he was homosexual, and Richie still insists that Billy returned his feelings:

RICHIE: I've been telling you. I did.
ROGER: Jive, man, jive!
RICHIE: No!
ROGER: You did bullshit all over us! ALL OVER US!
RICHIE: I just wanted to hold his hand, Billy's hand, to talk to him, go to the movies hand in hand like he would with a girl or I would with someone back home.
ROGER: But he didn't wanna; *he* didn't wanna.
RICHIE: He did.
ROGER: No, man.
RICHIE: He did, he did. It's not my fault. (p. 102–103)

Roger claims to understand Richie, but at the end he can only call Richie "a queer." The only compassion comes from a drunken sergeant who has been told he's dying of leukemia: "There's a lotta worse things in this world than bein' a queer. I seen a lot of 'em, too" (p. 107).

Rabe uses Richie to dramatize sex as the great destroyer of the male bond. Whites and blacks can get along as long as a common language can be found, but homosexuality is taboo. The history of oppression of blacks has not made them sympathetic toward homosexuals.

At the end of the play, Richie lies on his bunk weeping, though he does not understand why he is unhappy: "I don't know what's hurtin' in me" (p. 107). Richie is unable to put a name on his pain—is it pain at being homosexual? at being rejected? at seeing a love object die? at awareness at some level of his complicity in that death? or is it confusion in the face of the meaningless violence he has seen?

In the hermetic, all-male world of *Streamers,* the homosexual, the object of irrational fear and hatred, becomes a symbol of the chaotic, hostile forces men unleash on one another. In Rabe's world, the homosexual is neither innocent victim nor traitor, but, like everyone else, he is sealed in a world of misunderstanding. The homosexual, not the representative of white, heterosexist values, survives, but it is 1967, and he has not yet found his own society or waged his own war.

Resistance

Noel Greig and Drew Griffiths' *As Time Goes By* (1977), Martin Sherman's *Bent* (1979), and Doric Wilson's *Street Theater* (1982) move their gay characters from acquiescence of their status as outsiders or criminals to militant assertion of their gay identity, the beginning of gay liberation. The characters for the most part are fictional, but the settings and situations are evocations of crucial moments in gay history. In *As Time Goes By,* Victorian Englishmen flee to France to escape imprisonment in the wake of the Oscar Wilde scandal, and young Germans in 1934 try to flee Nazi Germany to avoid imprisonment and death. Among the English characters, Edward Carpenter provides a counterpoint of idealism and courage in the 1890s, and Magnus Hirschfield provides a model for self-acceptance for German homosexuals, but the fictional characters are not ready to live the example of their real prototypes. *Bent* focuses again on gay men in Nazi Germany, which has become a real historical site and a metaphor for oppression of gays, as the pink triangle worn by gay prisoners in concentration camps has become a symbol of gay identity and resistance. The Stonewall riot, which provides the finale for *As Time Goes By*, is the subject of Doric Wilson's *Street Theater*, a satire of closeted gays and a celebration of a central moment in modern gay history. Within these historical moments, the most positive act is the rejection of oppression from without and within and, in Richard Hall's words, "choosing sides": "Gay theater will bear witness to some sense of community, to a shared experience of choosing sides, that is a central fact of gay life. Events onstage will be joined somehow to our choices offstage. 'Us' under the spotlight will be different from 'them.' "[32] In all three plays, we watch characters move from seeing themselves as "them," the outsiders and criminals that society sees, to asserting an "us," a positive identity.

In a homosexual brothel in London in 1896, the brothel keeper begins his presentation of his stable of young men to an audience of noblemen by quoting Gaveston's speech from the first scene of *Edward II*. The young men, clad in Greek costumes, quote poetry by Edward Carpenter. Thus begins Noel Greig and Drew Griffiths' history play, *As Time Goes By*, an example of historical gay drama fulfilling its traditional function of education and assertion of a gay culture. The play creates a catalog of literary and historical personages and events, as the action moves from Victorian England to Nazi Germany to Stonewall, through Oscar Wilde and Edward Carpenter, through Magnus Hirschfield and Cole Porter and Ernst Rohm, to a number of 1969 gay types, in order to show that the history of gay liberation did not begin on Christopher Street in 1969. The play also, through its choice of events, defines what are seen as three key symbolic events in the one hundred years of pre-AIDS gay history: Oscar Wilde's trial, the Nazi purge, and Stonewall. Within this framework Greig and Griffiths' reading of history shows that love relationships are only possible for those willing to be "out" and opposed to capitalism, which bases all relationships on money and ownership.

Each of the major episodes of *As Time Goes By* takes place in a setting that is both a gay meeting ground and a symbol of economic exploitation—an 1896 London brothel in which poor boys are kept to amuse wealthy noblemen, a gay nightclub in Berlin in 1929, a Mafia-owned gay bar in New York—and each episode contrasts those who accept the status quo with the revolutionaries of the time.

As the wealthy Londoners are endangered by a police raid on their favorite brothel, Edward Carpenter and his working-class lover have found their "Uranian [the favored term of many nineteenth-century writers, for homosexuality] Utopia." The wealth of the Londoners allows them to support the system that oppresses them and, in the process, to oppress the boys they buy for sex. Greig and Griffiths scathingly satirize the point of view of the wealthy closet queens as they sail to France to avoid imprisonment:

> TREVELYAN: I agree with Oscar Wilde and his socialist friends, but I'll certainly not fight alongside them for my sexual rights, because I can afford to pay for them.
>
> REGINALD: Yes, at two sovereigns a time.
>
> TREVELYAN: And worth every farthing. Lovely boys. Now who can say we corrupted them.
>
> REGINALD: For goodness sake, we bought them.
>
> TREVELYAN: They were poor, they needed to earn a living. Some of them probably did it just for the cash, but I'm certain that if they'd means of their own they wouldn't be out courtin' the girls. No, they'd be throwing their legs up in the air just the same, but for other young boys. They'd all be running off to set up house together. How dull for us. We'd only have each other.[33]

In the second part, Greig and Griffiths present Berlin from 1929 to 1934 as an object lesson in the price of remaining apolitical by contrasting the courage of Magnus Hirschfield with the blindness of the typical bar queen. The central event is the destruction of Hirschfield's Institute of Sexual Science and the collapse of Hirschfield's gay movement, not because of the Nazis but because of the indifference of gays: "No, what we've got to do is stick together and make a cozy little nest for ourselves, and let the rest of the world go by"

(p. 50). The gay men of Berlin have no allies on the left or the right. As a friend tells Hirschfield: "The left supported you for the same reasons the Nazis are attacking your work. Power" (p. 47). At the end of the Berlin sequence, it is 1934 and everyone is fleeing for his life.

For Greig and Griffiths, Stonewall is a new chapter of a continuing saga, a chapter of unity and courage. The sequence is made up of monologues, signifying a fragmented community, until the denizens of the bar—a disaffected student, a drag queen mourning the death of Judy Garland, and a businessman who has lost his black lover to separatist politics—join to fight the police. Finally gay men refuse to flee and stay to fight those who would deny them a place.

The Stonewall scene acknowledges the importance of the rebellion to gay liberation in England and Europe. In Philip Osment's poignant panorama of English gay life in the eighties, *This Island's Mine,* a character remembers:

> Then came the rumours from New York
> Of riots in Greenwich Village,
> And a new sort of Pride was born
> Which quickly spread to Europe.[34]

The birth of that pride comes, in *As Time Goes By,* with a simple, definite "No!" shouted to a policeman.

The spirit of Marlowe's Gaveston lives: *As Time Goes By* celebrates the opulence and playfulness of gay culture through musical numbers and parodies. From the Greek extravaganza at the brothel to the Berlin nightclub show to the drag queen's lament for Judy Garland, the play displays the theatricality of gay life. In a typical gay cultural gesture, the play ends by appropriating the song "As Time Goes By" as a gay hymn: "A kiss is just a kiss/ A sigh is just a sigh,/ The fundamental things apply,/ As Time Goes By" (p. 70).

As Time Goes By was written by and for the gay community, providing a celebration of "oppression, resistance, survival, and heroic making." It counsels courage as a way of life for the gay man—for only in declaring himself and fighting his oppressors will he be free—and urges solidarity for a community united to affirm and protect itself. The play's heroes, from the celebrated Edward

Carpenter and Magnus Hirschfield to the ordinary denizens of Christopher Street, provide examples of courage.

Martin Sherman's *Bent* (1979) uses the Nazi period to frame a more specific agenda. Through presenting a harrowing picture of oppression from without and within, *Bent*, as a mainstream gay play, also calls for assimilation through assertion of conventional values. Max, the leading character, progresses from absorption in a negative version of the "gay lifestyle"—promiscuity, drugs, and the inability to embrace a love relationship fully—to an education in love for another man. The Holocaust provides a background of brutal oppression, but the real issue of the play is self-oppression, as manifested in behavior that would be considered typical for urban gay men in 1979. The opening of *Bent* is purposely ambiguous about its time period. We are warned to see homophobia, or heterosexism, as a constant possibility, but we are also encouraged to see Max's education in love as a gay *Pilgrim's Progress*.

At the beginning of *Bent,* Max is a rather unsettled thirty-four-year-old who shares a sparsely furnished apartment with his lover, Rudy, a dancer in a drag show. Max and Rudy's relationship is fashionably "open," though Rudy does not share Max's penchant for bringing home lovers for him and Max to share, nor for his flirtation with sadomasochism: "I know pain is very chic just now, but I don't like it, 'cause pain hurts."[35] References to cocaine, ménages à trois, and fashionable S&M activities underscore the parallels between 1934 Berlin and pre-AIDS urban gay life. However, a knock at the door brings Nazi soldiers, who kill the young SA officer Max had brought home the night before. Max and Rudy are forced to run for their lives. It is the morning after the Night of the Long Knives, and its aftermath will reinforce the lesson in self-oppression Max learned years before when his father fired a young worker Max loved: "Queers aren't meant to love" (p. 132).

After the Nazi invasion of the stage at the end of the first scene, the remaining short scenes of act 1 trace the two years from Max's flight to his arrival in Dachau and show Max's growing denial of his own sexuality, as a strategy for staying alive. In one scene, Greta, the opportunistic drag queen who employed Max and Rudy, denies his gayness, too: "Everyone knows I'm not queer. I got a wife and kids" (p. 93). Denial is survival.

In another scene, Uncle Freddie, a middle-aged closet queen who has maintained the proper image while secretly being a "fluff," comes to tell Max that his family will help him escape from Germany but will do nothing for Rudy, with whom Max has spent more than a year in hiding (living in tent colonies and in the forest), while Max tried to "swing a deal" to get them out of Germany. Max knows that to win the cooperation of his family, he will have to play by their rules: "Remember that marriage Father wanted to arrange. . . . Make the arrangements again. I'll marry her. Our button factories can sleep with her button factories. . . . If I want a boy, I'll rent him. Like you. I'll be a discreet, quiet . . . fluff. It's what Father always wanted" (p. 97). Neither Max nor Uncle Freddie is aware that "decent, quiet fluffs" are also an endangered species.

Although he gives up his family's offer of escape because he is committed to protecting Rudy, who is neither strong nor particularly bright, Max cannot admit to loving him: "What's love? Bullshit. I'm grown up now. I just feel responsible" (p. 97). Later, in a brief moment of happiness, Max and Rudy hold hands by the campfire in their forest hideout: a searchlight is turned on and they are immediately arrested. Max's edict, "Queers aren't meant to love," is again reinforced on the train to Dachau, when Max, in order to survive, must not only deny his relationship to Rudy—"If you want to stay alive, he cannot exist" (p. 105)—but also deal the deathblow to his lover.

Max must further betray his dignity and self-respect to prove he isn't "bent" by performing an act of necrophilia with an adolescent Jewish girl. Thus Max earns a yellow star—the badge of the Jew—rather than a pink triangle—the badge for the bottom of the Dachau pecking order in 1936—but in the process loses what remains of his self-respect: "You mustn't touch me. I'm a rotten person" (p. 112). By the end of the first act, Max is a picture of shame and self-hatred.

The short scenes that compose the second act are devoted to Max's reeducation by Horst, a young political activist who is a well-drawn version of a conventional character in gay drama and film: the proud gay who is the teacher, foil, and lover of the ambivalent hero (Saul in *As Is*, Felix in *The Normal Heart*, Peter in *An Early Frost* are other examples). During act 2, as Max and Horst perform the maddening task of moving rocks from one pile to another and back again, Horst teaches Max that to do more than survive, "You should be proud of *something*" (p. 118). The basis of that pride is the love Max has long forbidden himself. Because Max and Horst are not allowed to touch each other, or even look at each other, their relationship must progress solely through language, thus presenting an ironic reversal: usually it is not sex gay men are denied by a heterosexist society but the right to speak openly of their desire, the right to express their love.

For Max, speaking of sex is one thing, but love is alien territory. When Horst proclaims his love, Max can respond only with self-hatred: "Hate me. That's better. Hate me. Don't love me" (p. 132). Horst counters by asserting the telling difference between him and Max: "I love myself. Poor you, you don't love anybody" (p. 133). Horst also echoes Rudy in his rejection of Max's need to inflict pain as part of sex: "You don't make love to hurt" (p. 137), and he forces Max to enter the alien territory of real emotional intimacy signified by a loving, nonsexual embrace, even though this embrace must be in word, not in deed. Tenderness replaces rough sex and love replaces self-hatred, but in this world of oppression, Max's first real physical embrace of Horst comes after Horst has been fatally shot: "I love you. What's wrong with that? What's wrong with that?" (p. 147).

Horst dies running toward the soldier who is harassing him. His death is an act of defiance and resistance. Max puts on Horst's jacket, thus exchanging yellow star for pink triangle, and walks into the electrically charged fence. His suicide, too, is an act of resistance. He dies a proud, gay man. His identity has been forged and is proudly asserted. Dachau allows no riot against authority, but a man can assert his identity and choose his death. Shortly before he dies, Horst affirms a central lesson of gay history: "Well . . . what the hell. There are queer Nazis. And queer saints. And queer mediocrities. Just people. I really believe that. That's why I signed Hirschfield's petition. That's why I ended up here. That's why I'm wearing this triangle. That's why you should be wearing it" (p. 141).

For all its grim subject matter, *Bent,* like *As Time Goes By,* celebrates theatricality, from the song of the Berlin drag queen to the

celebrated verbal sex scenes, to the unabashedly melodramatic ending. Moreover, it never loses its sense of the ironic humor that
enables its characters to endure.

As both *As Time Goes By* and *Bent* use Nazi Germany as a
metaphor for gay oppression, both *As Time Goes By* and Doric
Wilson's *Street Theater* (1982) present the Stonewall riot as the
beginning of gay liberation and a true gay community. *Street Theater*
is also an exemplar of inside gay drama, written by a gay playwright
for gay audiences and performed, for part of its New York run, at
The Mineshaft, a Greenwich Village sex-on-premises leather bar.
During its run at The Mineshaft, *Street Theater* was being performed
not in some theater removed from the life of its audience but
literally within the gay male community, a kind of indoor street
theater. Jack, the leatherman who is one of the play's principal
characters, could have been one of The Mineshaft's regular custom-
ers. The bar itself, with its leather costumes, S&M trappings, and
the performance of sex as theater, showcased those theatrical aspects of gay life that the play celebrates.

Wilson's play seems to stem from a comment by playwright
William M. Hoffman, "The Stonewall Riots of 1969 might be viewed
as gay street theater,"[36] for *Street Theater* is a memorial to Stonewall
and also a celebration of the theater of gay life, presenting a catalog
of pre-Stonewall gay types: the catty drag queen, the leatherman,
the kid from the Midwest, the diesel dyke, student radicals, and
young and old closet queens—including Michael and Donald from
Mart Crowley's play, *The Boys in the Band* (1968), which was still
presenting a picture of gay self-hatred when the Stonewall riot took
place. It also presents caricatures of gays' adversaries: the under-
cover police who relish the assignment of entrapping gays and the
mafia-connected gay bar owner.

Street Theater begins with the voice of Murfino, the "cigar in the
mouth slob" who runs the Stonewall Inn for his "partners in New
Jersey."[37] Murfino sees himself as the narrating stage manager of
Thornton Wilder's *Our Town* (1938), which he acknowledges was
written by someone "of your lavender leaning" (p. 8), but the
allusions to *Our Town* only distance Wilson's play from that idealized picture of small-town life written by a closeted homosexual.
Nor will the stage of this uncloseted extravaganza remain bare, as it

does in *Our Town*. A diesel dyke and leatherman bring on scenery that colorfully depicts the Christopher Street of June 1969, and Murfino's voice is eventually drowned out by the voices of gay people.

The principal action of the play is the creation and mobilization of a gay community, which at the beginning seems a ludicrous fantasy: "You couldn't find two faggots who agree on the recipe for cheese fondue" (p. 28). In the first act, Wilson presents, in a series of comic confrontations and unsuccessful assignations, caricatures of the self-hatred that divides the community, most fully personified in Sidney, a middle-aged closet queen who revels in the masochism of unfulfilling relationships: "My dear man, you underestimate my capacity for self-destruction. When the wrong man comes along, I'll know him" (p. 45). Sidney is an older version of Michael and Donald, who, like their namesakes in *The Boys in the Band,* are victims of psychoanalysis: "You have no idea how good I feel about how bad I feel" (p. 22).

The climax of the second act is the Stonewall riot. At the end of the play, Sidney gives up the closet and joins the gays who are rebelling against police harassment. Only Michael and Donald remain on the side of their oppressors:

> DONALD: You faggots are revolting!!
> (SIDNEY, *horrified at* DONALD, *makes his decision, tosses his sunglasses in the gutter, joins* CEIL *and the others.*)
> SIDNEY (*to* DONALD *and* MICHAEL): You bet your sweet ass we are! (p. 77)

Sidney joins his fellow gays in "a grouping worthy of a statue in Sheridan Square" as the play ends. The police are silenced: the united gay men and women are the dominant voice, chanting "The street belongs to us."

The revolt dramatized in *Street Theatre* is not so much against outside forces as it is against the internalization of those forces. Internalized heterosexism maintains the closet and prevents community. The gay community that coalesces to resist exploitation and police harassment is a motley assortment of gay types. The Stonewall of *As Time Goes By* is linked to the struggles of blacks and women, part of a pattern of issues of identity and civil rights raised by the protests of the sixties. *Street Theater* focuses on the theater of gay life and the forging of its existence as a political reality.

As the plays about traitors focused on creating and maintaining masks, these plays focus on moments of unmasking. *As Time Goes By* moves from theater to the real life of gay oppression. *Bent* moves to a moment of honesty in which Max removes his disguise, the yellow star, and proudly dons the jacket with the pink triangle. At the end of *Street Theater,* Sidney doffs his dark glasses and joins the gay community. These unmaskings provide a positive counter to the dramas of duplicity that chronicle a sad chapter of gay history.

Heroic Making

Larry Kramer's list of culture heroes was basically one of artists and intellectuals. His "culture that isn't just sexual" is, with a couple of exceptions, a list of makers of high culture: philosophers, artists, writers, musicians. In gay drama, one alternative to the dramatization of criminals as rebellious gay martyrs is the depiction of gay artists as heroes. These biographical dramas establish and reinforce a gay canon. They educate gay audiences about men whose lives make them part of gay history while making sure the mainstream audience understands the centrality of homosexuality to the experience and work of these artists. The plays are also reminders of the major role gay artists have had in high culture and assertions of a continued investment in that culture, which drama itself represents. The common bond between gay and heterosexual members of the audience is an appreciation of the creative work of these men, for the plays assume a knowledge of the creative output of their subjects.

Since one function of these plays is to establish the link between homosexual desire and the work of these creative men, they are also love stories, chronicling the problems for creative gay men in establishing relationships in a world hostile to homosexual love. These biographical dramas, like the depictions of gay life discussed in the next chapter, place gay love relationships within a pattern familiar to all members of a mainstream audience, defy heterosexist assumptions that gay love is impossible, and sanction the display of such love.

Christopher Hampton's *Total Eclipse,* produced at the Royal Court in 1968, a daring work for its time, candidly depicts the turbulent, sporadic affair of the nineteenth-century French poets Arthur Rimbaud and Paul Verlaine. Rimbaud was a sixties hero (Jim Morrison declared that Rimbaud was a major influence on his work), and in choosing him as a subject, Hampton was focusing on a contemporary ideal of the antisocial artistic rebel. In terms of gay drama, *Total Eclipse* combines the dramatization of the homosexual as criminal and outsider with an exploration of the relationship between art and love.

The play begins with Verlaine's voice remembering Rimbaud's fascination with the underclass and his combination of beauty and power, which would lure Verlaine from his bourgeois womb: "He moved with the grace of a little girl at catechism. He pretended to know about everything, business, art, medicine. I followed him, I had to!"[38] After Rimbaud's death, Verlaine claims that "Rimbaud is trapped and living inside me" (p. 71), that Verlaine speaks with Rimbaud's voice. By beginning and ending with Verlaine's voice, the play underscores its focus on Verlaine's appropriation of Rimbaud. The final sentence of his first speech, "I followed him, I had to!" defines the compulsive nature of Verlaine's attraction to the teenage genius' beauty, his imagination, and his stronger will.

At the beginning of the play, Rimbaud enters the living room of Verlaine's in-laws, where Verlaine and his pregnant wife have resided since he gave up his civil-service position. Rimbaud is filthy, but he is also "extremely good looking: thin lips, cold, grey eyes" (p. 11). When Verlaine enters, he is "transfixed by Rimbaud's appearance" (p. 11) and overwhelmed by Rimbaud's articulation of his loathing for bourgeois cant and mediocre poetry. Verlaine is first seen as opposite to this personification of the starving, rebellious artist: he is "well dressed and looks like a civil servant with private means" (p. 11). He seems a balding, self-indulgent sentimentalist who doesn't have the courage to be a rebel. When Verlaine's wife agrees with her father's edict that Rimbaud leave the house (among other things, Rimbaud has been stealing objects d'art), Verlaine, drunk and enraged, throws her down and punches her in the face.

Although Verlaine cannot muster the courage to sever all ties with his wife, he becomes Rimbaud's companion and lover, half of an Odd Couple of nineteenth-century sentimentalist and modern, pessimistic realist. Verlaine all too easily relies on vague words like love, while Rimbaud realizes that "Complacency exists. But not love. It has to be reinvented" (p. 23). Love cannot be what "binds families and married couples together out of stupidity or selfishness or fear" (p. 23). Love must be "reinvented" out of physical desire and human need: Rimbaud sounds here like a 1968 sexual liberationist.

The action of the play revolves around the faltering attempts of the two men to forge a love relationship without the language or the models and, in Verlaine's case, without the strength of character to support such an endeavor. Rimbaud is constantly frustrated in his attempts to strengthen Verlaine: to make him leave his wife and her world, which is antithetical to the making of poetry, to force him to be more precise in his use of words, and to help him understand that poetry begins in pain. He tells Verlaine of being raped by four drunken soldiers: "It clarified things in my mind which had been vague. It gave my imagination textures. And I understood that what I needed, to be the first poet of this century, the first poet since Racine or since the Greeks, was to experience everything in my body" (p. 23). Verlaine must realize that the body is not merely the source of indulgence, sentiment, or nostalgia, and it is for this purpose that Rimbaud stabs his lover's hands with a knife: "The only unbearable thing is that nothing is unbearable" (p. 35).

While the audience at *Total Eclipse* sees no love scenes between the two men (though we are told of their anal intercourse), we do see a series of scenes chronicling a troubled homosexual relationship without a community to offer them support or a choice of more appropriate lovers. Verlaine vacillates between "respectability" and marriage on the one hand and debauchery with Rimbaud on the other. He is afraid, above all, to be alone, because "I don't exist without someone else" (p. 53). Rimbaud, who is incapable of supporting himself or of living his own philosophy, stays with Verlaine but rationalizes his dependency and inertia as free will: "You're here, living like this, because you have to be. It's your life. Drink and sex and a kind of complacent melancholy and enough money to soak yourself oblivious every night. That's your limit. But I'm here because I choose to be" (p. 49). When Rimbaud finally musters the courage to leave an unsatisfactory relationship, Verlaine shoots him in the hand:

> RIMBAUD *begins to laugh hysterically.*
> VERLAINE: Oh God, what have I done?
> RIMBAUD: You missed. (p. 55)

Verlaine turns the shooting into a melodramatic scene with the appropriate cliché; Rimbaud sees the shooting as another ludicrous failure. Rimbaud presses charges out of his anger that Verlaine will not let him leave freely but insists on possessing him. The resultant trial focuses more on sodomy than on the shooting, and Verlaine is sentenced to two years in prison.

The final meeting between the two poets also ends in violence. After imprisonment, divorce from his wife, and a not-very-convincing religious conversion, Verlaine wants to reestablish his relationship with Rimbaud, who has stopped writing and wants to make a final break out of their problematic relationship: "I no longer have any sympathy for you" (p. 61). Rimbaud's only means of escape from Verlaine's clinging, desperate embrace is a series of swift punches.

The final scene takes place fifteen years later. Rimbaud has died of cancer. His family is trying to destroy the poems that would sully his, and their, reputation and to ban the anonymous preface containing biographical details not consonant with their image of Rimbaud as a Christian convert. Verlaine, a fat, pathetic, middle-aged drunk, lives only for his sentimentalized memory of the past with Rimbaud: "We were always happy. Always, I remember. . . . He's not dead, he's trapped and living inside me" (p. 71). But it is Verlaine who is trapped within his distorted memories of Rimbaud that no longer have any relationship to truth: "We were always happy. Always. I remember" (p. 71). Verlaine is neither with wife nor male lover: he now is in the company of a "semiretired prostitute."

Total Eclipse is not only a chronicle of the unhappy relationship of two artists. It is also the depiction of a relationship for which the participants' culture or psyches did not equip them. Verlaine, however talented, could not escape his own weakness and dependence.

Rimbaud could not find a place for his sexuality or poetry. This picture of what contemporary pop psychology calls codependency is also an attack on past and present complacent, middle-class culture.

In *Total Eclipse*, Christopher Hampton employs the episodic structure and objective realism Osborne used in *A Patriot for Me* to depict the relationship of Verlaine and Rimbaud. The recurring images that give the play its power are of violence to the body, from the punching, stabbing, and shooting to Rimbaud's sister's lengthy description of the amputation of his cancerous leg. The living-through-the-body Rimbaud envisioned has more to do with pain than pleasure. The play does not show Verlaine and Rimbaud in their roles as poets beyond presenting a few artistic arguments and Rimbaud's physical attack on a mediocre poet, nor does it attempt an explanation of the relationship between their turbulent romance and their poetry. As a matter of fact, one is hard put to imagine Hampton's Verlaine writing poetry at all, much less poetry of the quality of his real counterpart. The mysteries of Rimbaud's life after his break with Verlaine are left unexplained. Yet, like *A Patriot for Me, Total Eclipse* is presented as a case study that does not veer from selected facts.

Noel Greig's *The Dear Love of Comrades* (1979) is a more positive picture of the forging of a gay life away from the norms of conventional society. Edward Carpenter, its protagonist, is a figure in the pantheon of gay history; a poet, socialist, and early writer on homosexuality. Carpenter tried to practice what he preached, attempting to found a Utopian gay community in the midst of Victorian England. Here the relationship between life and work is central: Greig's play focuses on the relationships of his central character, as he moves to the full experience of the homosexual love he writes about. The play shows the troubled relationships between Carpenter and each of the three working-class Georges who were his lovers (Adams, Hukin, and Merril) in the early nineties and presents their problems in living by Carpenter's ideals of nonpossessiveness. Adams and Hukin are married; though their wives are never seen, they offer a protective cover for their relationships with Carpenter. Adams, the most problematic of the lovers, cannot be cured of his capitalism: he wants Carpenter's farm to be profitable. Nor can he avoid feelings of possessiveness that the play attributes to his capitalistic principles of ownership. George Hukin is too much Carpenter's disciple, too much a believer in his philosophy, to be his satellite. He loves Carpenter but also loves his wife and George Merril. At the end, he demands that Carpenter practice what he preaches, first by not being jealous of Hukin's sexual relationship with Merril— Carpenter has difficulty ridding himself of feelings of jealousy and possession—and then by accepting and affirming his own sexual orientation. Hukin tells Carpenter: "Write till there's not a scrap of paper and the ink's run dry. One day it might all come true, but there's people living now who'll thank you much more for doing the *one thing* that you're not supposed to do. Which is to be homosexual. Not think and write and talk about it, but be it."[39] Hukin leaves Carpenter with the challenge he most fears, of living the life he has theorized with the earthy George Merril.

The Dear Love of Comrades is narrated by a character who represents the English author E. M. Forster, who in the 1940s gave a radio talk on Carpenter. Forster's hatred of his own homosexuality makes him Carpenter's opposite: "He [Carpenter] was also a homosexual, although I did not announce this fact over the airwaves. How could I admire in someone else a quality that I loathed in myself?" (p. 74). The prologue of the play begins with Carpenter and the three Georges singing a setting of Walt Whitman's "I Sing the Body Electric," the antithesis of Forster's description of his reaction to being "pinched on the bottom" by George Merril: "The electric shock that entered my spine did not reach my brain. I drew a veil between myself and the world" (p. 75). The juxtaposition of Forster's voice and Whitman's poem provides an ironic frame for the action of the play, but it is Whitman's words, and the voices of Carpenter and the three Georges that are, literally, the last word. Carpenter taught his working-class friends principles, but they taught the middle-class writer from Brighton to revel in a physical world, to "sing the body electric." Greig's play reinforces the traditional notion of working-class physicality vitalizing the middle and upper classes. It celebrates the class and age differences that were presented as evil in *The Green Bay Tree*.[40]

The Dear Love of Comrades is written in the nonlinear, non realistic style of many Gay Sweatshop plays, presenting a collage of scenes and songs whose roots are in Brecht. But where Brecht uses irony, Gay Sweatshop productions offer a more expansive, optimistic humanism, more Carpenter than Marx. On the one hand, Greig's play is a carefully researched documentary by a student of Carpenter's work; on the other, it is a finely shaped theater piece whose meaning comes from juxtaposition and repetition, not linear narrative. *The Dear Love of Comrades* celebrates a chapter of gay history before Stonewall that offers an alternative to the martyrdoms depicted in many historical dramas. The play gives historical perspective to the principles of gay liberation and reveals the links between that liberation and socialism. Like Hampton's play, it challenges by stressing the great difference between concept and actuality, between idea and life.

When Noel Greig read about Carpenter's life, he found not only subject matter but inspiration:

> Here was proof that a movement in which I held faith—the impulse towards a radical shift in the structures of society—held within its early stages an open advocation of something even closer to me—my own sexuality. Some sense of isolation dissolved—the feeling of having no personal part in the movements of history. In the early 1970's that starting point for many of us in the Gay Liberation Movement was the phrase "the personal is political." For myself Edward Carpenter gave this a historical dimension.[41]

Greig's play is not only an expression of his commitment but also a clarification of the values the Gay Sweatshop represented and of the style it developed.

Total Eclipse and *The Dear Love of Comrades* are set in the late nineteenth century, when homosexuality was just beginning to be an operative concept: the term "homosexuality" was coined in 1869; the action of *Total Eclipse* begins in 1871. Verlaine and Rimbaud, through their attraction to one another, were launched into uncharted territory. Edward Carpenter, at the end of *The Dear Love of Comrades,* which takes place in 1896, overcomes his fears and commits to living out the homosexuality he theorized in his writings. Unlike Edward Carpenter, who wrote about homosexual love, or Paul Verlaine, who made his relationship with Arthur Rimbaud a matter of public record, the English composer Benjamin Britten was reluctant to discuss his homosexuality. Only after Britten's death did his artistic collaborator and lover of almost forty years, tenor Peter Pears, openly discuss their relationship. Paul Godfrey's play, *Once in a While the Odd Thing Happens* (1990), places center stage the aspects of Britten's life that remained, while he was alive, an open secret.

The Britten-Pears relationship was something of a paradox. On one hand, it was one of the best known artistic and personal collaborations in musical history and in gay history; however, Britten could not see his homosexuality in positive terms. Unlike his sometime friend and collaborator, the poet W. H. Auden, Britten remained a closeted man and artist, yet he wrote a series of eloquent theater works about men who cannot find a positive outlook for their sexuality: Claggart and Vere in *Billy Budd,* Aschenbach in *Death in Venice,* Quint in *The Turn of the Screw,* and Peter Grimes. Musicologist Philip Brett has commented that Britten, in his work, expressed "his own shame and loneliness . . . so powerfully that he encapsulates the social experience of gay people since homosexuality was defined in 1869."[42] As such, Britten's operas are themselves central to twentieth-century gay theater.

However unable Britten was to find positive terms for his homosexuality, the texts he chose to set to music create a gay canon: Rimbaud's "Les Illuminations," Michelangelo's sonnets, W. H. Auden's poems, Henry James' *The Turn of the Screw* and "Owen Wingrave," Melville's *Billy Budd* (with a libretto by E. M. Forster), and Thomas Mann's *Death in Venice.* Even Britten's adaptation of George Crabbe's poem, "The Borough," into the opera *Peter Grimes* can be given a gay reading: an emotionally thwarted man is violent toward the boys to whom he is attracted, and his expulsion represents the exile of the "different" man from his community.

Building on the writings of Britten experts like Philip Brett and Clifford Hindley,[43] who have focused on the gay elements in the composer's work, Paul Godfrey, in *Once in a While the Odd Thing Happens,* gives the reticent Britten a voice and a language in which to express his love for Peter Pears and to describe the relationship between that love and his music, much of which was written for Pears to perform. Godfrey's preface to the published text of his play insists on its authenticity, developed out of interviews with people who were closest to Britten, including Pears and Britten's sister, Beth. Godfrey's claims for his play are complex and contradictory: "The play is fiction, but I have portrayed the characters as I believe they were and shown events as I understand them. The purpose was not to do a biographical drama but to use these specific figures to create a play with the widest resonance."[44] Though he lists his sources, Godfrey claims artistic license in his treatment of the facts, impressions, and memories of conversations that he amassed in his research. Godfrey did not want to be tied to the details of time and place that often limit biographical drama. He opts for the representational freedom of Gay Sweatshop playwrights rather than the literal detail of *Total Eclipse*. Most playwrights, I assume, aim for the "widest resonance," but in this case the aim is to create a play that aspires, in its use of free verse, to the emotive and suggestive power of Britten's music, which W. H. Auden describes in the play as "mercurial, but eloquent, yet uncomfortable" (p. 72).

Philip Brett has written that the gay man, "and in particular the artist, needs to come to terms with himself as well as society, and settle the linked questions of 'roots' and sexuality."[45] These related issues are the focus of Godfrey's play, which is structured on events in Britten's life in the decade leading to the premiere of his first grand opera, *Peter Grimes* (1945): the unhappy move to America, influenced by Auden; the development of the relationship with Pears and the break with Auden; the return to England and commitment to Aldeburgh, a village on the North Sea, as the locus for his life and work; and the dedication to the seemingly quixotic goal of creating English grand opera. Godfrey's Britten makes meaningful connections—between his sense of place and his art ("I should have known I could never live anywhere else" [p. 57]) and between his passion for Pears and his music. The unique quality of the Britten-Pears relationship is its complete merger of art and love. Britten puts Pears' voice "at the centre of everything" (p. 63), while Pears himself is "the source of my joy" (p. 64).

The play tracks the events of this ten-year period in a free-flowing succession of short episodes. Time and place are conveyed only by the language, not by realistic scenery or devices. The play's detachment from the realistic apparatus of scene-setting used by plays like *A Patriot for Me* and *Total Eclipse* mirrors Britten's own separation from the key events of the period, the Depression and World War II, to which he was a conscientious objector. Britten's commitment to his art separated him from history: during the war he devoted himself to writing *Peter Grimes*: "Little else matters but getting this done" (p. 62).

Godfrey's Britten is as steadfast in defending his personal life and work as he is to his principles as a conscientious objector. When a chorus member tells him he should cancel "your precious opera with your 'friend' in the starring role" so that opera lovers can celebrate the end of the war with a familiar work, Britten stands firm:

> BRITTEN: You do it!
> CHORUS: Careful, you may regret this one day.
>   When we come to round up people like you.
> BRITTEN: I am not ashamed!
>   *Exit* CHORUS
>   (I am ashamed?
>   No.)
>   Here
>   I am. (p. 80)

The chorister tries to make Britten the outsider, as the villagers of Aldeburgh do to Peter Grimes. Britten's simple "I am" is an eloquent expression of self-acceptance, tied to his love for Pears and pride in his work. The greatness of Britten's operas are linked to his love for Pears, "I wrote it for you, you know that" (p. 84), as they vividly portray men bereft of the kind of love Britten and Pears experienced.

Godfrey has written Benjamin Britten as a gay artist-hero. To do so, he omits the negative image of homosexuality Britten internalized and expressed in his work. Godfrey's Britten is proud and loving, if also, like his protagonists, willful and obsessed. This is a revisionist Britten, one contemporary gay men can unreservedly celebrate.

The production of *Once in a While the Odd Thing Happens* was itself a page of gay history. In the era of Clause 28, which above all bans government money for positive depictions of homosexuality as an alternative to family life, the government-funded National Theatre commissioned and presented a play that did just that. It is Britten's married sister, the representative of conventional family life in the play, who says of Britten's relationship with Pears, "I think such happiness is too rare to dismiss it" (p. 76). The word "odd" in Godfrey's title, which is the first line of a chorus from Britten and Auden's American folk musical, *Paul Bunyan* (1941), defines the relationship: considered "queer" by some, it is all too "uncommon."

Benjamin Britten's love for Peter Pears and his collaboration with Pears are inextricably connected to the experience of Britten's work, particularly on disc, where Pears' definitive interpretations have been recorded for posterity. History and literature have preserved the details of Edward Carpenter's life with George Merril and Paul Verlaine's sad, turbulent relationship with Arthur Rimbaud. The movement from the doomed relationship of Edward II and his "minions"; through the unhappy outsiders of *A Patriot for Me, Another Country,* and *Streamers;* to the violence and self-destruction of the poets in *Total Eclipse;* to the proud, angry self-assertion of the participants in the Stonewall rebellion and the loving relationships of Edward Carpenter and George Merril, Benjamin Britten and Peter Pears, offers a positive, even optimistic vision of gay history, affirming the centrality of the right to be gay and to love.

The new nuclear family in Harvey Fierstein's *Torch Song Trilogy*. Harvey Fierstein (r) as Arnold; Court Miller (l) as Arnold's vacillating lover, Ed; and Fisher Stevens as David, Arnold's gay foster son. Reprinted by permission of Hunt/Pucci Associates.

CHAPTER SIX

Fashioning
a Gay Self

In John Guare's *Six Degrees of Separation* (1990), the young black gay man whose acting of the role of Sidney Poitier's son has given him entree into an affluent, white home, tells his hostess:

> The imagination has moved out of the realm of being our link, our most personal link, with our inner lives and the world outside that world—this world we share. . . . Why has imagination become a synonym for style? I believe imagination is the passport we create to take us into the real world.[1]

Paul's comment can be seen as a gloss on the dramatic depictions of the stasis and progress of gay men I shall discuss in this chapter. These depictions present imagination first as a means of separation and isolation, then as a tool for forging a gay identity, and finally as a bridge to other people.

In the closet dramas discussed in part 2, the fate of the homosexual was isolation. Corrupted Julian controls the action at the end of Mordaunt Shairp's *The Green Bay Tree* (1933). Unlike his corrupter, Mr. Dulcimer, he is allowed to survive, but he is cut off from realism's version of the "real" world—of productive activity, marriage, and children. At the end of the play, Julian is arranging flowers, turning nature into art just as he, the homosexual as aesthete, is a work of art, created in the image of Mr. Dulcimer. In Tennessee Williams' plays, the gay artist who tries to join his vision to the real world is destroyed. In *Suddenly Last Summer* (1958), the poet Sebastian Venable is eaten alive by the boys he has had sex with. Allan Grey, another poet, is exposed by his wife; rejected and humiliated, he shoots himself. If we read Blanche DuBois as a crypto-gay character, we see a person who tries to redeem a threatening heterosexual world by turning it into theater. In the end, Blanche is not allowed to find a space in which to create a livable, tolerable world. Inge's Spencer Scranton, in *The Tiny Closet* (pub. 1962), can only hide in another closet when his locked closet is opened, revealing the women's hats that are the products of his imagination, his sexuality, and his gender identity. Like the closet, the parallel world of the imagination and of imaginative creation is not necessarily a safe haven.

"Realist" Stanley Kowalski shouts at Blanche in Williams' *A Streetcar Named Desire* (1947), "There isn't a goddam thing but imagination,"[2] as though imagination were the opposite of a stable truth. Gay drama centers on the conflict established in Blanche DuBois' cry, "I don't want realism. I want magic!" In Williams' play, the realism that crushes Blanche's performances is a fabric of lies and denials far more damaging than Blanche's theatrical illusions. Imagination can liberate, but imagination can also create and reinforce an isolated, hermetic world for the gay character. Many of the plays discussed in this chapter enact a pathology of the imagination, while others show the liberating possibilities of a gay man's imagination. I also postulate that a reassertion of imaginative, nonrealistic theater can liberate gay drama from the prosaic, conventional norms and strictures reinforced by realism.

In the plays discussed in this chapter, two related metaphors link the gay character's experience to the world of imagination: performance and writing.

Performance can entail the exaggerated acting of roles created and defined outside oneself, expressions of one's internalized heterosexism. Such negative exhibitions usually connect assumptions about oneself to a supposed fixed reality of gender identity that postulates that homosexuals aren't men. Exclusion from conventional representations of manhood or outright opposition to them can result in various exhibitions of identification with women: imitations of women—which means drag; identification with larger-than-life depictions of victimized women from opera, ballet, and camp movies (the Judy Garland cult being the most famous example in this area); or performing a stereotype of effeminacy. The problem for the gay character is to liberate himself from the stereotype of effeminacy without merely aping the behavior of heterosexual men. The ideal performance would be unmoored from conventional notions of masculinity and femininity—an imaginative self-creation possible onstage only outside the framework of realistic drama.

Another mode of performance is the play of anarchic wit, the virtuosic manipulation of language as a means of dismantling censorious judgments. As the exercise of wit has been for gay men a successful defensive measure—at times even a liberating tactic—wit, too, has been a liberating tactic in gay drama since the epigrams of Oscar Wilde's crypto-gay characters deflated the shibboleth of Victorian propriety. Doric Wilson's *Street Theater* of 1982 (discussed in chapter 5) recreates gay history through parody and satire; even the climactic moment is built on a pun, "You faggots are revolting," an expression of internalized heterosexism here converted into a call to arms.

Christopher Durang has based his most hilarious yet disturbing plays on parodies of the language of oppression. *Sister Mary Ignatius Explains It All For You* (1979) has a particularly virulent representative of the Catholic church unwittingly demonstrate how the theology and doctrine of her religion oppresses women and gay men, who "do that thing that makes Jesus puke."[3] For Sister Mary Ignatius, words aren't enough to purge the world of such sin, so she, carrying out her own inquisition, shoots the young man who has proudly proclaimed his gayness: "I've sent him to heaven!" (p. 206). In *Beyond Therapy* (1981), a female psychiatrist has an honest, if manic, reaction to a character's admission of gayness:

> COCKSUCKER! Oh, I'm sorry. It was just this terrible urge I had. I'm terribly sorry. (*Gleefully.*) COCKSUCKER! (*Screams with laughter, clutches Snoopy, rocks back and forth.*) COCKSUCKER! Whoops! Sorry. Oh, God, it's my blood sugar. Help, I need a cookie.[4]

Wit enables Durang's characters to parody and dismantle destructive language. But the effect is limited. It seldom helps them shape a positive vision of gay experience. Similarly, the wit of many characters in gay drama helps them dismantle oppressive language, but it is not the only imaginative tool necessary in constructing a positive self. Wit is often only an expression of futility.

Writing links the gay character to the world of art and to the written world of the play he inhabits. The protagonists of many gay dramas are failed writers, masters of language too often turned against themselves instead of being shaped into art. Only after mastering the articulation of a positive self-image, which requires revising a language that has, for gay men, been oppressive, is a character finally able to write.

The metaphoric actions of performance and writing are joined in the creation of the gay self, a work of art, the product of a critique, revision, and, to some extent, rejection of the self-image and the language that have been taught by an education in a heterosexist society. Only when the gay character has embarked on such a self-creation can he forge relationships that meaningfully and honestly connect him to other people—lovers, friends, family. Like the self, relationships and the languages of relationships must be forged anew out of words that have limited or negative meanings for gay men. A major example of this is the discourse of marriage and family.

Isolation

The most significant nurturing place for "inside" gay drama was the Caffe Cino in Greenwich Village, which for almost a decade presented a series of new dramas, many of them gay-oriented. The cafe, owned by a gay man, Joe Cino, was from 1958 until Cino's death in 1967 a workshop for a group of young gay playwrights, including Lanford Wilson, Robert Patrick, Doric Wilson, and William M. Hoffman.

Lanford Wilson's one-act play *The Madness of Lady Bright* (1964) was one of the first big hits of this fringe theater (164 performances) and proved that gay drama—and off-off Broadway itself—could be commercially viable. In this prototypical inside gay drama, a gay character imaginatively transforms his environment.

The setting for *The Madness of Lady Bright* is on "*the stage within a stage.*" The audience is not to forget that Wilson's play is just that— something enacted. The stage as frame also underscores the performative nature of Leslie Bright's life. Leslie fashions the space in which he lives as a reflection of himself, but doing so is an act of exclusion as well, of controlling the encroachment of reality. The walls of Leslie's one-room apartment are covered with signatures of the men Leslie has had in his bed. The names are a memorial to Leslie's sex life. The walls on which the names are inscribed are Leslie's memory: *The Madness of Lady Bright* really takes place inside its central character's mind.

The young man and woman who share the stage with Leslie portray the voices in Leslie's head, of his mother, of his past lovers, of imaginary companions, and the internalized voices of "normal" society. Having no real audience left, Leslie Bright imagines one, as he imagines his fellow performers. Leslie's head is also filled with music—Mozart, Judy Garland, *Giselle,* rock 'n' roll, and striptease accompaniments—heard sometimes separately, sometimes cacophonously. Leslie has not created the art that defines him; he has imported it from a space he does not wish to inhabit.

Images of performance and writing begin the play. The boy and girl are an imaginary audience for Leslie's monologue, but Leslie also has an urge to write down—to record—his utterances. He becomes inarticulate, however, the moment he tries to write:

> You are a pile of paper addresses and memories, paper phone numbers and memories, and you mean nothing to me. (*Trying to catch the line just said*) You—I am surrounded—I am left with (*Rather desperately trying to catch the right phrasing of the line to write it down*) a—with paper memories and addresses. (*Finding a piece of paper at the desk. With a pencil, bent over the desk*) I am—how?[5]

The play moves from this futility, which reflects Leslie Bright's loss of the ability to order his experience, to the imaginative enactment of real and imaginary scenes from the past, particularly reminiscences of Adam, the first signer of Leslie's wall and the man Leslie claims to have loved. Leslie's fixation on the one man memorialized on his wall with whom he didn't have sex is a prime manifestation of his self-hatred and masochism. Like many gay protagonists, he romanticizes the roles of victim and outcast, thus making his isolation both bearable and inevitable.

For Leslie, his drag is not only a performance of femininity related to his sense of failed masculinity—"But, whatever your dreams, there is no possibility whatever of your ever becoming, say, a lumberjack" (p. 181)—but it is also a veneer of eternal youth covering his aging body. As he puts on lipstick, he proclaims, "I will never be old" (p. 196). Leslie may be "built like a disaster," but his assumed femininity is the basis for his fantasies of beauty, love, and freedom. Leslie imagines himself as the ballet heroine, Giselle. Giselle is one of the Wilis, specters of young women who have died of unrequited love; they reappear every night to lure the men who abandoned them to dance to their deaths. Giselle, however, tries to save her faithless husband's life. Leslie identifies with Giselle, who, with the masochism of a male-created nineteenth-century heroine, continues to sacrifice for the man she loves. At the end of the play, Leslie tries to dance *Giselle* but collapses. Unlike Giselle, he is tied to a failing body. Throughout Leslie's dancing, the young man and woman dance together, an imagined couple and a complement to the visual image of Leslie's isolation.

With only memory and imagination, bereft of new experiences to feed on, Leslie is going mad, his mind deteriorating in counterpoint to the aging of his middle-age body: "I grow brittle and I break. I'm losing my mind, you know. Everyone knows when they lose their mind. But I'm so lonely" (p. 196). At the end, Leslie can only repeat "take me home," which becomes a pathetic cry for help, a plea for death.

With a nod in the direction of Samuel Beckett monologues like *Krapp's Last Tape* (1958), Wilson has fashioned a vivid theatrical portrait of a man disconnected from the outside world (no one answers the phone when Leslie calls except Dial-a-Prayer). Leslie's imagination, now out of control, frightens him. He hears the voices of people who have briefly loved him and the inescapable voices that molded his self-hatred. Leslie Bright is not loved. He doesn't even have the solace of the performer's substitution for love—adulation. *The Madness of Lady Bright* is a depiction of the imagi-

nation and theatricality that have made life bearable for this lonely
man, yet isolated him.

Wilson's comrade at the Caffe Cino, Robert Patrick, has written,
"I met here [in Greenwich Village], the kind of brave and brazen
gay men I longed for, but half the time they were so crippled by
identity crises and simple self-hatred that they couldn't maintain an
affectionate erection, much less a relationship."[6] In Patrick's *The
Haunted Host* (1964), this dilemma is not the core of classic American realistic melodrama, but of comedy. The setting is realistic, a
Greenwich Village apartment "set just above the main homosexual
cruising crossroads,"[7] but the action mixes fantasy and reality.
Again, writing and performance dominate the action. Jay, the protagonist, is a playwright whose life and work are now crippled by
the ghost of his lover, who committed suicide after Jay left him. The
lover, Ed, was a handsome young would-be writer who was also
Jay's protégé. Jay's way of showing his love for Ed was to pour his
own self and creativity into him. This act of "ghost-writing" figured
the ways in which Jay gave over his whole identity to his lover,
more a sign of self-hatred than of love. When he didn't feel that Ed
was returning all he had invested in the relationship, Jay ended it:
"What was I supposed to do, go on producing indefinitely for you
to keep on confiscating?"(p. 120).

When the play opens, Jay's home is in disarray and is still
dominated by Ed, whose picture hangs on the wall and whose
manuscripts cover Jay's desk. The chaotic room is an image of his
mind, stricken with grief and guilt. Jay has become a recluse,
conversing only with Ed's ghost. Into the hermetic world of this
drugged-out, manic, and self-hating failed writer comes Frank, who
is the spitting image of Ed, looking for a place to spend the night,
advice on his playwriting, and, though he claims to be heterosexual,
perhaps an exotic homosexual adventure. Jay tries desperately to
avoid responding to his unwelcome guest, the embodiment of his
ex-lover, sure that he is living through some awful punishment.

Jay's defense against this intruder is to perform, to camp, and to
cut off any chance for communication by carrying on a frenetic
monologue. When Frank asks for advice on his writing, Jay mounts
a filibuster, boring Frank to sleep by reading his own plays, a not-
too-subtle means to avoid helping Frank write. When Frank tries to

defend himself, Jay drugs him into unconsciousness. Above all, Jay fights the bids for artistic advice and the sexual ploys that are temptations to relive the past: "You want me to do it all over again! Jay, the mad scientist! You want me to praise you and pour myself into you and write your plays for you. You want me to take my brain out and put it into your body and make a corpse out of you and a ghost out of myself" (p. 132). Jay makes Frank, and himself, realize the sickness of his past relationship with Ed and why he cannot let history repeat itself: "The minute you try to live someone else's life for him, or let him live yours—it's suicide" (p. 135). In trying to avoid repeating a mutually destructive relationship, Jay avoids all affection, all contact, and has sealed himself in his apartment. Before Frank leaves, he says the one thing he thinks can "break" Jay: "I love you." The ideal of being loved may be frightening to Jay, but Frank is the wrong person to offer it.

Frank, eager at first to assert his heterosexuality, tries to cast Jay as the "other," but Jay's wit enables him to turn Frank's heterosexist judgments around and direct them back to their source:

FRANK: Tell me, did you ever see a psychiatrist?
JAY: You mean one of those people who tell you society is sick then offer to help you adjust to it? (p. 97)
. . . .
JAY: Tell me, Frank, how long have you been heterosexual? (p. 99)

Frank can only dismiss Jay's turning of the tables as sick, a standard heterosexist ploy.

Frank has all the makings of a realistic playwright. He wants to write "Honestly! Truthfully! Fearlessly!" (p. 115), based on his own experience—as if he has had any. He brings to his work what Jay would call the "cookie cutters" of conventional interpretation ("I took psychiatry") and generalizations from a white, heterosexual point of view ("trying to get you people to be serious is murder"). Jay has his own revelations, based on a point of view and experiences Frank cannot comprehend.

When Frank leaves, Ed's ghost leaves as well. Jay is ready to move out of the past. He throws into the wastebasket Ed's manuscripts, the remnants of an unhealthy relationship that wasn't a collaboration. Jay reaches a crucial turning point. He has gained enough understanding of the past and enough pride in himself to exorcise his ghost. Frank accused him of being tough, but toughness was essential for the survival of gay men in the 1960s—and beyond. When Frank asked Jay whether he was a homosexual, Jay responded, "I am THE homosexual," a glib remark but one showing the beginnings of the sense of pride that will allow Jay to write his own script instead of pouring himself into someone else's. Jay's witty, manic performance has both dismantled Frank's judgments and liberated Jay from constantly reliving his past series of self-destructive infatuations. At the final curtain, Jay, too, leaves the apartment. His exit from the scene suggests a re-integration into the gay society that teems right outside his apartment.

At the end of Mart Crowley's *The Boys in the Band* (1968), Michael leaves his apartment to go to midnight mass, hardly a place to give a gay man much positive reinforcement. Michael is a failed writer whose self-hatred keeps him from creative activity. Unlike Lanford Wilson and Robert Patrick, Crowley does not make anything of the metaphoric potential of his protagonist's profession or of the connection between his self-hatred and his inability to write. Michael's profession as writer is merely linked to a general sense of his articulateness. His only narratives are self-oppressing or misconstructions of others' lives. Language for him is always a weapon. Michael's home is the locus for the gathering of a group that represents middle-class urban gay society. In the course of the play, Michael assembles the group and dismantles it, reinforcing his own isolation.

I mentioned in the previous chapter how Michael and his friend Donald are parodied in Doric Wilson's *Street Theater* (1982). They are the most eloquent spokesmen for the men in power, "People like us don't have rights," Wilson's Michael says to his fellow gays, "we haven't earned them."[8] They are the only gay characters who attack the participants in the Stonewall riots from the sidelines: "You faggots are revolting!" Wilson realized *The Boys in the Band* was itself an important event in gay history and gay drama and that Michael and Donald are not merely malicious fictions but frequently encountered types of self-hating, closeted gay man who have internalized the language of their oppressors. After all, the self-hatred that Michael and his friends act out was present in *The Madness of*

Lady Bright and Patrick's own play, *The Haunted Host*. Yet *The Boys in the Band* has become for its detractors, particularly those who did not experience gay life before Stonewall, a paradigm of politically incorrect gay drama. For some, this antipathy to the play is based on its lack of a sense of the sadder elements of gay history. For others, the problem with *The Boys in the Band* is one of audience. Kaier Curtin notes that during the first weeks of its run, *The Boys in the Band* played to predominantly gay audiences but that eventually it attracted a large number of heterosexuals.[9] It is one thing to show a gay audience the dark side of its life; it is quite another to profit by parading this before a mainstream audience.

Many of the actors did all they could to distance themselves from their characters, thereby reinforcing stigmas against gay people. A *New York Times* feature article on one of the actors was entitled, "You Don't Have to Be One to Play One." As his wife pours his beer, actor Cliff Gorman tells the reporter, "I already knew how to lisp because I'd been telling gay jokes since I was a kid."[10] Gorman also pointed out that gay actors were asked to read for the part of Emory, whom the same *Times* article described as "The Definitive Screaming Queen" and refused. Acting gay was professionally risky: the reticence of the actors reflects the fact that being gay in 1968 was not something one advertised. This public distancing of actor and character helped maintain the distance between the play and its audience.

At the same time, as playwright William M. Hoffman has noted, "Whatever one thinks of it, *The Boys in the Band,* more than any other single play, publicized homosexuals as a minority group."[11] The very existence of such a performance was in some sense empowering. The production ran for years, and the original cast made a film version in 1970, which is still available on videotape. Heterosexuals may find the video a reassuring, if inaccurate, picture of the unhappy lives of "those people"; gay men can see it as a quaint period piece or a slice of pre-Stonewall gay life. Film critic Vito Russo believed that the film "summed up a generation of gay men who were taught to blame all their troubles on their homosexuality."[12]

The Boys in the Band follows the structural pattern of *The Haunted Host,* but in doing so inverts the traditional place of gay men in commercial drama: an outsider disrupts a hermetic, "realistic" society and leaves the stage at the climax of the action, but in Crowley's play this outsider is not expelled as the homosexual was in traditional drama. He leaves voluntarily, rejecting the world presented on the stage. The play's point of view is both that of the self-hating gay man and that of the outsider, who represents the audience on the other side of the fourth wall. What the outsider and the audience see and hear is purported to be a slice of life, the "off-stage" activities of closeted gay characters when they're not "playing straight." For the first time, mainstream audiences see gay men talk openly about their sexual predilections, dance together, kiss, and retire upstairs for sex. Characters acknowledge a common gay culture with their references to the plays of Tennessee Williams and Edward Albee and their homages to camp movie queens like Maria Montez. The silences and indirections of closet drama no longer prevail, but the play is still trapped within the normative sphere of realistic drama. The actions of the characters become performances, watched and judged by the "normal" outsider who offers society's judgments, which the characters too readily accept. Just as the fallen woman of nineteenth-century drama accepted and articulated the judgment of the patriarchs who decided her place in society, the boys in the band know that they are gay, alone, and unhappy—that they would be happier if they were straight. They can articulate these judgments with the solipsism and eloquence developed through years of psychotherapy, whose theories and strategies are presented without skepticism.

In the first scene between Michael and Donald, best friends who "tricked" together years ago when they were in college, Donald, degreed but doing menial work because he is too anxious and self-hating to pursue a career, defines himself as sick, "I'm not that well yet."[13] His sexual orientation is one expression of his "sickness." Michael, a compulsive shopper and reformed alcoholic (until the end of act 1), defines himself as "spoiled rotten, stupid, empty, boring, selfish, self-centered" because his overprotective, domineering mother "refused to let me grow up" (p. 23). The classic Freudian stereotype of arrested development is linked to psychoanalytic interpretation—"Christ, how sick analysts must get of hearing how mommy and daddy made their darlin' into a fairy" (p. 19)—without attacking or even questioning the role of the psychiatrist in maintaining that interpretation. Michael's sporadic dependence on the Catholic Church only intensifies his masochism. A heterosexist audience could see Michael and Donald as pathological and unproductive—intelligent men who have failed to fill a useful role in society. Thus they can be judged both sick and unmanly.

After fifteen minutes or so of masochistic self-analysis, Michael's party guests begin to arrive and, when assembled, are presented as a microcosm of the gay community: Emory, a mincing Nellie queen and interior decorator; Bernard, a black librarian who masochistically endures racial slurs; a bickering couple comprising Larry, a wayward, promiscuous artist, and "athletic-looking" Hank, a schoolteacher who has recently left his wife to move in with Larry; and a vapid, stupid, but beautiful hustler with a heart of gold: "I try to show a little affection—it keeps me from feeling like such a whore" (p. 174). The hustler is a birthday present for the guest of honor, Harold, a former ice-skater and self-described "thirty-two-year-old, ugly, pock-marked Jew fairy" who veils his own self-loathing under a cloud of marijuana smoke. Clearly the only things that connect the members of this bickering group are their gayness, their self-hatred, and their middle-class credentials. The only thing they share with their presumed audience is their position in the middle class. The vituperation and game-playing that ensue at Harold's birthday party owe a considerable debt to Edward Albee's *Who's Afraid of Virginia Woolf?* (1962)

The surprise arrival of the supposedly heterosexual Alan, Michael's former college chum, the only representative of the straight world, is the catalyst for cruelty from cruelty-prone Michael. When confronted with a roomful of homosexuals, Alan, "who is so pulled-together he wouldn't show any emotion if he were in a plane crash" (p. 29), lashes out at effeminate Emory with a catalog of homophobic epithets worthy of *Cat on a Hot Tin Roof's* Brick Pollitt:

> ALAN: (*Lashes out*) Faggot, fairy, pansy . . . (*Lunges at* EMORY) . . . queer, cocksucker! I'll kill you, you goddamn little mincing swish! You goddamn freak! FREAK! FREAK!
> (ALAN *beats* EMORY *to the floor before anyone recovers from surprise and reacts*)

By the end of the play, Alan has vomited, vehemently denied Michael's accusations that he had a homosexual affair in college, and vowed to return to the wife he has recently left, thanking Michael for shocking him back into his marriage. The play hints—merely hints—that Alan's leaving his wife and his behavior at Michael's party are signs of homosexual panic. Alan's continued presence at the party is at least a sign that he is as much as masochist as the others: "He was dying for somebody to let him have it and he got what he wanted" (p. 180). However, the shock of this nasty party has scared Alan back into a heterosexual commitment. Even if Alan has acknowledged homosexual impulses, the play does not question his return to a heterosexual life; it has to be happier than what he has seen at Michael's party and, after all, Alan has children.

Alan's presence brings to the fore all of Michael's guilt and self-loathing. He attacks his friends viciously and tries to destroy their illusions and frail self-respect, but he succeeds only in displaying his own misery. Harold, the birthday boy, who has repeatedly, accurately labeled Michael's behavior as "hateful," silences Michael's cruelty by making him face the truth about himself: "You are a sad and pathetic man. You're a homosexual and don't want to be. But there is nothing you can do to change it" (p. 173). After the guests have left, a guilt-stricken Michael goes off to midnight mass, leaving his friend Donald alone in the apartment reading a book. Donald will finish the bottle of brandy and drive back to Long Island. Though these two neurotics are best friends, neither could possibly have a relationship. They, like most of the characters in the play, are doomed to be alone until "we learn not to hate ourselves so much" (p. 178).

While positing unhappy isolation for most of its characters, *The Boys in the Band* also defined a subgenre of gay dramas about redefining the rules of gay men's relationships. The one couple in the play, Larry and Hank, are fighting over Hank's equation of relationship with monogamy. Hank and Larry have been lovers for two years. For Larry, it is an attempt at a long-term relationship after a history of sexual promiscuity. It is Hank's first gay relationship; he left his wife and children to be with Larry. Hank wants the same rules to prevail in his relationship with Larry that prevail in a heterosexual marriage; "till death do us part" and total sexual fidelity." The tension caused by this disagreement over the rules of their relationship causes cycles of bickering. The more Hank suspects Larry of infidelity, the more Larry asserts his right to have other lovers. Larry also would like Hank to be unfaithful, so that he would be free to follow his impulses. Larry doesn't believe the fidelity Hank wants is even possible: "The ones who swear their undying fidelity are lying. Most of them anyway—ninety percent of them. They cheat on each other constantly and lie through their teeth. I'm sorry, I can't be like that and it drives Hank up the wall" (p. 157). The couple's conflict is resolved by an agreement to try Larry's rules: "Respect—for each other's freedom. With no need to lie or pretend" (p. 160). The contract Hank and Larry establish is their solution to the conflict the gay liberationist sees between male need for sexual variety and the affectional need for a stable, loving relationship. Larry teaches Hank that love is not a matter of sexual possession or even sexual fidelity. Larry and Hank resolve their dispute, at least temporarily, and go upstairs to make love, the one happy ending in the play. In this resolution, Crowley asserts both the possibility of a relationship and the fact that the rules cannot be the same as they are for heterosexuals. Marriage is redefined but upheld, and Larry and Hank leave the neurotic game-playing. Crowley makes his positive judgments indirectly; Larry and Hank are the most "masculine" of the guests and the ones with active professions.

As for Michael, Donald, Emory, Bernard, and Harold, *The Boys in the Band* allows its heterosexual audiences a liberal compound of pity, tolerance, and superiority. Homosexual audiences saw that the characters' "problem" was not their sexual orientation but their "internalized homophobia," their acceptance of the judgments of family, medicine, law, and religion.

Doric Wilson's *Street Theater* (1982) shows that the Michael and Donald of Crowley's play, and their "real life" counterparts, were not immediately converted by the events of June 27, 1969. Larry Kramer's *Just Say No* (1988) depicts the Michaels and Donalds a generation later but turns the closeted, self-hating, but ever-so-well dressed gay men into the best friends and supporters of a certain ex-actress who is the First Lady of the United States and into enemies of the gay community. Kramer's version of Michael and Donald dread exposure because they would no longer be invited to the best parties. Larry Kramer and Doric Wilson see Michael and Donald as real devils that gay life and gay drama must exorcise.

The Boys in the Band was a bellwether for gay drama in a number of ways. It not only proved that uncloseted gay drama could be "commercial" (it ran over a thousand performances) but it also offered a formula for appropriating the conventions of realistic drama while demonstrating their limitations. The conventions can provide an effective means of presenting "problems" or affirming relationships, but they cannot depict what it means to act gay. In moving gay drama "uptown," Crowley's play moved it into the language of American realism, in which aberrant behavior has to be explained and cured. There is a plodding literal-mindedness about the play, the result of a drive to make sure the audience has a reason for everything and everyone, but such full explanations are characteristic of commercial plays. You can't blame Crowley for succeeding in the popular arena (he moved on to produce the successful television series "Hart to Hart," which began in 1979). The challenge for post–*Boys in the Band* and post-Stonewall gay dramatists is to find forms more suited to the creation of a positive gay self.

In the worlds of *The Madness of Lady Bright, The Haunted Host,* and *The Boys in the Band,* the gay world is a dangerously closed society. Domestic space becomes a refuge from a hostile, terrifying world. "Out there" are hostile heterosexuals; inside, gay men face their own private demons (created by the people out there). Isolated within the domestic space, the creative gay man is at a dead end. This isolation did not stop with Stonewall. Robert Patrick wrote in 1988, "*The Boys in the Band* was no fantasy. It still isn't, for that matter."[14] The AIDS epidemic becomes for some characters another reason to withdraw.

Terrence McNally's *The Lisbon Traviata* (1985/1989) weaves a disturbing set of variations on the themes of fantasy, performance, and isolation within a gay world at the height of what one character calls, "our very own bubonic plague."[15] Mendy and Stephen, its central characters, are holdovers from an earlier time, self-hating gay men who use elements of gay culture to encase themselves in a bearable world. Mendy and Stephen's escape and solace comes from that cornerstone of gay culture—opera. McNally, himself a regular on the "Opera Quiz" feature of the live Texaco Metropolitan Opera radio broadcasts, uses his two protagonists to analyze the gay man's fascination for opera and to draw its dangers vividly.

Jokes abound in the gay community about macho types in leather bars arguing over the merits of rival divas and describing the lobby of the Metropolitan Opera at intermission as the Easter Parade for gay men. To more than one generation of homosexual men opera offered not only a liberation but the chance to participate in a sport; the merits of various singers could be argued as another group of men might argue baseball statistics. Part of the imaginative experience of opera is the audience's substituting of an imaginary body for the body of the overweight, unglamorous diva. Opera, above all, purports to transcend bodies. Substituting one sex for another— imagining oneself as the larger-than-life character or as the performer—is the next logical step. Opera cries out for such rereading. The opera queen's identification is usually less with the role than with the performer: he projects himself onto the diva who can, through voice and force of will and personality, make an audience believe she is a grand, beautiful, tragic victim. One of New York City's great institutions is La Gran Scena Opera Company di New York, in which the all-male cast present scenes from the great operas filtered through a gay sensibility. The men are capable of singing all the great soprano roles and acting with all the magnificent excess of the great divas. The more one knows about opera, the more one can appreciate the detail of their parody of specific artists, but anyone who knows even the bare bones of the story can appreciate diva Vera Galupe-Borzkh (Ira Siff) singing Violetta's poignant "Addio del passato" from the third act of Verdi's *La Traviata* while caressing her lover's briefs. The male characters are fools, unworthy of sharing the stage with the grandly suffering diva who is an unlikely combination of vulnerability and toughness, of faith and cynicism. What Mme. Vera Galupe-Borzkh and her colleagues perform is the self-absorption of the diva—the total performer.

Generations of opera queens have idolized Maria Callas, the temperamental Greek-American soprano whose vocal limitations were overcome by force of will, intelligence, and fierce temperament; whose career languished early when vocal problems became insurmountable; and who died, alone, in Paris, having never recovered from the loss of her two great loves, her singing and her

Greek tycoon, Aristotle Onassis. Her story is itself operatic—grand, sentimental, a bit unbelievable, built on the suffering and loneliness of an extraordinary woman.

In *The Lisbon Traviata,* Stephen, a failed writer, and his friend, Mendy, live for opera, particularly for the memory of Maria Callas, around whom they have erected a mythology that has little connection to her or to their own reality. The "Lisbon Traviata" of the title is a pirated recording of Callas singing the part of Violetta in a Lisbon performance that Mendy has not yet heard and that fills the air at the end of the play. Mendy has given up wife and family to live hermetically sealed in a nineteenth-century setting, drapes shut, doors locked, listening to opera, as though doing so were his profession. Even his gay society centers on opera and Callas. His annual party is on Callas' birthday, and his friendship with Stephen is based on their mutual adoration of the Brooklyn-born diva.

The first act, set in Mendy's ornate, campy world, is comedy, dominated by an opera queen enacting his passion: "She's given me so much: pleasure, ecstasy, a certain solace, I suppose; memories that don't stop. This doesn't seem to be such a terrible existence with people like her to illuminate it" (p. 34). Mendy speaks of Callas in terms like "truth" and "intensity." Her singing provides feelings Mendy cannot get from his own life—from his estranged wife, his son, his friends. Yet he wonders why he can't find a lover. Beyond the closed drapes of Mendy's shrine to Callas is a troubled real world of men dying of a real disease, AIDS, but Mendy and Stephen are oblivious to real suffering. All emotions have been focused on their fantasy of Maria Callas. Mendy can think only of obtaining a recording of the Lisbon *Traviata.* At the end of the first act, the audience hears, with Mendy and Stephen, director Franco Zeffirelli's voice on a videotape of a documentary about the soprano: "There has been perhaps one faithful companion to Maria throughout her life, her loneliness. The price sometimes one has to pay for the glory and the success" (p. 49). Mendy and Stephen's loneliness is not connected to such glory, but to their own self-absorption. Where Mendy sees opera as a substitute for an emotional life he cannot have—"Opera doesn't reject me. The real world does" (p. 24)—Stephen, a writer and editor whose professional and personal life are on the rocks, sees his own emotional life as opera. The second act, which veers toward operatic pathos, depicts the end of Stephen's relationship with Mike, a doctor enmeshed in the real world of dying patients and dying friends—and in a new relationship. Mike tells Stephen: "You live in TOSCA. You live in TURANDOT. You live in some opera no one's ever heard of. It's hard loving someone like that" (p. 86). Stephen refers to Mike, his estranged lover, as "my life's salvation" (p. 87), but cannot even give Mike his full attention; he is impelled to focus on whatever opera is blaring from the stereo. Mike leaves because, "I just want to be away from you" (p. 85).

At the end, after Mike has left, Stephen loses himself in Callas' Violetta, the operatic version of *La Dame aux Camélias*, singing "Sempre libera"—"Always free"—an ironic commentary on Stephen's entrapment in his own fantasy world: "*He throws his head back with her as she reaches for a climactic high note but no sound comes out. . . . Callas is all we can hear*" (p. 88). Stephen's only union is with Callas: he will listen to her while avoiding his lover's attempts at connection.

On one level, *The Lisbon Traviata* is a satire on opera queens filled with diva jokes that only opera queens would understand. One can laugh at Mendy, who is a parody of a familiar type, but Stephen is neither funny nor sympathetic. His cruelty toward his fellow gays who have died of AIDS—"Wouldn't you rather be at a nice restaurant than sitting here moping over someone who probably, if the truth could be faced up to, even just a little bit, got what was coming to him" (p. 80)—is the expression of someone totally severed from reality and compassion. His desperate, futile attempts to humiliate Mike's new lover and to keep Mike from leaving are pathetic.

The second act is filled with messy verbal and physical violence, a contrast to the bloodless, noble deaths of opera. Mike punches Stephen for blaring opera on the stereo as a means of driving out Mike's new lover. Stephen threatens to stab Mike with a pair of scissors. Unconsciously, Stephen and Mike speak the lines from the final scene of Georges Bizet's *Carmen,* but without the music and within a Manhattan apartment, such operatic moments are banal.[16] Mike leaves the apartment for the real world of professional commitment, family (he is going to stay with his brother), and the potential of a relationship with a productive human being. Stephen, who no longer writes or even cares about his editing job, is alone and silent, bonded only to Maria Callas. Even his friend Mendy has beome only a voice on the phone.

Fathers and Sons

The protagonists of *The Madness of Lady Bright, The Haunted Host, The Boys in the Band,* and *The Lisbon Traviata* turn their domestic spaces into stages on which their own neuroses and fantasies are played out. Ultimately, these performances create or maintain isolation. Imagination is used by these gay characters to project themselves onto other people or to absorb others into themselves but not to create. In another group of plays, the protagonist liberates his imagination by forging links with a redefined family, albeit a non-traditional one.

In Albert Innaurato's *Coming of Age in Soho* (1984), a writer's reunion with his fourteen-year-old son leads to a reintegration for him of experience and art. At the beginning of the play, Bartholomew Dante, known to his friends as Beatrice, unsuccessfully isolates himself in order to try to find himself. This search first involves divesting himself of compromises with the outside world, "I want to stop working to define myself by every standard but mine."[17] His ultimate goal, though, is artistic expression. Beatrice is a writer whose books thus far reflect his own immaturity; he is best known for a children's book entitled *Little Boy Bound.* The link between work and creator is made abundantly clear in the first moments of the play, when a young man, tied to a chair, emerges from Beatrice's bedroom. In addition the book's title presents an image of its author's immaturity. Beatrice is also the creator of a video game, "Death in Venice," involving a chase between an old man, a young boy, and cholera. The game is a reflection of his life in the age of AIDS.

Beatrice has left his wife to start life over in a Soho apartment, but she, the ambitious daughter of a Mafia don, wants him back; she needs a husband to legitimize her campaign for political office. Beatrice is through with acting heterosexual: "If I wasn't acting a hundred percent, I was acting forty or fifty percent" (p. 30), but he also wants to avoid the stylized performance associated with acting gay: "I've forgotten how to respond naturally. I seem to camp automatically now, to expect insincerity, and admire finely wrought falsehood, and I shrug off everything" (p. 36). Beatrice's choice of nickname reflects the idea that finding oneself is in part a matter of working out one's sexual identification. He is not, as the name would suggest, a drag queen, but "conventionally masculine in manner" (p. 3). He is, as a matter of fact, both Bartholomew and Beatrice, both masculine and feminine, both public ('Bartholomew' is his pen name) and private.

Beatrice wants to "raise" himself, but his home is invaded by two teenage boys: Dy, a runaway preppie, and Puer, Beatrice's son by a brief marriage to a German radical. Dy has run away "to be free" (p. 9); Puer, to "feel less singular and alone" (p. 24). Beatrice falls in love with Dy but is disturbed by his lack of feeling toward his son's efforts to win his love. Beatrice tells Dy that "One of the problems of life" is "sorting out love and friendship and sex" (p. 28), which he manages to do as he works through his attachments to these two boys. Dy finally agrees to go back home, and Beatrice decides to let his son stay with him. At the end, Beatrice and Puer put the contents of Dy's journal of living with Beatrice, "Coming of Age in Soho," into the computer as a starting point for Beatrice's own writing: "Maybe there's something in there about me, or about us, or maybe about the three of us I can expand" (p. 77). As Puer types into the computer, Beatrice begins his writing: "It was the worst of times, but Bartholomew Dante began to come of age and this is his story" (p. 78).

At the end Beatrice is again Bartholomew, the author of *Little Boy Bound* is writing about coming of age, and the man who liked to tie boys up has freed himself and embraced his son. Coming of age is realizing one is both boy and man, both masculine and feminine. This drama of the maturation of man and artist is presented with an almost operatic mixture of realism and outlandish theater, from the invasions of Mafia goons who try to force Beatrice back to his wife to Puer's outlandish attempts at looking like the all-American boy. Character's names (Odysseus, Trajan, Puer) free them from the confines of realistic drama. The echo of Charles Dickens ("It was the best of times, it was the worst of times" is the first line of his

1859 novel, *A Tale of Two Cities*) in Beatrice/Bartholomew's last line is appropriate; Innaurato's play is Dickensian in its reliance on coincidence, its veering from comedy to pathos, its narrative freedom, and its generosity of spirit.

Harvey Fierstein's *Torch Song Trilogy* (1981) also moves its central character to an embrace of fatherhood. At the end of the trilogy a gay family has been forged, and Arnold's acceptance of love is linked to the acceptance by his ambivalent lover, Ed, of his own homosexuality. Arnold's troubled relationship with Ed is the through line that connects the three plays.

Each of the three plays in *Torch Song Trilogy* is written to be performed in a different style, moving from musical theater to domestic realism. The first play, *International Stud* (1978), alternates scenes and torch songs sung by "Lady Blues." The songs create the world Arnold inhabits. Instead of identifying with divas, like the protagonists of *The Lisbon Traviata,* Arnold identifies with the tough female voice of the torch singer, suffering and surviving unworthy men. Arnold is "the last of a dying breed,"[18] an old-style drag queen who makes his money singing torch songs in gay bars. When Arnold starts talking about what he wants in a man, "the international stud," he begins to sound like a torch-song lyric:

> A guy who knows what he wants and aint a'scared to go out and get it. A guy who satisfies his every need and don't mind if you get what you want in the bargain. Matter of fact, he aims to please. He'd be happy to be whatever you wanted him to be, 'cause you're happy bein' what he wants you to be. (p. 16)

Arnold does not yet see that what he wants in another man is what he must become. He does know that he needs this "stud" not for his on-stage female role but for his off-stage male one, "the part that's not so well protected" (p. 16).

Arnold's first monologue is addressed directly to the audience as he prepares to perform. In it he confesses the failing that makes a connection with the international stud—or becoming the international stud—impossible, the lack of self-love that prevents accepting love. We see Arnold's meeting with Ed Reiss as Ed's monologue. In essence, it is Ed's performance, the "line" he delivers to prospective "tricks" in gay bars; self-assured, clear in what he wants, though not without its red flags: "I'd ask you back to my place but I have this straight roommate. He's got a hangup about gays. . . . I date women too" (p. 18). This line signals Ed's inability to accept his homosexuality: "I've got to be proud of who I am" (p. 30). Ed has run away from Arnold precisely because he does love him and is terrified. He says sex with Arnold was "out of control" and refers to "losing" himself, both expressions of passion Ed finds terrifying, particularly when it means giving up ties to conventionality.

The simple platforms that make up the setting are stage "islands," allowing theatrical distance between Arnold and Ed to mirror their irreconcilable differences. A tape of their dialogue on their first night together is heard between choruses of one of Lady Blues' songs, as if the dialogue itself were the raw material for a torch song. Only in the final scene, in which Arnold takes control of the relationship by rejecting Ed's manipulative advances, are both actors visible in the same playing area. Ed, at that point in the throes of panic and indecision, wants Arnold to take charge and force him to give up Laurel, but Arnold has come to separate torch song from reality: "Maybe he's treating me just the way I want him to. Maybe I use him to give me that tragic torchsinger status I so admire in others. If that's true . . . then he's my International Stud. I love him. . . . But do I love him enough? What's enough? This is enough" (p. 43). Masochism should be left to performance, to torch songs. Arnold will not suffer through Ed's vacillations.

The monologues isolate their speakers, whose fears of commitment prevent honest dialogue. Yet, unlike Wilson's Lady Bright, Arnold has a real audience. The fourth wall of realistic theater has been razed and The International Stud begins and ends with direct address to the audience. The music, the torch songs, are not figments of Arnold's imagination but part of a metatheatrical performance. Fierstein has successfully mixed genres: drag act, cabaret, comic monologue, and dramatic scene.

Fugue in a Nursery (1979), the trilogy's second play, takes place at Ed's upstate New York farmhouse. Laurel, with whom Ed now lives, has invited Arnold up for the weekend in order to size up the competition (Laurel knows Ed is not over his feelings for Arnold). Alan, Arnold's lover, insists he and Arnold go; he knows Arnold has not recovered from Ed. Fugue in a Nursery is not presented within the conventions of realism. The setting is a gigantic bed, in which all the action takes place, underscoring the dominant role in sex of game-playing. The bed is a stage on which the four characters do a lot of acting. The scenes are accompanied by and interspersed with an instrumental quartet, each instrument representing one of the characters. The linear action is clearly defined, but the nonrealistic style of performance focuses on the interrelationships of characters and scenes.

Arnold's antagonist is Laurel, who rightly sees Arnold as a rival and wages a battle she only partially and temporarily wins. All of Laurel's relationships have been with gay or bisexual men, and she is not about to suffer another rejection. Arnold, on the other hand, has no intention of actually returning to Ed, no matter how strong his feelings are.

Alan, Arnold's new beau, is a beautiful, eighteen-year-old hustler who sees Arnold as both lover and parent. Alan has every reason to be insecure about Arnold, who never will say he loves Alan because he doesn't, or at least, because he won't admit he does:

> ARNOLD: So, maybe I don't love him, but I need that gorgeous imbecile, and I like to think that he needs me.
>
> . . . .
>
> ED: Don't you think he deserves to be loved?
> ARNOLD: Of course he does. Who doesn't. But who is? (p. 75)

Ed and Alan have, literally, a roll in the hay, an act that has less to do with their attraction to each other than with their feelings for Arnold. The aftermath is that Ed and Laurel get married, and Alan and Arnold make a formal commitment to their relationship. Both are compromised relationships. Ed's marriage is the result of Laurel's manipulation and his cowardice. Arnold still will not admit he loves Alan. The play ends with Arnold as writer and performer, singing his new torch song, which is both a rejection of Ed and a recognition of what his relationship with Alan will be:

> I can't live on love alone.
> Want somebody all my own. (p. 101)

The fact that the song is directed to Ed, not Alan, is a sign that he has not been forgotten:

> Keep my number by the phone
> Call me if you should atone. (p. 101)

Again, Arnold ends the play alone onstage, where he is in control of the action. Offstage, events and characters are messier and not so easy to manipulate.

The final play, *Widows and Children First* (1979), takes place five years later. Arnold is still grieving over the loss of Alan, killed by gay-bashers. Arnold's memories of Alan are of a more loving and reciprocal relationship than was evident in *Fugue in a Nursery*. This may be in part because, as Arnold admits, ". . . it's easier to love someone who's dead; they make so few mistakes" (p. 172).[19] It is also because a real love developed between Arnold and Alan during the five years they were together. Arnold is in the process of fulfilling his and Alan's ambition of adopting a gay son, and fifteen-year-old David is living with Arnold on a trial basis. So is Ed, who has left Laurel and "temporarily" moved into Arnold's living room. While the play moves toward the formation of a new nuclear family consisting of Arnold, Ed, and David, its focus is on Arnold's tempestuous break with his mother.

Widows and Children First is, as the title suggests, about "widows" and their children. One widow is Arnold's mother, and the play concerns in part her inability to establish a peaceful relationship with her gay son; the other is Arnold himself, "widowed" by Alan and trying to raise David, Arnold's streetwise foster son. The basic issues of the play are two related, politically charged issues for gay men: a young gay's right to a nurturing, gay-positive home and a gay man's right to be a surrogate parent to young gays.

The action has moved to a realistic setting, Arnold's apartment, thus moving into the most familiar territory of American drama, domestic realism, though, as is typical in gay drama, a member of the "normal" middle-class family is the outsider who is later to be removed from the scene. *Widows and Children First* depicts the conflict between parent and gay son that has since become the formula for television dramas about gay men, but Fierstein makes Arnold's mother a classic nightmare of a Jewish mama, powerful but unintentionally funny, in the grand tradition begun by Clifford Odets in *Awake and Sing* in 1935. Arnold's mother cannot see her son as a fit father for David nor her son's feelings of love and grief for Alan as equal to hers for her husband:

ARNOLD: How dare I say I loved him? You had it easy, Ma. You lost your husband in a nice clean hospital. I lost mine out there. They killed him there on the street. . . . Children. Children taught by people like you. 'Cause everybody knows that queers don't matter! Queers don't love! And those that do deserve what they get! (p. 145–46)

While he is still wounded by his mother's disapproval, she is angry that Arnold never really confided in her, even after she flew up to New York to attend Alan's funeral: "Maybe I could've comforted you" (p. 172). Arnold and his mother do share strength, temperament, stubbornness, and their status as widows.

As Arnold lays down the law to his mother, his new son sets terms for Arnold's relationship with him. Though Arnold has given this former battered child the only loving home he has ever known, David doesn't want to be an excuse for Arnold's isolation: "I'm tellin' you now: I'll walk if you try to use me as an excuse for sitting home alone, or to pick a fight with your mother or with Ed. Hey, you do what you gotta do. I aint judgin.' Just don't blame anybody but yourself" (p. 158). As David wants Arnold to understand that he has to take full responsibility for his life, Ed, now separated from Laurel and sleeping in Arnold's living room, wants Arnold to trust his love: "Arnold, the time I've spent here with you and David . . . it's been the closest thing to whatever it is I want" (p. 164). At the end, Arnold and Ed begin negotiating the sort of relationship they want, though they have no clear models: "Christ, I mean, I don't even know what this is supposed to be. I can't exactly buy a book or study some *Reader's Digest* article that's gonna tell me. All I know is whatever this is, it's not a grade B imitation of a heterosexual marriage" (p. 166).

Nothing is completely resolved at the end. Arnold is once again alone onstage, listening to a song on the radio that David has dedicated to him. Arnold, who needs "nothing from anyone except love and respect" (p. 152), will cautiously build a strong relationship with Ed. The ending intimates that a loving gay family is being forged, without the support of biological ties or received rituals.

Torch Song Trilogy advocates the right of gay men to have what the other 90 percent of society takes as its birthright—a loving home. Arnold, like Beatrice Dante in Innaurato's *Coming of Age in Soho,* has moved from loving a teenage boy to being a father to one. Yet the domestic realism of *Widows and Children First* reinforces a misconception that there is no difference between Arnold's family and a heterosexual family, that the gayness of Arnold, Ed, and David makes no appreciable difference. Could not Fierstein have used a dramatic idiom that suggested this home was going to be enlivened by its occupants' gayness, or at least by the imagination that shaped the first two plays? In *Widows and Children First,* the only music comes from the on-stage radio. While this might be a sign that Arnold has distanced himself from the role of torch singer in his own life, we miss the music. Moving Arnold from the world of experimental theater to that of Neil Simon may be comforting for a Broadway audience, but it is a reduction.

Growing Up to Music

The very title *Torch Song Trilogy* connects the action to music: two of its three plays are musical theater. The actions of all but one of the plays I have discussed in this chapter are set against or within forms of musical theater. In various ways, music has been a figure for both entrapment and liberation. In Wilson's *The Madness of Lady Bright,* the sound of Mozart wafting from another apartment is the cue for one of Leslie's theatrical transformations, as he turns his apartment into the lobby of a concert hall and imagines himself engaged in an intermission conversation. Yet Leslie is also aware that the music he hears is probably the accompaniment for a real tête à tête. Ultimately the music spinning out of Leslie's control is the most vivid metaphor of his madness. In McNally's *The Lisbon Traviata,* music is also a sign of the central characters' pathologies. The strains of Gustav Mahler's "Das Lied von der Erde" in Innaurato's *Coming of Age in Soho* represent first Beatrice's wish for solitude and later his loss of Dy. At a climactic moment, the strains of verismo opera accompany the threats of Beatrice's wife and her Mafia friends. In these plays, music is part of a culture with which gay men identify themselves. In Crowley's *The Boys in the Band,* dancing is one of the most important visible signs of homosexual behavior that is forbidden by "normal" society. Twice Alan's entrances interrupt dancing, a sign of the conflict between straight and gay society. Michael's only moment of happiness in the play is in the opening scene when he dances alone to bossa nova music being played on the radio.

If music and musical theater have been to gay playwrights such important aspects of the gay experience, offering positive and negative role models; if, as stated by the DJ in "Northern Exposure," a love of show tunes is a sign of homosexuality; musical theater should be a powerful medium for depicting the contemporary gay experience. I described in the previous chapter how London's Gay Sweatshop, following Brecht's example, used songs in their recreations of gay history, as part of a theatrical form that defied the constraints of realism. In America, William Finn's three musicals about the coming of age of Marvin—*In Trousers* (1979), *March of the Falsettos* (1981), and *Falsettoland* (1990)—are a compendium of the actions and themes of gay drama during the past three decades, but freed from the constraints of conventional drama. Of all the works discussed in this chapter, Finn's trilogy of musicals about Marvin present the richest, most complete picture of the emotional development of a gay man through his love for another man.

Finn's three musicals are not conventional Broadway musical extravaganzas. They are small in scale, with small casts and bands and simple, nonrepresentational scenery. Solos are rare in Finn's musical structure and are used like Shakespearean soliloquies to allow a character to explain himself. Most of the music is made up of elaborate ensembles that define relationships and conflicts. The artifice of song allows the thoughts of the characters to be voiced as "naturally" as their words. Like many contemporary composers of musicals, Finn through-composes (there is no dialogue), thus creating intimate operas written for Broadway voices. Finn, like Stephen Sondheim, uses music to set complex, sophisticated, witty lyrics at least as literate and precise as any script discussed in this chapter.

The three Marvin musicals are connected by Marvin's relationships with his nuclear family—his wife and son—and with his lover, Whizzer. They move from Marvin's first sexual encounter with Whizzer in 1979 to Whizzer's death from AIDS three years later. Each of the musicals tells the story of a key moment in this history.

In Trousers (1979) chronicles Marvin's move out of the conventional heterosexual world; he leaves his wife and son and moves in with Whizzer. The only characters other than Marvin are his high-school teacher, Miss Goldberg, his high-school sweetheart, and his wife, Trina. The emphasis is on figures from Marvin's adolescence because Marvin remains a spoiled, petulant adolescent, prone to fits when he doesn't get his way. The central moment is Marvin's starring role in a school play about Christopher Columbus. After meeting Whizzer, Marvin presents a new play about the discovery of the new world, in which Columbus has a shipboard romance with Amerigo Vespucci and names the new world after him. "The thing about explorers," Marvin says, "they discover things that are already there."[20] Marvin's new world is his homosexuality, but at first this is just another appetite to be satisfied. Sex with Whizzer is described joyously and graphically in "Whizzer Going Down," a contrast to the chaste avoidance of sex in most gay plays. However, Marvin's nonsexual expectations of his relationship with Whizzer are immature and unrealistic:

> Whizzer will act very parental,
> Completely gentle,
> Absolutely swell. (p. 71)

Whizzer's invisibility in *In Trousers* is a sign that he is now little more than a virtuosic sexual performer and the object of unrealistic expectations.

At the opening of *March of the Falsettos* (1981), Marvin wants to keep his entire universe intact:

> I want a tight knit family.
> I want a group that harmonizes.
> I want my wife and kid and friend
> To pretend
> Time will mend
> Our pain. (p. 98)

Wife and kid and friend have other ideas. Trina marries Marvin's psychiatrist, adolescent son Jason worries that he will grow up like his father (he already acts as petulant), and Whizzer, disgusted with Marvin's "family charades," packs his bags.

Marvin has poisoned his relationship with Whizzer with the assertions of conventional masculinity. In place of the ecstatic descriptions of sex in *In Trousers,* Marvin and Whizzer now fight. Like their chess games, Marvin sees his relationship with Whizzer as a series of contests he must win. Worse, he sees it as a conventional, patriarchal marriage:

> Whizzer's supposed to make the dinner—
> Make the dinner, look to screw.
> That's what pretty boys should do. (p. 129)

At the end, Marvin and his son, Jason, are alone onstage together. Marvin gives Jason a fatherly assurance, "You'll be, kid, a man, kid, whatever the song" (p. 175), but the principal question raised in *March of the Falsettos* is what does it mean to be a man. Manhood—conventional masculinity—is a set of baggage that the men of *March of the Falsettos,* gay and straight, must rethink. The title song, sung in falsetto by Marvin, Whizzer, Jason, and Mendel (Trina's new husband) is a challenge to sing without the voice—the vanity, competitiveness, and hierarchical demands—of conventional masculinity.

> Who is man enough to
> March of the Falsettos? (p. 153)

It is the masculine voice that keeps these men from giving and accepting love from anyone, that leads them to be frightened of love.

Falsettoland (1990) is, as its opening song states:

> About growing up,
> Getting older,
> Living on a lover's shoulder,
> Learning love is not a crime. (p. 185)

To the five characters of *March of the Falsettos,* Finn has added a lesbian couple: a doctor, Charlotte, and a caterer, Cordelia. Doctor and caterer become crucial characters in the two related actions of *Falsettoland,* Whizzer's illness and Jason's bar mitzvah.

Marvin and Whizzer are reunited when both go to see Jason play baseball (Jason likes Whizzer the best of the men in his life). Another song of their sex life shows how far Marvin has "been revised" since "Whizzer Going Down":

> It's been hot,
> Also it's been swell.
> More than not,
> It's been more than words can tell.
>
> . . .
>
> We take it day by day.
> What more can I say? (p. 216–217)

Love has made Marvin less articulate, less forceful. He trusts language less. The prevalence of AIDS among her patients has made Charlotte even more conscious of the limitations of language: "Something so bad that words have lost their meaning" (p. 219).

When Whizzer is hospitalized with an HIV-related illness, Marvin's ex-wife and son realize that Whizzer has become part of their family:

> Trying not to care about this man Marvin loves.
> But that's my life.
> He shared my life. (p. 224)

Trina articulates what all the characters have to accept: "Life is never what you planned" (p. 224).

At Jason's behest, his bar mitzvah is held in Whizzer's hospital room. There at this family gathering, Jason is hailed as:

> Son of Abraham, Isaac and Jacob
> Son of Marvin, son of Trina, son of Whizzer, son of Mendel.
> And godchild to the lesbians from next door. (p. 244)

Whizzer dies without a death scene, that celebration of victimization that typically culminates nineteenth-century opera. Whizzer is too tough to indulge in such melodramatics:

> Give me the balls to orchestrate
> A graceful leave.
> That's my reprieve. (p. 239)

At the end, Marvin sings a song to, and with, his memory of Whizzer, affirming not only their love but the man he has become because of that love:

> Who would I be
> If I had not loved you?
> How would I know what love is? (p. 245)

Marvin has matured enough to celebrate what he had instead of regressing to his earlier petulance and self-pity. Loving has come of age.

In the final chorus, characters sing that Falsettoland "is where we take a stand" (p. 248), and Finn's stand is uncompromising. He has celebrated the sexual component of Marvin and Whizzer's relationship, as well as their growth from sparring partners to friends. He has placed Marvin and Whizzer's relationship within a network of marriages and, in the process, created a new sense of family. Everyone, not just the gay protagonist, has come of age, a bittersweet process that means:

> Holding to the ground as the ground keeps shifting.
> Trying to stay sane as the rules keep changing. (p. 224)

Unlike the other protagonists discussed in this chapter, Marvin is not an artist—we don't know what his profession is—but he is presented within a self-reflexive work of art that, as musical theater tends to do, celebrates the acts of creation and performance as it celebrates the ways in which Marvin and the members of his family bravely forge their lives and the links between them. Marvin and his family are highly conscious of language. Created within a world of verbal and visual metaphor, the characters seem always aware of the power of metaphor and of their own experience as metaphor, a gift denied most inhabitants of the real or realistic worlds and harking back to the world inhabited by characters in Elizabethan drama.

Both of my chapters on openly gay drama have ended with works that defy the conventions of post-Ibsen representational theater and the compromises of the realistic, domestic problem play. Other forms are more suited to convey the gay experience as something richer than a social problem to be solved or a domestic intrusion to be expelled. Gay playwrights present their protagonists as artists, particularly as writers and performers, and it is in the world of admitted artifice—poetry, music, theater—that the richness and challenge of acting gay can be most fully depicted. Realism defines and reinforces limits. Works like Finn's Marvin trilogy and Paul Godfrey's *Once in a While the Odd Thing Happens* (1990) allow characters and audience to transcend every given except the free play of imagination possible in the theater. In this freedom, the protagonist can grow into gayness and learn to love.

A culture built on the necessity of acting—in which freedom from the constraints of conventional gender roles can mean the possibility of life of the imagination, in which alternative readings of musical theater offer a supportive mythology in an opulent parallel world, and in which a play of language defuses oppressive judgment—is best re-created by a theater freed from the literal-mindedness of most mainstream realistic drama. Marlowe's Gaveston said of Edward, "Music and poetry is his delight," then described an opulent theater that blurred gender and celebrated homoerotic desire. In the metatheatrical world of *Falsettoland* and other gay theatrical works by Martin Sherman, Neil Bartlett, Paul Godfrey, Doric Wilson, Philip Osment, Noel Greig, and Drew Griffiths, we see vividly the positive meanings of acting gay. Freed from the restraints of the structure, conventions, and assumptions of realistic drama, their works show us characters with complex protean identities. Theater in these works is not a slick metaphor for illusion. Theater is the mirror of the role-playing and stereotyping gay men experience every day. More important, it reflects the complex and multifaceted identities of people who have created their affirming personae. Gay theater cannot solve the problems of heterosexism or AIDS, but it can offer a liberating vision of what it means to be gay.

NOTES

Preface

1. This is Lanford Wilson as quoted in an interview with Robert Massa, *Village Voice* (June 28, 1988), p. 38.

2. For the most part I choose to use the word *heterosexism* instead of the more common *homophobia*. Richard Mohr's argument won me over:

> It is worth noting the problems with the term's [homophobia] adoption. At a minimum, it is vague. If it just means "fear of gays," modeled, say, on "xenophobia," why not just say so and save two syllables? More important, the coinage is morally misleading. Its use makes it sound as though bigotry is a mental illness, like agoraphobia, or a physical illness, like hydrophobia. But the bigot's problem is not disease, whether mental or physical. The bigot is not sick; he is immoral. . . . If antigay bigotry needs an abstract noun, "heterosexism," though awkward, at least sets the concept in the correct moral constellation, by placing it alongside "racism" and "sexism." Richard Mohr, *Gays and Justice,* (New York: Columbia University Press, 1988, p. 12)

I will use *homophobia,* then, only when I mean literally a phobia (uncontrollable, irrational fear) about homosexuality (Brick's in Tennessee Williams' *Cat on a Hot Tin Roof,* for instance). Otherwise I will use *heterosexism.*

3. On June 27, 1969, a number of lesbians and gay men actively fought police

harassment inside and outside the Stonewall Inn on Christopher Street at Sheridan Square in New York's Greenwich Village. The riot has come to mark the beginning of gay liberation in the United States. See John d'Emilio, *Sexual Politics,' Sexual Communities: The Making of a Homosexual Minority in the United States, 1940-1970* (Chicago: University of Chicago Press, 1983), 223–249.

4. A word about my practice of dating plays. The date listed in parentheses is that of the New York or London production. *The Green Bay Tree* was produced in both cities in 1933. Contemporary American plays tend to have a number of productions in regional theaters or workshops before they are produced in New York. I will list the date of the New York production. Publication information will be found in the notes.

1: Seeing Gay

1. Martin Esslin, *The Field of Drama* (London: Methuen, 1987), 60.

2. Herbert Blau, *Take Up the Bodies: Theater at the Vanishing Point* (Urbana: University of Illinois Press, 1982), 289.

3. Don Shewey, "The Actor as Object of Desire," *American Theatre* (October 1990), 7:30.

4. Herbert Blau, *The Audience* (Baltimore: Johns Hopkins University Press, 1990), 26.

5. The production took place at the Shakespeare Memorial Theatre, Stratford-upon-Avon, 1987, and at the Barbican Center, London, 1988.

6. William Shakespeare, *The Merchant of Venice,* in Stanley Wells, Gary Taylor, John Jowett, and William Montgomery, eds., *William Shakespeare: The Complete Works* (Oxford, England: Clarendon Press, 1988), 448. Further references to this play are to this edition.

7. The "shadow" of the "Elizabethan sin of Sodom . . . was never far from the flower-strewn world of Elizabethan friendship and it could never wholly be distinguished from it." Alan Bray, "Homosexuality and the Signs of Male Friendship in Elizabethan England," *History Workshop Journal,* no. 29 (Spring 1990), 16. Bray's recent essay unravels the complex relationship of physical intimacy, romantic language, male friendship, and sodomy in Elizabethan England.

8. For the classic reading of the fraught complex of homosociality and homosexuality and their relationship to women, see Eve Kosofsky Sedgwick, *Between Men* (New York: Columbia University Press, 1985).

9. For the central work in this area, see Alan Bray, *Homosexuality in Renaissance England* (London: Gay Men's Press, 1982).

10. Blau, *The Audience,* 53.

11. My use (my colleague Stanley Fish might say misuse) of the term *interpretive community,* needs some explication. To Fish, the interpretive community is "made up of those who share interpretive strategies, not for reading but for writing texts, for constituting their properties." "The meanings and texts produced by an interpretive community are not subjective because they do not proceed from an isolated individual but from a public and conventional point of view." Stanley Fish,

Is There a Text in This Class: The Authority of Interpretive Communities (Cambridge, Mass.: Harvard University Press, 1980), 14.

Is there a gay interpretive community in Fish's sense of the term? I would have to answer yes and no. For much of the period covered in this study, the self-image of gay men was a text written by dominant culture. Dramas reflect this internalized homophobia. Post-Stonewall gay writers and performers defy, challenge, and re-shape the middle-class American interpretive community that forms the audience for drama, but there is some question whether, in the process, they create another interpretive community.

On the other hand, many lesbians and gay men, from the time they knew they were "different," joined a shared pattern of rereading and writing that finds a space for their sexuality. When I speak of separate interpretive communities, I refer to the fact that a gay man is likely to read, say, a Tennessee Williams play differently from a heterosexual man. Moreover, gay writers are likely to be aware that they are writing for two audiences, gay and straight, with two different codes.

12. "The combination of themes—homosexuality and the horrors of Dachau—may be overwhelming." Lee A. Jacobus, Editor's Preface to Martin Sherman's *Bent,* in Jacobus, ed., *The Bedford Introduction to Drama* (New York: St. Martin's Press, 1989), 907. This syntactical equation of homosexuality and Dachau is classic, but it is particularly surprising from St. Martin's, a press that has been in the forefront of gay literature.

13. Martin Sherman, *Bent,* in Don Shewey, ed., *Out Front: Contemporary Gay and Lesbian Plays,* 127. Further references to *Bent* are to this text.

14. Simon Watney quotes an article in the *Sun,* a trashy London tabloid, about gay actor Michael Cashman's casting as the gay Colin on the hit soap opera "Eastenders": " 'There is no suggestion that actor Michael Cashman is gay in real life. He is simply playing a role.' " Watney comments on the "pathological insistence that the actor is distinct from the part he plays, as if to reassure readers that no actor who is gay in 'real life' could possibly appear on *Eastenders.*" *Policing Desire: Pornography, AIDS, and the Media* (Minneapolis: University of Minnesota Press, 1987), 87.

The same sorts of assertions appeared in the American press about Jack Coleman and William Campbell, the lovers on "Dynasty." The *Sun* article about Michael Cashman was particularly silly since the actor is openly gay.

15. Proposed by the Conservative government in 1987 and passed by Parliament in 1988, Section 28 forbids any local government to "intentionally promote homosexuality or publish material with the intention of promoting homosexuality" or "promote the teaching in any maintained school of the acceptability of homosexuality as a pretended family relationship." Thus government-supported theaters like the Royal National Theatre, the Royal Shakespeare Company, the Royal Court, and smaller theaters throughout the United Kingdom receiving local goverment subsidies could be enjoined from presenting plays that offered positive gay images. The National Theatre 1990 production of Sherman's *Bent* provided a test case in the most highly visible arena. The production was so successful that it moved from the National to the West End for a run limited only by Ian McKellan's other

commitments. See Jeffrey Weeks, *Coming Out: Homosexual Politics in Britain from the Nineteenth Century to the Present,* rev. ed. (London: Quartet Books, 1990), 237–248.

16. Martin Sherman's *A Madhouse in Goa* opened at the Lyric, in Hammersmith, March 1989, for a limited run, then moved to the West End for another limited run. It was directed by Robert Allan Ackerman. Rupert Graves played David; Ian Sears, Costos.

17. Martin Sherman, *A Madhouse in Goa* (Charlbury, England: Amber Lane Press, 1989), 28.

18. Richard Mohr, "Outing: A Problem in Gay Ethics" (unpublished draft), p. 10.

19. A word on the use of the term *gender.* In current theoretical writings, one's sex (male or female) relates to biological attributes. One's gender (masculine or feminine) is a social construction. Thus the gender order is not a natural hierarchy, but a socially constructed one that places heterosexual men above women and homosexual men.

This distinction gives another reason for the absurdity of the term *homosexual.* Homosexuality does relate to the act of sex and the same-sex object of desire, but definitions of homosexuality and discourse about homosexuality, being social constructions, are not stable descriptions of natural phenomena. They change from time to time and from society to society. Moreover, a homosexual is not only different from a heterosexual by reason of the sex of the object of his desire, he is also shaped by his own history of oppression, marginalization, or rejection because of his homosexuality.

20. "Some men, of course, will resist kissing. This resistance is often a last holdout against a full commitment to homosexuality ('cowboys don't kiss'). Hustlers who think of themselves as straight don't kiss. When young adolescent boys start fooling around with each other, they also often draw the line at kissing. As long as their lips don't meet they can believe that what they are doing is not homosexual, but just a way of getting their rocks off." Charles Silverstein and Edmund White, *The Joy of Gay Sex* (New York: Crown Publishers, 1977), 133.

21. C. A. Tripp, *The Homosexual Matrix* (New York, New American Library, 1977), 226.

22. Arthur Miller, *A View from the Bridge* (New York: Viking, 1960), 44. Further references are to this edition. The Broadway premiere, directed by Martin Ritt (September 1955), featured Van Heflin as Eddie and Richard Davalos as Rodolfo.

23. Some colleagues have argued with this characterization of Miller's attitude toward sexual politics. Others see my reference to Miller's "brutal patriarchy" as unsupported name-calling. For both groups I offer this clarification.

Arthur Miller sees wives as long-suffering creatures whose duty it is, not only to put up with their husbands' failures and cruelty but also to support staunchly their husbands' illusions or downright lies. In *Death of a Salesman* (1949), Linda Loman supports Willy even though he has consistently lied to her, bullied her, and cheated on her. That she should not only submit to this treatment but lionize the man who treats her this way is never questioned. Esther, at the beginning of *The*

Price (1968), is rightfully dissatisfied with her guilt-ridden, self-pitying husband, but ultimately Miller has her uphold the very illusions about his mean-spirited father and his duty toward his father that have been the source of his (and her) unhappiness. In *The Crucible* (1953), Elizabeth Proctor takes the blame for her husband's adultery and thus the responsibility for the whole mess with Abigail. Ultimately Proctor takes his stand not because of his wife but for his three sons.

Although the men are weak, the women are often presented as the cause of the problem the play depicts. In *The Crucible,* Abigail, after all, is the problem. It is not, as it was historically, a group of prepubescent girls who were empowered by their superstitious elders: it is a group of frustrated, unhappy adolescent girls, led by a girl who has slept with a man and developed what amounts to a "Fatal Attraction," evil, destructive infatuation for him. Female sexuality is as much the problem as male superstition. In *The Price,* the most violent image is of the mother vomiting on her husband's hands when he tells her all their money is lost.

24. Arthur Miller, *After the Fall* (New York: Viking, 1964), 98.

25. *The Boys in the Band,* by Mart Crowley, was first performed off Broadway at Theatre Four on April 14, 1968, under the direction of Robert Moore. Peter White was Alan, Robert La Tourneaux the hustler. The text was published in 1968 by Farrar, Straus & Giroux. The scene under discussion is on pages 81–83.

26. Lanford Wilson's *Fifth of July* opened at the Circle Repertory Theatre on April 27, 1978, under the direction of Marshall Mason. William Hurt was Ken Talley, Jeff Daniels his lover, Jed. It opened on Broadway, under Mason's direction, at the New Apollo Theatre, on November 5, 1980. Christopher Reeve (later succeeded by Richard Thomas) was Ken. Jeff Daniels (later John Dossett) was Jed. The original text was published by Hill and Wang, 1979 (the kiss is on page 11). The Broadway text, which is considerably revised, is available from Dramatists' Play Service, 1982 (the kiss is on page 8).

27. *Six Degrees of Separation,* by John Guare, opened at the Mitzi E. Newhouse Theater of Lincoln Center in New York, on May 19, 1990, under Jerry Zaks' direction. Stockard Channing was Ouisa; James McDaniel, Paul; David Eigenberg, the hustler. The play moved to the Vivian Beaumont Theater on October 28, with Courtney B. Vance in the role of Paul. The text was published by Vintage in New York, 1990. The scene under discussion is on pages 47–50, and further references are to this edition.

28. I cannot help but be curious about how blacks respond to Guare's play. It is clear from a white point of view why the dangerous stranger must be black, and from a heterosexual point of view why he is gay. But making him a gay black raises unanswered questions about the intense problems of black heterosexism.

29. Margaret Walters, *The Male Nude: A New Perspective* (Harmondsworth, England: Penguin, 1978), 17.

30. Barbara Freedman, *Staging the Gaze: Postmodernism, Psychoanalysis, and Shakespearean Comedy* (Ithaca: Cornell University Press, 1991), 1.

31. Walters, *The Male Nude,* 11.

32. Tennessee Williams, *A Streetcar Named Desire,* vol. 1, *The Theatre of Tennessee Williams* (New York: New Directions Publishing, 1971), 371.

33. Tennessee Williams, *Cat on a Hot Tin Roof,* vol. 3, *The Theatre of Tennessee Williams* (New York: New Directions Publishing, 1971), 30.

34. Robert Patrick, *T Shirts,* in William M. Hoffman, ed., *Gay Plays: The First Collection* (New York: Avon Books, 1979), 42. The play was first performed at the Out-and-About Theatre, Minneapolis, October 19, 1978, and directed by Richard E. Rehse. Further references are to the published text listed above.

35. Robert Patrick, *Mercy Drop and Other Plays* (New York: Calamus Books, 1979). The production was first performed at the WPA Theatre in New York in February 1973, under the direction of Hugh Gittens. Kevin Breslin played the boy, Johnny.

Patrick notes that in the original production of *Mercy Drop,* one of the leading characters who was to appear nude had to keep his clothes on because he contracted warts on his penis. "Rather than give science-fiction overtones to what is, after all, essentially a love story, he was allowed to retain his jumpsuit" (p. 3). The published script contains more production photos than is usually the case, many featuring nude shots of the lead actor. Patrick's Author's Note, explaining why the other actor is clad, not only explains the discrepancy between written text and photos but also offers an apology for providing less nudity than the words promise. The "audience" for the published text was to receive the same view of nudity as the theater audience.

36. Patrick, *Mercy Drop,* 78.

37. I don't want to suggest that male nudity happened only in gay drama. The Broadway success of the rock musical *Hair* in the sixties proved its commercial viability. It was also a feature of such unsuccessful commercial countercultural dramas as the short lived *Che,* by Lennox Raphael. A nude scene provided the climax of the highly successful *Equus,* by Peter Shaffer. Though the scene was a heterosexual "sex" scene, the focus was on the male character, and the sexual attraction of the older narrator-character for the boy who appears nude is not too well hidden (see chapter 3 of this book).

38. Terrence McNally, *The Lisbon Traviata* (New York: The Fireside Theatre, 1990), 88. The first New York production opened at the Theatre Off Park on June 4, 1985, under John Tillinger's direction, with Benjamin Hendrickson as Stephen and Steven Culp as the unclad Paul. A revised version was produced at the Promenade Theatre in October 1989, under Tillinger's direction, with Anthony Heald and John Slattery as Stephen and Paul.

39. Ben Jonson, *Epicoene, or The Silent Woman.* The play was directed by Danny Boyle for the Royal Shakespeare Company, Swan Theatre, Stratford-upon-Avon, in the summer of 1989. Jared Harris was Clerimont, Liza Hayden his "ingle." John Hannah was Epicene.

40. For the most cogent, witty discussion of this subject, see Stephen Orgel, "Nobody's Perfect: Or Why Did the English Stage Take Boys for Women," in Ronald R. Butters, John M. Clum, and Michael Moon, eds., *Displacing Homophobia* (Durham, N.C.: Duke University Press, 1989), 7–30.

41. Simon Trussler, Introduction to Ben Jonson's *Epicoene* (The Programme-

text for the Royal Shakespeare Company production) (London: Methuen, 1989), xiii.

42. Dyer notes how effeminate "queens" and mannish "dykes" are considered to be more like the opposite sex. "Yet they are not exactly masculine or feminine either. In gay usage, they may be an assertion of in-betweenism or more generally of a refusal of rigid sex role-playing; but in their use within the dominant culture they are more characteristically portrayed as people who in failing, because of not being heterosexual, to be real women or men, at the same time fail to be truly masculine or feminine in other ways." "Seen to Be Believed: Some Problems in the Representation of Gay People as Typical," *Studies in Visual Communication* (Spring 1983), 9:12.

43. Harvey Fierstein, *Torch Song Trilogy* (New York: Gay Presses of New York, 1980), 15. After the individual plays of the trilogy had their LaMama productions, *Torch Song Trilogy* was presented off off Broadway by The Glines on October, 16, 1981, in a production directed by Peter Pope and with Fierstein as Arnold. The production later moved off Broadway and then to a small Broadway house, the Helen Hayes Theatre.

44. Jerry Herman, "A Little More Mascara," in Fierstein's *La Cage aux Folles*. George Hearn played Albin/Zaza in the Broadway production, which opened at the Palace, under Arthur Laurents' direction, in August 1973.

45. It is interesting to note that the London production of *La Cage aux Folles* was not a success. Drag is much more a staple of British low comedy (see television shows like *Monty Python's Flying Circus* or *Benny Hill*) and is connected to the mockery and degradation of women. This celebration of American drag simply did not translate.

46. David Henry Hwang, *M. Butterfly* (New York: New American Library, 1988), 60. Further references are to this edition. *M. Butterfly* opened on Broadway in March 1988, in a production directed by John Dexter, with John Lithgow as Gallimard and B. D. Wong as Song. I write in chapter 3 about Dexter's ability, in production, to bring out the homosexual subtext in Peter Shaffer's plays, but in New York and London (with Anthony Hopkins), his production of Hwang's play assiduously avoided its subtext.

47. Charles Ludlam, *The Mystery of Irma Vep,* in *The Complete Plays of Charles Ludlam* (New York: Harper & Row, 1989), 795.

48. Derek D. Smith played Edgar, Jane, and Irma. Wil Love played the other characters in this production, which opened in May 1991.

49. "To interpret a text is not to give a (more or less justified, more or less free) meaning, but on the contrary to appreciate what *plural* constitutes it." Roland Barthes, *S/Z,* trans. Richard Miller (New York: Farrar, Straus, & Giroux, 1974), 5. While any theatrical adaptation limits the number of plural readings, and may add more, between the readings of adapter and audience member, the kind of reading Barthes describes is exactly what Bartlett gives the Balzac story. I have been interested to see that none of the interviews with Bartlett I have read cites Barthes' work. Perhaps Bartlett, who is a student and translator of French literature, did not want his work to appear too esoteric.

50. Neil Bartlett, *Sarrasine* (unpublished libretto), 1990. The musical score was composed by Nicholas Bloomfield. I am grateful to Neil Bartlett and *Sarrasine*'s producer, Simon Mellor, for letting me study the script and allowing me to quote from it.

51. Honoré de Balzac, *Sarrasine,* trans. Richard Miller, in Roland Barthes, *S/Z* (New York: Farrar, Straus, & Giroux, 1974), 252. In Balzac's story, Sarrasine is a sculptor, a perfect image for his rigid readings of those he wants to be his subjects.

52. Quoted in Gerard Raymond, "The Last Castrato: Neil Bartlett Adapts Balzac's Short Story, *Sarrasine*," *Theatre Week* (September 2–8, 1991), 22.

The protean nature of La Zambinella is effectively reflected in Nicholas Bloomfield's superb muscial score, which veers from quotations from eighteenth- and nineteenth-century opera to show tunes and Edith Piaf–like love songs. The instrumentalists who provide the background music and accompany the songs are onstage with the actors and, at times, interact with the characters.

53. Williams, *A Streetcar Named Desire,* 355.

2: AIDS Drama: Displacing Camille

1. Paula A. Treichler, "AIDS, Homophobia, and Biomedical Discourse," *October* (Winter 1987), 43:42. See also Treichler's essay "AIDS, Gender, and Biomedical Discourse: Current Contests for Meaning," in Elizabeth Fee and Daniel M. Fox, eds., *AIDS and the Burdens of History* (Berkeley: University of California Press, 1988), 190–266.

2. Simon Watney, "The Spectacle of AIDS," *October* (Winter 1987), 43:78.

3. Robert Chesley, *Hold,* in *Hard Plays/Stiff Parts: The Homoerotic Plays of Robert Chesley* (San Francisco: Alamo Square Press, 1990), 154. Further references to *Hold* are to this edition.

4. Robert Chesley, *(Wild) Person, Tense (Dog),* in *Hard Plays/Stiff Parts,* 133.

5. Robert Chesley, *Night Sweat,* in *Hard Plays/Stiff Parts,* 66.

6. Lanford Wilson, *A Poster of the Cosmos,* in M. Elizabeth Osborn, ed., *The Way We Live Now: American Plays and the AIDS Crisis* (New York: Theatre Communications Group, 1990), 74.

7. Jean Claude van Itallie, *Ancient Boys,* in *Gay Plays: An International Anthology* (New York: Ubu Repertory Theater Publications, 1989) 393.

8. Terrence McNally, *Andre's Mother,* in Osborn, ed., *The Way We Live Now,* 191.

9. William M. Hoffman, *As Is,* in Don Shewey, ed., *Out Front: Contemporary Gay and Lesbian Plays* (New York: Grove Press, 1988), 547.

10. Richard Greenberg, *Eastern Standard* (New York: Grove Weidenfeld, 1989), 63.

11. Sander L. Gilman, *Disease and Representation: Images of Illness from Madness to AIDS* (Ithaca, N.Y.: Cornell University Press, 1988), 2.

12. Charles S. Rosenberg, "Disease and Social Order in America: Perceptions and Expectations," in Fee and Fox, eds., *AIDS and the Burdens of History,* 27.

13. Alan M. Brandt, "AIDS: From Social History to Social Policy," in *AIDS and the Burdens of History*, 155.

14. See Jeffrey Weeks, *Sexuality and Its Discontents: Meanings, Myths, and Modern Sexualities* (London: Routledge & Kegan Paul, 1985).

15. Brandt, "AIDS," in *AIDS and the Burdens of History*, 151.

16. For a fuller discussion of AIDS and morality, see Simon Watney, "The Spectacle of AIDS," *October, 43* (Winter 1987), 71–86.

17. Susan Sontag, *AIDS and Its Metaphors* (New York: Farrar, Straus & Giroux, 1989), 72–73.

18. For a study of the relation of AIDS literature to the past and to memory, see John M. Clum, " 'The Time Before the War': AIDS, Memory, and Desire," *American Literature* (December 1990), 62:648–667.

19. I am thinking particularly of the Marwoods of George Lillo's *The London Merchant (1731)* and Gotthold Lessing's *Miss Sara Sampson (1755)*. This Marwood herself is a descendant of William Congreve's unhappy, destructive Marwood in *The Way of the World* (1700). The fallen woman, then, moves from seventeenth-century aristocratic comedy to eighteenth-century bourgeois "tragedy" to nineteenth-century romantic melodrama.

20. Alexandre Dumas, fils, *La Dame aux Camélias,* Edith Reynolds and Nigel Playfair, trans., in Stephen S. Stanton, ed., *Camille and Other Plays* (New York: Hill & Wang, 1957), 118. Further references to the play are to this text.

21. Alexandre Dumas, fils, *La Dame aux Camélias,* David Coward, trans. (Oxford, England: Oxford University Press, 1986), 11.

22. Dumas, fils, *La Dame aux Camélias* (the novel), 37–38.

23. Gilman, *Disease and Representation,* 256–257.

24. Catherine Clément, *Opera, or the Undoing of Women,* Betsy Wing, trans. (Minneapolis: University of Minnesota Press, 1988), 62.

25. In Nicholas Muni's 1991 contemporary staging of Verdi's *La Traviata* at the New York City Opera, Violetta, Verdi's version of Marguerite, dies of AIDS, not consumption. While reviewers noted that the audience giggled at the hospital ward death scene that had poor Violetta singing "Addio del Passato" with tubes in her nose, the production acknowledged the resemblance between the master narrative of *La Dame aux Camélias* and contemporary AIDS narratives.

26. My focus in this book is on gay men, but the causality I describe in this section has been applied to other "risk groups" for HIV infection. Drug addicts too are seen as suffering the wages of sin or of excessive appetite, which is seen as the same thing. The distribution of clean needles, like the distribution of condoms or safe-sex information, is resisted because some feel that preventing or denying the "sin" is preferable to saving the "sinner." Thus the category of "innocent" People With AIDS as if there are guilty People With AIDS.

Because there are a number of affluent gay men who support the theater, their experiences with AIDS are most often the stuff of drama. Even television drama tends to present AIDS as a disease of affluent men.

27. Gilman, *Disease and Representation,* 258. Gilman notes that from the En-

lightenment, the image of the syphilitic shifts from male to female, "but then only with the female as the image of the source of infection" (253–254).

28. Watney, "The Spectacle of AIDS," 73.

29. Charles Ludlam, "Observations on Acting," *American Theatre* (October 1990), 7:36.

30. There were a number of such couples in 1985, the year of the gay on network television. The prototypes were Stephen Carrington and Luke Fuller on *Dynasty*, a couple that bore many resemblances to Michael and Peter, who appeared later the same year.

31. *Our Sons* was written by William Hanley, directed by John Erman. It aired on ABC.

32. John J. O'Connor, "Gay Images: TV's Mixed Signals," *New York Times* (May 19, 1991), sec. 2, p. 32.

33. Larry Kramer, *The Normal Heart* (New York: New American Library, 1985), 71.

34. The Gay Sweatshop is Britain's leading gay theater group. It began producing gay drama in London and on tour in 1974 and is still active. For a comprehensive history of this important group, see Philip Osment, "Finding Room on the Agenda for Love: A History of Gay Sweatshop," in *Gay Sweatshop: Four Plays and a Company* (London: Methuen, 1989).

35. Andy Kirby, *Compromised Immunity*, in Osment, ed., *Gay Sweatshop: Four Plays and a Company* (London: Methuen, 1989), 57. Further references are to this edition.

36. Richard Greenberg, *Eastern Standard* (New York: Grove Weidenfeld, 1989), 19. Further references are to this edition.

37. van Itallie, *Ancient Boys*, in *Gay Plays*, 368.

38. William M. Hoffman, *As Is*, in Shewey, ed., *Out Front*, 520. Further references are to this edition.

39. Edmund White, "Esthetics and Loss," in John Preston, ed., *Personal Dispatches: Writers Confront AIDS* (New York: St. Martins Press, 1989), 149.

40. Robert Chesley, *Jerker, or the Helping Hand*, in Shewey, ed., *Out Front*, 453. Further references are to this edition.

41. Harvey Fierstein, *Safe Sex* (New York: Atheneum, 1988), 57–58. Further references are to this edition.

42. Larry Kramer, *The Normal Heart*, 114. Further references are to this New American Library edition.

43. Larry Kramer, *Reports from the Holocaust: The Making of an AIDS Activist* (New York: St. Martins Press, 1989), 186.

44. Alisa Solomon, "AIDS Crusaders Act Up a Storm," *American Theatre* (October 1989), 6:39.

45. Stephen Chapot, "Liz Taylor, Live," in Preston, ed., *Personal Dispatches,* 95.

46. There have been a number of works based on the AIDS quilt. For those who have not seen the quilt, the HBO telefilm, available on video, *Common Threads: Stories From the Quilt,* is a superb introduction to the significance of the quilt. It is also a fine documentary of a chapter in gay life, to be seen in the context of other

major documentaries, such as *Before Stonewall* and *The Times of Harvey Milk*. Also useful as an introduction is *The Quilt: Stories From the NAMES Project* (New York: Pocket Books, 1988). I was also instructed by the text of Richard Mohr's illustrated lecture, "TEXT(ile): Reading the NAMES Project AIDS Quilt."

47. This production, *Unnatural Acts,* was developed by Jeffrey Storer and Ed Hunt, artistic directors of the Manbites Dog Theater of Durham, North Carolina. The Durham production was transferred for a limited run to Joseph Papp's New York Shakespeare Festival at the Public Theater.

48. Solomon, "AIDS Crusaders," 40.

49. Bruce Nussbaum, *Good Intentions: How Big Business and the Medical Establishment Are Corrupting the Fight Against AIDS* (New York: Atlantic Monthly Press, 1990).

50. Burroughs-Wellcome, a pharmaceutical corporation whose American headquarters are in Research Triangle, between Raleigh and Durham, North Carolina, are the producers of AZT, until October 1991 the only antiviral drug approved for use against HIV. Burroughs-Wellcome was the first target of AIDS activists, in 1987, because of the exorbitantly high price of AZT. Bowing to demonstrations and press coverage of the protest, they lowered the price by 20 percent, but it is still high. For a full description of the controversy, see Bruce Nussbaum, *Good Intentions: How Big Business and the Medical Establishment Are Corrupting the Fight Against AIDS* (New York: Atlantic Monthly Press, 1990).

Jesse Helms, former television commentator, is the ultraconservative senator from North Carolina. Characteristically, Helms began his 1990 run for reelection with an antigay speech. He has also been the strongest spokesman against the National Endowment for the Arts funding of projects with homoerotic content.

51. Douglas Crimp, *AIDS Demo Graphics* (Seattle, Wash.: Bay Press, 1990), 19.

3: Closet Pederasts

1. Their statement was reprinted in *American Theatre* (March 1991), 7:50.

2. Philip Brett, "Britten and Grimes," in Philip Brett, ed., *Benjamin Britten: Peter Grimes* (Cambridge, England: Cambridge University Press, 1983), 189.

3. Three arguments on outing are particularly forceful. Richard Goldstein, "The Art of Outing: When Is It Right to Name Names," *Village Voice* (May 1, 1990), 33–37; Gabriel Rotello, "Why I Oppose Outing," *Outweek* (May 29, 1991), 10–11,64; Richard Mohr, "Outing: A Problem in Gay Ethics," draft of a chapter from a forthhcoming book (1991).

4. Eve Kosofsky Sedgwick, *Epistemology of the Closet* (Berkeley: University of California Press, 1990), 7.

5. African-Americans became truly uncloseted in 1917, when black actors played blacks for the first time on Broadway, but plays about the taboo of miscegenation had been salacious theatrical material since Dion Boucicault's nineteenth-century melodrama, *The Octoroon* (1859). Various forms of incest dominated American "serious drama" in the twenties and thirties. See Clum, *Ridgely Torrence* (New York Twayne, 1972).

6. While there are many fine histories of the development of the concept of the homosexual and the development of the language of homosexuality in the nineteenth century, two are landmark works: Michel Foucault, *The History of Sexuality*, Robert Hurley, trans., vol. 1, *An Introduction* (New York: Pantheon, 1978); and Jeffrey Weeks, *Sexuality and Its Discontents: Meanings, Myths, and Modern Sexualities* (London: Longman, 1980).

7. Jonathan Katz, *Gay American History* (New York: Avon Books, 1976), 139.

8. Katz, *Gay American History*, 138.

9. In the published edition of Osborne's *A Patriot for Me* are printed the cuts and alterations requested by the Lord Chamberlain. Three entire scenes about Colonel Redl's homosexual activities are to be cut, as well as such minor details as references to "clap" and "crabs." Even a scene with Redl and a woman together in bed "must not be played with the couple both in bed." John Osborne, *A Patriot for Me* (London: Faber and Faber, 1965), 128. Since Osborne refused to agree to the cuts, the Royal Court Theatre was turned into a private club for the run of the play. Such "clubs" were not under the Lord Chamberlain's jurisdiction.

10. Richard Dyer, "Seen to Be Believed: Some Problems in the Representation of Gay People as Typical," *Studies in Visual Communication* (Spring 1983), 9:2.

11. Jeanie Forte, "Realism, Narrative, and the Feminist Playwright," *Modern Drama* (March 1989), 32:117.

12. Jill Dolan, "Lesbian Subjectivity in Realism: Dragging at the Margins of Structure and Ideology," in Sue-Ellen Case, ed., *Performing Feminisms: Feminist Critical Theory and Theatre* (Baltimore: Johns Hopkins University Press, 1989), 46.

13. Alan Sinfield, "Closet Dramas: Homosexual Representation and Class in Postwar British Theater," *Genders* (Fall 1990), 9:115.

14. Kaier Curtin, *We Can Always Call Them Bulgarians* (Boston: Alyson, 1987), 178. Curtin quotes a *New York Times* interview with Shairp at the time of the New York opening of *The Green Bay Tree* (November 12, 1933): "The idea which grew into *The Green Bay Tree* came to Mr. Shairp one day when he was walking in Hampstead Heath, near his home, he saw a man and a boy driving together, and something in the boy's wistful expression suggested to him the theme which is the basis for the play. When he returned home he told his wife he had found a new subject and then went directly to work." In recent years, Hampstead Heath has been a famous cruising area.

15. Mordaunt Shairp, *The Green Bay Tree*, in Michael Wilcox, ed., *Gay Plays* (London: Methuen, 1984), 33. Further references to the play are to this edition.

16. "In some schools such as Harrow, where Terence Rattigan was a pupil, it became fashionable for boys in rebellion against school values 'to proclaim their genuine or affected homosexuality.' This pattern allowed the cultivation of leisure-class male homosexuality as a possible, unspecific, unavowed component within a general, Bohemian, artistic, and theatrical stance. It was these cultivated gentlemen who sought lower-class partners. And partly because they were the producers of books and plays and—eventually, hesitantly, and obliquely—alluded to the matter, this became the expected pattern of homosexual relations." Alan Sinfield, "Closet

Dramas: Homosexual Representation and Class in Postwar British Theater," *Genders* (Fall 1990), 9:113.

17. Peter Burton, Introduction to Shairp, *The Green Bay Tree, Gay Plays,* 53.

18. Jed Harris cut this final flower-arranging from the Broadway production, as if the sight of a man arranging flowers was too shocking. Julian sends Trump out for the flowers and sits alone onstage, smoking a cigarette, as the curtain falls.

19. Martin Gottfried, *Jed Harris: The Curse of Genius* (Boston: Little Brown, 1984), 142.

20. Gottfried, *Jed Harris,* 143.

21. Gottfried, *Jed Harris,* 143. The legendary animosity Laurence Olivier had for Jed Harris developed during rehearsals of *The Green Bay Tree.* Harris' brutal treatment of actors infuriated Olivier, who later claimed that he based his characterization of Shakespeare's *Richard III* on Harris. Olivier also claimed that he hated playing Julian: "He was weak, indecisive, despicably without backbone. I never felt comfortable playing him, and I began to despise myself for his disagreeable qualities" (quoted in Thomas Kiernan, *Sir Larry* [New York: Times Books, 1981], 101). Note that Olivier hates the character's weakness, not his sexuality.

22. Curtin, *We Can Always Call Them Bulgarians,* 186.

23. Noël Coward, *Design for Living* (Garden City, N.Y.: Doubleday, Doran & Co., 1933), 12. Further references to *Design for Living* are to this edition.

24. John Lahr, *Coward the Playwright* (London: Methuen, 1982), 83. Lahr's discussion of *Design for Living* is as disapproving of the central trio as Ernest is, and in 1982, he would still refer to the bisexuality of the play's heroes as "abnormal sexuality." Fortunately, Lahr was not in a position to do the disservice to Coward that he did to Joe Orton.

25. Noël Coward, Introduction to *Play Parade,* vol. 1 (London: Heinemann, 1934), xvii.

26. According to Leslie Halliwell, the film, directed by Ernst Lubitsch, with Gary Cooper (hardly one's idea of a sophisticated Coward leading man), Frederic March, and Miriam Hopkins had only one line left from Coward's play, thanks to pressure on Paramount from the Legion of Decency, the Catholic pressure group (*Halliwell's Film Guide: 7th Edition* [New York: Harper & Row, 1989], 265).

27. John Osborne, *Look Back in Anger* (New York: Penguin, 1982), 19. Further references are to this edition.

28. Peter Shaffer, *Five Finger Exercise* (New York: Samuel French, 1958).

29. Shelagh Delaney, *A Taste of Honey,* in Henry Popkin, ed., *The New British Drama* (New York: Grove Press, 1964), 97. Further references to the play are to this text.

30. Harry and Bill's meeting in *The Collection* is not the only Pinter meeting that has overtones of a homosexual pickup. The meeting of the protagonists on Hampstead Heath is an inside joke that got a laugh in the original London production of *No Man's Land* (1975). Aston's bringing Davies home in *The Caretaker* (1960) has similar overtones.

31. Simon Trussler, *The Plays of Harold Pinter* (London: Victor Gollancz, 1973), 111.

32. John Mortimer, Introduction to Georges Feydeau, *Three Boulevard Farces* (Harmondsworth, England: Penguin, 1985), 9.

33. C.W.E. Bigsby, *Joe Orton* (London: Methuen, 1982), 17.

34. Peter Shaffer, *Black Comedy and White Lies* (New York: Stein and Day, 1967).

35. In 1967 the British government decriminalized private consensual sex between men over the age of twenty-one, except prisoners and members of the military. In a kind of catch-22, the consensual act of sex, so long as it was private, was legal, but any invitation to have sex was not. Recently, Clause 25 of the Criminal Justice Bill listed among serious violent crimes that are to receive tougher prison sentences a number of consensual homosexual activities.

36. Quoted in John Lahr, *Prick Up Your Ears* (New York: Knopf, 1978), 156.

37. Lahr, *Prick Up Your Ears*, 35n.

38. Lahr, *Prick Up Your Ears*, 215.

39. Bigsby, *Joe Orton*, 67.

40. Joe Orton, in John Lahr, ed., *The Orton Diaries* (New York: Harper & Row, 1986), 125.

41. Lahr, ed., *The Orton Diaries*, 256.

42. Lahr, *Prick Up Your Ears*, 276.

43. Lahr, *Prick Up Your Ears*, 276.

44. The film of Lahr's biography was directed by Stephen Frears and released in 1987.

45. Alan Bennett, Introduction to *Prick Up Your Ears: The Screenplay* (London: Faber, 1987): "Dramatizing the act of writing is never easy: the paper ripped from the typewriter and flung into the wastepaper basket. . . . But how else do you do it?" (p. vii).

46. Bennett, *The Screenplay*, ix.

47. Orton, in Lahr, ed., *The Orton Diaries*, 125.

48. Orton, in Lahr, ed., *The Orton Diaries*, 251.

49. Orton, in Lahr, ed., *The Orton Diaries*, 251.

50. Jonathan Dollimore, "The Challenge of Sexuality," in Alan Sinfield, ed., *Society and Literature, 1945–1970* (New York: Holmes & Meier, 1983), 51.

51. Joe Orton, *What the Butler Saw*, in *The Complete Plays* (New York: Grove Weidenfeld, 1976), 370. Further references to Joe Orton's plays are to this text.

52. Dollimore, "The Challenge of Sexuality," 54–55.

53. Lahr, *Prick Up Your Ears*, 205.

54. Orton, in Lahr, ed., *The Orton Diaries*, 53. Williams obviously had more admiration for Orton than Orton had for him. According to Orton, Williams saw the New York production of *Entertaining Mr. Sloane* (1964) twice and "says it's the funniest play he's ever seen" (*The Orton Diaries*, 157). Williams dedicated a late play, "The Blonde Europeans," to Orton. In May 1967, Orton and Halliwell stayed in the Tangiers flat in which Williams had written *Suddenly Last Summer* (1958). For Orton, it was decorated in "the kind of taste I abhor" (*The Orton Diaries*, 157).

55. Alan Sinfield, "Who Was Afraid of Joe Orton," *Textual Practice* (Summer 1990), 4:271.

56. Lahr, *Prick Up Your Ears,* 156.

57. Simon Shepherd, *Because We're Queers: The Life and Crimes of Kenneth Halliwell and Joe Orton* (London: Gay Men's Press, 1989). "In his plays Orton continually infiltrated the action with images of sexy boys. These images are carefully set up, created in front of us, and thus become fetishistic" (p. 102).

58. Shepherd, *Because We're Queers,* 102–103.

59. Orton, in Lahr, ed., *The Orton Diaries,* 45.

60. Orton, in Lahr, ed., *The Orton Diaries,* 145.

61. Lahr, *Prick Up Your Ears,* 134.

62. Orton, in Lahr, ed., *The Orton Diaries,* 203.

63. Lahr, *Prick Up Your Ears,* 130.

64. John Lahr sees a good deal of Kenneth Halliwell, Orton's longtime companion, in Wilson (Lahr, *Prick Up Your Ears,* 128–138). According to Lahr's constantly negative reading of Halliwell, Wilson is the closest approximation to Halliwell's self-destructive personality, and the circumstances of Wilson and Frank's life, like their difference in age, seem autobiographical. *Ruffian on the Stair* began as an adaptation of a novel Orton and Haliwell coauthored, *The Boy Hairdresser.*

65. Shepherd, *Because We're Queers,* 165.

66. Shepherd, *Because We're Queers,* 165.

67. Sinfield, "Who Was Afraid of Joe Orton," 167.

68. Peter Shaffer, *Equus* (Harmondsworth, England: Penguin, 1977), 108.

69. For a more traditional reading of the religious dimension of these plays, see John M. Clum, "Religion and Five Contemporary Plays: The Search for God in a Godless World," *South Atlantic Quarterly* (Autumn 1978), 77:418–432.

70. One might say further that the relationship between the two women in Shaffer's *Lettice and Loveage* (1988) could be added to his catalog of closeted homosexual relationships.

4: American Dreams

1. Paula Treichler, "AIDS, Gender, and Biomedical Discourse: Current Contests for Meaning," in Elizabeth Fee and Daniel M. Fox, eds., *AIDS: The Burdens of History* (Berkeley: University of California Press, 1988), 205.

2. There is a study to be written on the relationship between the homosexuality of many of the male movie stars of the fifties (Clift, Dean, Mineo, Hunter, Hudson, to name just a few) and changing images of masculinity. The ménage à trois played out by James Dean, Sal Mineo, and Natalie Wood in *Rebel Without a Cause* (1955) had not only a potentially gay element (which is why Mineo/Plato had to be killed off) but also a really gay element. It also raises the issue of interpretive communities, for the homosexuality of these figures was "common knowledge" among gays, who then could provide their own subtext to films starring these actors (think of the turbulent relationship between Hudson and Dean in *Giant* (1956), for instance).

3. In the telefilm *Rock Hudson,* the star's agent, Henry Willson (played by Andrew Robinson), is the villain of the piece for destroying Rock's relationships

with men to protect his stardom. Willson also arranges Rock's marriage when rumors start getting out of control. Hudson eventually fires Willson so that he can have a love life. In the telefilm, Hudson is the nice guy made unhappy by sharks. Marc Christian, the lover who sued Hudson's estate because Hudson did not tell him he had AIDS, is a selfless lover duped by Rock's evil secretary, who is devoted to protecting Rock's straight image.

4. Richard Mohr, "Outing: A Problem in Gay Ethics," draft of a chapter from a forthcoming book (1991), 17.

5. Robert Anderson, *Tea and Sympathy* (New York: Random House, 1953), 3. Further references to *Tea and Sympathy* are to this edition.

6. For example, in the 1982 film *Making Love,* the gay writer, played by Harry Hamlin, quotes Laura's final line to the married doctor he has just initiated into the joys of gay sex. It is the only camp line given to this homogenized character.

7. In the film adaptation, Hollywood "justice" prevailed, and Laura became a "fallen woman" because of her salvation of Tom. The film ends with Tom, ten years older and married, reading a letter from Laura in which she states that what they did was wrong. The film, of course, also removes any hints of homosexuality, overt or latent, from the teachers.

8. Mohr, "Outing," 20.

9. Loring Mandel, *Advise and Consent* (New York: Samuel French, 1961), 17.

10. Allan Berube, *Coming Out Under Fire: The History of Gay Men and Women in World War II* (New York: The Free Press, 1990).

11. This is also true to some extent of his short stories, in which furtive sex is treated in poignant, if elliptical language, but he still seemed more comfortable dealing candidly with homosexuality in the more private form of the short story and lyric poem than in the theater, where public disclosure became the object of terror. I deal with the relationship of the stories to the plays in an essay; see John M. Clum, " 'Something Cloudy, Something Clear': Homophobic Discourse in Tennessee Williams," in Ronald R. Butters, John M. Clum, and Michael Moon, eds., *Displacing Homophobia* (Durham, N.C.: Duke University Press, 1989), 149–169. For a discussion of Williams' short stories, see also Claude J. Summers, *Gay Fictions: Wilde to Stonewall* (New York: Continuum, 1990), 133–155.

12. Tennessee Williams, *A Streetcar Named Desire,* vol. 1, *The Theatre of Tennessee Williams* (New York: New Directions Publishing, 1971), 354. Further references to *A Streetcar Named Desire* are to this text.

13. Richard Dyer, "Stereotyping," in Richard Dyer, ed., *Gays and Film* (New York: Zoetrope, 1984), 32.

14. This may be why *A Streetcar Named Desire* is continually quoted in gay drama. A classic example is George's cry "Flores para los muertos" in Edward Albee's *Who's Afraid of Virginia Woolf?,* which seems to be there as an homage to Williams and a recognition of the closeted gay dimension of his own play. In early 1991, the gay male theater group, Bloolips, and the lesbian theater collective, Split Britches, presented *Belle Reprieve,* their cross-dressed version of *Streetcar* with Bette Bourne as Blanche.

15. Tennessee Williams, as quoted in Michael Bronski, *Culture Clash: The Making of a Gay Sensibility* (Boston: South End Press, 1984), 115.

16. The best recent discussion of the meaning and implications of camp, a sythesis and extension of previous definitions—one pertinent to my discussion of *Streetcar* and other gay drama—can be found in Jonathan Dollimore's *Sexual Dissidence: Augustine to Wilde, Freud to Foucault* (Oxford: Oxford University Press, 1991). Camp, for Dollimore, "renders gender into a question of aesthetics. Common in aesthetic invovement is the recognition that what seemed like mimetic realism is actually an effect of convention, form, or some other kind of artifice. . . . Camp comes to life around that recognition; it is situated at the point of emergence of the artificial from the real, culture from nature" (p. 311–312).

17. Evidence suggests that the homosexual connotations of the words I cite here were part of American gay slang in 1947 and that Williams knew the "code." In the letters he wrote to Donald Windham before *Streetcar* was written (Donald Windham, ed., *Tennessee Williams' Letters to Donald Windham, 1940–1965* [New York: Holt, Rinehart, & Winston, 1976]), Williams refers to his young, casual sexual partners as "trade," another term appropriated into gay slang from the jargon of prostitution, and speaks often of his propensity for "chicken"—boys—a preference he clearly shares with Blanche. According to Harld Wentworth and Stuart B. Flexner's *Dictionary of American Slang* (2d supplemental ed. [New York: Thomas Crowell, 1975]), straight meant heterosexual as early as 1945. Eric Partridge's *A Dictionary of Slang and Unconventional English, Eighth Edition* (New York: Macmillian, 1984) claims that "quean" was used to identify an effeminate homosexual as early as the late nineteenth century. The term comes from "quean," a British term for a prostitute. According to Kaier Curtin (*We Can Always Call Them Bulgarians*, pp. 73–78), characters in Mae West's *The Drag* (1927) called themselves "queens" and spoke of their penchant for "rough trade." The evidence for "trick" and "turn the trick" is more circumstantial. Since by 1947 Williams had already written about male prostitutes, whose slang was surely that of their female counterparts, he would surely know their slang.

> He learned a great deal from the bold homosexuals. Like jazz musicians and dope addicts, they spoke in code. The words "fairy" and "pansy" were considered to be in bad taste. They preferred to say that a man was "gay" while someone quite effeminate was a "queen." As for the manly youths who offered themselves for seduction while proclaiming their heterosexuality, they were known as "trade," since they usually wanted money. Gore Vidal, *The City and the Pillar* (New York: E.P. Dutton & Co., 1948), 156.

18. Harold Beaver, "Homosexual Signs (In Memory of Roland Barthes)," *Critical Inquiry* (Autumn 1981), 8:106.

19. Beaver, "Homosexual Signs," 106.

20. Tennessee Williams, *Suddenly Last Summer,* in vol. 3, *The Theatre of Tennessee Williams* (New York: New Directions Publishing, 1971), 351. Further references to *Suddenly Last Summer* are to this edition.

21. Tennessee Williams, *Cat on a Hot Tin Roof,* in vol. 3, *The Theatre of Tennessee*

Williams (New York: New Directions Publishing, 1971), 15. Further references to *Cat on a Hot Tin Roof* are to this edition.

22. Recent productions, like Howard Davies' superb 1988 production at the National Theatre of Great Britain, which he recreated with a different cast for Broadway in 1990, have removed Williams' euphemistic obscenities and replaced them with their real counterparts.

23. In Richard Brooks' screenplay for the 1958 movie, direct references to homosexuality are removed, making Brick's problems alcoholism and arrested development.

24. Tennessee Williams, "The Critic Says Evasion; I Say Mystery," *New York Herald Tribune* (April 17, 1955), sec. 4, p. 2. Reprinted in Maria St. Just, ed., *Five O'Clock Angel: Letters of Tennessee Williams to Maria St. Just, 1948–1982* (New York: Penguin, 1990), 110. Lady St. Just does not mention that the piece was published—only that Williams gave it to her for safe keeping.

It is interesting to see that Williams would defend his "mystery" while candidly explaining his play. It is also interesting to note the use of the word *must* instead of the more neutral *will* in describing Brick's "heterosexual adjustment." Williams' dictum for Brick is in line with medical and moral thinking in the mid–1950s. How much did the playwright really buy into such attitudes?

25. Tennessee Williams, "Too Personal?," preface to *Small Craft Warnings,* in vol. 5, *The Theatre of Tennessee Williams* (New York: New Directions Publishing, 1976), 220. Further references to *Small Craft Warnings* are to this edition.

26. Williams, as quoted in Donald Spoto, *The Kindness of Strangers: The Life of Tennessee Williams* (Boston: Little Brown, 1985), 355.

27. Tennessee Williams, *Vieux Carré,* in *The Theatre of Tennessee WIlliams, Volume 7* (New York: New Directions, 1980), 178.

28. Quoted in Donald Spoto, *The Kindness of Strangers: The Life of Tennessee Williams* (New York: Ballantine Books, 1985), 319.

29. Tennessee Williams, Introduction to William Inge, *The Dark at the Top of the Stairs* (New York: Random House, 1958), vii–viii.

30. The complex relationship between Williams and Inge is discussed in biographies of both writers. Williams was instrumental in getting Inge's early work produced, but in the 1950s Williams saw Inge as his antagonist in an intense rivalry that extended to comments on Inge's personal style. Williams was disturbed by Inge's success and despised his closeted, "gentlemanly" behavior: "Inge may be [agent] Audrey's [Wood's] gentleman playwright, but I prefer to remain her degenerate playwright" (Spoto, *The Kindness of Strangers,* 251).

31. William Inge, *Come Back, Little Sheba,* in *Four Plays* (New York: Grove Press, 1958), 23. The play was first presented on Broadway, February 1950.

32. William Inge, *Picnic, Four Plays,* 90. First produced on Broadway, February 1953. In Mart Crowley's *The Boys in the Band,* a character says of the hunky, vapid hustler who comes to the party to be Harold's birthday present: "He looks right out of a William Inge play to me." (New York: Farrar, Straus, & Giroux, 1968), 77.

33. "Such material could not have found wide public approval in the sexually

reticent Eisenhower era when it was being composed, but the therapeutic value of writing it was probably very significant to Inge." Ralph F. Voss, *A Life of William Inge* (Lawrence, Kans.: Uniersity Press of Kansas, 1989), 144.

34. William Inge, *The Tiny Closet*, in *Summer Brave and Eleven Short Plays* (New York: Random House, 1962), 189. Further references to *The Tiny Closet* are to this edition.

35. William Inge, *The Boy in the Basement*, in *Summer Brave and Eleven Short Plays*, 163. Further references to *The Boy in the Basement* are to this edition.

36. Inge's dislike for actors burns through a number of his plays, particularly, *A Social Event*.

37. William Inge, *Where's Daddy* (New York: Random House, 1966), 31. The play was first produced on Broadway, March 1966.

38. Georges-Michel Sarotte, *Like a Brother, Like a Lover: Male Homosexuality in the American Novel and Theatre from Herman Melville to James Baldwin* (Garden City, N.Y.: Doubleday Anchor, 1978), 108.

39. Howard Taubman, "Modern Primer: Helpful Hints To Tell Appearances From Truth," *New York Times* (April 28, 1963), sec. 2, p. 1.

40. Tennessee Williams' *The Milk Train Doesn't Stop Here Anymore* (1963), in its first, less campy version, directed by Herbert Machiz, was first presented on Broadway in January 1963, with Hermione Baddely and Paul Roebling. (A revised, Kabuki-style howler with Tallulah Bankhead and Tab Hunter opened a year later. Later still came the film version, *Boom!* (1968), in which Liz Taylor camps it up, with Noël Coward playing the witch—on the stage a female part, in the film a bitchy queen—a rare case of film unclosing a gay subtext.) While the *Times* mildly approved of the 1963 version, the play did contain, in the handsome young man as angel of death (if not in the cartoon women), one of Howard Taubman's telltale signs of homosexual drama: "The character who passes this miracle for her is one of those handsome, pallid young men with a dead heart who has become a fashionable symbol for some of our playwrights." (Review of *The Milk Train Doesn't Stop Here Anymore*, *New York Times* [January 18, 1963], p. 7). In his April article, cited in note 39, Taubman would make clear the homosexual subtext underneath this fashionable symbol.

41. Edward Albee, *Who's Afraid of Virginia Woolf?*, in *Selected Plays of Edward Albee* (New York: Nelson Doubleday, 1987), 120. Further references are to this edition.

42. Richard Schechner, "Who's Afraid of Edward Albee?," in C.W.E Bigsby, ed., *Edward Albee: A Collection of Critical Essays* (Englewood Cliffs, N.J.: Prentice-Hall, 1975), 64. I am fascinated by Schechner's ability to ascertain not only the sexual orientation of Albee's audience but also their sexual potency.

43. Schechner, "Who's Afraid," in Bigsby, ed., *Edward Albee*, 65.

44. Philip Roth, "The Play That Dare Not Speak Its Name," in Bigsby, ed., *Edward Albee*, 105.

45. Roth, "The Play That Dare Not," Bigsby, ed., *Edward Albee*, 109.

46. Stanley Kauffmann, "Homosexual Drama and Its Disguises," *New York Times*

(January 23, 1966), sec. 2, p. 1. The article was reprinted in Kauffmann, *Persons of the Drama* (New York: Harper & Row, 1976), 291–294.

47. Stanley Kauffman, "On the Acceptability of the Homosexual," *New York Times,* February 6, 1966, sec. 2, p. 1. The essay was reprinted in Kauffmann, *Persons of the Drama,* 295–298.

48. The review was reprinted in Stanley Kauffmann, *Theater Criticisms* (New York: Performing Arts Journal Publications, 1983), 98–100.

49. Kauffmann, *Theater Criticisms,* 150.

50. Georges-Michel Sarotte, *Like a Brother, Like a Lover* (Garden City, N.Y.: Doubleday Anchor, 1978), 142.

51. Sky Gilbert, "Closet Plays: An Exclusive Dramaturgy at Work," *Canadian Theatre Review* (1989), 59:55–58.

52. Gilbert, "Closet Plays," 57–58.

53. Gilbert, "Closet Plays," 58.

54. Foster Hirsch, "Evasions of Sex: The Closet Dramas," in Philip C. Kolin and J. Madison Davis, eds., *Critical Essays on Edward Albee* (Boston: G. K. Hall, 1986), 130.

55. The one play that transcends this sort of reading, though it doesn't completely escape it, is *A Delicate Balance* (1966). I might add here that the key to reading Albee is in the adaptations, particularly of Carson McCullers' *The Ballad of the Sad Cafe* (1963).

56. Edward Albee, *The Zoo Story,* in *Selected Plays,* 12.

57. Alan Sinfield, "Who Was Afraid of Joe Orton?" *Textual Practice* (Summer 1990), 4:273–274.

58. "I do know I felt I was Johnny while I was writing it. I identified with him completely. . . . About a year later I was watching a production of the play at the Mark Taper forum in Los Angeles when I realized I was Frankie." Introduction to *Three Plays by Terrence McNally* (New York: Penguin, 1990), xi.

59. Quoted in the frontispiece of *Three Plays by Terrence McNally.*

60. Frank Rich, "2 Terrence McNally Couples Struggle to Love, Against the Odds" (rev. of *Lips Together, Teeth Apart*), *New York Times* (June 26, 1991), sec. B, p. 3.

61. Otis Stuart, "Measuring the Times: Terrence McNally Straddles the Sexual Divide," p. 93.

62. Quoted in Otis Stuart, "Measuring the Times: Terrence McNally Straddles the Sexual Divide," *Village Voice* (September 3, 1991) p. 93.

63. Terrence McNally, Introduction to *Three Plays by Terrence McNally,* ix.

64. Craig Lucas, "A Gay Life in the Theater," *American Theater* (November 1990), 7:24–29, 68.

65. Craig Lucas, *Prelude to a Kiss* (New York: Dutton, 1990), 31.

66. Lucas, *Prelude to a Kiss.*

67. I have pluralized this catch-all term *the gay experience* to convey my understanding of the myriad, contradictory elements it inadequately names. There are only gay experiences. As for the gay sensibility, I am drawn to Jonathan Dollimore's argument: "I shall suggest that there is a sense in which the very notion

of a homosexual sensibility is a contradiction in terms. I am interested in an aspect of it which exists, if at all, in terms of that contradiction—of a parodic critique of the essence of sensibility as conventionally understood." *Sexual Dissidence: Augustine to Wilde, Freud to Foucault* (Oxford: Oxford University Press, 1991), 308.

5: Dramatizing Gay History

1. Robert Wallace, "To Become: The Ideological Function of Gay Theatre," *Canadian Theatre Review* (Summer 1989), 8.

2. Don Shewey, "Pride in the Name of Love: Notes on Contemporary Gay Theater," Introduction to *Out Front: Contemporary Gay and Lesbian Plays* (New York: Grove Press, 1988), xxv.

3. Philip Brett, Postscript to Philip Brett, ed., *Benjamin Britten: Peter Grimes* (Cambridge, England: Cambridge University Press, 1983), 191.

4. Eve Kosofsky Sedgwick, "Pedagogy in the Context of an Anti-Homophobic Project," *South Atlantic Quarterly* (1990), 89:142.

5. Christopher Marlowe, *Edward the Second* (New Mermaids Edition) (London: Ernest Benn, 1967), 34. Further references to *Edward II* are to this edition.

6. Larry Kramer, *The Normal Heart* (New York: New American Library, 1985), 114.

7. For an articulate argument for homosexuality as a social construction, see David Halperin, *One Hundred Years of Homosexuality and Other Essays on Greek Love* (New York: Routledge, Chapman & Hall, 1990).

8. Larry Kramer, *The Normal Heart*, 114.

9. This is a statement by director Nicholas Hytner in the program for the Royal Shakespeare Company production of *Edward II* in 1990.

10. Jonathan Goldberg, "Sodomy and Society: The Case of Christopher Marlowe,"*Southwest Review* (Autumn 1984), 69:377.

11. This is Gerard Murphy as quoted in " 'Sweet Lies': Terrence Michael Stephenson Talks to Director Gerard Murphy and Actor Simon Russell Beale About the RSC's New Production of *Edward II*," *Gay Times* (August 1990), 36.

12. Alan Bray's *Homosexuality in Renaissance England* (London: Gay Men's Press, 1982), is the seminal work on this subject. His 1990 essay, "Homosexuality and the Signs of Male Friendship in Elizabethan England," *History Workshop Journal* (Spring 1990), 1–19, complicates a reading of *Edward II* by showing how expressions of love and affection between men were common signs of favor in the Elizabethan court and were not necessarily signs of sodomy: "Marlowe describes in this play what could be a sodomitical relationship, but he places it wholly within the incompatible conventions of Elizabethan friendship, in a tension which he never allows to be resolved" (p. 10).

13. Purvis E. Boyette, "Wanton Humor and Wanton Poets: Homosexuality in Marlowe's *Edward II*," *Tulane Studies in English* (1977), 22:36. A typical "traditional," "enlightened" view of homosexuality in *Edward II* can be found in Sharon Tyler, "Bedfellows Make Strange Politics: Christopher Marlowe's *Edward II*," in James Redmond, ed., *Themes in Drama, 7: Drama, Sex, and Politics* (Cambridge,

England: Cambridge University Press, 1985), 55–68. For recent, classic homophobic criticism, see Ronald Huebert, "Tobacco, Boys and Marlowe," *Sewanee Review* (Spring 1984), 92:206–224, in which is found the following gem: "For Gaveston: showily dressed, ostentatiously vain, flirtatious or bitchy as the mood strikes him, eager to parade his coy submissiveness when the king is at his side, rapaciously greedy for power when he isn't, Gaveston, in short, is the stereotypical homosexual" (p. 214).

14. Stephen Orgel, "Nobody's Perfect: Or Why Did the English Stage Take Boys for Women?," in Ronald R. Butters, John M. Clum, and Michael Moon, eds., *Displacing Homophobia: Gay Male Perspectives in Literature and Culture* (Durham, N.C.: Duke University Press, 1989), 16.

15. Bray, "Homosexuality and the Signs of Male Friendship," 9.

16. Bruce R. Smith, Homosexual Desire in Shakespeare's England: A Cultural Poetics (Chicago: University of Chicago Press, 1991), 213.

17. Simon Shepherd, *Marlowe and the Politics of Elizabethan Theatre* (London: Harvester Press, 1986), 198.

18. In a number of recent productions, Lightborn has been played by the same actor who played Gaveston. This, I think, is appropriate. George L. Geckle, *Text and Performance: Tamburlaine and Edward II* (Atlantic Highlands, N.J.: Humanities Press International, 1988), 100. Though the stage directions are confusing, the sixteenth-century historian Holinshed tells us that Edward was murdered by having a hot poker inserted in his anus. The RSC production of 1990 enacted this graphically.

19. Claude J. Summers, "Sex, Politics, and Self-Realization in *Edward II*," in Kenneth Friedenreich, Roma Gill, and Constance B. Kuriyama, eds., *"A Poet and a Filthy Play-maker": New Essays on Christopher Marlowe* (New York: AMS Press, 1988), 236.

20. Bruce R. Smith sees Edward's martyrdom as his greatest performance: "Without doing a thing, Edward emerges as the Noble Sufferer. Thanks to all his practice in role-playing, the master rises to the occasion magnificently." *Homosexual Desire in Shakespeare's England: A Cultural Poetics*, 218.

21. Hugh Whitemore, *Breaking the Code* (New York: Fireside Theatre, 1987), 104.

22. Larry Kramer, *The Normal Heart*, 114.

23. Alan Bennett's double bill of plays about Guy Burgess and Anthony Blount, *An Englishman Abroad* and *A Question of Attribution,* were presented under the title *Single Spies* by the National Theatre of Great Britain in 1988 and published by Methuen in London the same year. The production was successful enough to be moved to the West End. I don't discuss the plays in this chapter because they do not deal with the relationship of the characters' sexuality to their treason.

24. See chapter 3, note 9 for a description of the cuts the Lord Chamberlain ordered.

25. Redl's story is also depicted in the 1984 Hungarian film *Colonel Redl.*

26. John Osborne, *A Patriot for Me* (London: Faber & Faber, 1965), 19. Further references to *A Patriot for Me* are to this edition.

27. Arnold P. Hinchcliffe, *John Osborne* (Boston: G.K. Hall, 1984), 80.

28. Julian Mitchell, *Another Country* (Ambergate, Derbyshire, England: Amber Lane Press, 1982), 24. Further references to *Another Country* are to this edition.

29. It is ironic that Julian Mitchell's screen version of *Another Country* plays up the teenage love between Guy and his beloved Harcourt (who is never seen in the play) but cuts most of the political discussion.

30. Some of my gay students tell me that many fraternities accept homosexual brothers but demand they protect the heterosexual image of the fraternity by staying away from campus gay groups and gay demonstrations.

31. David Rabe, *Streamers* (New York: Alfred A. Knopf, 1977), 59. Further references to *Streamers* are to this text.

32. Richard Hall, "The Elements of Gay Theater," in Richard Hall, *Three Plays for a Gay Theater* (San Francisco: Grey Fox Press, 1983), 153.

33. Noel Greig and Drew Grifiths, *As Time Goes By,* in *Two Gay Sweatshop Plays* (London: Gay Men's Press, 1981), 27–28. Further references to *As Time Goes By* are to this edition.

34. Philip Osment, *This Island's Mine,* in Philip Osment, ed., *Gay Sweatshop: Four Plays and a Company* (London: Methuen, 1989), 94.

35. Martin Sherman, *Bent,* in Don Shewey, ed., *Out Front: Contemporary Gay and Lesbian Plays* (New York: Grove Press, 1988), 85. Further references to *Bent* are to this edition.

36. William M. Hoffman, Introduction to William M. Hoffman, ed., *Gay Plays: The First Collection* (New York: Avon, 1979), xxix.

37. Doric Wilson, *Street Theater,* in Shewey, ed., *Out Front,* 7. Further references to *Street Theater* are to this edition.

38. Christopher Hampton, *Total Eclipse* (London: Faber, 1981), 9. Further references to *Total Eclipse* are to this edition.

39. Noel Greig, *The Dear Love of Comrades,* in *Two Gay Sweatshop Plays* (London: Gay Men's Press, 1981), 140. Further references are to this edition.

40. The concept of homosexual relationships bridging differences in age and class remains strong in England. The gay relationship depicted in 1987 and 1988 on the British TV soap opera "Eastenders" was between Colin, a fortyish middle-class outsider to the working-class neighborhood in which he lived, and Barry, an eighteen-year-old who sold records from a stall in a street market. Colin's flat was, stereotypically, much more contemporary in style than those of his neighbors. The relationship was quickly ended after howls of protest over a scene that showed Colin and Barry in bed together.

41. This is Noel Greig as quoted in Philip Osment, " 'Finding Room On the Agenda For Love': Introduction," in *Gay Sweatshop: Four Plays and a Company* (London: Methuen, 1989), xliii.

42. Lawrence Mass, "Homosexuality and Music: A Conversation with Philip Brett," *Christopher Street* (September 1987), 24. Thanks to my colleague, Michael Moon, for calling my attention to this article.

43. Philip Brett has written a number of articles on Benjamin Britten and compiled a collection of essays on *Peter Grimes.* Clifford Hindley has written several

essays on gay themes in Britten's work, including: "Love and Salvation in Britten's *Billy Budd*," *Music and Letters* (1989), 70:363–381 and "Contemplation and Reality: A Study in Britten's *Death in Venice*," *Music and Letters* (1990), 71:511–523.

44. Paul Godfrey, Preface to *Once in a While the Odd Thing Happens* (London: Methuen, 1990), n.p. Further references to *Once in a While the Odd Thing Happens* are to this edition.

45. Philip Brett, "Britten and Grimes," in Philip Brett, ed., *Benjamin Britten: Peter Grimes* (Cambridge, England: Cambridge University Press, 1983), 187.

6: Fashioning a Gay Self

1. John Guare, *Six Degrees of Separation* (New York: Vintage, 1990), 34.

2. Tennessee Williams, *A Streetcar Named Desire*, in vol. 1, *The Theatre of Tennessee Williams* (New York: New Directions Publishing, 1971), 398.

3. Christopher Durang, *Sister Mary Ignatius Explains It All For You*, in *Christopher Durang Explains It All For You* (New York: Grove Weidenfeld, 1983), 195. Further references to the play are to this edition.

4. Christopher Durang, *Beyond Therapy*, in *Christopher Durang Explains It All For You*, 272.

5. Lanford Wilson, *The Madness of Lady Bright*, in William M. Hoffman, ed., *Gay Plays: The First Collection* (New York: Avon Books, 1979), 180. Further references to *The Madness of Lady Bright* are to this edition.

6. Robert Patrick, Preface to *Untold Decades* (New York: St. Martin's Press, 1988), xiv.

7. Robert Patrick, *The Haunted Host*, in Ed Berman, ed., *Homosexual Acts: A Volume of Gay Plays* (London: Inter-Action, 1975), 84. Further references to *The Haunted Host* are to this edition. The performance history of *The Haunted Host* is a minihistory of gay drama. The original production in 1964 was directed by Marshall W. Mason, who later became artistic director of the Circle Repertory Company and directed Lanford Wilson's plays and William M. Hoffman's *As Is* (1985). The two characters of *The Haunted Host* were played by Patrick and Hoffman. Ten years later, in 1974, it was one of the first plays coproduced by London's Gay Sweatshop. In 1991, a New York revival starred Harvey Fierstein, who had made his first nondrag appearance in a 1975 production of the play.

8. Doric Wilson, *Street Theater*, in Don Shewey, ed., *Out Front: Contemporary Gay and Lesbian Plays* (New York: Grove Press, 1988), 58.

9. Kaier Curtin, *We Can Always Call Them Bulgarians* (Boston: Alyson, 1987), 328.

10. Judy Klemsrud, "You Don't Have to Be One to Play One," *New York Times* (September 29, 1968), sec. 2, p. 3.

11. William M. Hoffman, Introduction to *Gay Plays: The First Collection* (New York: Avon, 1979), xxvii.

12. Vito Russo, *The Celluloid Closet: Homosexuality in the Movies*, 2d ed. (New York: Harper & Row, 1987), 176.

13. Mart Crowley, *The Boys in the Band* (New York: Farrar, Straus & Giroux, 1968), 13. Further references to *The Boys in the Band* are to this edition.

14. Patrick, Preface to *Untold Decades,* xv.

15. Terrence McNally, *The Lisbon Traviata,* in *Three Plays by Terrence McNally* (New York: Penguin Plume, 1990), 85. Further references to *The Lisbon Traviata* are to this edition.

16. In an earlier version of the play, Stephen stabs Mike with a pair of scissors: "I'm surprised more people don't stab their lovers. Instead, they yak, yak, yak. Where does that get them? Nowhere. But look at us. The final duet." (Terrence McNally, *The Lisbon Traviata,* in Shewey, ed., *Out Front,* 417). This ending is in many ways more logical, if less "realistic." Stephen finally turns his life into opera.

17. Albert Innaurato, *Coming of Age in Soho,* in *Best Plays of Albert Innaurato* (New York: Gay Presses of New York, 1987), 7. Further references to *Coming of Age in Soho* are to this edition. In its first incarnation, the central character was a woman, Gioconda. At producer Joseph Papp's suggestion, the leading female character was changed into a male character.

18. Harvey Fierstein, *Torch Song Trilogy* (New York: Gay Presses of New York, 1980), 15. Further references to *Torch Song Trilogy* are to this edition.

19. In the film, Arnold's relationship with Alan becomes central and is clearly a relationship built on mutual love.

20. William Finn, *In Trousers, The Marvin Songs* (New York: The Fireside Theater, 1991), 80. Further references to *The Marvin Songs* are to this edition.

ANNOTATED LIST
OF RESOURCES

Rather than offering a bibliography that repeats information on primary and secondary material offered in the notes, I present below a selective annotated reading list of published gay drama, as well as information on other bibliographical resources. An asterisk (*) denotes that the play is discussed in this book.

Anthologies

Berman, Ed., ed., *Homosexual Acts: A Volume of Gay Plays.* London: Inter-Action Imprint, 1975.
——. *Gay Plays: An International Anthology.* New York: Ubu Repertory Theatre Publications, 1989.
Hoffman, William M., ed., *Gay Plays: The First Collection.* New York: Avon, 1979.
Osborn, M. Elizabeth, ed. *The Way We Live Now: American Plays & the AIDS Crisis.* New York: Theatre Communications Group, 1990.
Osment, Philip, ed., *Gay Sweatshop: Four Plays and a Company.* London: Methuen, 1989. Containing Osment's superb essay on the history of London's Gay Sweatshop.

Shewey, Don, ed., *Out Front: Contemporary Gay and Lesbian Plays*. New York: Grove Weidenfeld, 1988.

Wilcox, Michael, ed., *Gay Plays*. London: Methuen, 1984.

——. *Gay Plays: Volume Two*. London: Methuen, 1985.

——. *Gay Plays: Volume Three*. London: Methuen, 1988.

——. *Gay Plays: Four*. London: Methuen, 1990.

Plays

The following is a reading list of published plays that form a gay dramatic canon. Versions listed are those most easily obtainable (hardcover first editions of plays discussed in this text are listed in the notes). If the work appears in one or more of the anthologies listed above, the anthologized version is noted. I also note video versions of the plays listed. An asterisk indicates that the play is discussed in this book.

Albee, Edward. *The American Dream, The Zoo Story, Who's Afraid of Virginia Woolf*. In *Selected Plays of Edward Albee*. Garden City: Nelson Doubleday, 1987.*

——. *Tiny Alice*. New York: Atheneum, 1965.

Anderson, Robert. *Tea and Sympathy. Famous American Plays of the 1950's*. New York: Dell, 1962.*

Baraka, Imamu Amiri (LeRoi Jones). *The Baptism & The Toilet*. New York: Grove, 1967. Baraka's vision of racial hatred among young men set against homosexual desire.

Bartlett, Neil. *A Vision of Love Revealed in Sleep* (in Wilcox, *Volume Four*). Bartlett, distinguished translator, novelist, playwright, and director, creates—with the collaboration of composer Nicholas Bloomfield—unique, sophisticated musical theater pieces that are collages of high culture celebrating an old-fashioned notion of "the gay sensibility." Detractors dismiss Bartlett/Bloomfield collaborations as outdated high camp. Those of us who admire them find them powerful, stimulating theatrical extravaganzas, using elements of nineteenth-century culture to define contemporary gender and sexual identity. *A Vision . . .* is a theatrical version of a prose poem by Victorian painter Simeon Solomon. The latest work by Bartlett and Bloomfield, *Sarrasine* (1990), is discussed in the text.

Bennett, Alan. *Single Spies and Talking Heads*. New York: Summit Books, 1990. *Single Spies* comprises two one-act plays offering bittersweet portraits of British spies Anthony Blount and Guy Burgess.

Bentley, Eric. *Round 2* (in Wilcox, *Four*). A New York gay version of Viennese playwright Artur Schnitzler's comedy of sexual manners, *La Ronde*.

Bowne, Alan. *Forty-Deuce*. New York: Sea Horse Press, 1981. A grim, realistic picture of the life of teenage street hustlers around Times Square.

Brecht, Bertolt. *Baal* and *The Life of Edward the Second of England*. trans. William E. Smith and Ralph Manheim. In *The Collected Plays of Bertolt Brecht*, Vol. I. New York: Vintage, 1971. *Baal* is an early play in which the antihero's homosexuality underscores his outsider status. Brecht's free adaptation of Marlowe's *Edward II* loses the eloquence of the original, but is a gritty, powerful variation. Gaveston is definitely the commoner the barons describe.

Bumbalo, Victor. *Adam and the Experts.* New York: Broadway Play Publishing, 1990.

———. *Niagara Falls and Other Plays.* New York: Calamus Books, 1984. *Niagara Falls* is a truly funny pair of one acters about an Upstate New York Italian American family's response to the homosexuality of the son, from his father's disapproval to his newly married sister's envy of what strikes her as a charmed life.

Busch, Charles. *Four Plays.* Garden City: Fireside Theatre, 1990. Busch is a lover of camp low culture—fifties beach movies and B horror films—but his theater pieces are more than spoofs of what is already funny. They send up gender stereotypes in complex ways. The collection includes the long-running *Vampire Lesbians of Sodom.*

Chesley, Robert. *Hard Plays/Stiff Parts: The Homoerotic Plays of Robert Chesley (Night Sweat, Jerker, Dog Plays).* San Francisco: Alamo Square Press, 1990.*

———. *Jerker, or the Helping Hand.* (in Shewey).*

———. *Stray Dog Story.* New York: JH Press, 1984.

Churchill, Caryl. *Cloud Nine* (New York version). New York: Methuen, 1984. An important mixture of feminism and gay politics often performed in professional and university theaters, though now its politics have been dated by AIDS. An American version, directed by Tommy Tune, was a long-run off-Broadway success.

Coward, Nöel. *Design for Living, Coward: Plays: Three.* London: Methuen, 1979.*

Cristofer, Michael. *The Shadow Box.* New York: Avon, 1977. An often-produced story of inmates of a cancer hospice and their loved ones, featuring a gay writer, his dreary male lover and his lively, feckless ex-wife. Soap opera drivel, which merely switches the stereotypes of flighty gay male and devoted wife.

Crowley, Mart: *The Boys in the Band.* New York: Farrar, Straus, & Giroux, 1968. The film version is still available on video.*

Durang, Christopher. *Christopher Durang Explains It All for You.* New York: Grove Weidenfeld, 1983. A collection of Durang's early plays, including *Beyond Therapy* and *Sister Mary Ignatius Explains It All for You.* Brilliant satires on the forces of heterosexism. There is an awful film version of *Beyond Therapy* available on video.

Eagleton, Terry. *Saint Oscar.* London: Field Day, 1989. The most recent Oscar Wilde play, by a famous literary critic. Eagleton is less interested in seeing Wilde as a martyr than he is in understanding the connections between Wilde's politics and his behavior.

Elyot, Kevin. *Coming Clean.* London: Faber, 1984. British comedy about what happens when a gay couple hires a houseboy.

Fierstein, Harvey. *Forget Him* (in Shewey).

Fierstein, Harvey. *Safe Sex.* New York: Atheneum, 1987.* There is a video of the third, weakest play of the trilogy, *On Tidy Endings,* with Fierstein and Stockard Channing.

——. *Torch Song Trilogy.* New York: Gay Presses of New York, 1980.* The film version is available on video.

Finn, William. *The Marvin Songs (In Trousers, March of the Falsettos, Falsettoland).* Garden City: Fireside Theatre, 1991.* The original cast albums of *March of the Falsettos* and *Falsettoland* are available on CD.

Gellert, Roger. *Quaint Honor* (in Wilcox, *Volume Two*). 1958 pioneering English play about schoolboy romance.

Genet, Jean. *The Maids and Deathwatch.* Translated by Bernard Frechtman. New York: Grove, 1954. *Deathwatch* is Genet's only play with gay characters.

Gill, Peter. *Mean Tears and In the Blue.* Birmingham, England: Oberon, 1987. *Mean Tears* is a powerful depiction of a gay version of co-dependency. The one-act *In the Blue* is a celebrated series of variations on the beginning and end of a gay relationship.

Godfrey, Paul. *Once in a While the Odd Thing Happens.* London: Methuen, 1990.*

Gray, Simon. *Butley, Plays: One.* London: Methuen, 1986. The witty depiction of an English professor who cannot cope with homosexual or heterosexual relationships. Most of Gray's plays involve at least one homosexual character, reflecting Gray's mixed feelings about homosexuality.

Greenberg, Richard. *Eastern Standard.* New York: Grove Weidenfeld, 1989.* Greenberg's *American Plan* was produced by the Manhattan Theatre Club in 1990 and will, I hope, be published soon. It is a Jamesean picture of a very American young man, with a gay romance in his past, who becomes involved with a worldly Jewish matron and her neurotic daughter. A more complex picture of innocence and experience than the New York critics saw.

Greig, Noel. *The Dear Love of Comrades, Two Gay Sweatshop Plays.* London: Gay Men's Press, 1981 (also in Osment).*

——. and Griffiths, Drew. *As Time Goes By, Two Gay Sweatshop Plays.* London: Gay Men's Press, 1981.*

Guare, John. *Six Degrees of Separation.* New York: Vintage, 1990.*

Hall, Richard. *Three Plays for a Gay Theater.* San Francisco: Grey Fox Press, 1983. Contains Hall's important essays on gay drama.

Hampton, Christopher. *Total Eclipse.* London: Faber, 1969.*

Herbert, John. *Fortune and Men's Eyes.* New York: Grove, 1967. Sex and power among teenagers in prison. A much-performed play (even made into a poorish film) by a major Canadian playwright.

Hoffman, William M. *As Is* (in Shewey and Osborn).* There is a lugubrious video version, well acted but directed too heavily.

——. and Holland, Anthony. *Corbury: The Queen's Governor.* (in Hoffman). A mix of history and theatrical fantasy centering on the transvestite colonial governor of New York.

Inge, William. *The Boy in the Basement* and *The Tiny Closet, Summer Brave and Eleven Short Plays.* New York: Random House, 1962.*

Innaurato, Albert. *Best Plays of Albert Innaurato.* New York: Gay Presses of New

York, 1987. Contains *Gemini,* Innaurato's long-run play about a Harvard graduate in the throes of homosexual panic, and *Coming of Age in Soho.**

Jonson, Ben. *Epicoene, or The Silent Woman.** Available in a number of editions of Jonson's plays. The RSC text, published by Methuen (1989), contains Simon Trussler's insightful essays.

Katz, Jonathan. *Coming Out.* New York: ARNO, 1975. A docudrama of gay and lesbian history and historical figures by the author/compiler of the essential reference volume, *Gay American History.*

Killingworth, Gerald. *Days of Cavafy* (in Wilcox, *Four*). A presentation of scenes from the everyday life of the great poet.

Kirby, Andy. *Compromised Immunity* (in Osment).*

Kondoleon, Harry. *The Fairy Garden* (in Shewey). Kondoleon is something of a surrealist, building gentle, dreamlike fantasies out of domestic situations. A playwright who cannot be properly appreciated without seeing his work.

———. *Zero Positive* (in Osborn). Kondoleon's whimsical comedy about AIDS and death manages to stay this side of cloying and to be genuinely affirming.

Kramer, Larry. *Just Say No.* New York: St. Martins, 1989.*

———. *The Normal Heart.* New York: New American Library, 1985.*

Lorca, Federico Garcia. *The Public and Play without a Title.* New York: New Directions, 1983. *The Public* is Lorca's only gay play.

Lucas, Craig. *Prelude to a Kiss.* New York: Dutton, 1990. The hit comedy by the openly gay playwright-filmmaker (*Longtime Companions*). An example of contemporary "closet drama," the fantasy depicts a body switch of a bride and elderly man at a wedding reception, and the ensuing problems for the groom.*

Ludlam, Charles. *The Complete Plays.* New York: Harper & Row, 1989. Ludlam's plays, like those of Charles Busch, must be seen to be appreciated, but the volume at least is a record of his many scripts.

MacDonald, Robert David. *Chinchilla* and *Webster.* In *Three Plays by Robert David MacDonald.* London: Oberon Books, 1991. Two backstage dramas about sexual and theatrical politics. *Chinchilla* depicts a Diaghalev-like impressario. *Webster* is a rather fantastic, but vibrant, portrait of the great Jacobean dramatist who, in MacDonald's play, had a craving for boy actors (the boys make Eve Harrington seem self-sacrificing). A vivid conjectural picture of backstage life in a Jacobean playhouse.

Mann, Emily. *The Execution of Justice* (in Shewey). Docudrama about trial of Dan White for murdering Harvey Milk and Mayor George Moscone. One wishes for a bit more imagination. Overshadowed by the film documentary *The Times of Harvey Milk.*

Mason, Timothy. *Bearclaw* (in Wilcox, *Volume Two*). Well-crafted play about the relationship of a gay native American nursing home orderly with a "difficult" senior citizen.

———. *Levitation* (in Wilcox, *Volume Three*). Begins as a classic American back porch drama, but gently and effectively becomes more poetic. What Thornton Wilder might have written if he could have dealt with his homosexuality.

McGuinness, Frank. *The Carthaginians*. London: Faber, 1989. Five people, including a flamboyant queen, occupy a Derry graveyard.

——. *Innocence: The Life and Death of Michelangelo Merisi, Caravaggio*. London: Faber, 1987.

McNally, Terrence. "Andre's Mother" (in Osborn).*

——. *The Ritz and Other Plays*. McNally's bathhouse farce in a volume with his early plays. Although it is a bit slow, Richard Lester's film of *The Ritz* (available on video) does have the original cast and gives a better sense of the play than reading the script will.

——. *Three Plays*. New York: New American Library, 1990. Includes the revised version of *The Lisbon Traviata* * (original version in Shewey) and McNally's hit play, *Frankie and Johnny in the Clair de Lune*. By the time this book is published McNally's recent play, *Lips Together, Teeth Apart,* will probably be in print.

Mitchell, Julian. *Another Country*. Ambergate, Derbyshire: Amber Lane Press, 1982.* The film version, available on video is an enjoyable romance—quite different from the play.

Morris, Sidney. *If This Isn't Love*. New York: JH Press, 1982. Popular romantic comedy about the vicissitudes of a gay couple over twenty-five years.

Moss, Simon. *Cock-Ups*. London: Faber, 1984. An imaginative dramatization of the last days of Joe Orton and Kenneth Halliwell.

Orton, Joe. *The Complete Plays*. New York: Grove Weidenfeld, 1976.* *Entertaining Mr. Sloane* is included in Hoffman, but one should read all of Orton's plays.

Osborne, John. *A Patriot for Me*. London: Faber, 1965.*

Osment, Philip. *This Island's Mine* (in Osment). A panoramic theater piece in Gay Sweatshop style. Scenes of gay life in England in the 1980's.

Patrick, Robert. *The Haunted Host,* (in Berman).*

——. *Mercy Drop and Other Plays*. New York: Calamus, 1979.* A satire of television's "This Is Your Life" turns into a dark satire on American values.

——. *T Shirts* (in Hoffman).* A biting satire on the emptiness of gay nonrelationships in the 1970s.

——. *Untold Decades: Seven Comedies of Gay Romance*. New York: St. Martin's, 1988.

Pintauro, Joe. *Plays by Joe Pintauro*. New York: Broadway Play Publishing Company, 1989. The gay playlets in this collection also appear in Wilcox, *Four*.

Rabe, David. *Streamers*. New York: Knopf, 1977.* Robert Altman's fine film version is available on video.

Shairp, Mordaunt. *The Green Bay Tree* (in Wilcox, *Volume One*).*

Sherman, Martin. *Bent*. (in Shewey).*

——. *A Madhouse in Goa*. Ambergate, Derbyshire: Amber Lane Press, 1989.* A powerful double bill, produced successfully in London with Vanessa Redgrave and Rupert Graves, about personal, political, artistic, and ecological betrayal.

——. *Passing By* (in Wilcox, *Volume One*). Lovers contract hepatitis together. A Pre-AIDS romantic comedy.

——. *When She Danced*. Ambergate, Derbyshire: Amber Lane Press, 1988. Loved by British critics in its three London productions (most recently a West End hit in 1991, with Vanessa Redgrave as Isadora and Michael Sheen as the gay Greek pianist), but dismissed by New York critics. A depiction of one of the last days of Isadora Duncan. The gay character has the last word on Isadora.

Stevens, David. *The Sum of Us*. New York: Fireside Theatre, 1991. A recent hit off-Broadway as well as in Australia.*

van Itallie, Jean Claude. *Ancient Boys* (in Ubu)*

Vogel, Paula. *The Baltimore Waltz*. The full-length text can be found in *American Theatre* (September 1991). Excerpts are in Osborn. A witty, touching play about the relationship of a man, dying of AIDS, and his sister. The play quickly moves out of the conventions of realism into fantasy. It is one of the best AIDS plays thus far.

Wasserstein, Wendy. *The Heidi Chronicles and Other Plays*. New York: Penguin, 1990. Heidi's best friend is a gay pediatrician.

Whitemore, Hugh. *Breaking the Code*. New York: Fireside Theatre, 1987.*

Wilcox, Michael. *Lent*. London: Methuen, 1983. A reminiscence of adolescence by one of Britain's leading gay playwrights.

——. *Massage and Other Plays*. A paedophile and a rent boy.

——. *Rents*. Wilcox's celebrated depiction of Edinburgh rent boys (hustlers).

Wilson, Doric. *Forever After*. The muses of comedy and tragedy, played by drag queens, interfere in a gay romance.

——. *A Perfect Relationship*. Wilson is one of the most pungent satirists of the pre-AIDS gay scene, both loving and understanding its absurdities.

——. *Street Theater* (in Shewey)*

Wilson, Lanford. *Burn This*. New York: Hill and Wang, 1987. Heterosexual passion and homosexual caution. A romance for the late twentieth century.

——. *5th of July*. New York: Hill & Wang, 1978. Revised "Broadway" version, New York: Dramatists Play Service, 1982.*

——. *The Madness of Lady Bright* (in Hoffman).*

——. *A Poster of the Cosmos* (in Osborn).*

Bibliographies of Gay Drama

Helbing, Terry, ed. *Gay Theatre Alliance Directory of Gay Plays*. New York: JH Press, 1980. Descriptive list of plays to 1980.

Loeffler, Donald L. *An Analysis of the Treatment of the Homosexual Character in Dramas Produced in the New York Theatre from 1950 to 1968*. New York: Arno Press, 1975, pp. 188–201.

Shewey, Don. *Out Front: Contemporary Gay and Lesbian Plays*. New York: Grove Weidenfeld, 1988. List of produced and published gay drama listing publisher or, for unpublished plays, producing theater.

Publications

The following periodicals offer regular coverage of gay drama.

American Theatre is the best periodical on our theater, with solid articles on gay drama and dramatists. Many issues contain a full-length play.

The *Village Voice* contains coverage of New York theater, including gay drama and performance art.

Many gay newspapers and magazines contain theater coverage. *The Advocate,* which has improved enormously over the past year, is the national gay magazine. There is some theater coveage, which tends to focus on the West Coast. Local gay newspapers such as the *New York Native,* and the *Washington Blade* contain area theater coverage.

In England, the weekly magazine *Time Out* is the best record of gay drama. The *Gay Times* has some arts coverage.

Canadian Theatre Journal and *Canadian Drama* have offered solid coverage of Canadian gay drama. Both often print playscripts.

INDEX

ACT-UP, 78, 80–81, 82

Advise and Consent (Mandel), 148

After the Fall (Miller), 15–16

Albee, Edward, 118, 121, 127, 139, 149, 153, 175, 176–189, 255, 256

Alexander, Bill, 5–7

Almodóvar, Pedro, 26–27

Amadeus (Shaffer), 135

The American Dream (Albee), 139, 153, 177, 185

American Gigolo (Schrader), 9

Ancient Boys (Van Itallie). 45, 66

Anderson, Robert, xiii, 139, 142–147

Andre's Mother (McNally), 45

Andrews, Julie, 60, 62

Another Country (film), 299

Another Country (Mitchell), 209, 210, 214–217, 242

Apted, Michael, 110

Are You Being Served?, 115–116

As Is (Hoffman), 45, 63, 67–71, 74, 75, 79, 228

As Time Goes By (Greig/Griffiths), 202, 223, 224–227, 229, 230, 231–232

Auden, W. H., 153, 191, 239, 240, 242

Awake and Sing (Odets), 268

Bad Habits (McNally), 191

Baldwin, Alec, 191

The Ballad of the Sad Cafe (Albee), 178

Balzac, Honore de, 33–36

Banderas, Antonio, 26–27

Barthes, Roland, 34, 283

Bartlett, Neil, 33–36, 276, 304

Bates, Alan, 110

Baxter, Stanley, 118

Beale, Simon Russell, 196 (*illus.*)

Beaver, Harold, 153

Beckett, Samuel, 250

Bennett, Alan, 118–119

Bent (Sherman), xiv, 7–9, 25–26, 181, 202, 223, 224, 227–230, 232, 279

Bergman, Ingmar, 177

Berube, Allan, 148

The Best Man (Vidal), 148
Beyond Therapy (Durang), 247
Bigsby, C. W. E., 115, 117–118
Billy Budd (Britten/Forster), 239
Billy Budd (Melville), 135, 239
Black Comedy (Shaffer), 116–117, 135
Blau, Herbert, 3, 4, 7
Bloomfield, Nicholas, 33, 284
Bourne, Bette, 2 (illus.), 34, 292
The Boy in the Basement (Inge), 167–168,
    170–172, 173
Boyette, Purvis E., 204
Boyle, Danny, 27–29
The Boys in the Band (Crowley), 16–17,
    52, 182, 230, 231, 253–259, 263,
    270- 271, 294; and Inge, 294
Brandt, Allan M., 46, 47
Bray, Alan, 204, 205, 278, 297
Breaking the Code (Whitemore), 208–209
Brecht, Bertolt, xiii, 238, 271, 304
Brett, Philip, 87, 199, 239, 240
Britten, Benjamin, 238–242
Burgess, Guy, 210
Burroughs-Wellcome, 287
Burton, Peter, 95
Busch, Charles, 32–33, 151, 305

Caffe Cino, 248, 251
La Cage Aux Folles (Fierstein/Herman),
    xii, 29, 30–31
Caird, John, 114–115
Callas, Maria, 26, 260–263
Camille (Ludlam), 48–49, 54, 67
camp, def., 153–154, 293
The Captive (Bourdet), 89–90
The Caretaker (Pinter), 289
Carpenter, Edward, 94, 224, 225, 226–
    227, 236–238, 242
Cashman, Michael, 9, 279
Cat on a Hot Tin Roof (Williams), 23, 141,
    156–162, 173, 176, 220–221, 256
Center Stage (Baltimore), 33
Chapot, Stephen, 79
Charleson, Ian, 40, 161
Che (Raphael), 282
Chesley, Robert, xii, 25, 38 (illus.), 41–
    43, 44, 71–73, 79

The Children's Hour (Hellman), 106, 143,
    147
Clément, Catherine, 51
Clift, Montgomery, 145
"closet dramas," def., xiii
Cohn, Roy, 147
The Collection (Pinter), 107–114, 289
Come Back, Little Sheba (Inge), 23, 153,
    167
Coming of Age in Soho (Innaurato), 263–
    265, 270, 301
Compromised Immunity (Kirby), 45, 63–
    65, 75
Consenting Adult (McGreevey), 78
Coward, Noël, xiv, 84 (illus.), 86, 93,
    99–104, 128, 133
Cowen, Ron, 54–60
Crimp, Douglas, 81
Crowley, Mart, 16–17, 52, 182, 230,
    253–259
The Crucible (Miller), 106
Curtin, Kaier, 254

La Dame aux Camélias (Dumas), xiv, 39,
    45, 48–53, 54, 59, 67, 76, 262
La Dame aux Camélias (Dumas) (novel),
    50, 51
The Dark at the Top of the Stairs (Inge),
    166
Day, Doris, 141
Dean, James, 141, 145
The Dear Love of Comrades (Greig), 236–
    238
Death in Venice (Britten/Piper), 239
The Death of Bessie Smith (Albee), 177
Deathtrap (Lumet), 11
Deathwatch (Genet), 178
Delaney, Shelagh, 106–107
A Delicate Balance (Albee), 183, 186
Design for Living (Coward), xiv, 84 (illus.),
    86, 93, 99–104
Design for Living (film), 289
Dexter, John, 135–136
Dolan, Jill, 92
Dollimore, Jonathan, 120, 124, 296–297
The Drag (West), 89, 90
Drury, Allen, 148

Dumas, Alexandre, fils, xiv, 39, 48–53, 76
Durang, Christopher, xii, 247–248
Dyer, Richard, 91, 150, 283
Dynasty, 78

An Early Frost (Cowen), 54–60, 62, 74, 77, 78, 199, 228
Eastenders, 299
Eastern Standard (Greenberg), 45, 65–67, 69, 75
Edward II (Marlowe), 196 (*illus.*), 200, 202–208, 210, 213, 224, 242, 276, 297–298
Entertaining Mr. Sloane (Orton), 85, 126–128
Epicoene, or the Silent Woman (Jonson), 27–29, 30
Equus (Shaffer), 22, 133–135, 136, 282
Esslin, Martin, 3

Faggots (Kramer), 76
Falsettoland (Finn), 39, 245, 271, 273–275, 276
Fatal Attraction (Dearden/Lyne), 27
Fierstein, Harvey, xii, xiii, xiv, 10–11, 29–30, 73–74, 80, 87, 181, 244- (*illus.*), 265–270
Fifth of July (L. Wilson), 17–18, 36, 190
Finn, William, 39, 245, 271–276
Fish, Stanley, 278–279
Five Finger Exercise (Shaffer), 105–106, 116, 121, 134, 135
Forster, E. M., 62, 94, 146, 237
Forte, Jeanie, 92
Frankie and Johnnie in the Clair de Lune (McNally), 189, 190, 191
Frears, Stephen, 119
Freedman, Barbara, 20
Funeral Games (Orton), 118, 120

Garber, Victor, 54
Garbo, Greta, 48, 53
Garland, Judy, 72, 99, 226, 247, 249
Garland, Robert, 99
Gay Sweatshop, 63, 237–238, 240, 271, 286
Gazzara, Ben, 55, 59

gender, def., 280
Genet, Jean, 178–179, 180, 181
Gere, Richard, 9
Giant, 79, 141
Gilbert, Sky, 182–183, 186
Gill, Peter, 130–131, 132, 306
Gilman, Sander L., 46, 50, 52
Giselle (Adam), 249, 250
The Glass Menagerie (Williams), 164, 165
Godfrey, Paul, xiii, 239–242, 276
Goldberg, Jonathan, 203, 204
Gorman, Cliff, 254
La Gran Scena Opera Company di New York, 260
Grant, Hugh, 61, 62
Graves, Rupert, 10
The Green Bay Tree (Shairp), xiii, 85, 92–99, 102, 103, 104, 105, 107, 108, 109, 135, 142, 145, 146, 154, 155, 161, 172, 221, 237, 245–246, 288–289
Greenberg, Richard, 45, 65–67, 306
Greig, Noel, xiii, 202, 223, 224–227, 236–238, 276
Griffiths, Drew, 202, 223, 224–227, 276
Guare, John, xii, 18–22, 245
Guttenberg, Steve, 191

Hair (MacDermot, Ragni, Rado), 22
Hall, Peter, 6
Hall, Richard, 224
Halliwell, Kenneth, 118, 119
Hamlet (Shakespeare), 40
Hampton, Christopher, 233–236, 238
Hanley, William, 60–63
Hannah, John, 28
Harris, Jed, 85, 98–99, 161, 289
The Haunted Host (Patrick), 251–253, 254, 259, 263, 300
Hedda Gabler (Ibsen), 185
Hellman, Lillian, 106, 143
Helms, Jesse, 81, 287
Herman, Jerry, xii, 29
heterosexism, def., 277
Hinchcliffe, Arnold P., 214
Hindley, Clifford, 239
Hirsch, Foster, 183

Hirschfield, Magnus, 224, 225–226, 227, 229

Hitchcock, Alfred, 99

Hobson, Harold, 117–118, 120

Hobson, Laura Z., 78

Hoffman, William M., xii, 45, 63, 67–71, 79, 230, 248, 254

Hold (Chesley), 41–43

The Homecoming (Pinter), 117

homophobia, def., 277

The Homosexual Matrix (Tripp), 12

Hudson, Rock, 78, 82, 139–141, 147

Hunt, Edward, 80

Hunter, Tab, 145

Hutton, Timothy, 191

Hwang, David Henry, 31–32

Hytner, Nicholas, 203

Ibsen, Henrik, xiii

The Importance of Being Earnest (Wilde), 95, 103

In Trousers (Finn), 271, 272, 273

Inadmissable Evidence (Osborne), 214

Inge, William, xiii, 22, 23, 149, 152, 153, 158, 161, 166–174, 175, 179, 180, 182, 183, 184–185, 186, 189, 246; and Williams, Tennessee, 294

Inman, John, 115

Innaurato, Albert, xii, xiii, 263–265

"inside" plays, def., xii

Isherwood, Christopher, 86

Ivanek, Zeljko, 61

Jarman, Derek, 86, 202

Jerker, or the Helping Hand: A Pornographic Elegy (Chesley), 71–73, 79

Jones, Cleve, 79

Jonson, Ben, xi, 27–29, 120, 170

Just Say No (Kramer), 80, 258–259

Kauffman, Stanley, 179–181, 183

Kirby, Andy, 45, 63–65, 75

Klein, Beverly, 2 (*illus.*), 34

Kondoleon, Harry, 307

Kramer, Larry, xii, xiv, 45, 63, 75–77, 79, 80–81, 82, 197, 200–201, 209, 232, 258–259

Krapp's Last Tape (Beckett), 250

Kristeva, Julia, 48

La Cage aux Folles (Fierstein/Herman), xii, 29, 30, 31

Lahr, John, 102, 118–119, 128, 130, 289, 291

Laughton, Charles, 99

Law of Desire (La Ley del Deseo) (Almodóvar), 26–27

Liberace, 53–54, 82

Liberace: Behind the Music, 53–54

Lips Together, Teeth Apart (McNally), 189, 190, 191

The Lisbon Traviata (McNally), 27, 189, 190, 259–263, 265, 270, 301

Longtime Companion (Lucas/Rene), 11–12, 13, 191

Look Back in Anger (Osborne), 104–105, 214

Loot (Orton), 117, 118, 120–121, 125–126, 132

Lord Chamberlain, 85, 90, 92, 96, 103, 104, 142, 210, 219, 288

Lucas, Craig, xii, 11–12, 191–192

Ludlam, Charles, 33, 48–49, 53, 54, 151

Lunt, Alfred, and Fontanne, Lynne, 84 (*illus.*), 100

M. Butterfly (Hwang), 31–32

MacDonald, Robert David, 307

MacDowell, Malcolm, 110

MacIntosh, Cameron, 86

A Madhouse in Goa (Sherman), xiv, 9–10

The Madness of Lady Bright (L. Wilson), 248–251, 253–254, 259, 263, 270

Making Love (Sandler/Hiller), 11, 292

Malcolm (Albee), 179

Mandel, Loring, 148

March of the Falsettos (Finn), 271, 272–273

Margret, Ann, 60, 62

Marlowe, Christopher, xii, 196, 200, 201, 202–208, 226, 276

Mason, Marshall W., 18

Mason, Timothy, 307

Maurice (Forster), 62, 94, 146

McCarthy, Sen. Joseph, 143, 147
McCowen, Alec, 86
McKellan, Ian, 9, 86, 202
McNally, Terrence, xii, 27, 45, 189–191, 259–263
Melville, Herman, 155
The Merchant of Venice (Shakespeare), 5–7, 114
Mercy Drop (Patrick), 24–25, 282
Merril, George, 236–238, 242
A Midsummer Night's Dream (Shakespeare), 114–115
The Milk Train Doesn't Stop Here Anymore (Williams), 295
Miller, Arthur, 13–16, 106, 142, 149, 280–281
Miller, Court, 244 (*illus.*)
Mitchell, Julian, 209, 214–217
Moffett, D. W., 59, 77
Mohr, Richard, 11, 140, 147–148, 277
Molina, Alfred, 119
Morrison, Jim, 233
Mortimer, John, 114
Murphy, Gerard, 202, 203–204, 206–207
My Beautiful Laundrette (Kureishi/Frears), 119
The Mystery of Irma Vep (Ludlam), 33

Names Project Quilt, 78, 79–80
Natural Affection (Inge), 167, 175, 177
New York City Opera, 285
New York Review of Books, 181
New York Shakespeare Festival, 79, 80
New York Times, 62, 75, 76, 77, 175, 176, 179, 180, 254
Night Sweat (Chelsey), 43
No Man's Land (Pinter), 289
The Normal Heart (Kramer), xiv, 63, 75–77, 79, 80, 197, 200–201, 228
Northern Exposure, 197–200, 271
Nussbaum, Bruce, 81

O'Connor, John J., 62–63
Odets, Clifford, 268
Oldman, Gary, 119
Olivier, Laurence, 92, 98, 289

Once in a While the Odd Thing Happens (Godfrey), 239–242, 276
O'Neill, Eugene, 176, 183
opera, and gay men, 260
Orgel, Stephen, 205
Orpheus Descending (Williams), 23, 153, 167
Orton, Joe, 85, 86, 103, 108, 114, 117–133, 164, 181; and Williams, Tennessee, 290
The Orton Diaries, 128–129
Osborne, John, 90, 104–105, 209, 236, 288
Osment, Philip, 226, 276
Our Sons (Hanley), 60–63, 199
Our Town (Wilder), 230–231
outing, def., 87, 287
"outside" dramas, def., xii

Papp, Joseph, 79, 80
Patrick, Robert, xii, 23–25, 248, 251–253, 259, 282
A Patriot for Me (Osborne), 90, 209, 210–214, 236, 240, 242, 288
Paul Bunyan (Britten/Auden), 242
Pears, Peter, 239–242
Peter Grimes (Britten/Piper), 239, 240, 241
Picnic (Inge), 23, 153, 167, 189
Pinter, Harold, 85, 103, 107–114, 117, 129
Porter, Cole, 224
A Poster of the Cosmos (L. Wilson), 43–44
Prelude to a Kiss (Lucas), xii, 191–192
Prick Up Your Ears (film)(Bennett/Frears), 118–119
Prick Up Your Ears (Lahr), 118
problem play, def., xiii
public schools, (British), homosexuality in, 288–289

Quinn, Aidan, 138 (*illus.*)

Rabe, David, 217–223
Rattigan, Terence, 133
Rebel Without a Cause (Stern/Ray), 291
Redl, Alfred, 210–214

Reports From the Holocaust (Kramer), 80
Rich, Frank, 189–192
Richard II (Shakespeare), 202
Rimbaud, Arthur, 233–236, 238, 242
The Ritz (McNally), 191
Rock Hudson (Turner), 291–292
Rosenberg, Charles, 46
Roth, Philip, 178–179, 181
Rowlands, Gena, 55
Royal Court Theatre, 90, 210, 233
The Royal Hunt of the Sun (Shaffer), 135–136
Royal National Theatre, 9, 40, 161, 241–242, 279
Royal Shakespeare Company, 5, 27, 114, 202
The Ruffian on the Stair (Orton), 129–133
Russo, Vito, 254

Safe Sex (Fierstein), 73–74
Sanders, George, 99
Sarotte, Georges-Michel, 181–182
Sarrasine (Bartlett/Bloomfield), 2 (*illus.*), 33–36, 284
Schechner, Richard, 178
Section 28, def., 279
Sedgwick, Eve Kosofsky, 88, 200
Shaffer, Peter, 22, 63, 105–106, 116–117, 133–136, 282
Shairp, Mordaunt, xiii, 92–99, 103, 135, 145, 245, 288
Shakespeare, William, xi, xiii, 5–7, 40, 114–115, 202
Shepherd, Simon, 127, 133, 205
Sherman, Martin, xiv, 7–10, 25–26, 86, 181, 202, 223, 227–230, 276, 308–309
Shewey, Don, 3–4, 199
Sinfield, Alan, 92, 126, 133, 189, 288–289
A Single Man (Isherwood, dramatized by Michaelion), 86, 123
Sister Mary Ignatius Explains It All For You (Durang), 247
Six Degrees of Separation (Guare), xii, 18–22, 32, 36, 245
Slapstick Tragedies (Williams), 179

Small Craft Warnings (Williams), 123, 162–164
Smith, Bruce R., 205, 298
Solomon, Alisa, 78
Sondheim, Stephen, 271
Sontag, Susan, 47
Spoto, Donald, 165
stereotypes, homosexual, 91–92
Stevens, David, 192
Stevens, Fisher, 244 (*illus.*)
Stonewall Riots, 202, 224, 226, 230–232, 238, 242, 253, 254, 258, 259; def., 278–279
Storer, Jeffrey, 80
Streamers (Rabe), 217–223, 242
Street Theater (D. Wilson), 202, 223, 224, 230–232, 247, 253, 258
A Streetcar Named Desire (Williams), 3, 22, 35, 36, 138 (*illus.*), 149–154, 157, 163, 176, 186, 189, 193, 246
Strindberg, August, 185
Stuart, Otis, 191
Suddenly Last Summer (Williams), 154–156, 157, 161, 246
The Sum of Us (Stevens), 192
Summers, Claude, 207
Sunday, Bloody Sunday (Gilliatt/Schlesinger), 11
Sweet Bird of Youth (Williams), 23, 153, 167

T Shirts (Patrick), 23–24
Talley's Folly (L. Wilson), 189–190
A Taste of Honey (Delaney), 106–107
Taubman, Howard, 175–177, 178, 182
Taylor, Elizabeth, 79, 141
Tea and Sympathy (Anderson), xiii, 139, 142–147, 154, 156, 158, 161
Tea and Sympathy (film version), 292
Testory, Francois, 2 (*illus.*), 34
Thatcher, Grant, 196 (*illus.*)
This Island's Mine (Osment), 226
Tie Me Up, Tie Me Down (Átame) (Almodóvar), 26–27
Tiny Alice (Albee), 178, 188
The Tiny Closet (Inge), 167–170, 171, 172, 246

Torch Song Trilogy (Fierstein), xiv, 10–11, 181, 192, 244 (*illus.*), 265–270

Torch Song Trilogy (film) (Fierstein/Bogart), 17

Total Eclipse (Hampton), 233–236, 238, 240, 242

La Traviata (Verdi), 48, 51, 260, 285

Treichler, Paula, 39, 40, 41, 139

Tripp, C. A., 12

Tristan und Isolde (Wagner), 7

Trussler, Simon, 108

Turing, Alan, 208–209

The Turn of the Screw (Britten/Piper), 239

Twelfth Night (Shakespeare), 114

Unnatural Acts (Hunt/Storer), 80

Vampire Lesbians of Sodom (Busch), 32–33

Van Itallie, Jean Claude, 45, 66

Verdi, Giuseppe, 48, 51, 76

Verlaine, Paul, 233–236, 238, 242

Vidal, Gore, 148

Vieux Carre (Williams), 164–165

A View from the Bridge (Miller), 13–15, 16, 18, 36, 142

Vogel, Paula, 309

Voss, Ralph, 167

Wales Padlock Act, 89, 92

Wallace, Robert, 199

Walters, Margaret, 20, 21

Watney, Simon, 41, 52, 279

Welcome Home, Bobby (Bromberg), 78

Welles, Orson, 119

West, Mae, 89

What the Butler Saw (Orton), 117, 118, 120, 121–125, 127, 132

Where's Daddy? (Inge), 167, 172–173, 179

White, Edmund, 71

Whitemore, Hugh, 208–209

Whitman, Walt, 94, 237

Who's Afraid of Virginia Woolf? (Albee), 121, 153, 176, 177, 178, 181, 182, 183, 185–189, 256, 292

Wilde, Oscar, 95, 103, 118, 128, 153, 202, 223, 224, 225, 247

Wilder, Thornton, 230

Williams, Tennessee, xii, xiii, 3, 22–23, 105, 122, 123, 125, 127, 141, 149–166, 167, 173, 174, 175, 176, 177, 179, 180, 183, 184, 185, 186, 189, 193, 246, 255, 292, 294, 295; gay slang in, 293; and Inge, William, 294; and Orton, Joe, 290

Wilson, Doric, xii, 202, 223, 224, 230–232, 247, 248, 253, 258, 259, 276

Wilson, Lanford, xi, xii, 17–18, 43–44, 189–190, 192, 248–251, 253

Wojewodski, Stan, Jr., 33

Zeffirelli, Franco, 261

The Zoo Story (Albee), 177, 184, 185